Monetary Policy Frameworks for Emerging Markets

Monetary Policy Frameworks for Emerging Markets

Edited by

Gill Hammond

Director, CCBS, Bank of England, UK

Ravi Kanbur

T.H. Lee Professor of World Affairs, Cornell University, USA

Eswar Prasad

Tolani Senior Professor of Trade Policy, Cornell University, USA

Edward Elgar

Cheltenham, UK • Northampton, MA, USA

Published by
Edward Elgar Publishing Limited
The Lypiatts
15 Lansdown Road
Cheltenham
Glos GL50 2JA
UK

Edward Elgar Publishing, Inc.
William Pratt House
9 Dewey Court
Northampton
Massachusetts 01060
USA

A catalogue record for this book
is available from the British Library

Library of Congress Control Number: 2009925929

PEFC
PEFC/16-33-111
CATG-PEFC-052
www.pefc.org

ISBN 978 1 84844 442 3

Printed and bound by MPG Books Group, UK

Contents

Contributors

Philip Abradu-Otoo, Economist, Monetary Policy and Financial Stability Department, Bank of Ghana

Dr Christopher Adam, Reader in Development Economics, University of Oxford, UK

Dr Wenersamy Ramos de Alcântara, Senior Quantitative Researcher, International Reserves Operations Department, Central Bank of Brazil

Dr Janine Aron, Centre for the Study of African Economies, Department of Economics, University of Oxford, UK

Professor Edward Buffie, Professor of Economics, Indiana University, USA

Paulo Vieira da Cunha, Principal, Tandem Global Partners and Visiting Scholar, Columbia University, USA (formerly Deputy Governor of the Central Bank of Brazil)

José De Gregorio, Governor, Central Bank of Chile

Dr Piti Disyatat, Team Executive, Bank of Thailand

Diana Dragutinovic, Minister of Finance, Serbia (formerly Vice-Governor, National Bank of Serbia)

Professor David Fielding, Department of Economics, University of Otago, New Zealand

Professor Marvin Goodfriend, Professor of Economics, Tepper School of Business, Carnegie Mellon University, USA

Professor Charles Goodhart, Financial Markets Group, London School of Economics, UK

Gill Hammond, Director of the Centre for Central Banking Studies, Bank of England, UK

Dr Denny H. Kalyalya, Deputy Governor, Operations, Bank of Zambia

Professor Ravi Kanbur, T.H. Lee Professor World Affairs, International Professor of Applied Economics and Management and Professor of Economics, Cornell University, USA

Professor Eduardo Levy-Yeyati, Head of Latin American Research, Barclays Capital, and Barcelona Graduate School of Economics, Spain

Dr Rakesh Mohan, Deputy Governor, Reserve Bank of India

Professor John Muellbauer FBA, Nuffield College, University of Oxford, UK

Dr Luděk Niedermayer, Former Deputy Governor, Czech National Bank

Dr Bandid Nijathaworn, Deputy Governor, Bank of Thailand

Professor Stephen O'Connell, Eugene M. Lang Research Professor, Economics Department, Swarthmore, College, USA

Dr Michael Patra, Senior Advisor to the Executive Director, International Monetary Fund

Catherine Pattillo, Deputy Division Chief, Western Hemisphere Department, International Monetary Fund, USA

Daniela Silva Pires, Deputy Head, External Debt and International Relations Department, Central Bank of Brazil

Professor Eswar Prasad, Nandlal P. Tolani Senior Professor of Trade Policy, Department of Applied Economics and Management, Cornell University; Senior Fellow, Brookings Institution; and Research Associate, National Bureau of Economic Research, USA

Dr Sukudhew Singh, Assistant Governor, Bank Negara Malaysia

Dr Nii Kwaku Sowa, Director-General, Securities and Exchange Commission, and Member, Monetary Policy Committee, Bank of Ghana

Federico Sturzenegger, Kennedy School of Government, Harvard University, USA and Universidad Torcuato Di Tella, Argentina

Acknowledgements

We would like to thank all those who participated in the workshop which inspired this volume and who contributed chapters to this volume. The financial and administrative support from the Bank of England and Cornell University in hosting the workshop is also gratefully acknowledged. We have received excellent secretarial support from Chris Chaplin at the Bank of England and administrative support from Sue Snyder at Cornell which we acknowledge with appreciation.

Gill Hammond
Ravi Kanbur
Eswar Prasad

PART I

Frameworks for Monetary Policy

1. Monetary policy challenges for emerging market economies*

Gill Hammond, Ravi Kanbur and Eswar Prasad

1.1 INTRODUCTION

Emerging market economies have now become one of the most dynamic and economically important groups in the world economy. As these economies become larger and more integrated into international trade and finance, they face an increasingly complex set of policy challenges. Given their important role in the world economy in terms of population and sheer economic size, addressing these challenges effectively has important economic, social and political implications even beyond their national borders.

Monetary policy is typically the first line of defense against a number of internal and external shocks that these economies are now exposed to, so it is important to get it right. However, emerging market economies face a number of difficult challenges in designing monetary policy frameworks that work well in terms of promoting monetary and financial stability. Despite their rising economic might, many emerging market economies still have relatively underdeveloped financial markets and institutions, per capita incomes that still lag far behind those of advanced industrial economies, and a significant fraction of their population are still living in poverty. This puts a number of constraints on the effective formulation and implementation of macroeconomic policies.

Does existing economic theory provide lessons that are pertinent for designing effective monetary policy frameworks in emerging markets? What can be learnt from cross-country studies and from experiences of individual countries that have adopted different approaches? While country-specific circumstances and initial conditions matter a great deal in formulating suitable frameworks, are there clear general principles that can serve as a guide in this process?

To address some of these issues and create a forum for a dialogue between senior policymakers and academics, the Bank of England and Cornell University organized a conference in London on 17–18 July

2007. The conference produced a rich and productive set of interactions amongst senior central bank officials from a large number of emerging market central banks and academics working on different aspects of monetary policy formulation. The chapters in this volume represent a selection of papers presented at the conference.

The discussions at the conference were very wide-ranging. A sampling of the issues covered includes the following: What are the particular challenges faced by central banks in emerging markets? What are the pros and cons of different monetary policy frameworks? Has rising openness to trade and financial flows made monetary policy less effective in achieving domestic objectives? How should monetary policy respond to shocks of uncertain nature (demand/supply; transitory/permanent)? What institutional frameworks can help in increasing the effectiveness of monetary policy transmission in less developed economies? What role do policies towards capital account liberalization have in devising appropriate monetary policy strategies? How should monetary policy in emerging market economies respond to large exogenous shocks such as the worldwide surge in food and fuel prices, or the possible spillovers from financial shocks such as the subprime crisis in the United States?

The chapters in this book tackle some of these difficult issues. The contributors recognize that there are unlikely to be clear or general answers to many of the questions confronting central bankers in these challenging times. Nevertheless, the contributions of both academics and policymakers facilitate a revealing discussion of the interaction between theory and practice. For instance, theoretical work on the optimality of an inflation target as the prime objective of monetary policy has been influential in guiding the increasing adoption of inflation targeting regimes around the world (see De Gregorio, Chapter 3, this volume). But the discussion also highlights the substantial gaps that still exist between what can be learnt from existing theoretical and empirical research and the practical challenges that confront central bankers.

In this chapter, we provide an overview of the main issues discussed, linking them to broader debates in the academic literature as well as an assessment of how individual countries have chosen to respond to specific policy challenges and what the consequences have been. We discuss many controversies where there are still sharp differences in views between and amongst theorists and practitioners. We also delineate a few key analytical issues where there is still a yawning gap between theory and practice. In the process, we set out a broad agenda for further research in this area.

1.2 BACKGROUND

To set the stage for the discussions in this book, we begin by reviewing the objectives of monetary policy, the particular challenges faced by central bankers in emerging market economies, and some recent developments that have heightened these challenges.

1.2.1 Objectives of Monetary Policy

There is a general recognition in the academic literature and in advanced industrial economies that the primary role for monetary policy is price stability (see Bernanke et al., 1999). Other objectives such as promoting growth and employment are seen as secondary to this. This has been reflected in increasing independence for central banks and new laws that give central banks statutory responsibility for price stability (for example, Ghana, as discussed by Sowa and Abradu-Otoo in Chapter 16 of this volume). The rationale is that the best way that a central bank can promote growth and employment is by keeping inflation low and stable.

Central banks are also responsible for financial stability; this has come to the fore during the credit crisis that started in 2007. Even those central banks that are not responsible for prudential regulation are usually responsible for maintaining the stability of the financial system as a whole. In response to the current market turbulence, the financial stability objective has become more pre-eminent, with monetary policy aimed at restoring and maintaining the stability of the financial system. Indeed, the dual role expected of monetary policy in responding to a financial stability shock – the credit crunch – at the same time as a price stability shock – highly volatile oil and commodity prices – has posed particularly challenging dilemmas for central banks. On the institutional side, some central banks are being given a greater role in promoting financial stability.

The situation is rather more complex in emerging market economies, however. While price stability is seen as important in these economies as well, financial stability is a key responsibility since in most emerging markets central banks are also responsible for prudential regulation (Nijathaworn and Disyatat, Chapter 2, this volume; and Singh, Chapter 7, this volume). Moreover the political economy context in these countries makes it much harder for central banks to be insulated from other objectives, including the promotion of output and employment growth.

This is the essence of the challenge facing central bankers in emerging market economies: while it has only one instrument – usually short-term interest rates – monetary policy in many emerging market countries is seen as responsible for promoting high growth, keeping inflation low and stable, and maintaining financial stability (Goodfriend and Prasad, Chapter 8 in this volume, discuss this with specific reference to China). And even this one instrument is subject to a variety of constraints.

1.2.2 Constraints on Monetary Policy in Emerging Markets

Central banks in emerging markets face a unique set of challenges. These are in part institutional and in part technical, but both of these act as severe constraints on monetary policy implementation.

The key institutional constraint is the lack of central bank independence. In some countries, this takes the form of the central bank being statutorily under the purview of the finance ministry. In some countries where the central bank is in principle independent, there is still the reality that it can be buffeted by various political forces, especially the finance ministry (as argued by Dragutinovic, in the case of Serbia, Chapter 12, this volume). Hence, central banks are always treading a fine line in terms of maintaining their legitimacy and independence in difficult circumstances.

Furthermore, irrespective of the degree of statutory independence, operational independence of the central bank is in some cases circumscribed by constraints such as an exchange rate objective. Maintaining the exchange rate at a particular level or within a specific range can often limit the scope that the central bank has in using policy instruments such as the interest rate to pursue an independent domestic monetary policy aimed at managing domestic activity and inflation (Goodfriend, 2004).

Fiscal dominance is another key problem facing emerging market central banks. In many of these countries, long-term fiscal discipline is lacking and monetary policy is often an adjunct to fiscal policy, particularly since the latter is seen as having important redistributive functions. An unsustainable fiscal policy, characterized by continuing high levels of government budget deficits and public debt, acts as a severe constraint on monetary policy as the central bank then has to take account of the government's debt management objectives in setting interest rates, rather than focusing exclusively on the price stability objective. It also makes it harder to manage inflation expectations (see Sims, 2005).

Moreover, monetary policy is often hampered by a weak transmission mechanism related to the underdevelopment of the financial system (for example the case of Zambia, discussed by Kalyalya, Chapter 17, this volume). In particular, a fragile banking system can make it difficult for a central bank to use policy interest rates aggressively to achieve domestic objectives, as large changes in interest rates can have potentially devastating consequences on the balance sheets of weak banks.

The lack of well-developed financial markets means that the interest rate channel of monetary policy transmission is less effective. Further, the lack of market integration within these countries means that there are asymmetrical regional responses to monetary policy, as shown by Fielding in Chapter 14 of this volume. Consequently, the lags in the effects of monetary policy on economic activity are even longer and more variable than in industrial economies. The absence of deep and liquid financial markets also means that there is limited feedback from the market about monetary policy – central banks in industrial economies rely on these market signals for feedback about the effects of their policy actions on market sentiment and expectations.

Other institutional rigidities can also undermine the effectiveness of monetary policy. For instance, inflexible labor markets can lead to substantial inflation persistence, which again makes it harder for monetary policy to manage economic activity reliably.

1.2.3 Other Challenges

One structural change that is making it more difficult to isolate monetary policy from external influences is the increasing openness of the capital account in emerging market economies. Even in countries that have *de jure* capital controls, financial flows are increasingly able to find their ways around those controls. Greater trade openness, the rising sophistication of domestic and international investors, and the sheer volume of financial flows have all made it increasingly difficult to keep capital bottled up when the incentives for it to cross national borders are strong enough. A prime example is that of China where, despite the determined efforts of the authorities to tighten controls on inflows, money has been pouring in through different channels in recent years (see Prasad and Wei, 2007). An open capital account of course makes it much harder to maintain an independent monetary policy when the central bank is also trying to manage the exchange rate (this is the Mundell–Fleming 'impossible trinity').

A different type of problem of capital flows arises in heavily aid-dependent low-income economies, particularly in Africa. Aid flows are significant, but can be volatile, depending on political and other factors. How should governments, and monetary policy, respond to these volatile flows to the government? Buffie et al. (Chapter 6, this volume) argue that a key aspect is how credibly the government can commit to time paths of expenditure and absorption. If an aid boom is perceived to be temporary, the markets' fear of the looming fiscal problems can lead to capital outflows and inflation. An appropriate strategy, it is argued, could be to reduce deficits to some extent along with purchases of internal debt. In

Chapter 13 of this volume, Adam et al. further support the case for temporary reserve accumulation in the face of aid-driven capital flows.

Recent circumstances have made monetary policy formulation even more challenging in emerging markets. Rising worldwide food and energy prices in 2007 and the first half of 2008 created a dilemma for central bankers in these economies who were endeavoring to manage inflationary expectations while they are under political pressures to avoid stifling growth by tightening monetary policy. This episode highlights the difficulties in formulating strategies for responding to commodity price shocks. Existing theoretical models yield what seems like a naive and simplistic answer, that central banks should target only the core component of the price index and let prices for food and energy, which tend to be flexible prices, adjust according to market conditions. In less developed economies, expenditure on food tends to constitute a large share of total consumption expenditure, which makes it difficult for central banks in these economies to be seen as leaving those prices to market conditions.

In addition to institutional constraints, central banks in emerging market economies face a number of technical challenges in implementing monetary policy and particularly inflation targeting. In an inflation-targeting regime, the central bank needs the technical capacity to model the economy, understand the transmission mechanism and forecast inflation and output. Structural changes in the economy, such as greater openness, mean that modeling and forecasting techniques must evolve, and that the past can be a less reliable guide to the future. These issues are discussed by Aron and Muellbauer in Chapter 15 of this volume in the case of South Africa. Central banks also need good macroeconomic data to inform their decisions. Finally, they need a communication strategy as an integral part of their inflation-targeting framework, as argued for example by Niedermayer for the Czech Republic (Chapter 11, this volume).

1.3 OPTIONS FOR MONETARY POLICY FRAMEWORKS

Each country has specific institutional features and circumstances that determine how monetary policy decisions are formulated and implemented. Nevertheless, it is possible to identify a set of broad frameworks that have been used by emerging market and other economies. We begin by evaluating these options, in terms of their durability and effectiveness in achieving monetary policy objectives.

1.3.1 Managed Exchange Rate

The exchange rate provides a nominal anchor that is quite useful for some countries, especially those with low levels of financial and institutional development, and/or central banks that lack credibility (Husain et al., 2005). For economies that are highly open to trade, which is the case for many emerging markets, high nominal exchange rate volatility complicates domestic macroeconomic management and can have adverse effects on investment, employment and output growth. Given these potential advantages, many emerging markets have chosen to use the exchange rate as a nominal anchor to varying degrees.

A strict version of a managed exchange rate is a hard peg (currency board or dollarization), although there are a variety of other intermediate versions (for an early discussion of exchange rate regime options for emerging markets and the constraints on some of these regimes in a world of mobile capital, see Williamson, 1998). The common feature is that this option involves the loss of monetary autonomy and the 'importing' of monetary policy from abroad. The virtue is that pegging the domestic currency to the currency of a country whose central bank has credibility in maintaining low and stable inflation helps keep domestic inflation low. However, experience has shown that, even with a hard peg, fiscal discipline and sound structural policies are necessary to deliver good inflation and growth outcomes. Otherwise, currency pegs quickly become unsustainable.

Other forms of a hard peg include monetary unions such as the euro area. The logic of this approach is that linking monetary policy among a group of similar countries may facilitate a common response to common shocks, while acting as a disciplining mechanism on other policies in individual countries. There is also some evidence that currency unions promote trade and investment flows within the union. Some argue that the benefits from currency blocs means there will be an inevitable move by regional countries to monetary unions, and far fewer individual currencies in the future. For a good summary of the literature see de Grauwe (2000). The downside is that, in periods when business cycles across countries in the union are not well synchronized or when they get hit with different shocks, navigating a common monetary policy could be difficult.

A different option is to have an exchange rate that is tightly managed against one currency or a basket of other currencies. This arrangement can co-exist with an open capital account only in countries such as Singapore that have high levels of financial development and other good policies. But this is not an easy combination for most emerging markets to manage.

In general, managed exchange rate regimes require a large array of capital controls since large volumes of flows can make exchange rate management very difficult, in addition to stripping away monetary policy autonomy. There are of course currency boards such as Hong Kong and countries with exchange rate targets and well-disciplined macro policies (for example, Singapore) that are able to manage their exchange rates effectively while keeping their capital accounts fully open. But in most other developing economies, especially those with weak macro policies and underdeveloped financial markets, capital controls are seen as an important buffer required to mitigate exchange rate volatility.

1.3.2 Flexible Exchange Rate and Monetary Targeting

This usually involves a managed float, where the currency is managed within a relatively tight band, although the size of this band varies across countries and, within countries, over time. Examples are Bangladesh, Sri Lanka, Tanzania, Uganda and Zambia (Kalyalya, Chapter 17 in this volume, discusses the Zambian case). Monetary aggregates provide visible targets that are relatively easy to measure, making them appealing to economies with underdeveloped financial systems. One complication is that monetary aggregates are increasingly distorted by financial integration and globalization. Moreover, in economies where the rate of productivity growth is highly volatile, there is no stable relationship between monetary aggregates, on the one hand, and economic activity and inflation on the other. Consequently, many of these countries are in fact looking to move towards an alternative regime such as inflation targeting, but lack the institutional and technical prerequisites. Goodhart (Chapter 4 in this volume) challenges the view that money does not matter, arguing that there continues to be a strong empirical relationship between money and prices.

1.3.3 Inflation Targeting with Managed Float

Many countries have adopted inflation targeting but manage the exchange rate, ostensibly to 'lean against the wind' in smoothing out short-term volatility in exchange markets. In practice, this approach often involves substantial exchange market intervention as countries have a fear of letting their currencies float freely. Examples of countries that the International Monetary Fund (IMF) classifies as 'inflation targeters with managed float' constitute a diverse group, including Colombia, Ghana, Indonesia, Romania and Thailand (see Sowa and Abradu-Otoo on Ghana, Chapter 16 in this volume, and Nijathaworn and Disyatat on Thailand, Chapter 2 in this volume).

A variant of this is the approach adopted by the Reserve Bank of India

(RBI), which does not have a formal inflation objective but whose senior officials nevertheless mention the range of inflation that they are comfortable with in an attempt to anchor inflationary expectations. The RBI also manages the exchange rate quite actively at times, and its senior officials have argued that this is a pragmatic approach that gives them a degree of freedom in running monetary policy effectively (Mohan and Patra, Chapter 9 in this volume).

1.3.4 Inflation Targeting with Exchange Rate Flexibility

More and more countries, both from the group of advanced industrial economies as well as the emerging market economies, are moving towards this monetary regime. Even a number of countries that at present have one of the other regimes discussed above, have indicated that they view this regime as the endgame for the evolution of their own monetary frameworks.

Indeed, part of the apparent inevitability of moving to this regime is that, in every country, capital accounts are becoming increasingly open over time in de facto terms, irrespective of the capital control regime. This makes it harder to manage exchange rates for any sustained period without exposing the exchange rate regime to speculative attacks. The Chinese experience suggests that it may yet be possible to maintain a tightly managed exchange rate while the capital account is becoming more open, but only by maintaining extensive financial repression, which in turn has large welfare costs (see Prasad, forthcoming).

In tandem with the moves by central banks to adopt some form of inflation targeting, the academic literature has by and large come around to the view that this alternative is the best one for most advanced and middle-income economies. The inflation target provides a clear anchor for monetary policy, while exchange rate flexibility provides room for an independent monetary policy and a buffer against certain external shocks.

Rose (2006) marshals evidence that this regime seems to deliver the best outcomes in terms of output growth, low inflation and also lower exchange rate volatility than alternative regimes. He also notes that this regime is the most durable of the lot. However, it may be premature to declare that this is the best alternative; after all, it has not been around for very long and may not have been tested sufficiently under conditions of extreme duress. Furthermore, many countries introduced inflation targeting after 1990, a period when inflation has generally been moderate around the world. In terms of durability, the fact is that many countries lack credible alternatives since many of them turned to this regime after the breakdown of alternatives such as a fixed exchange rate regime. Nevertheless, experience indicates that in countries that have adopted inflation targeting, inflation expectations are better anchored and inflation persistence is lower (Levin et al., 2004).

Is the shift towards inflation-targeting regimes well advised? We now provide a critical review of the theoretical and empirical evidence of the appropriateness of this regime for emerging market economies, and the potential complications faced by central banks that do adopt inflation targeting (see Mishkin, 2000, for an excellent alternative summary of these issues).

1.4 BENEFITS OF AN EXPLICIT INFLATION OBJECTIVE

There is a great deal of evidence, from both individual country experiences and cross-country studies, that a central bank that is focused on price stability can be most effective at delivering good monetary and macro outcomes.[1] Low and stable inflation has large macroeconomic benefits – it would stabilize gross domestic product (GDP) growth, help households and firms make long-term plans with confidence, increase investment, and thereby allow monetary policy to make its best possible contribution to long-term employment and output growth. It would also have financial market benefits – for instance, by enabling the development of a long-maturity bond market, which would assist in infrastructure financing and public debt management.

Monetary policy that has a single clearly defined objective may be the best contribution that monetary policy can make to macroeconomic and financial stability and, therefore, to long-term growth. By contrast, trying to do too much with one instrument is a recipe for ineffectiveness, especially in difficult times. Moreover, the notion that monetary policy can itself increase long-term growth through activist policies is problematic – in fact, faith in that belief led to stagflationary episodes (economic stagnation coupled with high inflation) in the US in the 1970s and 1980s.

Monetary policy nevertheless has a key role to play in encouraging investment in physical capital and galvanizing productivity gains, mainly by ensuring macroeconomic stability. Transparency and predictability of monetary policy are essential ingredients for achieving liquid financial markets, reducing fragility of financial firms and stabilizing capital flows. A stable macroeconomic environment not only helps make cross-border capital flows more stable by giving domestic and foreign investors more confidence in a country's fundamentals, but it also helps in dealing with the inevitable vagaries of those flows.

It is sometimes argued that the process of switching to an objective of price stability entails a loss in output growth. This is true in countries where an inflation target has been used as a device to bring down inflation from a high level and to build credibility for a central bank that has lacked inflation-fighting credentials. One of the earliest inflation targeters – New Zealand – suffered this problem. An early form of inflation targeting was introduced in early 1988 in an attempt to bring inflation down from around 15 percent in the mid-1980s. Inflation was brought down to 2 percent by 1991, although with an adverse impact on growth and employment during that period. Output losses were also experienced at the time of the introduction of inflation targeting in some Latin American economies. But in every one of these cases, inflation targeting was seen as a solution to high inflation and lack of central bank credibility. However, there is no reason why, if inflation is low and the central bank has a reasonable degree of credibility, switching to a focus on price stability rather than multiple objectives should have output costs.

One lesson from these episodes is that inflation targeting may not necessarily be the best monetary policy framework for bringing inflation down from high levels. This is because it depends on the ability to forecast inflation, which is more difficult when inflation is high and volatile. So a central bank risks losing credibility by getting the forecast wrong and having large target misses. Nevertheless, some countries like Chile and Israel have still used inflation targeting successfully in purging entrenched high levels of inflation from their economies, More generally, however, inflation targeting is regarded as a good framework for keeping inflation low (Mishkin and Schmidt-Hebbel, 2005).

It is also argued by some that making low and stable inflation the objective of monetary policy creates a deflationary anti-growth bias, wherein inflationary pressures would be dealt with swiftly and decisively, but deflationary pressures would not be resisted as aggressively (McKinnon, 2006, implicitly makes this point in his discussion of Chinese exchange rate policy). In fact, there is no reason why there should be an asymmetric approach to inflation versus deflation. The Bank of England for example explicitly has a symmetric point target for inflation. In other countries where the inflation target is specified as a range, the norm is to treat the floor of the target range as seriously as the ceiling. Put differently, if growth falters, it is also likely to bring inflation down below the floor of the inflation objective, allowing the central bank to ease monetary policy. In this case again, the ability of the central bank to move aggressively with its policy instrument to maintain price stability (and thus growth), rather than being hamstrung by an exchange rate objective, is crucial (see Goodfriend, 2004).

Inflation targeting is sometimes seen as a rigid framework that ties the hands of central bankers and constrains their decision-making in some respects. In practice, however, the monetary policy frameworks of most central banks do give them discretion in reacting to shocks as to how quickly they aim to bring inflation back to target after a shock. And the frameworks have evolved such that most are now described as 'flexible inflation targeting'.

In sum, focusing on low and stable inflation does not mean that short-term fluctuations in output and employment growth will be ignored in monetary policy formulation. This objective provides a framework for thinking about how other macro developments affect inflation and, therefore, how monetary policy should react to those developments. This provides some degree of flexibility to central bankers in reacting to different types of shocks and how persistent they are likely to be. Moreover, it can increase the independence and effectiveness of monetary policy by setting more realistic expectations about what monetary policy can and cannot achieve, and by focusing attention on future inflation (which monetary policy can influence) rather than current inflation (which it cannot), as monetary policy can have an effect only with a lag. Finally, transparency about the monetary policy process allows financial market participants to plan for the already high volatility they need to deal with without it being augmented by policy volatility.

One should also not oversell the benefits of this regime. In particular, it is worth making the point that adopting an inflation-targeting regime by itself will not confer credibility on a central bank (Mishkin and Schmidt-Hebbel, 2005). But this regime has often been adopted as part of a package of measures aimed at building stronger institutions. It provides a framework in which policymakers can make a greater political commitment to price stability and, as in the case of Latin America, better fiscal policies. Thus, while inflation targeting may not be a macroeconomic panacea in itself, it can serve as a catalyst for a broader set of reforms that can increase the credibility of the central bank and deliver better outcomes on inflation and macroeconomic stability more generally.

1.5 PROBLEMS WITH AN EXPLICIT INFLATION OBJECTIVE

In practice, inflation targeting poses a number of challenges for central bankers. One recent policy challenge for many emerging markets has been dealing with the volumes and volatility of capital inflows and outflows. Indeed, in some circumstances, these flows can drive monetary policy into a corner – for instance, in the cases of many economies in Asia that experienced large capital inflows during 2005–07 (Singh, Chapter 7, this volume). This stoked domestic inflation, but central bankers in many of these countries found it difficult to raise interest rates to manage domestic inflation as that would have drawn in more inflows. Exchange rate appreciation would of course serve as a shock absorber in these circumstances, but many of these economies were wary of allowing their exchange rates to fluctuate by a wide margin, which complicated matters.

A related problem other than just the sheer volume of inflows is that it can be difficult to separate out long-term versus short-term speculative inflows. Unfortunately, reimposition of capital controls to limit inflows, even in a selective manner, is not without problems; it often ends up being not just ineffective but even counterproductive as it injects uncertainty into an already unsettled environment. A case study of this is provided by the example of Thailand, which in December 2007 tried to impose a tax on short-term portfolio inflows. The market reaction was swift and brutal, with the stock market plunging by over 15 percent in one day, forcing the government largely to rescind the controls.

What are the policy options for emerging markets facing such circumstances, and how do the viable options vary for different types of economies? In the face of a surge in inflows, the central bank has a few options to control inflation.

First, allow the exchange rate to appreciate. Exchange rate flexibility facilitates adjustment to relative prices, freeing up monetary policy to focus on the inflation objective. The downside is that the cost of hedging such exchange rate volatility falls on the private sector. In many emerging markets, financial underdevelopment means that currency derivatives and other instruments for hedging currency risk may not be available, putting an especially onerous burden on small and medium-sized enterprises that may not have easy access to hedging opportunities via international financial markets.

Second, intervene against appreciation. Some central banks in emerging markets have chosen to intervene aggressively in exchange markets to avoid excess volatility and also what they perceive as divergence from fundamentals. But prolonged intervention can cause a surge in reserve accumulation, which then exposes central banks to the risks of currency mismatches on their balance sheets and potentially large carrying costs on their reserve portfolios. In addition, this puts the onus on central banks to sterilize the intervention as the liquidity inflows would otherwise undermine domestic price stability. Sterilization of course has quasi-fiscal costs since the rate of return that has to be paid on sterilization bonds is typically higher than that earned on liquid instruments such as industrial country Treasury bonds that reserves are kept in. Such costs can mount very quickly as sterilization levels increase. These problems with intervention are emphasized by Goodfriend and Prasad (Chapter 8, this volume) for China. However, the discussion of Brazil by da Cunha et al. (Chapter 10, this volume) shows that in some circumstances temporary reserve build-up through intervention need not have large costs and can be part of a strategy that incorporates exchange rate smoothing. Levy-Yeyati and Sturzenegger (Chapter 5, this volume) further strengthen the case for temporary intervention by presenting evidence on the link between relative undervaluation and growth.

Third, impose restrictions on capital inflows. This is becoming an increasingly unviable option as de facto financial openness increases. Selective and targeted controls are a seductive option for a central bank that is concerned about specific types of flows, but these tend to be ineffective as there are inevitably large loopholes to get around these controls. Comprehensive controls have large costs to the economy and also tend to lose their effectiveness fairly quickly. But it remains an open question whether it is a viable, or ultimately counterproductive, short-run strategy for countries to hold onto whatever controls they have and thereby insulate themselves to the best possible extent against volatile capital flows (see Williamson, 2006).

Fourth, reduce restrictions on capital outflows. This is an appealing alternative to counterbalance inflows and take some of the pressure off the exchange rate. It may also have the advantage of generating many of the indirect benefits of financial openness that have been touted by various authors, including domestic financial development and opportunities for international portfolio diversification by domestic investors. One problem is that, once controls on outflows are weakened in good times, it may be difficult to reverse this in bad times when domestic and international investors are withdrawing due to a change in sentiment about an economy's prospects. This implies that opening up to outflows should be done in a controlled manner rather than as a one-shot full liberalization (see Prasad and Rajan, 2008).

The deepening of the financial crisis in the latter half of 2008 showed the fickleness of capital flows to emerging markets, with many of these economies facing significant outflows after a prolonged period of inflows. Many of the points discussed above in the context of a surge in inflows can be applied symmetrically to the case of outflows. One crucial difference, of course, is that large exchange rate depreciations can potentially be devastating for emerging markets, especially those that have large amounts of foreign-currency denominated debt. Perhaps this strengthens the case for greater focus on exchange rate management, at least in terms of preventing abrupt, massive depreciations of the domestic currency.

1.6 DIFFICULT CHOICES AND OUTSTANDING ANALYTICAL QUESTIONS

How should an emerging market central bank go about picking from the menu of tough choices laid out above? As the country-specific chapters in this volume make clear, monetary policy on the ground is of course a matter of judgment rather than mechanical rules, although academic knowledge has an important role in providing guidance on the relative merits and demerits of these choices. But only limited progress has been made so far in providing clear analytical guidance on these issues. And there are other related issues, where again much analytical work – both theoretical and empirical – remains to be done.

Until the financial crisis roiled world markets, many emerging markets that had been experiencing rapid productivity growth relative to their major industrial-country trading partners were experiencing pressures for real exchange rate appreciation. What then are the relative costs, for instance, of accepting real exchange rate appreciation through nominal appreciation or inflation? For example, Levy-Yeyati and Sturzenegger (Chapter 5, this volume) suggest that there are growth benefits to some undervaluation. Is it really true that holding down the nominal exchange rate results in inflation taking on the burden of adjustment? To answer such questions, a great deal more work needs to be done to understand whether the interest rate channel or the exchange rate channel is more important in emerging markets for transmitting the effects of monetary policy actions.

One response to the sort of conundrum laid out above is to argue that it is better for central bankers to adopt a pragmatic and flexible approach rather than a rule-bound framework. India's central bankers, for instance, have an inflation objective but do actively manage the exchange rate at times (also see Yi, 2001 for a Chinese central banker's views on this issue). Some policymakers seem to feel that this type of approach gives them a degree of operational freedom since they can keep market participants guessing and avoid giving markets one-way bets. But there are some potentially negative effects of such an approach, which have been in evidence in the Indian context. It makes outcomes of monetary policy actions less predictable since the market is never entirely sure of how to interpret individual policy actions, therefore leading to market overreactions in some circumstances. This reduces the effectiveness of the monetary transmission mechanism. It also increases overall policy uncertainty, which is not good for anchoring inflation expectations, or for growth and stability.

A different set of questions enters into the complicated relationship between monetary policy and financial markets. How should monetary policy react to asset price bubbles? Are there conflicts between the monetary policy and financial stability objectives? What are the implications for the optimal regulatory structure for banks and other financial institutions – is it better for the central bank not to be the direct regulator of banks, freeing it up to take monetary policy decisions without having to be constrained by worries about the repercussions on the banking system? (For a practitioner's perspective on these issues, see Reddy, 2008.)

Events in 2007 and 2008 showed that faced with a looming financial crisis, a central bank cannot ignore the banking system when pursuing its monetary policy objective (see Mohan, 2007 for a related discussion). Events related to the US bailout of Bear Stearns and the failure of Northern Rock in the UK show that conventional wisdom does not always hold – the US Federal Reserve won at least a few plaudits for rescuing a non-bank institution while the Bank of England's reputation was damaged even though it was not the regulator of the bank in question.

There are also a number of practical issues that need to be confronted in the context of an inflation-targeting regime. For instance, what is the right inflation rate to target? Theory tells us that monetary policy should target the inflexible component of price index – that is, core inflation – and not attempt to offset certain relative price shifts that have no long-run implications for general Consumer Price Index (CPI) inflation. In practice almost all inflation-targeting central banks target the headline measure of inflation. In emerging market economies, the reality is that a large part of the consumption basket of average household is accounted for by food and energy. The price of food, in particular, can rise rapidly, putting central bankers in a quandary since targeting core inflation then becomes politically unacceptable. Moreover, rising food and fuel prices have economic consequences that a central bank cannot ignore. For example, they may create upward pressure on wages as workers strive to maintain real incomes. Such second-round effects may result in higher inflation becoming entrenched and require a larger monetary policy response to bring inflation back to target. A different complication arises when there is a large divergence between inflation based on regional CPI or between urban and rural CPI inflation. What price index should central bankers really focus upon and why? What are the trade-offs in terms of credibility and ease of communications versus effective monetary control of choosing different price indexes as the target?

Clearly, the list of unanswered questions far outnumbers those for which we have more or less arrived at plausible answers that both academics and practitioners can agree upon.

1.7 BRIDGING THE GAPS BETWEEN THEORY AND PRACTICE

How can academic research contribute to improving the formulation of monetary policy and addressing in a concrete way the difficult challenges that central bankers face? Many practitioners feel that the academic literature has failed to come to grips with the complexities and messiness of policymaking in the real world. Mervyn King (2005), for instance, has gently noted that in some respects monetary practice is ahead of monetary theory. The discussion in the preceding sections has laid out a number of issues where theory has not provided clear-cut answers. But there are challenges in another dimension as well – incorporating the knowledge from existing theory (and related empirical evidence) into the policymaking process.

Some obvious challenges in these two dimensions are as follows. Analytical models currently used by central banks have serious limitations. For instance, neo-Keynesian models that are still widely used in many policy institutions typically have very little role for money, despite a broad consensus that in the long run inflation remains a monetary phenomenon (Goodhart, Chapter 4 in this volume). Dynamic stochastic general equilibrium models hold out a lot of promise in terms of formulating monetary policy but often have a limited role for the financial sector and for commodity prices (see Goodfriend and King, 1997; Goodfriend, 2002 [2004]; Woodford, 2003). So the available models are not very helpful in thinking about how central banks should react to shocks such as sharp changes in food or fuel prices, or dislocation in financial markets. On the financial stability side, the development of macro models in which the real and financial sectors are linked together that can help seriously analyze issues of financial and macro stability in a general equilibrium context is still in its infancy.

At the same time, theoretical models have not yet done a good job of figuring out how to model the formation of inflation expectations, which is a key input into monetary policy formulation. Despite the potency of the Lucas critique, models with backward-looking expectations still dominate, in part because of their tractability relative to models with forward-looking expectations.

Despite these caveats, the chapters in this volume are also testament to the progress that can be made on these challenging issues through a process of interactive dialogue between central bankers and academics.

NOTES

* The views expressed here are those of the authors and not necessarily those of the Bank of England.

1. The general discussion in this section draws on material from the volume edited by Bernanke and Woodford (2005). For a more specific discussion of these issues for emerging markets see Jonas and Mishkin (2005), and for a skeptical view on the relevance of inflation targeting for these economies see Blanchard (2005).

REFERENCES

Bernanke, Ben, Thomas Laubach, Fredrick Mishkin and Adam Posen (1999), *Inflation Targeting: Lessons from International Experience*, Princeton, NJ: Princeton University Press.

Bernanke, Ben and Michael Woodford (eds) (2005), *The Inflation Targeting Debate*, Chicago, IL: University of Chicago Press.

Blanchard, Olivier (2005), 'Discussion of Inflation Targeting in Transition Countries: Experience and Prospects', in Ben Bernanke and Michael Woodford (eds), *The Inflation Targeting Debate*, Chicago, IL: University of Chicago Press.

Goodfriend, Marvin (2002), 'Monetary Policy in the New Neoclassical Synthesis: A Primer', *International Finance,* Summer, pp. 165–92; reprinted (2004), *Economic Quarterly*, Federal Reserve Bank of Richmond, Summer, pp. 21–45.

Goodfriend, Marvin (2004), 'Understanding the Transmission of Monetary Policy', manuscript, Federal Reserve Bank of Richmond, presented at Joint China–IMF High Level Seminar on China's Monetary Policy Transmission Mechanism, Beijing, May.

Goodfriend, Marvin and Robert King (1997), 'The New Neoclassical Synthesis and the Role of Monetary Policy', in Ben Bernanke and Julio Rotemberg (eds), *NBER Macroeconomics Annual*, Cambridge, MA: MIT Press.

de Grauwe, Paul (2000), *Economics of Monetary Union*, Oxford: Oxford University Press.

Husain, Aasim, Ashoka Mody and Kenneth Rogoff (2005), 'Exchange Rate Durability and Performance in Developing versus Advanced Economies', *Journal of Monetary Economics*, **52**, pp. 35–64.

Jonas, Jiri and Frederic S. Mishkin (2005), 'Inflation Targeting in Transition Countries: Experience and Prospects', in Ben Bernanke and Michael Woodford (eds), *The Inflation Targeting Debate*, Chicago, IL: University of Chicago Press.

King, Mervyn (2005), 'Monetary Policy: Practice Ahead of Theory', Mais Lecture, http://www.bankofengland.co.uk/publications/speeches/2005/speech245.pdf.

Levin, Andrew T., Fabio M. Natalucci and Jeremy M. Piger (2004), 'The Macroeconomic Effects of Inflation Targeting', *Reserve Federal Bank of St Louis Review*, **86** (4), pp. 51–80.

Mishkin, Frederic S. (2000), 'Inflation Targeting in Emerging-Market Countries', *American Economic Review, Papers and Proceedings*, **90** (2), pp. 105–9.

Mishkin, Frederic S. and Klaus Schmidt-Hebbel (2005), 'Does Inflation Targeting Make a Difference?', manuscript, Columbia University.

Mohan, Rakesh (2007), 'Recent Financial Market Developments and Implications For Monetary Policy', Valedictory Address at IIF's Inaugural Asia Regional Economic Forum, 20 September.

Prasad, Eswar (forthcoming), 'Is the Chinese Growth Miracle Built to Last?', *China Economic Review*.

Prasad, Eswar and Raghuram Rajan (2008), 'A Pragmatic Approach to Capital Account Liberalization', NBER Working Paper No. 14051; forthcoming in *Journal of Economic Perspectives*.

Prasad, Eswar and Shang-Jin Wei (2007), 'The Chinese Approach to Capital Inflows: Patterns and Possible Explanations', in Sebastian Edwards (ed.), *Capital Controls and Capital Flows in Emerging Economies: Policies, Practices, and Consequences*, Chicago, IL: University of Chicago Press.

Reddy, Yaga V. (2008), 'Monetary and Regulatory Policies: How to Get the Balance Right', Speech at the Bank for International Settlements (BIS), 29 June.

Rose, Andrew (2006), 'A Stable International System Emerges: Bretton Woods, Reversed', CEPR Discussion Paper No. 5854.

Sims, Christopher (2005), 'Limits to Inflation Targeting', in B. Bernanke and M. Woodford (eds), *The Inflation Targeting Debate*, Chicago, IL: University of Chicago Press.

Williamson, John (1998), 'Crawling Bands or Monitoring Bands: How to Manage Exchange Rates in a World of Capital Mobility', *International Finance*, **1** (1), pp. 59–79.

Williamson, John (2006), 'Why Capital Account Convertibility in India Is Premature', *Economic and Political Weekly*, 13 May, pp.1848–50.

Woodford, Michael (2003), *Interest and Prices: Foundations of a Theory of Monetary Policy*, Princeton, NJ: Princeton University Press.

Yi, Gang (2001), 'The Framework of China's Monetary Policy', manuscript, People's Bank of China, Beijing, presented at the PBC–IMF International Seminar on Monetary Policy Operations, May, Suzhou, China.

2. The pursuit of monetary and financial stability in emerging market economies

Bandid Nijathaworn and Piti Disyatat*

2.1 INTRODUCTION

The attainment of monetary and financial stability is a goal at the forefront of policymakers' agendas everywhere. Yet the route to this end and the challenges involved can be significantly different in emerging markets compared to more developed economies. This chapter discusses the underlying cause of these differences and highlights the key implications for how monetary and financial stability should be pursued in the emerging market context. Viewed from this broader perspective, it becomes clear that not only are short-term stabilization efforts fundamentally limited in their ability to deliver on this front, but they may even hinder the attainment of these goals over the long term.

2.2 THE UNIQUE CONTEXT OF EMERGING MARKET ECONOMIES

The attainment of monetary and financial stability is something that policymakers everywhere place at the forefront of their agendas. Yet it is important to be reminded that they are only a means to an end. Monetary and financial stability are desirable only insofar as they are prerequisites for welfare-enhancing macroeconomic outcomes, and along this dimension, the context in which monetary and financial stability are pursued in emerging markets is quite distinct from that in developed economies. Thus in order to appreciate the challenges and practical aspects of managing monetary policy and financial stability in emerging economies, it is important to be aware of the key features that are unique to policymaking in this setting.

A stylized fact regarding emerging markets is the significantly higher

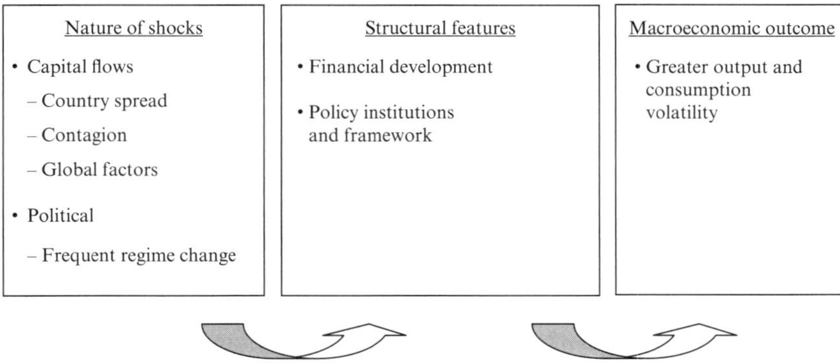

Figure 2.1 Determinants of macroeconomic outcomes

income and consumption volatility that they experience relative to developed economies. Evidently, output and consumption in emerging markets are an order of magnitude more volatile than in developed economies both in terms of levels and growth rates, despite the fact that average levels and growth rates of these variables are higher in developed economies. More strikingly, not only is consumption more volatile in emerging markets, but it is also more volatile in relation to income. As documented in Aguiar and Gopinath (2007), consumption is around 40 percent more volatile than income at business cycle frequencies for emerging markets, while the ratio is less than one for developed economies. The same is true when comparing relative volatility in growth rates of consumption and income (Kose et al., 2005). Such heightened volatility in macroeconomic outcomes that emerging market countries experience undoubtedly has adverse implications for welfare. In particular, the fact that consumption is so volatile – in itself as well as in relation to income – suggests the existence of serious limitations in the ability of economic agents in these countries to smooth consumption in response to shocks.

A large part of the explanation for higher macroeconomic volatility rests with key differences in the nature of shocks hitting emerging economies as well as the way in which their economic systems propagate those shocks. Figure 2.1 depicts how observed macroeconomic outcomes are the result of this interaction between the nature of shocks and the structural features of the economic system. From this perspective, there are key differences between emerging markets and developed economies that fundamentally influence the trade-offs and types of issues that policymakers face in managing monetary and financial stability.

Firstly, the nature of shocks that emerging markets experience is often quite different from what is experienced by developed economies.

A particularly pertinent example in this context is capital flow shocks. By virtue of their limited access to capital relative to growth potential, emerging market economies are natural recipients of capital inflows from capital-rich economies. These inflows are attracted by prospects of higher return and provide the necessary funding of investments that facilitate economic development, especially when the inflows are of the type that bring technological transfers and managerial expertise. At the same time, the procyclical nature of these flows can sometimes manifest themselves in 'sudden stops' that have adverse implications on consumption volatility (Calvo and Reinhart, 1999). This is a reflection of the fact that access to international capital markets has a procyclical element. Reinhart (2002), for example, finds that sovereign bond ratings are procyclical. Since these ratings have an important bearing on the spreads on bonds of emerging economies, this implies that costs of borrowing on international markets are procyclical as well. Indeed, it is a well-documented fact that country spread shocks are important drivers of business cycles in emerging market economies (Uribe and Yue, 2006). In addition, more pronounced information asymmetries in emerging market countries may make them more susceptible to contagion effects that drive large swings in capital flows unrelated to changes in fundamentals. Finally, the fact that capital flows are sensitive not just to domestic conditions in the recipient countries but also to macroeconomic conditions in industrial countries makes emerging market countries more susceptible to a wide array of global shocks.

Political instability and policy uncertainty are also more pronounced in emerging market countries. This is sometimes a reflection of the highly fragmented political landscape in these countries where a large number of small interest groups compete for policy leverage. The end result can be frequent regime switches and dramatic reversals in monetary, fiscal and trade policies. Such shocks can manifest themselves in terms of large observed shocks to trend growth that, in turn, lead to greater macroeconomic volatility. Aguiar and Gopinath (2007) provide convincing empirical evidence in this regard. More generally, a high degree of political uncertainty also feeds back into country spreads that exacerbate capital flow volatility and ultimately, business cycle fluctuations.

The second key difference between emerging market countries and their counterparts in the developed world has to do with structural features of the economic system that influence how various shocks are propagated through the economy. While there are many key differences in this regard, two features are especially important in the context of monetary and financial stability: (1) financial development; and (2) the institutional framework of monetary and financial supervision policy.

One of the most vital foundations of modern economies is the process of channeling resources to their most productive uses. Whether an economy functions smoothly and efficiently or not depends much on the manner in which the financial system performs this task. A strong banking sector with highly disciplined risk management helps to mitigate the risks of financial imbalances while the existence of a deep and liquid financial market that offers a breadth of financial instruments improves the ability of the economy to absorb shocks. More generally, the level of development of an economy's financial sector has a fundamental bearing on social welfare insofar as it determines the ability of agents to smooth out their consumption profile in the face of fluctuations in income. As such, a substantial part of the observed differences in macroeconomic outcomes between emerging market and developed economies can be attributed to the disparate levels of financial sector development in these two groups of countries. Indeed, a number of empirical studies indicate that financial development, especially greater financial access, is associated with lower macroeconomic volatility.[1]

The institutional framework of monetary and financial supervision policy also has an important influence on the extent to which various shocks make their way through the economy. Importantly, in a setting where there is substantial political instability, a weak central bank that lacks independence is likely to be manipulated for short-term political ends with adverse macroeconomic consequences. At the same time, a weak financial supervision framework increases the risk of financial imbalances building up – especially in situations where substantial capital flows drive up asset prices and generate favorable conditions for credit expansion – that may ultimately lead to severe economic dislocations. In contrast, a credible policy framework and enshrined central bank independence provide the necessary preconditions for alleviating the impact of shocks on the economy. For example, by anchoring the public's long-run inflation expectations to the target level, a credible inflation-targeting framework helps to mitigate the impact of temporary supply shocks on inflation and allows the central bank more leeway to adjust its policy instrument to cushion any negative impact on output.

Overall, then, the unique combination of shocks and structural features of the economic system in emerging markets give rise to a macroeconomic backdrop that is characterized by significantly higher output and consumption volatility than in developed economies. The period leading up to and immediately following the 1997 crisis is a prime example of this interaction. Rapid movements in capital flows into and out of emerging markets interacted with financial system underdevelopment, deficient bank supervision, and balance sheet weaknesses, resulting in a boom–bust cycle. In contrast, the experience of developed economies is more generally characterized by one where large shocks typically result in substantial asset price volatility and substantial financial losses that are not accompanied by significant disruption to either short-run or long-run economic growth. A rigorous assessment of the challenges of monetary and financial stability in emerging markets must explicitly recognize this underlying difference in economic backdrop.

2.3 MONETARY POLICY AND FINANCIAL STABILITY: THE LONG AND SHORT OF IT

In light of the unique agglomeration of factors in emerging markets outlined above, the pursuit of monetary and financial stability in emerging markets has two key facets: (1) addressing immediate short-run concerns emanating from various shocks; and (2) implementing structural reforms to ensure that financial stability becomes embedded in the underlying economic structure in the long run. The former concerns the challenge of maintaining economic stability through appropriate policy settings and actions to offset the various shocks hitting the economy at any given point in time. The latter focuses on strengthening the institutional framework for monetary policy and financial supervision as well as fostering financial sector development that improves the ability of the system to absorb shocks by itself in a way that minimizes the impact on the real economy without the need for policy intervention. Given the significant gap that emerging market countries have in this respect relative to developed economies, it becomes more crucial that the pursuit of monetary and financial stability in emerging markets be accompanied by a vigilant focus on making progress on structural reforms. In what follows, some specific challenges to monetary and financial stability in emerging markets from both the short- and long-run perspectives are discussed.

2.3.1 Short-Run Stabilization Challenges

Against the backdrop of a global liquidity glut in recent years, the search for yields among international investors has intensified, resulting in a resurgence of capital inflow into emerging markets and a pick-up in asset price volatility.[2] Given the high degree of dependence on foreign trade and inadequate experience with or willingness to use modern financial risk management tools at the firm level, these asset price fluctuations have become a prominent policy issue in emerging market countries. Within this context, large capital flows into financially shallow markets put pressure on emerging market central banks to lower interest rates or increase sterilized intervention activities in the foreign exchange market. This may even induce authorities to impose prudential measures, which can range from credit policy to capital account restriction on short-term inflows. A core issue that emerging market central banks face in the short run, therefore, is how best to contain financial vulnerabilities that accompany an influx of short-term capital.

Given these developments, there are three key challenges that emerging market policymakers must face in the near term: (1) dealing with the cost and constraint of coping with capital inflows; (2) finding a set of tools that can help assess the build-up of financial vulnerabilities; and (3) complementing monetary policy with prudential measures to prevent potential financial instability.

First, for those under a managed floating regime, lowering interest rates to reduce the relative attractiveness of the country to capital inflows may be an appropriate way to ensure price stability. But concerns of fast appreciation may not subside as exchange rates tend to behave more like asset prices than relative goods prices in practice. That means the nominal effective exchange rate can appreciate for a while in the short run, even after the central banks cut interest rates repeatedly. This is an element of the well-known exchange rate disconnect puzzle. The risk is that a central bank may cut the interest rate by too much, sowing the seeds for inflation and an asset price boom in the future as well. An obvious important technical challenge to emerging market central banks, then, is to improve their ability to forecast inflation and output and be more precise about the range of possible natural rates of interest, which vary through time.

Resisting the appreciating momentum of the exchange rate through interest rates alone may not be sufficient. A widely adopted practice that is assumed to be effective in the short run is through sterilized intervention. Sterilized intervention, however, entails quasi-fiscal costs from swaps or bond issuance, which adds to the liability side of the consolidated public sector balance sheet. Since the debt is in local currency, there is an inflation risk attached to it should there be future fiscal stress. There is also a potential for the market to raise doubts about monetary policy independence and therefore increase the risk of policy uncertainty. In the same vein, accumulating international reserves can also lead to possible damage to central bank credibility in some countries, as they incur balance sheet losses when assets and liabilities are marked to market in local currencies.

In sum, the challenge of containing the effects of capital inflows on asset prices may pose risks to future inflation and financial stability in emerging markets. This challenge seems to suggest the potential for complementing monetary policy with prudential measures, which is discussed below. The extent of the challenge depends crucially on the ability of the economy to cope with asset price fluctuation. It also depends critically on the ability of the real sector to adjust to the pace of the appreciation today as capital inflows continue.

The second challenge in the near term concerns the ability of emerging market central banks or financial supervision authorities to identify and quantify risks of potential financial instability in advance. Stress testing is one of the most powerful tools with which to assess financial stability *ex ante*. If implemented effectively across the financial industries, stress testing can help curb destabilizing activities and prepare financial institutions to deal with macroeconomic or financial shocks. Unfortunately, financial institutions and regulators in emerging economies have lagged behind their counterparts in advanced economies, especially on credit and liquidity risk stress testing.

A priority for regulators in emerging economies is therefore to move faster to increase the use of stress testing. They should also push financial institutions to invest in human resources and technology to conduct macro stress testing at least on an annual basis. Regulators and monetary policymakers must increase coordination in assessing macroeconomic and financial stability in an integrated fashion, in order to arrive at more relevant and convincing macro stress testing scenarios.

Finally, the third challenge, the role of prudential measures, seems to be pressing in light of the possible contradictory effect that financial globalization may impart on monetary policy effectiveness. This contradiction can be summed up as follows. Through both goods and asset price arbitrage, globalization is weakening individual central banks' ability to affect the trajectory of domestic real interest rates beyond relatively short horizons. On the contrary, to the extent that high asset prices are driven by low risk premia, they may become more sensitive to changes in perceived levels of risks. Just as a portfolio of assets with longer duration becomes more sensitive to interest rate changes, so past low interest rates may have contributed to 'excessive' rises in prices of assets that reflect very long horizon returns, such as equities or bonds. In the same vein, future monetary policy tightening may be potent enough to set the stage for their large fall.

While it is unclear how effective domestic monetary policy can be in checking excessive asset price volatility, it could mean that there is a more prominent role for macro-prudential measures. To counter the procyclicality of the credit market, emerging market authorities tend to use discretionary prudential measures such as targeted capital ratio, additional capital requirement, forward-looking provisioning requirement and loan-to-value conditions. These options have to cope with regulatory forbearance, timing effectiveness, market distortions and modelling of early warning systems, which includes the interplay between real and financial sectors.

The primary challenge in this respect concerns how emerging market central banks can move forward and utilize more forward-looking risk-based prudential measures or built-in stabilizers that mechanically link the risk limits such as capital ratio, provisioning, loan-to-value ratios to credit growth, property price movement or the length of economic cycle. This approach should have advantages over its discretionary counterpart in reducing regulatory forbearance (see Borio et al., 2001). However, calibrating policy tools of this type in practice has so far proven difficult, especially in emerging markets where data availability is limited and large structural breaks are present.

2.3.2 Long-Run Structural Reforms

From a longer-term perspective, the attainment of monetary and financial stability is determined predominantly by embedded structural features of the economy. These not only matter with regard to how shocks are propagated through the system but also influence the effectiveness with which policy stabilization efforts are able to cushion the economy from such shocks. This section discusses the roles that financial sector development and policy institutions and frameworks play in this respect.

2.3.2.1 Financial development

The strategy to ensure that the risk management capacity of the economy dynamically evolves with changing risk is to enhance the risk management ability of economic agents, and key to this would be via strengthening the efficiency and robustness of the financial system. The long-term strategy for emerging economies to enhance economic and financial resiliency should embrace the following considerations.

The importance of a well-balanced financial structure An efficient and well-balanced financial system will serve to enhance the efficiency and stability of the economy by ensuring efficient market information analysis, risk assessment, price discovery and allocation of resources and risks, as well as provide for market discipline and an improved risk culture of all players. The development of the financial system should also foster depth and breadth in terms of diversified types of market participants and intermediaries, with diverse underlying demand, risk profile and tolerance, decision horizon and market strategy. These underlying features will allow the system to manage and absorb shocks better as the market would be less prone to one-way market conditions and possesses greater liquidity.

It is important for the emerging economies to develop efficient domestic capital markets and derivatives markets as well as to have access to the international financial markets, so as to have more balanced and diversified financial systems. A more complete financial system will also contribute towards building a stronger banking system, as it will also facilitate risk management of the banking system itself. The experience of the Asian crisis pointed to the critical importance of the development of a long-term local currency debt market. In relation to this, BIS Committee on the Global Financial System's 'Report on Financial Stability and Local Currency Bond Markets' (BIS, 2007) identified that the lack of a long-term debt market may lead to increased risk from: concentration of credit and maturity risks in the banking system, as lack of markets may lead to the mispricing of risk and excessive delay in correcting large exposures; increased vulnerabilities from capital inflows; more limited macroeconomic policy instruments due to the lack of a non-inflationary domestic source of public sector financing; inability to cope with financial distress, as in the event of financial distress, bond market price adjustment accelerates the restructuring process in the aftermath of a financial crisis; and an inadequate range of assets for local investors.

The importance of strong financial market infrastructure Developments in emerging markets have proceeded in this direction, capital markets have grown in size, and the use of derivatives, including securitizations, has also expanded. While much progress has been observed, many of these developments are still at a nascent stage, and progress can take a substantial length of time where there are structural and institutional weaknesses.

Among the key issues for emerging markets are the structural weaknesses which can create disincentive and moral hazard, such as from actual or perceived state guaranty or insurance, such as for exchange rate, bank deposit or investment returns as well as forbearance of bad loans and debt forgiveness. These features create the risk of moral hazard and excessive risk-taking, as well as distorting related markets and hampering private market solutions. The presence of such distortions will therefore contribute to a build-up of financial vulnerability, hinder the growth of a market solution for tackling risk and complicate policy actions in events of crisis management.

These features are of critical importance as they are the underlying cause of risk on a systemic level, pervasive across all sectors. Progress in correcting these, however, may be slow, and can prove to be the major Achilles heel of emerging markets. For example, replacing deposit guaranty by a partial insurance system requires significant institutional strength and capacity to spearhead the legal framework to set up deposit insurance law and organization, but at a more fundamental and subtle level, it requires the authority to build up its reputation and send consistent and credible signals of not bailing out failed institutions. A significant learning curve exists in both the public and private sectors in creating a better credit and risk culture.

Market-driven financial market developments also need the support of critical infrastructure, namely:

1. Information that allows efficient decision-making and pricing on various asset markets – financial as well as related markets such as the real estate market – which are still markedly lacking in many emerging markets, and may be an area for public support. Information related to credit risk also needs to be improved for credit risk modelling, as this remains inadequate due to the comparatively nascent state of risk management development in emerging markets. Some institutions such as credit bureaus need to tackle fundamental issues of efficient market solutions to information sharing and pricing rules to ensure the efficient market provision of information.
2. Legal reform to ensure an enabling environment for innovation in products and business models of the financial system. The emerging market authorities need to support the development of risk management products and markets by providing an enabling regulatory environment, such as by using risk-based regulations, that does not hinder any products but rather ensures suitable risk capital and risk management. However, financial regulations and laws in emerging markets may be outdated and not allow many types of financial products, or to the contrary, they may not give the authority power to ensure the proper risk-based regulations necessary to ensure financial soundness and market integrity. In the worse cases, the regulation itself may be a source of risk if it distorts proper risk adjustment.
3. Human resources with proper competency in modern financial and risk management are scarce and are becoming a bottleneck for development. The authority may need to step in to facilitate training and the accredition of professional standards, if this has external benefits.
4. Accounting standards and disclosure standards that meet international standards, which may be controversial and expensive to implement.
5. Market education of key stakeholders, to ensure a proper risk culture and a reasonable understanding in risk management relevant to their needs.

The existence of a significant gap in emerging markets towards a more efficient and robust financial system Significant progress has been made by emerging markets in the past ten years, much of which has been catalyzed by comprehensive economic reform in which market-oriented economic and financial liberalization have been the main features. These developments are closely related to the process of globalization, while in Asia they are also the outcome of adjustment in response to the economic and financial crisis. A number of studies have been carried out a decade after the Asian crisis to evaluate the progress made in financial sector reform and developments. For example the World Bank's 'East Asian Finance: The Road to Robust Markets' (Ghosh, 2006) observed the following:

1. Diversification. Although the East Asian financial markets have deepened, they lag behind other regions of comparable per capita income in terms of bond markets, particularly corporate bond markets, while the role of equity markets varies across countries but overall has room to improve to match other regions.
2. Efficiency. The banking systems have improved, in association with structural strengthening associated with recapitalization and increased foreign ownership. Equity market efficiency lags behind other regions, while bond markets are hampered by liquidity problems in secondary markets.
3. Risk and soundness. The banking systems and equity markets are in general more robust than in the previous decade, but there are risks from risk-concentration in public banks and the shift of risk to non-banks which may be unregulated.

Thus, despite these developments, a significant gap still exists when compared to the role played by the financial markets in the developed economies, while challenges to financial stability, including those related to globalization, are mounting in emerging markets. It is therefore imperative that the emerging markets devise a proper strategy and process to drive reforms and ensure that their financial system development evolves to meet these challenges.

2.3.2.2 Policy institution and framework

The cross-country experiences of building up economic systems that have the ability to withstand increasingly intensified shocks associated with globalization indicate that a well-developed and balanced financial sector needs to be complemented by robust domestic institutions. With regard to monetary and financial stability, such domestic institutional strength is grounded in: (1) a credible monetary framework that effectively anchors the public's expectation of inflation; and (2) effective financial supervision policy and domestic financial institutions' capacity for sound risk management.

With regard to the monetary policy framework, it is a fact that central banks in emerging markets often have less institutional independence and are less shielded from direct and indirect political pressures in the conduct of policy. These interferences come in the forms of direct reporting of the central bank to the Ministry of Finance, the authority of the latter in appointing the central bank Governor, board members, and/or the Monetary Policy Committee members, through budgetary control, or through forced financing of the fiscal deficits as required by law. Such lack of independence comes at a great cost in terms of lower central bank credibility and a less favorable trade-off between inflation and output volatility.

Less obviously, but equally important, central banks in emerging markets also suffer from a relative lack of transparency in their policy formulation process. This ranges from unclear policy objectives, unspecified policy targets and irregular monetary policy meetings and announcements, as well as the absence of published meeting minutes and voting records of the monetary committee members. Without a clear understanding of the implicit policy response function, weaknesses in monetary policy transparency contribute to policy uncertainty and can exacerbate the impact of shocks on macroeconomic volatility.

With regards to financial supervision, emerging markets also generally trail behind developed economies in terms of the strength of their regulatory frameworks. Moreover, the risk management capacity of financial institutions in emerging market countries faces capacity constraints related to the unavailability of critical data, less supportive legal infrastructure, less adequate accounting standards and severe constraints on the available pool of local talent. These shortcomings inevitably have adverse consequences on the overall financial stability of the system. With less effective supervision and limited capacity to manage risk, the ability of the economic system to absorb volatility from global markets is then compromised. In the face of large capital inflows intermediated through the banking sector, for example, a substantial portion of the funds may be misallocated and end up as non-performing assets. The resultant weakened state of commercial banks' balance sheets then contributes towards more pronounced economic fluctuations.

Thus, for emerging markets, it is important to put greater emphasis on the building up of necessary institutions with regards to effective supervision. On this front, many countries are currently facing the challenges of implementing the Basel II Accord in three main areas: (1) a stronger risk management culture; (2) improved information systems and capacity building; and (3) greater stakeholder involvement. These will be discussed in turn below.

Stronger risk management culture The objective of Basel II is to strengthen the soundness and stability of the banking system through more risk-sensitive capital requirements and rigorous internal risk assessment process. Because Basel II is developed from the current practice among banks in developed countries, some banks in emerging markets may have a large gap to fill. For example, in moving away from collateral-based to credit-based loan approval, banks must focus more on the ability of customers to pay. While this requires a different set of expertise that focuses more on project evaluation than collateral management, loan decisions can be more forward-looking and overall credit should become less susceptible to the fluctuations in collateral prices.

Information system resources and capacity building The most important foundation for achieving financial stability through capital adequacy is information. Whereas developed countries generally already have in place the necessary infrastructure in this regard, financial institutions in emerging countries have to build the system from the ground up, involving areas such as data collection, storage, analysis and ways to embed the information effectively in the decision-making process. Motivated by several minimum requirements in Basel II, banks in emerging countries have invested significantly in the information technology infrastructure and processes to accumulate detailed and high-quality credit data that span a sufficiently long history. With the raw data, banks must develop the capacity to analyze and transform them into usable risk management tools. This step may take more time and effort because it involves building a knowledge base for quantitative analytical skills and the ability to apply international best practice to the unique local settings of emerging market countries. To keep up with the banks, the regulators must also develop their own technical capacity to supervise banks with these more advanced internal risk assessment processes.

Involvement of stakeholders An indirect effect from Basel II implementation is that other players in the wider financial industry will play more active roles in the banking sector, reinforcing the efficiency of risk management in the system. For instance, the simple approach of Basel II ties the amount of required capital to ratings by external credit assessment institutions (ECAIs) which would enable the ECAI's strength in terms of the wealth of data and expertise in credit risk assessment to be drawn on to improve the market efficiency in risk management. Unfortunately, only a few large companies in emerging countries are rated. At the outset, therefore, a significant challenge for regulators lies in the process of ECAI recognitions and risk-weight mapping processes as they must ensure stability of the banking system while at the same time fostering the development of local ECAIs and the bond market. With the increased incentive to be rated from Basel II, it is hoped that the demand for ECAIs will eventually attain the critical mass necessary for them to become an important source of credit information in the financial market. Improved transparency and market information is also a crucial element in strengthening market discipline by a broad set of stakeholders in the financial system, consistent with Pillar III of Basel II.

Overall, the discussion in this section highlights the challenges that emerging market countries must face up to in the process of building up robust domestic institutions and frameworks that are necessary for the maintenance of monetary and financial stability in the long run. Some of these involve amending existing laws, reforming the central bank and financial supervision authority, restructuring the commercial banking system and nurturing local talents. These efforts will undoubtedly take considerable time and patience, but it is a road that has to be taken. The next section discusses some of the main considerations in the emerging market context that influence the effectiveness with which these reforms are implemented.

2.4 FROM HERE TO THERE: THE CHALLENGE OF IMPLEMENTING STRUCTURAL REFORMS

While the two facets of monetary and financial stability discussed above are present in all economies, the interaction between them and the tensions that arise in terms of where the policy emphasis is placed are arguably more complex, with greater welfare implications in the emerging market context, not least because the gains to be had from structural reforms are much higher in these countries. It is therefore also important to focus on the process of implementing structural reforms and how to ensure that they remain on track. This section discusses some of the complexities that arise in this regard and highlights some of the lessons learned from previous reform efforts.

The most prominent conclusion from a reading of the literature on structural reforms is that they are difficult to implement. The first problem is that the gains from reforms are hard to quantify because they are often indirect and thus rarely fully appreciated by the wider public. The enshrinement of central bank independence, for example, helps to insulate monetary policy from short-term political opportunism and paves the way for monetary stability in the long run, but making a case for this in a non-technical manner to a wide audience with conflicting interests often proves a communication challenge for the central banks. The fact that many structural reforms entail short-run costs compounds the problem. The opening up of the domestic banking sector to foreign competition, for example, brings long-run benefits in terms of improved banking services but may adversely impact on domestic banks' profitability in the short run. This time mismatch between the costs and benefits of reforms is a prime reason why they are hard to sell. Where the costs and benefits accrue to different segments of the economy, as in this example, the difficulty of instilling reforms is exacerbated since it is hard to create satisfactory compensation schemes, while those who lose out tend to be concentrated within the particular industry which has been liberalized and thus more cohesive and effective in organizing political opposition to the reforms.

There are, however, general empirical regularities on the conditions that make reforms more likely.[3] These include: (1) a period of economic downturn or crisis that focuses the public's mind on the need for reform; (2) sufficient fiscal room to compensate the losers; (3) the success of previous reforms that may create competitive pressure for reforms in other areas; (4) the longer the length of time remaining in office for the government, the more likely it is that reforms will be undertaken; and (5) external pressure, in the form of either foreign reform efforts that increase competitive pressure domestically, or membership in an international economic organization that requires reform as part of the admission criteria.

Even if the obstacles to selling the reforms have been overcome, the practical aspects of implementing them pose further challenges. One of the most important issues in this respect concerns the proper pace and sequencing of structural reforms. In the context of financial sector reforms, for example, the underlying challenge is the proper mitigation of the additional risks that are injected into the financial system as markets develop and become more sophisticated. These risks consist of both financial risks borne by market participants as well as macroeconomic risks that may be associated with greater financial market volatility. Indeed, inappropriate setting of priorities among the reform measures or an overly rapid pace of change can result in financial instability in the short run. More generally, initiatives in the areas of financial sector development, monetary policy regime and capital account liberalization are all closely related, and designing appropriate reforms in one area requires careful consideration of how to proceed with the others. These and other issues are discussed extensively in the large literature on this subject and will not be repeated here.[4] Suffice to say that the consensus on the importance of structural reform efforts does not carry over with the same strength to the issue of the appropriate pace and sequencing of policy changes. Nonetheless, it should be stressed that a frequent outcome of debates on this issue is excessive inertia in reaching an agreement and actually starting the process of change. The more protracted the transition period, the greater the eventual costs to the economy in terms of deferred benefits from stronger fundamentals.

In the context of emerging markets, the main stumbling block for structural reforms is the high degree of political fragmentation. The need to accommodate many, and sometimes conflicting, interests not only slows the reform process but also often leads to compromised solutions that fail to address the original underlying goal of the reform. Against this backdrop it is vital to have a well-thought-out strategy for the timing and manner of instigating structural reforms. In terms of timing, the political climate in which structural reforms are pursued is a key determinant of the eventual outcome. For example, if reforms of the laws governing central bank mandates and responsibilities are undertaken in a climate where public perception of the central bank is negative, the outcome can be an institutional framework with less central bank independence. The manner with which reforms are proposed and packaged can also have an important bearing on the outcome. In cases where several reform goals are placed together in one package that is put before lawmakers, the risk is that one element of the package on which consensus cannot be reached may derail the whole package of reforms. Worse, extensive debate and bargaining may lead to compromises in some areas in order to achieve consensus on others, resulting in a significantly compromised package of reforms that may even be counterproductive. These risks are more acute in the fragmented political landscape of emerging market countries.

Finally, a recurrent theme that underlies much of the discussion in this chapter is the intricacy of achieving monetary and financial stability while at the same time maintaining the delicate balance of short-run stabilization efforts and long-run structural reforms. This is perhaps the toughest challenge for emerging markets in this regard. In particular, a heavy focus on maintaining immediate financial and economic stability can often hinder efforts to deliver these very same goals in the long run. Thus, ensuring that the outcome of such trade-offs turns out favorable to the attainment of monetary and financial stability in the long term is perhaps the toughest challenge for emerging markets in the present context.

2.5 CONCLUSION

Despite the challenges outlined above, the overall direction of change in emerging market countries in the past ten years is fundamentally reassuring. Much has been achieved in terms of strengthening the monetary frameworks and financial systems development, and reducing vulnerability to external shocks through the accumulation of sizable foreign reserves cushions, as well as significant restructuring of external debt currency denominations and maturity profiles. These changes make it more likely that the process towards further global financial integration will bring substantial benefits in terms of growth and fewer risks in terms of financial distress, and ultimately contribute towards a more stable macroeconomic outcomes.

NOTES

* The views expressed in this chapter are those of the authors and do not necessarily represent those of the Bank of Thailand or Bank of Thailand policy. We would like to thank Ashvin Ahuja, Sarawan Angklomkliew, Jaturong Jantarangs, Nawaporn Maharagkaga, Don Nakornthab, Kobsak Pootrakool, Mathinee Subhaswadikul and Supradit Tangprasert of the Bank of Thailand for their substantial contribution to the drafting of this paper and its final product.

1. Cecchetti et al. (2006) provide empirical evidence for OECD countries that increased access to credit enables households to smooth their consumption, which in turn reduces the volatility of consumption and output growth. See also Larrain (2004) and Raddatz (2003). Similarly, the evidence regarding international financial integration suggests that moving towards the latter ultimately will bring benefits of enhanced risk-sharing that leads to reduced consumption volatility (Kose et al., 2006).
2. This global liquidity glut may have stemmed from various factors, both structural and cyclical. A few examples of structural factors include: a demographic shift from working-age to older population, which swells up the volume of pension funds that need to fulfill their obligation to retirees; the rise of sovereign wealth funds in the era of high international reserves under rigid exchange rate arrangements; technological innovation and the decline in telecommunication, transport and other financial transaction costs from credit risk transfer mechanisms; and capital account liberalization – that have over the years eliminated a significant degree of cross-border financial friction. At the same time, the liquidity glut is also due in no small part to accommodative monetary policy in advanced economies, whether one looks from the angle of low interest rate or high money growth.
3. See OECD (2007), IMF (2004) and Rajan (2004) for a fuller discussion.
4. See, for example, World Bank and IMF (2005), IMF (2005), and Arbache (2004) and the references therein.

REFERENCES

Aguiar, M. and G. Gopinath (2007), 'Emerging Market Business Cycles: The Cycle Is the Trend', *Journal of Political Economy*, **115** (1), pp. 69–102.

Arbache, J. (2004), 'Do Structural Reforms Always Succeed?', United Nations University Research Paper No. 2004/58.

Bank for International Settlements (BIS) (2007), Committee on the Global

Financial System, 'Report on Financial Stability and Local Currency Bond Markets'.

Borio, C., C. Furfine and P. Lowe (2001), 'Procyclicality of the Financial System and Financial Stability: Issues and Policy Options', BIS Papers No. 1, March.

Calvo, G. and C. Reinhart (1999), 'Capital Flow Reversals, the Exchange Rate Debate, and Dollarization', *Finance and Development*, **36** (September), pp. 13–15.

Cecchetti, S., A. Flores-Lagunes and S. Krause (2006), 'Financial Development, Consumption Smoothing, and the Reduced Volatility of Real Growth', AEA 2007 Conference Papers.

Ghosh, S. (2006), *East Asian Finance: The Road to Robust Markets*, Washington, DC: World Bank.

International Monetary Fund (IMF) (2004), *World Economic Outlook: Advancing Structural Reforms*, April, Washington, DC: IMF.

International Monetary Fund (IMF) (2005), Independent Evaluation Office Report, 'Evaluation of the IMF's Approach to Capital Account Liberalization', Washington, DC.

Kose, M., E. Prasad, K. Rogoff and S. Wei (2006), 'Financial Globalization: A Reappraisal', IMF Working Paper 06/189, Washington, DC.

Kose, M., E. Prasad and M. Terrones (2005), 'Growth and Volatility in an Era of Globalization', *IMF Staff Papers*, **52**, pp. 31–63.

Kose, M., E. Prasad and M. Terrones (2006), 'How do Trade and Financial Integration Affect the Relationship between Growth and Volatility?', *Journal of International Economics*, **69**, pp. 176–202.

Larrain, B. (2004), 'Financial Development, Financial Constraints, and the Volatility of Industrial Output', Federal Reserve Bank of Boston Public Policy Discussion Papers 04-06.

OECD (2007), *Going for Growth 2007*, Paris: OECD.

Raddatz, C. (2003), 'Liquidity Needs and Vulnerability to Financial Underdevelopment', World Bank Policy Research Working Paper No. 3161, November.

Rajan, R. (2004), 'Why Are Structural Reforms So Difficult?', *Finance and Development*, June, pp. 56–7.

Reinhart, C. (2002), 'Credit Ratings, Default and Financial Crises: Evidence from Emerging Markets', *World Bank Economic Review*, **16** (2), pp. 151–70.

Uribe, M. and V. Yue (2006), 'Country Spreads and Emerging Countries: Who Drives Whom?', *Journal of International Economics*, **69**, pp. 6–36.

World Bank and IMF (2005), *Financial Sector Assessment: A Handbook*, Washington, DC: World Bank.

3. Implementation of inflation targets in emerging markets

José De Gregorio*

3.1 INTRODUCTION

The main objective of the great majority of central banks in the world is controlling inflation. In some cases financial stability is an added objective; in others, employment or economic development objectives are also included. In the case of Chile there are two explicit objectives, namely, price stability and the 'normal functioning of external and internal payments'. The latter objective, taken from the central bank's charter, corresponds to financial stability,[1] which involves two dimensions. The first is the stability of the domestic financial system, which in simple terms may be described as avoiding financial distress and dealing with it when it occurs. The second is the normal functioning of the system of payments to and from the rest of the world, which in simple terms means avoiding balance-of-payments crises and difficulties of access to international financial markets.

To address the price stability objective, Chile follows an inflation-targeting scheme. Chile is part of a worldwide trend in which a large and growing number of countries have adopted this approach to conducting their monetary policy (International Monetary Fund, 2005, Chapter 4). In an inflation-targeting regime, the central bank publicly announces a numerical objective regarding inflation, which may be either a specific number or a range. Although the target range itself is quite clearly defined, generally the percentage of the time that the central bank expects inflation to lie within the range is not made explicit, and of course one cannot expect inflation always to stay within the range, since inflationary or deflationary shocks will inevitably lead to deviations.[2] However, the central bank does generally set an explicit horizon within which the target is to be met and deviations are to be corrected.

In this chapter I intend to clarify some issues regarding the definition of inflation objectives and the conduct of monetary policy under inflation-targeting schemes. In particular, I will address the widespread but incorrect perception that such schemes imply that the central bank does not consider unemployment or output growth in conducting its policy. Although it is well understood in academic circles that the central bank does take these into account, it is less well understood among policymakers, and even less among the general public. I also discuss some issues concerning the use of inflation targets in practice, in particular the role of public communication and the exchange rate. To summarize, I attempt to show that:

- The inflation objective can be described in terms of a desired distribution for inflation. This may be thought of as defining an average value for inflation and its variability (variance). But in practice the target is defined by a mean value or a range.
- Setting the target as a mean and a variance is equivalent to defining the target in terms of a range and the percentage of the time one expects inflation to be in the range. This is comparable to setting the target around an inflation projection for the future, where the future time frame, or 'policy horizon', depends on the variance of the inflation target. The greater the fraction of time inflation is sought to be within the range, the shorter the policy horizon must be.
- A flexible inflation-targeting scheme, in which the target is defined along with a time horizon, reflects an objective function of the central bank that values not only price stability but also output and employment stability. In particular, a direct relationship also exists between the policy horizon and the central bank's tolerance of deviations of inflation from the target, on the one hand, and the importance attributed by the authorities to output deviations, on the other.
- Exchange rates are an important element in an inflation-targeting regime in an open economy as long as fluctuations in the value of the currency have effects on inflation. Although many countries with floating exchange rates and low inflation have seen a decline in the pass-through from exchange rate fluctuations to changes in domestic prices, large exchange rate swings may still have effects on inflation, and hence should be considered when making monetary policy decisions.

3.2 DEFINING THE RANGE FOR THE INFLATION TARGET AND THE POLICY HORIZON

The inflation target is fixed over a stated time horizon because it is recognized that inflation cannot be controlled in the short term, since monetary policy acts with a lag. Furthermore, and as discussed further below, a gradual adjustment of inflation when it deviates from the target avoids the costs, in terms of reduced economic activity, that would be incurred if inflation were returned to its target immediately. In other words, even if monetary policy did not operate with a lag, it would still be desirable to adjust gradually.[3] Moreover, in general, when the inflation target is specified in the projection horizon, explicit reference is made to a precise point, which always corresponds to the center of the target range.

This section develops a simple framework that explicitly shows the different ways of defining a given inflation target. In the first subsection, the central bank is assumed to take inflation as given, and some equivalences are shown in the definition of the inflation target that are useful for understanding its formulation. The next subsection complements this discussion by adding economic structure and endogenizing the inflation process.[4]

3.2.1 A Simple Framework for Understanding the Inflation Target

Consider a central bank whose target for inflation is defined as a range between $\overline{\pi}$ and $\underline{\pi}$, with its center equal to $\pi^* = (\overline{\pi} + \underline{\pi})/2$. Some central banks define the target in this way: for example, in Canada, Israel and New Zealand this range is from 1 to 3 percent, in South Africa it is from 3 to 6 percent, and in Chile the range is from 2 to 4 percent.[5] Other countries define the target as a single number, without specifying a range: for example, the United Kingdom sets a target of 2 percent, and Norway and Iceland 2.5 percent.

One can think of the inflation target and its range as corresponding to a probability distribution for inflation, with the objective understood as an expected value and a variance.[6] However, in reality most central banks define a range rather than a variance, because a range is more easily understood by the general public. Also, defining a distribution rather than a range requires much more information and certitude than central banks have in practice. As this section should make clear, in order for these two concepts, range and variance, to be equivalent one must define not only the range, but also the fraction of time that inflation is expected to be within the range – in other words, its probability of being within the range at a given time. I will denote this probability by x. In practice the value of x is not defined, although as shown here, when a policy horizon is defined, the tolerated variability of inflation is given implicitly.

Once a target range is known, the first question to ask is what this range means. Central banks are reluctant to be specific, but it is useful to think of the central bank as wanting inflation to lie within the range x percent of the time. It suffices to specify these two parameters – the target range and the percentage x – to establish both the center of the range (that is, the expected value of inflation) and the variance. Specifically, given the assumption of a known symmetric distribution (for example, a normal distribution), and given the range and the percentage of the time inflation is expected to be within the range, one can immediately determine the variance of inflation. The greater the value of x, the lower the variance of inflation must be.

As shown by Svensson (1997), the inflation target may be operationalized by setting the objective in terms of an inflation projection over a given horizon, which in practice is usually between four and eight quarters. One reason for such a relatively long horizon is that monetary policy affects inflation with a lag. A second is that adjusting inflation rapidly to its target would entail undesired costs in terms of reduced economic activity and high unemployment, even if inflation were perfectly controllable. In other words, inflation-targeting models do take unemployment into account. In fact, in the following section it is assumed, for the sake of simplicity, that the central bank determines inflation instantaneously, yet the optimal adjustment is still gradual.

Another relevant equivalence is that between the variance of inflation from its target and the policy horizon. Suppose that inflation follows a first-order autoregressive, or AR(1), process given by:[7]

$$\pi_t - \pi^* = \rho(\pi_{t-1} - \pi^*) + \varepsilon_t, \tag{3.1}$$

where ε_t is an independent and identically distributed (i.i.d.) random shock with a mean of zero and a variance of σ_ε^2, and ρ is the autocorrelation coefficient, which is between zero and one. The expected value of inflation is π^* and its unconditional variance is:[8]

$$\sigma_\pi^2 = \frac{\sigma_\varepsilon^2}{1 - \rho^2}. \tag{3.2}$$

In making its monetary policy decisions, the central bank projects inflation into the future. The central bank observes ε_t, but from $t + 1$ forward, the best it can do is to assume that this shock will be zero. The inflation projection one period ahead, conditional on all of the information available at time t, will thus be $\rho\pi_t + (1 - \rho)\pi^*$, and the projection T periods ahead will be:

$$E_t\pi_{t+T} = \rho^T\pi_t + (1 - \rho^T)\pi^*. \tag{3.3}$$

As the horizon lengthens (that is, as T rises), ρ^T approaches zero and the inflation projection approaches π^*. Consider now the case where the central bank announces that it wishes inflation to be around π^* in period T. More precisely, it wants the forecast of inflation to converge to π^*. In this respect, the objective of the central bank is the convergence of $E_t\pi_{t+T}$, where the relevant information set contains π_t. Therefore the conditional forecast $\rho^T\pi_t + (1 - \rho^T)\pi^*$ is the variable on which the operational objective of the central bank is based.

Given that only as T goes to infinity does the projection fully converge to π^*, it is assumed that a tolerance margin is allowed, expressed as the variance of the conditional forecast s. As a consequence, the variance of projected inflation that is obtained from equation (3.3) is:

$$T = \frac{\log s - \log \sigma_\pi^2}{2\log \rho} \tag{3.4}$$

$$= \frac{\log s - \log \sigma_\varepsilon^2 + \log(1 - \rho^2)}{2\log \rho}. \tag{3.5}$$

In the latter expression it should be noted that, given that $s < \sigma_\pi^2$ and $\rho < 1$, both the numerator and the denominator are negative; accordingly, T is well defined, since it is necessarily positive. It follows that the greater the variance of target inflation, σ_π^2, or in other words, the greater the range of inflation for a given x, the longer the policy horizon over which the conditional forecast is expected to converge toward π^*. Likewise, the greater the value of ρ, the longer the policy horizon, since the increased persistence of inflation slows down its convergence to the center of the target range.

In brief, it has been established that defining an inflation objective in terms of its mean and variance is equivalent to defining a range within which inflation is expected to remain during a given percentage of the time. This, in turn, is directly related to the projection horizon over which inflation is expected to converge toward its expected value. Therefore, if one knows the inflation distribution, and assuming inflation follows an AR(1) process like that described in equation (3.1), we have established that all three definitions of the target shown below are equivalent:

1. The inflation target has an expected value of π^* and a variance of σ_π^2.
2. The inflation target is given by the range $[\underline{\pi}, \overline{\pi}]$ in which it is expected to be x percent of the time.
3. Projected inflation is expected to be around π^* with a variance of s over a horizon of T periods ahead.

If one defines all the parameters of any one of these three definitions, one can then determine the parameters of the other two. Therefore, if one knew the economy's behavior exactly, it would be impossible to separate the inflation-targeting decision from the policy horizon. However, in reality this behavior is not known with accuracy, and this explains the lack of numeric precision in all parameters of the objective function. Moreover, it may be argued that specifying these parameters may lead to inconsistency, precisely because of the uncertainty that exists with respect to the actual structure of the economy. For example, the target may be defined in terms of definition 1 or 3, but the value of T could be inconsistent with the target specified in definition 2, simply because the economy's structure is not fully known.[9]

As an alternative to defining all of the inflation target's parameters precisely, central banks have moved to increase transparency and provide public explanations of their deviations from the target in their periodic inflation reports, also called monetary policy reports. For example, whenever inflation in the United Kingdom deviates from its target, the Governor of the Bank of England writes a formal letter to the Chancellor of the Exchequer to give an account of why the deviation has occurred. All these arrangements replace a more mechanical and explicit behavior with respect to the inflation target, in a world with much more uncertainty than is assumed in the models, with a public and transparent rendering of accounts. This practice recognizes that there are risks and contingencies that central banks' projection models cannot predict; nor can all policy responses to more complex scenarios than simple deviation of inflation from its target – particularly those associated with financial stability – be anticipated. It reflects the need to balance a well-defined rule, by which the central bank's performance can be evaluated, with proper flexibility in a real world that contains much uncertainty.

3.2.2 Is Inflation All that Matters?

Whereas the previous section assumed that the central bank takes the inflation process as given, this section goes further and adds structure to the economy, to understand where inflation comes from and how it relates to the output gap. This is done by deriving equation (3.1) above from the fundamental parameters of the economy, which in this case are given by preferences between unemployment and inflation along a Phillips curve. The value of ρ is determined by the monetary authorities, who gradually adjust inflation so as to reduce the cost of that adjustment in terms of output. The possibility of demand shocks is ignored.

Here I will use the model presented in De Gregorio (1995), which allows the optimal course of inflation to be derived from a social loss function, where the losses derive from inflation and output gaps, plus a Phillips curve that incorporates indexation of inflation. I will assume that the central bank has determined an optimal inflation rate π^*, but that it adjusts inflation gradually toward this rate in order to reduce welfare losses.

The social loss function is given by:[10]

$$L = a(y - \bar{y})^2 + (\pi - \pi^*)^2, \tag{3.6}$$

where y is gross domestic product (GDP) and $\bar{y}$ its full-employment level. It should be noted that here there is no inflationary bias as in Barro and Gordon (1983), since the central bank's preferences are socially optimal (Rogoff, 1985).[11]

Inflation is determined by the following Phillips curve:

$$\pi_t = \alpha\pi_{t-1} + (1 - \alpha)\mathrm{E}_{t-1}\pi_t + \delta(y - \bar{y}) + v. \tag{3.7}$$

The term v corresponds to an i.i.d. inflationary shock with zero mean and variance σ_v^2. This Phillips curve incorporates persistence of inflation through the term $\alpha\pi_{t-1}$, which may be interpreted as the result of indexation of prices and salaries. A simple case is that of certain regulated utility prices, which are indexed to past inflation. The persistence term could also represent the outcome of overlapping decisions on prices and salaries as in the extension of Taylor (1980) proposed by Fuhrer and Moore (1995).[12] The parameter α can also be interpreted as related to the credibility of the inflation target. If the public is confident of the authorities' commitment to the inflation target, expectations will be more forward-looking than if credibility is lacking, in which case the public may assume that past inflation will tend to be more persistent. The Phillips curve's slope is δ and, to simplify the notation, its inverse is defined as θ.

Solving for the output gap in the Phillips curve and replacing it in the objective function, we have that the first-order condition for the central bank's optimization is given by the following (subscript t is eliminated, and instead subscript -1 is used for a one-period lag):

$$\pi - \pi^* = \frac{1}{1 + a\theta^2}[\alpha a\theta^2(\pi_{-1} - \pi^*) + (1 - \alpha)a\theta^2(\mathrm{E}_{t-1}\pi - \pi^*) + a\theta^2 v]. \tag{3.8}$$

Taking expectations from the above expression to solve for rational expectations of inflation, and replacing this expression in the same first-order condition, we obtain the following expression for optimal inflation:

$$\pi - \pi^* = \frac{1}{1 + \phi}(\pi_{-1} - \pi^*) + \frac{v}{1 + \phi\alpha}, \tag{3.9}$$

where:

$$\phi \equiv \frac{1}{a\theta^2\alpha}. \tag{3.10}$$

Optimal inflation has the same form assumed in equation (3.1), where the autocorrelation coefficient and the error depend on the fundamental parameters of the model and on the inflationary shock. That is:

$$\rho = \frac{1}{1 + \phi} = \frac{a\theta\alpha}{1 + a\theta^2\alpha} \text{ and } \varepsilon = \frac{v}{1 + \phi\alpha}. \tag{3.11}$$

It should be noted that expected inflation is equal to the central value of the target range, π^*, and the variance is:

$$\sigma_\pi^2 = \left(\frac{a\theta^2}{1 + a\theta^2}\right)^2 \frac{\sigma_v^2}{1 - \rho^2}. \tag{3.12}$$

From these equations it can be easily verified that ρ and σ_π^2 are increasing functions of a, α and θ, and that σ_π^2 is increasing in the variance of the inflationary shock (σ_v^2). In section 3.2.1 it was shown that increasing the variance of target inflation is similar to extending the policy horizon or widening the target range, all else being equal. An increase in the variance of inflation produces the same results. Since an increase in any of the three parameters (a, α, θ) increases both σ_π^2 and ρ, one can conclude that increases in those parameters also lengthen the policy horizon T, as can be seen from equation (3.5).

These results can be interpreted as follows:

- When the central bank is not concerned about unemployment (that is, $a = 0$), the value of ρ will be zero, and expected inflation will adjust to π^* in each period. Therefore the policy horizon collapses to zero: the central bank attempts to meet the inflation projection in each period. In this case inflation would equal π^*, because monetary policy would fully offset the effect of any inflationary shock. As a increases, the policy horizon lengthens or, similarly, the inflation target variance increases.
- The greater the volatility of inflationary shocks, the greater the variance of target inflation, which in turn generates a longer policy horizon.
- Something similar occurs when the degree of backward-lookingness, measured by α, increases, as this also produces a slower adjustment and greater variability of the inflation target – the target range increases.
- When the slope of the Phillips curve decreases (δ falls and θ rises), the output gap has a smaller impact on inflation. Therefore the

central bank will accept a greater inflation variance, or a longer policy horizon, because it does not want to vary the output gap too much to offset inflationary shocks.

Why does all this happen? Because even though the central bank defines its objective in terms of an inflation target, it also considers the costs, in terms of unemployment, of attaining the target. In other words, having an inflation target does not mean that unemployment costs are disregarded. It should be noted that although, in this model, monetary policy operates without lags, the inflation target is not intended to be met in the short term.

To sum up, the persistence of inflation declines, and the policy horizon shortens, in response either to a decline in a, that is, an increase in inflation aversion; or to a decline in α, the degree of indexation; or to an increase in the slope of the Phillips curve $\delta = 1/\theta$, that is, a decline in θ. The decline in inflation persistence should also be accompanied by a decline in the variance of inflation, as long as the variance of the inflation shock (σ_v^2) remains constant.

The advantage of specifying the macroeconomic stability objective in terms of an inflation target is that it avoids the inconvenience of defining two objectives that might be inconsistent. For example, defining a limit for output variation along with an explicit inflation target could make both objectives incompatible with the economy's structure.

There are additional complications when the target is specified in terms of the activity level, since full-employment output is not known with certainty, and therefore pursuing very low unemployment could lead to the traditional inflationary acceleration; or, conversely, underestimation of full-employment output could lead to too rapid a deceleration of inflation or even deflation.

However, the fundamental reason for choosing an inflation-targeting regime is that otherwise inflation would be undetermined. Monetary policy deals with prices and inflation. Defining an inflation target provides an anchor for inflation.

3.3 ISSUES IN INFLATION TARGETING: INSTITUTIONS AND EXCHANGE RATES

In this section I will address two relevant issues for the implementation of inflation targets. The first is the use of public communication to report on the fulfillment of the inflation target. This is particularly relevant given that central banks do not have full control over inflation. I also discuss the limits to transparency, as well as the role of the exchange rate in the inflation-targeting regime. There is a natural place for exchange rate policy, and even exchange rate stabilization, in an inflation-targeting regime, once one takes into account the inflationary consequences of exchange rate fluctuations. I also discuss the role of foreign exchange intervention as an exceptional measure.

3.3.1 Communication and Transparency as Substitutes for Precision

Given the results presented above, inflation-targeting central banks should define their objectives by stating a target range for inflation and indicating the percentage of the time they intend inflation to lie within that range. This is equivalent to saying that they should announce the mean and variability of inflation. Additionally, convergence of inflation to the target can be defined as an intermediate objective, in a policy horizon that takes into account both the costs of attaining the target and the lags with which monetary policy operates. In general, this horizon is defined as from one to three years. However, the definition of the target is not precise. It is not completely clear what fraction of the time (x in the model) the central bank expects inflation to be within the tolerance range, nor is the central bank precise about the distance from the center of the band it expects the forecast to be (s in the model).

In practice, there is uncertainty regarding the transmission mechanisms of monetary policy and the structure of the economy: the 'true' parameters of the model in section 3.2 are unknown. This is particularly valid in emerging market economies, because of their frequent structural and policy changes. This makes it difficult to be precise in defining all of the parameters of the inflation target. When monetary policy is anchored by a fixed exchange rate or by targeted monetary aggregates, monitoring is very simple. It suffices to see whether the exchange rate is at the announced level or whether the monetary aggregates follow the announced path. With this information in hand, the public can evaluate whether the monetary policy objectives are being met. However, exchange rate and monetary anchors are less and less frequently used, since they are less efficient as a means of conducting monetary policy. Currently, most central banks instead set interest rates and pursue an implicit or explicit inflation target. Monitoring inflation is easy, but explaining deviations from the target is a more difficult task.

Inflation usually does deviate to some degree from the target. In Chile this has been the case since 2007, a period that has witnessed a sharp increase in food prices and a continuing rise in the oil price. But such deviations can have different causes: they may be due to some genuinely uncontrollable event or influence (such as a food price shock), or they may be due to the central bank failing to adopting a monetary policy consistent with its inflation target. For this reason, public communication and accountability are particularly important under an inflation-targeting scheme. This is why most central banks that have adopted inflation targets prepare periodic inflation reports to inform the public about actual inflation performance and explain its consistency with monetary policy decisions. This increases the credibility of monetary policy and strengthens commitment to the inflation target.

But predictability and transparency can also improve the effectiveness of monetary policy. Predictability is desirable because it avoids abrupt adjustments in asset prices. Also, it allows that the monetary policy and its expected future path be transmitted to the entire yield curve. In fact, monetary policy determines the interbank interest rate quite accurately, but aggregate demand depends on longer-term rates. Working capital depends on rates ranging from three months to one year, and investment on even longer-term rates. To the extent that monetary policy signals and strategy provide useful information for the market as it forms its expectations, the whole yield curve will be affected, and consequently monetary policy will be more effective.

Transparency also has its limits, and these are precisely related to the effectiveness of monetary policy, its decision-making independence, and the need for monetary policymakers' deliberations to be as frank and productive as possible. For example, in many countries the minutes of monetary policy meetings do not indicate which members take one position or another. This is reasonable, because what is more important is the tenor of the discussion, and revealing names could discourage members from speaking candidly at meetings, thus affecting the central bank's capacity to act with genuine independence. Full transcripts of the discussions are good for transparency and accountability, but these can be provided after a relatively long lag: the Federal Reserve Board, for example, releases transcripts after five years. How transparency is implemented in each country is specific to each case and its institutional tradition, but effective monetary policy in an inflation-targeting framework invariably requires a high degree of transparency.

Finally, adoption of an inflation target in emerging market economies poses certain institutional requirements. The first is an independent central bank that is empowered to establish a policy horizon that extends beyond the political and electoral horizons. Also necessary is a solid fiscal situation, to avoid the subordination of monetary policy to fiscal policy and so eliminate the possibility of inflationary financing, which undermines the credibility of the inflation target.

3.3.2 The Role of the Exchange Rate and Asset Prices

Another key element in an inflation-targeting regime is the exchange rate regime. If the economy is financially fully open, one cannot simultaneously adopt an independent monetary policy (that is, set the policy interest rate) and control the exchange rate – this is the well-known 'impossible trinity'. Therefore a floating exchange rate regime is a prerequisite for an effective inflation-targeting scheme. However, exchange rate fluctuations, in particular periods of persistent appreciation or depreciation, may create additional risks to macroeconomic stability that may require additional policy action.

After the bursting of the dot-com bubble in the United States some years ago, there was considerable discussion of whether the Federal Reserve should have raised interest rates pre-emptively, even in the absence of signs of rising inflation, so as to prevent the bubble from continuing to grow. This question has become even more urgent with the bursting of the housing bubble and the financial crisis that followed. Those who believe that pre-emptive action should have been taken argue that such action could have prevented, or at least attenuated, the financial crisis and economic slowdown that followed the bursting of the bubbles. Those on the other side maintain that monetary policy would have been neither effective nor necessary, because a slowdown would have followed even if the bubble had deflated gradually, and nor is there any certainty that an increase in interest rates could have prevented the bubbles.

This is certainly a second-order problem compared with the dilemma most emerging market economies face: namely, what to do about the exchange rate. Most countries have a preference for a 'competitive' real exchange rate, one that gives an advantage to the country's exports in foreign markets. This preference is natural in the wake of the many disastrous experiences with massive currency overvaluation under schemes of exchange rate inflexibility. Many considerations justify a flexible exchange rate regime, and this is not the place to discuss them.[13] I will focus here only on the role of the exchange rate in an inflation-targeting regime.

There has been much discussion of whether the exchange rate should or should not affect monetary policy decisions, that is, the setting of the policy interest rate.[14] In the context of a Taylor rule, the question is whether or not the exchange rate should be an argument in the rule. In a more general context, it is important to remember that, rather than any mechanical rule for setting the interest rate, what needs to be considered is what trajectory of interest rates is consistent with the inflation target. To the extent that the exchange rate affects the inflation outlook, it is a relevant variable to consider when deciding monetary policy. Its effect on consumer price inflation is much more evident than its effect on the prices of other assets, such as house or stock prices. Suppose, for instance, that the currency appreciates sharply and unexpectedly. Even if the pass-through coefficient is relatively low, as it is particularly in countries that have an inflation target set by an independent central bank, such an appreciation should reduce inflationary pressure and therefore create room for a monetary easing, which should in turn reduce exchange rate pressure and provide a better guarantee of achieving the inflation target.[15]

Thus the exchange rate does affect monetary policy decision-making, but it does so because of its effect on inflation, without additional considerations of competitiveness or exchange rate volatility. Therefore when the exchange rate has an effect on inflation projections, monetary policy should take it into account. For example, if the currency depreciates and the depreciation begins to affect inflation, an increase in the interest rate will contribute to attaining the inflation target both through its impact on investment expenditure and consumption of durable goods, and through its effect on the exchange rate. In addition, such a move on the part of monetary policy should stabilize the exchange rate. In any event, it is worth stressing the importance of analyzing the reasons behind exchange rate movements. If the depreciation is due to an adverse external scenario, it may have less of an impact on the inflation outlook and, accordingly, the monetary policy reaction would not necessarily be an increase in the interest rate.

Nevertheless, the direct effects of exchange rate fluctuations on inflation are not the only way the exchange rate can affect monetary policy decisions. Most central banks also have the objective of safeguarding financial stability. In Chile this objective is described in the central bank charter as the 'normal functioning of internal and external payments'. This is interpreted as meaning that the central bank must seek to avoid financial and exchange rate crises and extreme turbulence, as well as financial and exchange rate imbalances that could jeopardize macroeconomic stability. Undoubtedly one way to help ensure financial stability is through the adoption of a flexible exchange rate, but this does not preclude the possibility of exchange rate bubbles threatening financial stability.

An exchange rate bubble is more complicated to deal with than an asset price bubble. If the authorities are certain that, for example, a housing bubble exists, they can increase interest rates in order to prick the bubble. But in an emerging market economy, if the currency is experiencing a bubble, leading to a severe appreciation, raising interest rates could worsen the problem by encouraging an increase in carry trade. However, central banks can use other tools to stabilize the foreign exchange market. In particular, they can intervene directly by increasing or reducing their holdings of foreign exchange reserves. But this must be an exceptional measure, linked to changes in the position of international liquidity, and undertaken within a predefined period of time.

More concretely, current experience, in Chile in particular,[16] suggests that three main conditions must be met when implementing foreign exchange intervention in the context of an inflation-targeting regime with a commitment to control inflation. First, it cannot pursue a specific value for the currency, because then the inflation target would be subordinated to the exchange rate objective, thus falling victim to the 'impossible trinity'. Second, the depreciation that is expected to occur in the wake of the intervention must be consistent with the inflation outlook; otherwise credibility will be undermined. Implementing a mechanical rule for intervention, independent of the value of the currency, preserves monetary autonomy to use interest rates to control inflation. Third, the intervention must be completed within a predefined period: as already stated, intervention is an exceptional measure, and announcing a date for its termination strengthens the commitment to keep the intervention transitory. Experience also confirms that pursuing a mechanical rule for intervening, with some degrees of technical freedom, may be desirable to avoid speculation against the central bank.

Finally, a word about the objective of having a 'competitive' real exchange rate that promotes exports. This discussion is similar to that on the natural unemployment rate, in that the fundamental determinants of the exchange rate are beyond the scope of monetary policy. If the authorities tried to hold the exchange rate permanently to a level inconsistent with its fundamentals, the result could be inflation, which would restore the real exchange rate to its equilibrium level. As argued before, when the authorities are relatively certain that the exchange rate has overreacted, and provided there are no inconsistencies with the inflation target, transitory intervention may provide some relief. But a permanent attempt to avoid an appreciation will lead to inflation, so that a real appreciation takes place after all, through higher inflation and not through a nominal exchange rate adjustment. In addition, as experience shows, such an attempt may encourage the entry of short-term capital, generating additional exchange rate pressure.

Monetary policy cannot affect the real exchange rate in the medium or the long run, since it is determined by its fundamentals, such as the degree of trade openness, productivity growth, fiscal policy, net international assets and the terms of trade. Interest rate changes induce exchange rate fluctuations, but as long as they are incorporated properly in the context of an inflation-targeting regime, the movements of interest rates should be stabilizing. The exchange rate, in turn, functions as a shock absorber.

3.4 CONCLUDING REMARKS

As I hope to have shown, targeting inflation on the basis of a range within which inflation is expected to stay most of the time is similar to fixing an objective for projected inflation over a given policy horizon, or indicating an expected value and a variance for inflation. Either way, the definition actually used by central banks is not quite accurate, since the structure of the economy is not known with sufficient certainty to allow precise definition of the target parameters. Moreover, some margin of flexibility must be allowed to address situations that are impossible to anticipate.

On the other hand, defining the monetary authority's objective in terms of an inflation target does not mean that the business cycle, particularly unemployment, is irrelevant to it. This is reflected in the fact that the target is not intended to be met always and under all circumstances, and in the fact that the target is established in the context of a policy horizon generally of one to three years.

This chapter has used a simple analytical model to clarify these points but has omitted some relevant aspects of monetary policy practice, although these should not change the conclusions. The economy is subject to many kinds of shocks besides inflationary ones. This chapter has not considered in detail the credibility of the central bank, but the very decisions it makes and the formulation of its objective reveal information about its ability to contain inflation, as well as about its commitment to the target. Incorporating these aspects adds much more complexity, but generally their implications point in the direction of rigorously meeting the target, since the more credibility the central bank enjoys, the less costly are the adjustments to achieve the inflation target. In terms of the model presented here, credibility can be thought of as reducing inertia and the degree of indexation, thus enabling a faster return of inflation to the target range when deviations occur. It can also be shown that increased credibility on the inflation objective allows a reduction in the variability not only of inflation, but also of output (De Gregorio, 2007). Indeed, this is what the world has witnessed with the Great Moderation.[17]

In this chapter the need for optimal gradualism has been justified by inflation persistence. Excessive activism, in the sense of having a very short policy horizon, can be viewed as leading to greater volatility of interest rates and asset prices, which could lead to instability in the financial system. In a more general dynamic stochastic model, one could conceive of an optimal monetary policy whose horizon varies depending on the nature and magnitude of the shocks it encounters. In actual practice, the problem may be solved with escape clauses that allow for deviations from the target in exceptional situations, for example when financial stability is threatened.

The analysis of the model was presented in the context of a closed economy. Extension to an open economy and interactions with the exchange rate should not change the main conclusions of this discussion, but they certainly add new sources of fluctuation. This issue has been treated informally here in the light of accumulated experience in emerging markets. In any event, incorporating elements of an open economy could provide an additional reason to adopt a medium-term horizon. If the central bank adopted a very short horizon or a very narrow target range, the principal mechanism of monetary policy pass-through to inflation would be the exchange rate rather than aggregate demand. This, in turn, could generate deviations of the exchange rate that might affect the external equilibrium of the economy – an important concern for emerging market economies subject to strong fluctuations in external financing. I have also discussed the role of the exchange rate in the context of an inflation-targeting regime. As long as changes in exchange rates affect inflation, the exchange rate should be one of the variables that central banks take into account when deciding the stance of monetary policy. Doing so may also have a stabilizing effect on exchange rate fluctuations. However, in emerging markets there may be reasons to use additional instruments in periods of excessive fluctuation that threaten financial stability – financial market turbulence like that stemming from the US subprime mortgage crisis is a pertinent example. In such a case, intervention in the foreign exchange market may be advisable as long as it is consistent with the inflation target. This has a parallel with discussions in industrial countries on preventing bubbles from generating financial fragility.

No distinction has been made here between core inflation, which is calculated for a subset of goods in the consumer price index (CPI), and so-called headline inflation. In general, inflation targets refer to headline rather than core inflation, although the latter tends to be more stable. Although theory tends to prefer core inflation, there are reasons (which are not fully rational from an analytical standpoint) why central banks prefer headline inflation. In the first place, use of any of the various alternatives to headline inflation would pose a problem of credibility and public understanding. In addition, if one were to eliminate goods whose prices are more volatile, such as fuels, from the target measure of inflation, the result would only be to reinforce the second-round effects of a shock on such prices. In other words, if the central bank wishes to minimize second-round effects, it should be willing to respond to cost shocks, even if the response is not immediate. Accordingly, fixing the target in terms of headline inflation provides an anchor to all prices.

Central banks do not directly control inflation, as assumed in the model presented here, but do so through the interest rate, which in turn affects aggregate demand and output. To generalize the results, it would be sufficient to specify aggregate demand, which could be affected through the interest rate so as to meet the expected inflation trajectory. However, the main results would not be altered, because it is inflationary shocks that generate the trade-off between inflation and unemployment.

Finally, it could be argued that a flexible inflation-targeting policy is inconsistent with a central bank mandate that is limited to price stability and financial stability. In fact, given that this mandate does not explicitly include output stability, as considered in the model presented here, one could conclude that the horizon should be kept at its minimum. This argument, however, contains two deficiencies. First, a monetary policy that targets inflation in each period, disregarding its effects on output, may undermine financial stability. Such a policy would lead to extreme volatility of interest rates and of output. This, in turn, could increase financial vulnerability, for example by inducing abrupt changes in the financial positions of firms and households. Second, central banks also have more general objectives relating to the overall welfare of the population. In the case of the Central Bank of Chile, its charter says explicitly that: 'When passing its resolutions, the Board shall consider the general orientation of the Government's economic policies.' This 'general orientation' has to do with improving the welfare of the population, which necessarily implies taking into account the costs both of inflation and of output and employment fluctuations when pursuing monetary policy. In short, although inflation may seem to be the only concern of monetary policy in an inflation-targeting regime, this chapter has shown that this is not the case. Output and unemployment fluctuations are implicitly incorporated by allowing inflation to adjust gradually to its objective.

Consequently, a policy of flexible inflation targeting does consider full employment among its objectives. However, it is still preferable to organize monetary policy around a flexible inflation target. Doing so provides a nominal anchor to the economy, which in turn strengthens monetary policy credibility, a crucial element to minimize the costs of attaining price stability.

NOTES

* I am grateful to Luis Felipe Céspedes, Eduardo Engel, Jordi Galí and Andrea Tokman for their valuable discussions and comments, and to Christopher Neilson for superb research assistance.

1. In fact, Title III of the Organic Constitutional Law explicitly refers to the central bank's authority to regulate the financial system and the capital market, as well as to its powers to safeguard the financial system's stability.

2. Schemes of this type are known as 'flexible inflation targets', as opposed to 'strict inflation targets', because inflation is returned gradually to the target range when deviations from the conditional forecast occur; see Svensson (1999).
3. This argument is valid for supply shocks, which are the kind I analyze here. A more general model would allow for demand shocks, which require a different policy response. For the sake of simplicity, this chapter omits demand shocks, as they do not change the conclusions.
4. A more general presentation of the model with additional discussion can be found in De Gregorio (2007), on which this part of the chapter is based.
5. The exact phrasing of the target may differ across countries. For example, in some countries the target is stated as a range, whereas in others it is the center of the target plus or minus a deviation.
6. In what follows, I assume that inflation has a known symmetric distribution – specifically, a normal distribution – which is fully defined by its expected value and its variance.
7. I assume that ρ is known, and in the next section it is treated as endogenous. However, if ρ is uncertain, the value estimated by the central bank will affect the variability of inflation, and this effect will depend on whether ρ is under- or overestimated (Amano, 2007).
8. It suffices to take the variance of both sides of equation (3.1), where the unconditional variances of inflation and past inflation are the same and equal to σ_{π}^2.
9. One might argue that estimating equation (3.1) is easy, and that from there the target may be determined with accuracy, but the relationship between inflation and monetary policy should be also known. The assumption of an AR(1) process is made for expository purposes, but in reality the univariate process could be more complicated. Furthermore, defining the target based on the estimation of reduced-form equations is a prime example of the Lucas critique.
10. This is a simplification of a more general loss function that could be more formally derived following Woodford (2003, Chapter 6). Where indexation is present, the utility function will be somewhat different, but the main qualitative results presented in this chapter should not change.
11. Strictly speaking, from a welfare point of view the relevant objective is to minimize the present value of losses rather than the value in each period. The solution to that problem is significantly more complex; the details are presented in De Gregorio (2007). The assumption of a static loss function implicitly assumes that the central bank has no ability to commit to future policies, and so it optimizes period by period.
12. For more details, see Walsh (2003), Chapter 5.3. The existence of indexation is what complicates the solution of the problem when an intertemporal loss function is assumed. In the event that $a = 0$, the static and the intertemporal solutions are the same.
13. See Larraín and Velasco (2001) and Edwards and Levy-Yeyati (2005).
14. See, for example, Ball (1999).
15. Chile has several times confronted abrupt changes in the exchange rate with inflationary and monetary policy implications, which were explicitly mentioned in the statements after the relevant monetary policy meetings (December 2005 and February, March and April 2008).
16. Since Chile started floating the exchange rate in 1999, there have been three intervention episodes. Those of 2001 and 2002 occurred in the presence of major turmoil in the region and strong depreciation pressures (see De Gregorio and Tokman, 2007). The latest, which is ongoing at the time of writing (second semester 2007), began in the presence of a rapid appreciation in the context of high uncertainty in world financial markets due to the US subprime mortgage crisis, and with the purpose of increasing international reserves in the face of a reduction in international liquidity during the last few years.
17. The Great Moderation was first discussed by Kim and Nelson (1999) and Blanchard and Simon (2001). For a discussion of the various hypotheses offered to explain

the Great Moderation and, in particular, the role of better monetary policy, see De Gregorio (2008).

REFERENCES

Amano, R. (2007), 'Inflation Persistence and Monetary Policy: A Simple Result', *Economic Letters*, **94** (1), pp. 26–31.
Ball, L. (1999), 'Policy Rules for Open Economies', in J.B. Taylor (ed.), *Monetary Policy Rules*, Chicago, IL: University of Chicago Press.
Barro, R. and D. Gordon (1983), 'A Positive Theory of Monetary Policy in a Natural-Rate Model', *Journal of Political Economy*, **91** (4), pp. 589–610.
Blanchard, O. and J. Simon (2001), 'The Long and Large Decline in US Output Volatility', *Brookings Papers on Economic Activity*, **32** (1), pp. 135–64.
De Gregorio, J. (1995), 'Policy Accommodation and Gradual Stabilizations', *Journal of Money, Credit and Banking*, **27** (3), pp. 727–41.
De Gregorio, J. (2007), 'Defining Inflation Targets, the Policy Horizon and the Output–Inflation Tradeoff', Working Paper No. 415, Central Bank of Chile.
De Gregorio, J. (2008), 'The Great Moderation and the Risk of Inflation: A View From Developing Countries', Documento de Política Económica No. 24, Central Bank of Chile.
De Gregorio, J. and A. Tokman (2007), 'Overcoming Fear of Floating: Exchange Rate Policies in Chile', in N. Batini (ed.), *Monetary Policy in Emerging Markets and Other Developing Countries*, New York: Nova Science Publishers.
Edwards, S. and E. Levy-Yeyati (2005), 'Flexible Exchange Rates as Shock Absorbers', *European Economic Review*, **49** (8), pp. 2079–2105.
Fuhrer, J. and G. Moore (1995), 'Inflation Persistence', *Quarterly Journal of Economics*, **110** (1), pp. 127–60.
International Monetary Fund (2005), *World Economic Outlook*, Washington, DC: International Monetary Fund.
Kim, C.-J. and C. Nelson (1999), 'Has the US Economy Become More Stable? A Bayesian Approach Based on a Markov Switching Model of the Business Cycle', *Review of Economics and Statistics*, **81** (4), pp. 608–16.
Larraín, F. and A. Velasco (2001), 'Exchange Rate Policy for Emerging Markets: The Case for Floating', Essays in International Economics No. 224, Princeton University.
Rogoff, K. (1985), 'The Optimal Degree of Commitment to an Intermediate Monetary Target', *Quarterly Journal of Economics*, **100** (4), pp. 1169–89.
Svensson, L. (1997), 'Inflation Forecast Targeting: Implementing and Monitoring Inflation Targets', *European Economic Review*, **41** (6), pp. 1111–46.
Svensson, L. (1999), 'Inflation Targeting: Some Extensions', *Scandinavian Journal of Economics*, **101** (3), pp. 337–61.
Taylor, J. (1980), 'Aggregate Dynamics and Staggered Contracts', *Journal of Political Economy*, **88** (1), pp. 1–23.
Walsh, C. (2003), *Monetary Policy and Theory*, 2nd edn, Cambridge, MA: MIT Press.
Woodford, M. (2003), *Interest and Prices*, Princeton, NJ: Princeton University Press.

4. Whatever became of the monetary aggregates?*

Charles Goodhart

My title intentionally harks back to Maurice Peston's slim, but excellent, 1980 book entitled *Whatever Happened to Macro-economics*. In this book, a compilation of three lectures, Maurice asks how much then remained of traditional Keynesian macroeconomics in the aftermath of the monetarist counter-revolution, and of the development of Lucasian rational expectations. Maurice was much more impressed by the new contributions of the rational expectations school than he was by those of the more traditional monetarists.

Indeed, time has appeared to prove Maurice to be correct in this appreciation. After all, the monetary aggregates, the money supply in one, or other, of its various guises, should presumably play a major role in any monetarist scheme of affairs. As Mike Woodford (2006) has recorded: '[N]owadays monetary aggregates play little role in monetary policy deliberations at most central banks.' In contrast, a detailed treatment of expectations, and how these may be generated, lies at the heart of the current neo-Keynesian analysis.

My own thesis is that this downgrading of the role of the monetary aggregates in current models, and in forecasting future inflation, has gone too far. At this point a couple of personal caveats may be in order. I am far from being a card-carrying monetarist. Not only did I strenuously oppose Friedman's monetary base control mechanism and his K-per cent rule for monetary growth, but I have been credited, though without much justification (for example in *The Times* obituary of Milton Friedman, 17 November 2006), with having undermined monetarism by pointing out the likely instability of demand for money functions when turned into targets. That said, I was shocked when successive Conservative UK governments in the 1980s and 1990s could pass almost seamlessly from the view that control over broad money was the essential centrepiece of macro policy, the medium-term financial strategy (MTFS), to subsequently paying little or no attention to monetary developments in later years. By the same token I am concerned that some of the key features of a monetary, and of a truly Keynesian, economy are ignored in the neoclassical (neo-Keynesian) consensus.

A second caveat is that Woodford, and his supporters such as Uhlig (2006) and Gali (2006) at the recent European Central Bank (ECB) conference in Frankfurt (9–10 November 2006) on The Role of Money, had, I now believe, two separate purposes. The first was to deny the benefit of having a separate monetary analysis, the famous two pillars of the ECB. Insofar as monetary effects were important in preparing forecasts, and deciding policy, they should be integrated into a single, overall analysis of the prospects for the economy. I have no quarrel with this. It is the further, second line of argument, that we can in practice virtually ignore developments in the monetary aggregates in the conduct of monetary policy, focusing instead solely on a key policy determined interest rate, that I do want to question.

The starting point for Woodford (2006), as also for a somewhat similar, earlier article by B. McCallum (2001), 'Monetary Policy Analysis in Models without Money', is the basic, now widely accepted, new-Keynesian model of three equations, consisting of an IS-type aggregate expenditure function, a Phillips curve-type aggregate supply function, and a Taylor-type central bank reaction function, showing how central banks set interest rates.

In both the IS and the Phillips supply curve, expectations play a leading role; and whether they are forward- or backward-looking, rational or bounded, forms the core of a huge literature, but one which is not relevant to my thesis here. So I shall more simply write these as:

$$\tilde{y} = y_t - y^* = f(E\tilde{y}, R - E\pi) + u_t \qquad (4.1)\ (\text{IS})$$

$$\pi_t = f(E\pi, \tilde{y}) + v_t \qquad (4.2)\ (\text{AS})$$

where $\tilde{y}$ is the output gap, y is current real output, y^* is the natural, or equilibrium, or sustainable level of output, R is the nominal interest rate, E is the expectations operator, π is the rate of inflation, and u and v are error terms.

This is complemented by the Taylor type reaction function:

$$R_t = a + b_1(\pi_t - \pi^*) + b_2\tilde{y} \qquad (4.3)$$

where π^* is the target inflation rate.

Let me make two brief peripheral comments on this. First, it seems odd that the private sector is shown as responding to future expectations, but in equation (4.3) the central bank appears to be reacting only to current events. This latter is surely wrong. All inflation-targeting central banks make, and respond to, inflation forecasts. I have tried elsewhere to show that a proper forward-looking specification of reaction functions can make a large difference to the estimated coefficients (Goodhart, 2005).

Second, this three-equation model may only work satisfactorily during relatively calm periods of stable economic developments, a 'fair-weather' model. The zero bound to nominal interest rates suggests that this model may have limited usefulness during periods of deflationary pressures. Moreover, during turbulent periods, whether of severe deflation or inflation, expectations will not be anchored, will differ quite markedly from person to person, and be subject to potentially rapid and sharp revision. Under these circumstances one cannot assess what real rates of interest may be, so growth rates of the monetary aggregates may well be a better guide to the effects of monetary policy on the economy than either nominal, or an estimate of real, interest rates.

Be that as it may, this three-equation model determines the level of interest rates (real and nominal), the output gap, and both inflation and the price level (given the inflation target and the starting point). The system has a determinate equilibrium, so long as the central bank reacts sufficiently strongly to inflation in adjusting nominal interest rates. There appears to be no need to look at what is happening to money in this system to achieve the main macroeconomic variables of importance to social welfare.

In practice however money can be, and generally is, present in this model, since a demand-for-money function is fully consistent with the above three equations, as in equation (4.4):

$$M_t/P_t = f(y, R, \pi) + w_t \tag{4.4}$$

where P_t is the price level and w_t another error term. Note, however, that so long as the central bank sets interest rates, as is the generality, the money stock is a dependent, endogenous variable. This is exactly what the heterodox post-Keynesians, from Kaldor through Vicky Chick and on through Basil Moore and Randy Wray, have been correctly claiming for decades, and I have been in their party on this. Certainly if the demand for money function fits perfectly, and if its arguments are correctly set out in equation (4.4), then you learn nothing more from looking at money than you already knew from looking at inflation, output and interest rates.

There is a minor caveat to this, which is that money stock data, or elements of it, may come out earlier, or be less subject to (initial) measurement errors than data on output. If so, M could act as an early indicator variable for y, or even for Py. There have been a few instances of such indicator relationships: for example fluctuations in cash holdings (and M0), at least for a time, seemed to precede movements in personal consumption in the UK. I would not, myself, however want to put much weight on any such leading indicator properties.

But much the same is true of output, or of inflation; they too are endogenous, dependent variables. If their functional relationships held perfectly, then one would learn nothing more from looking at output, or inflation, outcomes than one already knew from a knowledge of its functional (structural) relationship. In reality, however, a great deal of time and effort is spent on analysing whether the deviation of output or inflation from forecast is due to one kind of shock or another, for example transient or permanent, demand or supply shock. Why do we not care as much about shocks to the demand for money function, whether deviations of the money stock from its expected value are caused by demand or supply forces, for example by a credit crunch?

One great advantage of central banks running monetary policy by setting interest rates, rather than via the monetary base, is that demand-side shocks to desired money holdings are automatically accommodated. So if one was to assume that all monetary shocks are demand-side, then movements in the money supply indeed tell one nothing. Note, however, that demand-side shocks to the real economy are also relatively easy to handle, in theory at least.

But it is not true that all shocks to money are demand-side. The bulk of money is in the form of commercial bank liabilities, and banks can behave very differently over time. The form of their liabilities, their capital base, their confidence and their risk appetite can and does alter over time, both cyclically and more permanently. The whole question of whether certain segments of the economy can access funds beyond their current income depends crucially on the behaviour of the banks. If there is a supply shock to money, with certain groups now getting more, or less, access to funding – for example when banks provide mortgages to a wider group of households on easier terms – will this not feed back into the IS curve? Of course it will. I shall revert to this in more depth later on.

But, first, I want to turn to two other issues. The first of these relates to the much closer long-run, low-frequency relationship between money and prices than is observed at higher-frequency, shorter-run periods, when the relationship is obscured by a variety of shocks. Michael Woodford accepts in his (2006) Frankfurt paper, slightly grudgingly for my taste, this longer-term relationship, but argues that it is an inherent consequence of having a reasonably stable long-run demand-for-money function. Thus, if we first difference equation (4.4):

$$\mu_t - \pi_t = b_1 dy_t + b_2 dR_t + dw_t \tag{4.5}$$

(see his equation 3.3), it can be easily shown 'that every term on the right-hand side of (3.3) is stationary, so that $\mu_t - \pi_t$ is predicted to be stationary'. So the growth rates of the money stock and of prices must, in the medium and longer run, move in tandem.

That is surely correct, but Woodford then goes on to argue that looking at inflationary outcomes by themselves is just as good, or better, than looking at (longer-term) monetary outcomes by themselves or, even better, jointly. This latter is not demonstrated by his model. Thus he attacks the Gerlach (2003, 2004) two-pillar Phillips curve estimate of inflation by arguing that the cointegration of inflation and money means that money growth must be correlated in the longer run with inflation; but the real question is whether attention to monetary trends adds anything beyond what is also already visible in inflationary trends.

If two variables are cointegrated, then if they begin to deviate there must be some forces, or factors, restoring the relationship. But these forces, or factors, may impinge primarily, or even perhaps solely, on one or other of the two variables. One reason for the emphasis that monetarists place on the stylized fact that this long-run relationship between monetary growth and price inflation continues to hold despite there having been many differing money supply regimes is that it makes it much more difficult to believe that the error correction mechanism is solely, or overwhelmingly, from money holdings adjusting passively to pricing developments, rather than vice versa. Of course, this is not a completely persuasive argument. Even under the gold standard there were numerous forces leading monetary growth to adjust to transaction requirements, for example via incentives to find more gold and/or financial substitutes for gold when monetary conditions had become tight. Even so, the likelihood that all such adjustment has been via passive monetary accommodation without any adjustment of inflation to monetary forces, especially in hyperinflationary circumstances, seems highly improbable.

A subsidiary argument is that it is really inflation, and not the statistics on the rate of growth of M3 or M4, that we really care about. So, even if there should be some effect of excess money balances (in the sense of money balances well above that consistent with desired low inflation and sustainable output) on subsequent output and inflation, we can still wait to see if it does actually feed through into higher inflation, and then take countervailing action.

But even if one should agree with this 'wait and see' argument, the faster past growth of money should at least be a warning that the future monetary policy decisions of the central bank might need to be more restrictive, in the sense of higher interest rates held for longer, than might otherwise be the case. Furthermore the 'wait and see' position depends on a number of arguable propositions, for example:

1. that demand shocks to money holdings are much more prevalent (and possibly longer lasting) than supply shocks;
2. that lags between monetary policy action and its effect on inflation are short enough that one can afford to wait until inflation actually appears in the data; and/or that the extent of monetary action necessary to stabilize inflation (once it has started – after a lag – to move away from target) will not then destabilize the financial system and/or the real economy;
3. that we can, and do, measure inflation correctly.

Unlike most other economists, I do have doubts as to whether we measure inflation correctly. A question arises as to how far, if at all, asset price increases, especially of housing prices, ought to enter the index from which inflation is measured. For a variety of reasons, monetary expansion may be more closely related to asset price inflation than to the inflation of goods and services prices. If inflation is (incorrectly) measured, to exclude all such asset price inflation, then the links between money growth and (true) inflation may be understated.

Moreover, in the longer run there should be cointegration between wealth and income and expenditure. Insofar as monetary fluctuations are closely associated with those in wealth-holdings, then the resultant disturbance to the wealth–income ratio is likely to have consequent effects on income flows and expenditure, and in due course on goods and services inflation.

At this point I begin to move away from the simple three/four neo-Keynesian equation system with which we began. The first amendment, naturally, from what I have been saying already, is to put asset prices and wealth into the model. For obvious reasons, the wealth–income ratio should be an argument in the expenditure function, and wealth should probably be the scale variable in the demand for money function. Finally, there should be asset demand and supply functions, where the demand for assets may in turn be a function of shocks to the supply of money, as well as to expectations of future earnings, of future monetary policies and of future asset prices themselves.

That said, I doubt whether anyone connected with monetary policy would deny the effect of the housing market, and of the equity market, on the forecast future for output and inflation. But why should we go any further than that, and link the process back to monetary growth specifically? This also raises the much debated issue of whether central banks, or anyone else, should be concerned about asset prices, except as they impinge on forecast values of real output and inflation.

Amongst the main arguments against using monetary policy to offset asset price fluctuations are:

1. that asset prices do not all move together in lockstep; and
2. that a member of a Monetary Policy Committee (MPC) is never in a strong position, *ex ante*, to claim that any particular asset price is out of line with fundamentals (a bubble).

But so long as there is a reasonably close relationship between monetary growth and asset prices in general, at least over some periodicities, these objections can be sidestepped. The authorities are then responding to an excessively fast rate of growth of monetary balances in general, and not to any particular set of asset prices, for example to M3 growth in the euro-zone rather than to housing prices in Spain, a point that Otmar Issing has made several times (2002, 2005).

Let me turn, finally, to my main point. This is that the so-called neo-Keynesian basic model is based on intertemporal utility maximization by a representative agent, based on the assumption that all debts are ultimately paid in full, otherwise known in the jargon as the transversality condition. But this means that everyone is perfectly creditworthy. Anybody's IOU can, and would, be accepted in exchange. There is no need for commercial banks, and there are none in Woodford's (2003) iconic book, *Interest and Prices*. Indeed it is hard to see why there should be any need for a specific monetary asset, since everybody's IOUs can be used for exchange purposes. All fixed-interest financial assets are effectively identical, and there is one single interest rate in any period, though it may shift over time as borrowing and savings propensities alter. Moreover nobody, and no firm, is liquidity constrained, ever. Indeed the conditions necessary for a no-default system to operate – either complete financial markets for every possible contingency or perfect information – are, I believe, identical to those that will allow a full Arrow–Debreu–Hahn Walrasian equilibrium to operate. As we know, money is not necessary in such a system.

Thus, by basing their model on the transversality condition, the neo-Keynesians are turning their model into an essentially non-monetary model. So it is no surprise that monetary variables are inessential in it. In reality, many agents in the economy, both persons and smaller companies, cannot sell assets, since they do not have sufficient saleable assets, or borrow, except at exorbitant interest rates. They are effectively liquidity constrained, with their expenditure limited to their current income and their few current assets. As Maurice Peston write in his 1980 book (Chapter 1):

> In Keynes's *General Theory* consumption is determined by income to a very considerable extent because the latter constrains the former. The poor household has no liquid or marketable assets and can hardly borrow. It can only spend its income.

It is that constraint that modern neo-Keynesian theory assumes away. Perhaps as we all become richer, and come to own more assets, such constraints will in practice bind less and less, and then money and commercial banks – and traditional Keynesian analysis – will indeed become less important. But I do not believe that that time has yet come. For a recent excellent empirical article on this, see Nier and Zicchino (2006). For the time being, the degree to which the current income, plus liquid asset, constraint bears on current expenditure depends to a considerable extent on the willingness of, and the terms on which, banks will lend to the private sector. This is a key reason why I believe that the rate of growth of bank lending to the private sector is at least as important a monetary aggregate as broad money. Obviously it makes no real difference whether an established company sells a bond to, or raises a loan from, a bank, but a small company or a person can usually only borrow from a bank, and then only in loan form.

So, shifts in bank willingness to extend such loans, as banks become more, or less, risk averse, will have the effect of shifting the constraints affecting the economy. In particular, when the growth rate of the money stock is declining, whole segments of the economy that were previously not income constrained may suddenly become so, and at a time when income is probably also dropping.

Furthermore, when default becomes possible, risk premia come into play. There ceases to be one single interest rate, as in the basic neo-Keynesian model, but instead there is a whole schedule of interest rates, depending on the perceived riskiness of the borrower. Generally in depressions interest rates on safe, liquid government debt instruments decline, but risk premia rise. It can then be ambiguous whether, overall, interest rates have risen or fallen. The reverse is true in booms; the official policy rate may rise, but risk premia may fall. Against this background it would be short-sighted not to cross-check for the combined effect that a combination of official policy measures and changing risk aversion may have, by looking carefully at the time path of the monetary aggregates.

As Lord Peston (1980) asked, again in Chapter 1: 'How far was the problem of [achieving and maintaining] full employment one of dealing with or failing to cope with risk and uncertainty?' I agree, but a measure of the willingness to face such risk and uncertainty is given by evidence of the growth rates of the money and credit aggregates. Keynesian economics emphasized income constraints and risk and uncertainty. I have argued here that evidence on how the economy is coping with these factors can be

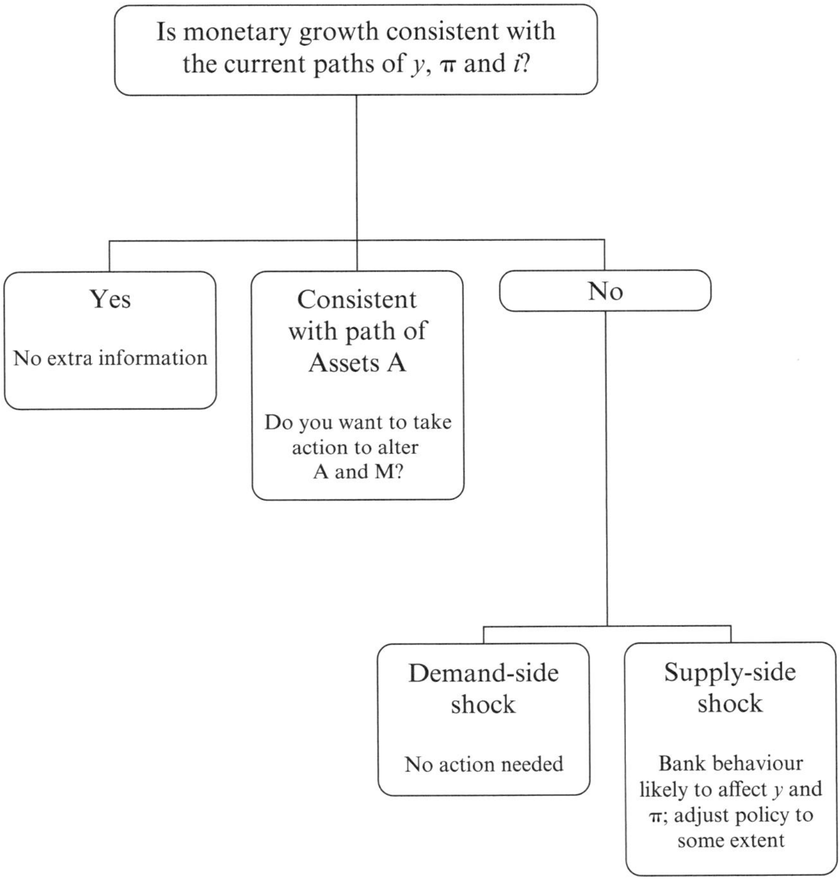

Figure 4.1 Decision tree: how to respond to monetary data

given by examining the growth rate of the money and credit aggregates. In my view anyone who believes that default, risk aversion and income constraints matter, whatever brand of Keynesian or monetarist, ought to concern themselves with the messages emanating from the monetary aggregates. To be sure such messages are often garbled by noise, especially from short-run demand shocks, so that such interpretation will be an art. Nevertheless it is an art worth attempting.

Let me now conclude with trying to set out a decision tree on how to respond to monetary data (Figure 4.1). By now the diagram should be easy enough to follow. The harder part, no doubt, is to know at any time exactly in which box we find ourselves.

NOTE

* As adapted from the Peston Lecture in honour of Maurice, Lord Peston, delivered at Queen Mary College, London, on 28 February 2007. This article was first published in the *National Institute Economic Review*, April 2007, **200**, pp. 56–61.

REFERENCES

Gali, J. (2006), Discussion of 'Money and Monetary Policy: the ECB Experience 1999–2006', by B. Fischer, M. Lenza, H. Pill and L. Reichlin, presented at the Fourth ECB Central Banking Conference at Frankfurt, The Role of Money: Money and Monetary Policy in the Twenty-First Century, 9–10 November.

Gerlach, S. (2003), 'The ECB's Two Pillars', CEPR Discussion Paper 3689.

Gerlach, S. (2004), 'The Two Pillars of the European Central Bank', *Economic Policy* **40**, pp. 389–439.

Goodhart, C.A.E. (2005), 'The Monetary Policy Committee's Reaction Function: An Exercise in Estimation', *Topics in Macroeconomics*, **5**, http://www.bepress.com/cgi/viewcontent.cgi?article=1240&context=bejm.

Issing, O. (2002), 'Monetary Policy in a Changing Economic Environment', presented at Rethinking Monetary Policy, a Symposium organised by the Federal Reserve Bank of Kansas City.

Issing, O. (2005), 'Monetary Policy and Asset Prices', in *Schwerpunktthermen und Serien*, Börsen-Zeitung and Barclays Capital booklet (Verlag Börsenzeitung).

McCallum, B. (2001), 'Monetary Policy Analysis in Models without Money', *Federal Reserve Bank of St Louis Review*, **83** (4), pp.145–60.

Nier, E. and L. Zicchino (2006), 'Bank Weakness and Bank Loan Supply', Bank of England, *Financial Stability Review*, December, pp. 85–93.

Peston, M. (1980), *Whatever Happened to Macro-economics?*, Manchester: Manchester University Press.

The Times (2006), 'Obituary of Milton Friedman', 17 November, pp. 78–9.

Uhlig, H. (2006), Discussion of 'How Important is Money in the Conduct of Monetary Policy?', by M. Woodford, presented at the Fourth ECB Central Banking Conference at Frankfurt, The Role of Money: Money and Monetary Policy in the Twenty-First Century, 9–10 November.

Woodford, M. (2003), *Interest and Prices*, Princeton, NJ: Princeton University Press.

Woodford, M. (2006), 'How Important is Money in the Conduct of Monetary Policy?', presented at the Fourth ECB Central Banking Conference at Frankfurt, The Role of Money: Money and Monetary Policy in the Twenty-First Century, 9–10 November.

5. Fear of appreciation: exchange rate policy as a development strategy*

Eduardo Levy-Yeyati and Federico Sturzenegger

5.1 INTRODUCTION

In 2005, four middle-income developing countries (Indonesia, Romania, the Slovak Republic and Turkey) joined the group of 21 economies that officially run inflation-targeting regimes in the context of freely floating exchange rates.[1] While this trend has been heralded as the triumph of floating regimes, many countries (China, Malaysia, Thailand and Argentina, to name a few) are still actively pursuing active exchange rate policies. In fact, the trend seems to point this way, with floating regimes accounting in 2004 for only 19 percent of all countries, down from 26 percent in 2000 according to the International Monetary Fund (IMF)'s regime classification. Additionally, international reserves in most developing countries are growing when even at a historical high, and two emerging economies (Argentina in 2005, Thailand in 2006) introduced controls on capital inflows to countervail the appreciation of their currencies. Are we re-enacting the fear of floating of the 1990s, or is this a new breed of active exchange rate policy? If so, are its premises validated in the data?

We tackle these questions in two ways. First, we trace the evolution of exchange rate regimes over the recent period based on an updated version of Levy-Yeyati and Sturzenegger's (2005) (hereafter LYS) de facto exchange rate regime classification, to document the prevalence of a 'fear of appreciation' – namely, the tendency to intervene to depreciate (or to postpone the appreciation of) the local currency. Indeed, we find that the convergence to the float-cum-inflation-targeting (FIT) paradigm adopted by many emerging in recent years is not taking place across the board, as the share of non-floats (intermediates, conventional and hard pegs) still represents 75 percent of the sample, exactly the same share as in 2000.

Does this imply that 'fear of floating' continues to prevail in the developing world despite the favorable global context and the reduced currency exposure? To get a full answer to that question, it is crucial to note a semantic nuance that has been understated in the recent exchange rate regime literature: fear of floating, as originally defined by Calvo and Reinhart (2002), entails a clearly asymmetric exchange rate policy. Since only depreciations trigger fears of financial distress or inflation pass-through, under fear of floating the intervention response should be stronger for (if not limited to) upward exchange rate movements. More generally, the incentives and implications to intervene in order to avoid an appreciation are radically different from those related to avoiding a depreciation: where the latter focus on short-run financial crises, the former is usually predicated on long-term economic growth. Similarly, the context conducive to one or the other differs: whereas fear of floating would tend to arise in times of financial turmoil, fear of appreciation will likely be triggered by economic bonanzas. At any rate, treating interventions in a symmetric way – in particular, attributing any intervention to fear of floating as has been previously the case in the literature – may lead to overstating the incidence of financial factors; more so in recent years when fear of appreciation appears to have prevailed. Indeed, fear of appreciation, as documented here, could be seen as the reverse – rather than the continuation – of fear of floating practices.

After refining the characterization of non-floating regimes, we are ready to evaluate the implications of fear of appreciation in terms of economic performance – and, in particular, whether the neo-mercantilist rhetoric underscoring this policy delivers on its promises in terms of export growth and import substitution – for developing economies where the premise of temporary protection to domestic industries applies more naturally.

The mercantilist view that exchange rate policy – more precisely, a temporarily undervalued currency – could be used to protect infant industries as a development strategy has a long tradition in economic theory and has recently enjoyed a minor revival. The issue of undervalued exchange rates has received considerable attention as a result of China's reluctance to float its exchange rate, a strategy presumed to be aimed at preserving the competitiveness of China's exports.[2] In academic circles, the role of depreciated real exchange rates for stimulating growth has been discussed in Rodrik (2007) and has also been found important in growth accelerations (Hausmann et al., 2005; Johnson et al., 2006). On the contrary, overvaluations have been associated to poor economic performance, for example through 'Dutch disease' effects of foreign aid (Rajan and Subramanian, 2006) or to explain the disappointing growth dividends of financial integration (see Prassad et al., 2006). Despite this indicative evidence, neo-mercantilist views have been saluted, at best, with skepticism.

To assess the economic impact of fear of appreciation, we identify two types of foreign exchange interventions: one aimed at defending the domestic currency (as in the traditional fear of floating), and one aimed at depressing it (as in fear of appreciation). In turn, with this finer definition of intervention at hand, we explore the economic implications of intervention empirically, including its effect on the real exchange rate and (cyclical and trend) output growth. As opposed to what is usually argued, we find a benign effect of fear of appreciation, arising not from export-led expansions or import substitution, but rather from increased domestic savings and investment rates. Finally, to examine this result from a different perspective, we look at how the contributions to growth from the different components of aggregate demand change with fear of appreciation. Again, we find that undervaluation does not seem to affect the tradable sector (through the export promotion and import substitution channels) but leads to greater contributions from domestic savings and investment.

We interpret these results in light of Díaz Alejandro's (1965) thesis that an undervalued exchange rate transfers resources from low- to high-income agents with a higher propensity to save; to the extent that these resources are saved and invested at home (as opposed to diverted abroad, as Díaz-Alejandro assumed originally) the redistributive effects of an undervalued currency should be expansionary.

5.2 DE FACTO REGIME CLASSIFICATION: UPDATING

In Levy-Yeyati and Sturzenegger (2001) we introduced a de facto classification of exchange rates that relied on clustering country-year observations on the basis of three classifying variables: the movements of the nominal exchange rate within each year, the movements in central bank reserves (intended to capture interventions in exchange rate markets) and changes in the rate of change of the exchange rate (to capture crawling-peg regimes).[3] The use of reserves changes distinguished our classification from later attempts at classifying exchange rate regimes that relied solely on exchange rate volatility,[4] and was critical to characterize exchange rate policy – as opposed to exchange rate volatility. It was this measure of foreign exchange intervention that allowed us to tell whether a stable exchange rate was the result of an active policy aimed at limiting exchange rate volatility (as is often assumed), or just the reflection of a stable environment in the context of a flexible exchange rate that does not impose any constraint on macroeconomic policy. In turn, the direction of the intervention will be the key variable to identify fear of floating from fear of appreciation in the finer regime classification that we propose here.

Central bank interventions are notoriously difficult to measure and they usually differ from a simple measure of reserve variation. To approximate as closely as possible the intervention impact of changes in reserves, we subtract government deposits at the central bank from the central bank's net foreign assets. More specifically, we define net reserves in dollars as:

$$R_t = \frac{Foreign\,Assets_t - Foreign\,Liabilities_t - Gov.\,Deposits_t}{e_t} \tag{5.1}$$

where e indicates the price of a dollar in terms of local currency.[5] In turn, our measure of intervention for country s and year j is defined as the annual average of the absolute value of monthly interventions (months are indexed by t), that is, the average absolute change in net international reserves relative to the monetary base in the previous month, both measured in US dollars:

$$MR_{s,j} = \sum_{t=1}^{12} \frac{1}{12} \frac{|R_{s,j,t} - R_{s,j,t-1}|}{\left(\frac{Money\,Base_{s,j,t-1}}{e_{s,j,t-1}}\right)}, \tag{5.2}$$

where the monthly absolute change in reserves is normalized by the monetary aggregate (both measured in the same currency) to capture the monetary impact of the intervention.

Using this measure of intervention, together with data on the volatility of exchange rates, we updated the LYS dataset to cover the period 1974–2004 and, based on new information, completed the classification for a number of undisclosed basket pegs. As a result, the new dataset includes 179 countries and 4189 observations, covering 82 percent of all country-year observations for the period.[6]

We can use the measure in (5.1) to benchmark actual interventions by type of regime against a 'typical' intervention under a float, which can be proxied by the distribution of the intervention variable R for Australia, Japan and the US, three countries that are often considered the closest to textbook floating regimes (Figure 5.1).[7] As can be seen, while pegs generally exhibit heavier intervention than floats, there are still many pegs with limited intervention – relative to the benchmark floats – a fact that can reflect the success of pegs in pre-empting market pressure, or the fact that many countries choose to peg only when they do not anticipate that the peg will be subject to considerable shocks.

Figure 5.2 shows the distribution of exchange rates over recent years. The graph shows that regime choices have remained remarkably stable, particularly since 1990. This evidence looks unkind to the bipolar view that forecast the disappearance of intermediate regimes, although it shows a very slight increasing trend in floating regimes. Furthermore, as noted in the introduction, de facto floats continue to represent less than one-quarter of the total sample.[8]

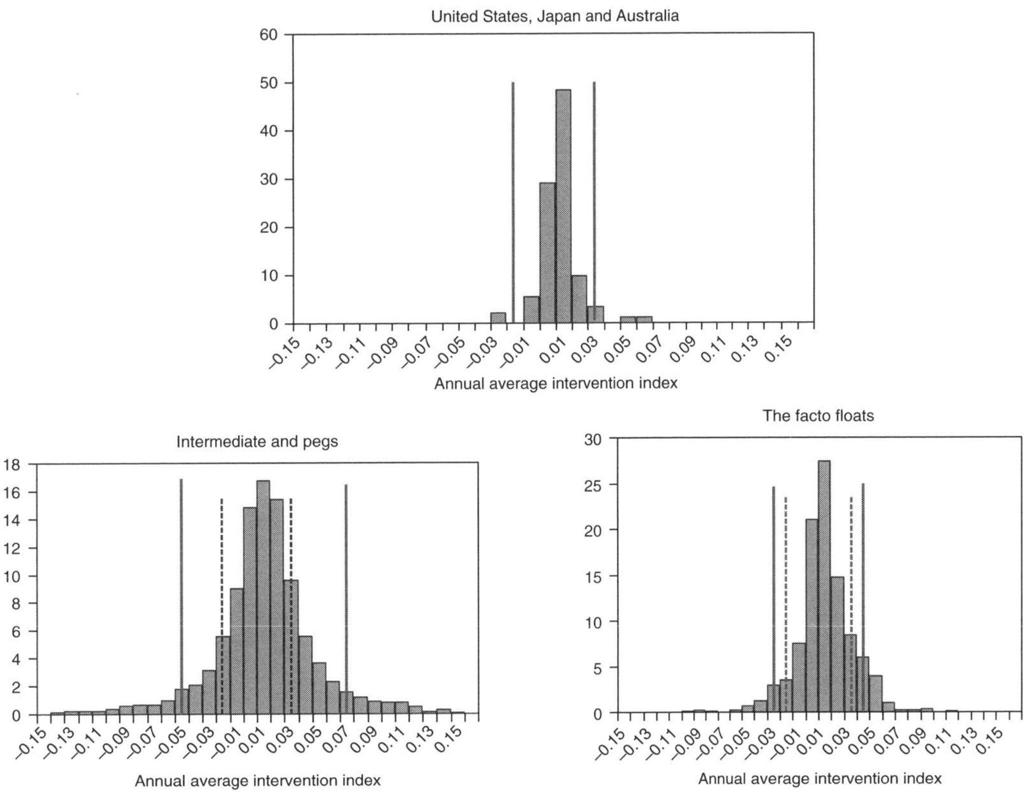

Figure 5.1 Foreign exchange interventions under different exchange rate regimes

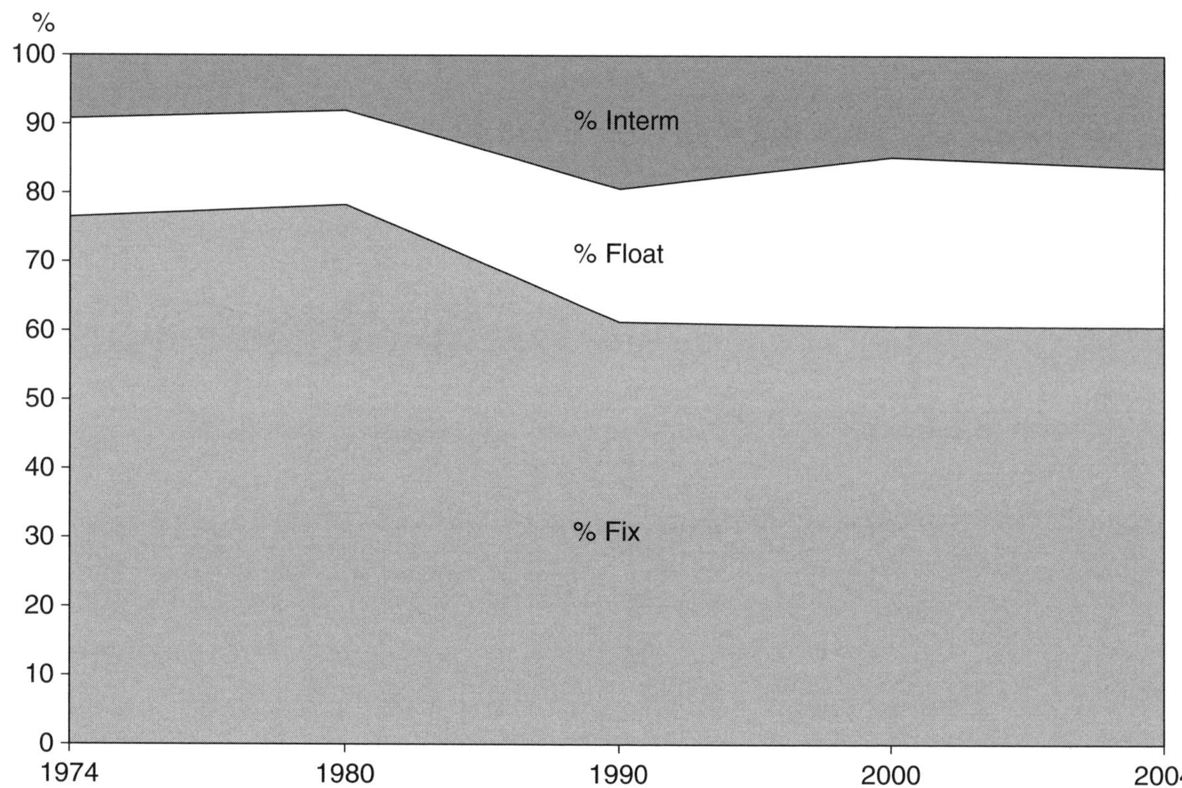

Figure 5.2 *Regime choice (1974–2004) based on LYS classification – all countries*

5.3 FEAR OF APPRECIATION

As noted in the introduction, the nature of de facto intermediate and pegged regimes involves a clear asymmetry. While the prototypical case of fear of floating would exhibit a low tolerance to exchange rate depreciations, there is little in the story to motivate the defense of a depreciated real exchange rate through (often unsterilized) reserve accumulation. Grouping both types of interventions together when studying the implications of the regime choice is likely to misrepresent them.

Because the LYS classification is already built on actual interventions, we can identify these two types of intervention with only minor additional work. The simplest way to do so is to sort out countries according to whether they intervene to depress or to defend the exchange rate, that is, whether the intervention in (5.2) is positive or negative. We capture this dichotomy in a new measure of intervention *Int*1, defined as the annual average of the monthly interventions:

$$Int1_{s,j} = \sum_{t=1}^{12} \frac{1}{12} \frac{(R_{s,j,t} - R_{s,j,t-1})}{\left(\frac{MBase_{s,j,t-1}}{e_{s,j,t-1}}\right)}, \tag{5.3}$$

which now will be negative or positive according to whether the central bank is selling or purchasing the foreign currency.

Figures 5.3 and 5.4 distinguish among intermediate regimes by indicating the percentage of cases where intervention is positive. As the figures show, the direction of intervention has changed dramatically (and predictably) over time. The debt crisis years found most developing countries selling foreign currency to defend their exchange rate anchors, while in recent years (with the unsurprising exception of crisis year 1998) countries have increasingly intervened in the opposite direction. As it turns out, conventional fear of floating is today represented by less than 20 percent of intermediate regimes. The same story emerges when interventions are detrended (to factor out the positive intervention that may be associated with the long-run growth of output and monetary aggregates), and when very small reserves changes are filtered out (with the cut-off defined as the 95 percent confidence interval of the distribution of interventions in benchmark floats Australia, Japan and the US, usually seen as models of floating regimes). Results are comparable when the exercise is replicated for the joint sample of intermediate and pegged regimes.

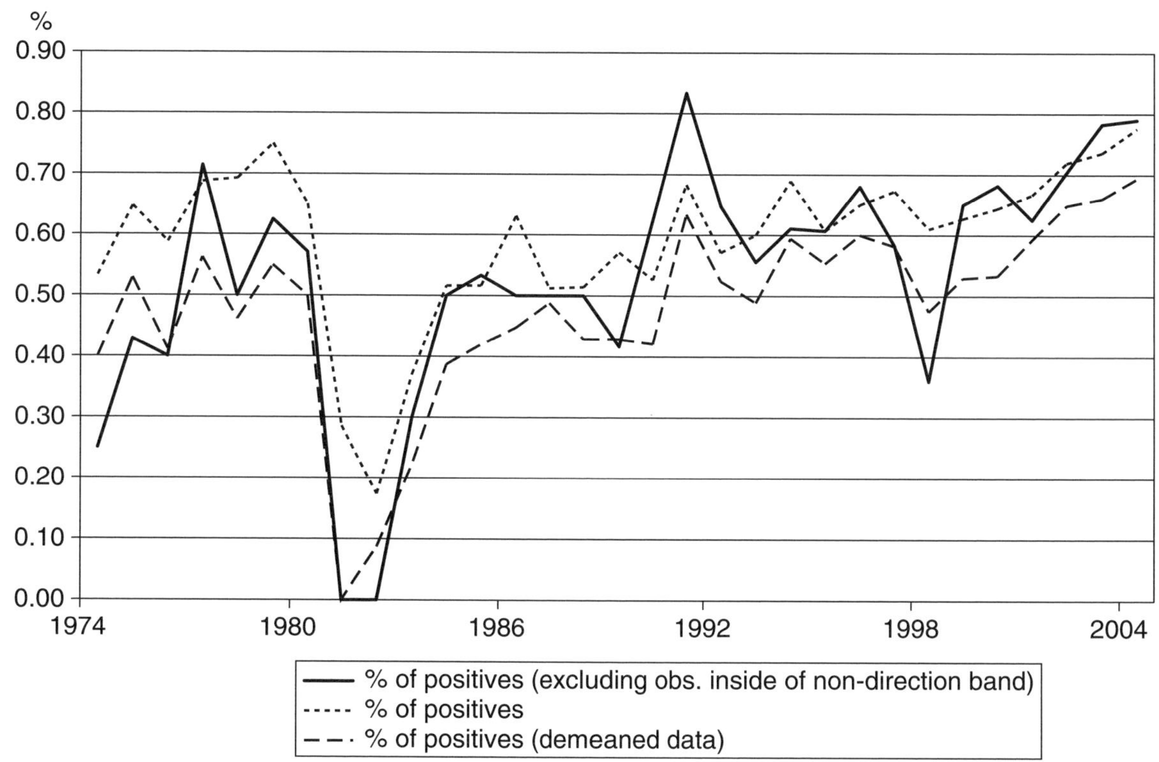

Figure 5.3 *Percentage of countries with a positive annual average of intervention index – only intermediate regimes (variable Int.1)*

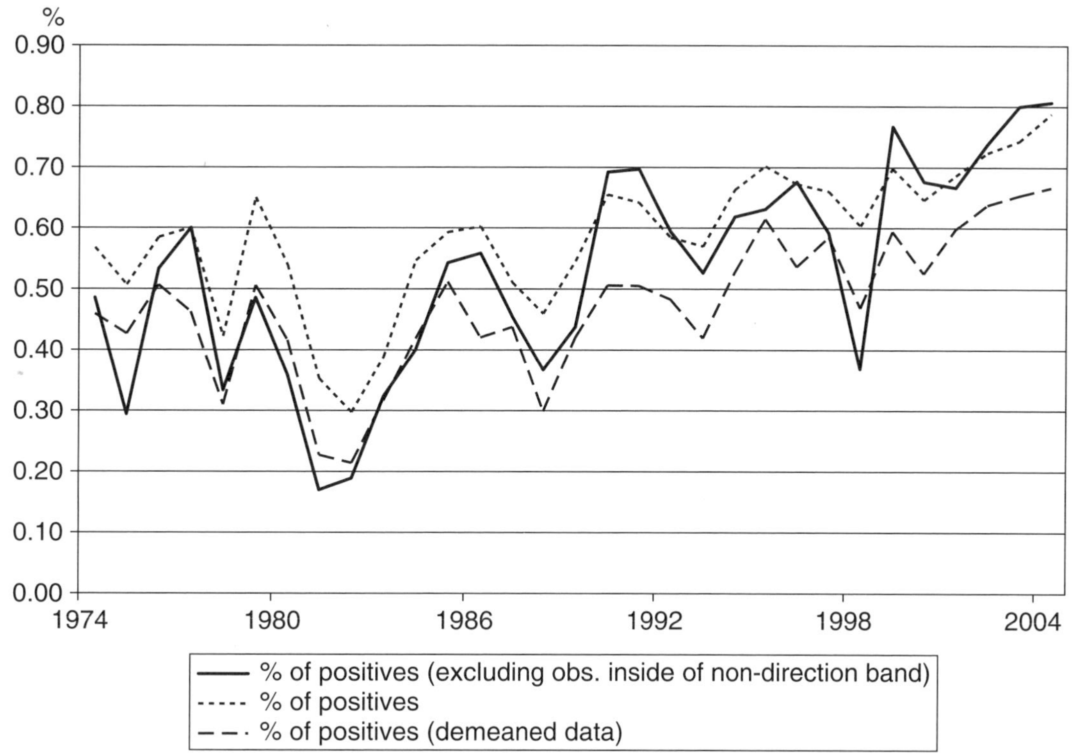

Figure 5.4 *Percentage of countries with a positive annual average of intervention index – intermediate and pegs (variable Int.1)*

5.4 FEAR OF APPRECIATION AND THE REAL ECONOMY

Having shown that fear of appreciation has been the prevailing pattern in recent years among countries with an active exchange rate policy, the next step is to understand the motives behind this choice, and to evaluate whether these motives are empirically validated. In particular, it is worth exploring whether these interventions have a significant and lasting effect on real variables despite the traditional view that nominal interventions are unlikely to have a real economic impact.

Economic performance tends to be positively correlated with a number of variables (such as capital inflows or terms-of-trade shocks) that tend in turn to lead to real appreciations and the accumulation of reserves. This aspect is particularly relevant for our intervention measure because increases in output tend to induce increases in money demand, which in turn may be met by either increases in domestic credit or increases in international reserves.[9] Moreover, the stock of reserves may grow with monetary aggregates if reserves are held for precautionary motives.[10] In either case, to the extent that our simple intervention measure may capture this growth-induced increase in reserves as intervention, it may be biased by endogeneity problems.

To address this potential concern, we adopt a conservative strategy: we modify our intervention measure to filter out the effect of changes in money demand. Specifically, we define first the ratio of reserves to broad money (M2):[11]

$$R2_{s,j,t} = \frac{Foreign\ Assets_{s,j,t}}{M_{s,j,t}} \tag{5.4}$$

and then we compute a new intervention measure, *Int*2, as the annual average change of this ratio:

$$Int2_{s,j} = \sum_{t=1}^{12} \frac{1}{12}(R2_{s,j,t} - R2_{s,j,t-1}). \tag{5.5}$$

Notice that a positive *Int*2 implies a strong degree of intervention, because for intervention to be positive reserve accumulation must exceed the increase in monetary aggregates. Thus, positive values of this 'strong intervention' measure cannot be interpreted as a response to an increase in money demand. For robustness, in the empirical tests that follow we use both intervention measures.

5.4.1 The Real Exchange Rate

The first critical link to be explored empirically is the one between intervention and real appreciations, that is, whether interventions indeed manage to preserve a depreciated real exchange rate. We do this in Table 5.1, where we run a panel regression of the log changes of the real exchange rate on key determinants of the exchange rate: terms of trade, the output of trading partners and capital inflows.[12] All regressions include year dummies to control for global factors such as international liquidity or risk appetite, as well as country fixed effects. Finally, we include estimates for two- and three-year non-overlapping intervals to test for cumulative effects. Our sample, here as well as in the following tests, comprises all developing economies.

Our benchmark specification is given by:

$$y_{i,t+s} - y_{i,t} = \beta\,(1/s) \sum_{j=t,t+s} Int_{i,j} + \gamma' \mathbf{X}_{i,t...t+s} + \mu_{t+s} + \theta_i + \varepsilon_{i,t+s}, \quad (5.6)$$

where y is the log of the real exchange rate, $\mathbf{X}$ is a vector of controls including the log difference of the terms of trade, the log difference of the trade-weighted average of the gross domestic product (GDP) of the country's trading partners, and the ratio of the financial account over GDP (to measure capital inflows), and μ, θ, ε are, respectively, the year and country dummies and the error term.

Exchange rates and reserves tend to change dramatically and endogenously over periods of financial distress that may lead to strong positive correlations (for example, a reserve drain followed by a currency collapse) that could be misleadingly construed as a policy choice. To make sure that these extreme events do not contaminate our results, in all regressions we exclude extreme values of the intervention measure and the dependent variable.[13]

Table 5.1 shows our results. We find the expected positive effect of intervention on the real exchange rate: the contemporaneous effect is positive and significant. The results indicate that a 10 percent increase in the reserves-to-broad money ratio leads to a contemporaneous 1.69 percent increase in the real exchange rate, and that the effect almost doubles if intervention is sustained over two years. The estimated effect is smaller (but still significant) for *Int*1. The effect appears to decline (and ceases to be significant) beyond the second year.

It is important to note at this point that reverse causality should not be a concern here: since positive interventions are likely to be triggered by real appreciations, endogeneity, if anything, would offset the positive

Table 5.1 *Panel regression of the log changes of the real exchange rate on key determinants of the exchange rate the terms of trade, the output of trading partners, and capital inflows*

Variables	[1]	[2]	[3]	[4]	[5]	[6]
*int*1. Index (*t*)	0.036*		0.109**		0.048	
	(0.022)		(0.055)		(0.072)	
*int*2. Index (*t*)		0.169**		0.262**		0.208
		(0.075)		(0.120)		(0.169)
Control variables						
ΔLog(*ToT*)	0.000	0.000	0.000	−0.001	−0.002	−0.002
	(0.001)	0.000	(0.001)	(0.001)	(0.002)	(0.001)
Trading partners	−0.008	−0.007	−0.011	−0.007	−0.013	−0.011
growth	(0.005)	(0.005)	(0.008)	(0.008)	(0.014)	(0.012)
Financial account to	−0.012***	−0.010***	−0.013***	−0.013***	−0.017***	−0.014***
GDP	(0.002)	(0.002)	(0.003)	(0.002)	(0.004)	(0.003)
Observations/Countries	1350/76	1433/80	675/76	778/80	485/76	549/80
R-squared	0.989	0.99	0.99	0.991	0.99	0.991
Mean dep. var.	3.718	3.733	3.733	3.733	3.733	3.733
St. dev. dep. var.	2.414	2.475	2.489	2.489	2.475	2.475

Notes:
$y(t, t + s)$ corresponds to the average over the period t to $t + s$ of the variable y.
Except otherwise indicated, all controls are averages for the period over which the dependent variable is measured.
All regressions included country fixed effects and time dummies.
Robust standard errors in parentheses.
* Significant at 10%; ** significant at 5%; *** significant at 1%.

correlation found in the table. Similarly, to the extent that mercantilist interventions occur when potentially unobservable 'good things happen', it is unlikely that omitted variables can account for the observed positive coefficient: on the contrary, uncontrolled favorable external factors would tend to weaken the positive association between intervention and the real exchange rate.

5.4.2 Output Growth

Does fear of appreciation have any influence on economic activity? If so, is it related with short-lived and quickly reverted cyclical fluctuations, or does it contribute to long-lasting output expansions? To explore this issue empirically, we face two methodological problems. On the one hand, there is the already noted positive link between the growth of output and monetary aggregates, which we address here introducing a second intervention variable (*Int*2) that traces reserve accumulation in excess of monetary expansions.[14] On the other hand, there is the possibility that interventions and growth respond to common factors. Favorable conditions (both domestic and external) are expected to lead to both faster growth and stronger demand for domestic assets, creating appreciation pressures. Moreover, growth itself can stimulate capital inflows that add to the appreciation bias. In both cases, fear of appreciation may lead the monetary authorities to intervene, inducing a positive association between intervention and economic performance that may be incorrectly interpreted as the result of a positive growth effect of intervention.

Our additional controls (terms of trade, external demand shocks and capital inflows) should help alleviate this potential problem. We also control for initial wealth (proxied by the initial per capita GDP) and population growth. As before, we include country dummies, and year dummies to capture the effect of global factors such as international liquidity or risk appetite. We also control for initial wealth (proxied by the initial per capita GDP) and population growth.

One potential caveat of the present analysis is the possibility that an association between intervention (that is, growing reserves) and growth captures the recovery that typically follows a financial crisis or, conversely, a protracted output contraction after a boom. While extreme events are already excluded from the regression, the results may nonetheless capture the aftermath of the crisis. To make sure that this is not the case, we add the initial output gap (computed as the Hodrick–Prescott (HP)-filtered, cyclical component of output) as an additional control.[15]

Table 5.2 reports the results. The intervention effect appears to be consistently significant and economically important: a 10 percent intervention

Table 5.2 Intervention and growth (sample of 1974–2004, dependent variable: % of change of the real GDP)

Variables	Δ%GDP (t + 1)	
	[1]	[3]
*Int*1. Index (t)	1.269***	
	(0.270)	
*Int*2. Index (t)		1.790**
		(0.810)
Control variables		
Lagged dep. var.	0.292***	0.307***
	(0.032)	(0.031)
LGDP_HP_cycle (t)	−38.124***	−40.016***
	(3.046)	(3.038)
ΔLog(*ToT*)	0.038***	0.038***
	(0.006)	(0.006)
Population growth	0.22	0.215
	(0.147)	(0.152)
Financial account to GDP	0.039*	0.062***
	(0.020)	(0.021)
Trading partners growth	0.206**	0.215***
	(0.083)	(0.083)
GDP (t)	−0.17	0.103
	(0.674)	(0.700)
Observations/Countries	1496/84	1577/88
R-squared	0.442	0.436
Mean dep. var.	3.59	3.519
St. dev. dep. var.	4.099	4.165

Notes:
$y(t, t + s)$ corresponds to the average over the period t to $t + s$ of the variable y.
Except otherwise indicated, all controls are averages for the period over which the dependent variable is measured.
All regressions included country fixed effects and time dummies.
Robust standard errors in parentheses.
* Significant at 10%; ** significant at 5%; *** significant at 1%.

is associated with a 0.14 percent increase in the growth rate in the following year. As expected, for the stronger *Int*2, the associated increase ranges from 0.18 percent to 0.29 percent. The results are subject to (at least) two potential criticisms. The first is related to the fact that, by working with short one- and three-year windows, our findings may be the reflection of short-lived cyclical effects on GDP. Moreover, if intervention is induced by economic expansions driven by domestic real shocks not captured by the additional controls, the positive intervention–growth link may be in part reflecting a reverse causality not fully eliminated by the lagging of the independent variables. On a more conceptual ground, the mercantilist view is based on the infant-industry premise that temporary protection leads to permanent effects in terms of competitiveness. More generally, the case for active exchange rate policy is certainly stronger if the effects of temporary intervention prove to be persistent.

We address these points in Table 5.3, where we rerun the baseline specification of Table 5.2 for output cycle and trend, respectively, where the latter are constructed, alternatively, using the Hodrick–Prescott (HP) filter and the Baxter–King's (BK) band-pass procedure, and add the first three lags of the intervention variable. The main results, which do not diverge qualitatively across methodologies, show a positive and significant effect on the long-run component (the effect on the cyclical component is significant only for the first intervention variable). The number, again, indicates sizeable economic effects: based on the BK decomposition, a 10 percent increase in *Int*1 and *Int*2 leads, respectively, to cumulative 0.15 percent and 0.6 percent increases in long-run growth over four years. All things considered, the evidence suggests a robust, persistent and economically important effect of intervention on economic growth.

The fact that the link between intervention and growth identified here still holds for long-run output trends should help dispel part of the natural skepticism associated with growth regressions. This notwithstanding, in order for the argument to be convincing, it needs to provide a clear empirical characterization of the channel through which this link materializes. Hence the second criticism mentioned above, to which we turn next.

5.5 INTERVENTION AND GROWTH: HOW DOES IT WORK?

If we accept for a moment the implication of the previous findings – namely, that there is indeed an effect of exchange rate intervention on growth – then where does this effect come from? Is it by promoting import substitution and stimulating the production and export of more sophisticated manufactures previously overpriced relative to international competitors, as the mercantilist view predicates? Does it induce a shift in the production structure that moves the economy to high-productivity-growth tradable sectors? While this is certainly the prime suspect in this case, when we replicate the specifications of Table 5.3 for the growth of imports and export volumes as dependent variables (adding GDP growth to filter the influence of economic activity on trade), the results are rather

Table 5.3 Intervention and growth, adjusting for output cycle and trend (sample of 1974–2004, dependent variable: % of change of the real GDP)

Variables	Trend (% change)				Cycle (% change)			
	BK		HP		BK		HP	
	(t + 1)				(t + 1)			
	[1]	[2]	[3]	[4]	[5]	[6]	[7]	[8]
*Int*1. Index (*t*)	0.562***		0.270***		0.599***		1.078***	
	(0.164)		(0.104)		(0.222)		(0.269)	
*Int*1. Index (*t*-1)	0.598***		0.345***					
	(0.165)		(0.106)					
*Int*1. Index (*t*-2)	0.354**		0.238**					
	(0.169)		(0.104)					
*Int*1. Index (*t*-3)	0.117		0.196*					
	(0.168)		(0.105)					
*Int*2. Index (*t*)		1.555***		0.969***		–0.451		0.814
		(0.54)		(0.33)		(0.712)		(0.803)
*Int*2. Index (*t*-1)		1.810***		0.818***				
		(0.52)		(0.31)				
*Int*2. Index (*t*-2)		1.892***		0.861***				
		(0.504)		(0.303)				
*Int*2. Index (*t*-3)		1.177*		0.788**				
		(0.659)		(0.344)				
Control variables								
LGDP_BK_trend (*t*)	–3.157***	–2.894***						
	(0.478)	(0.492)						

LGDP_HP_trend (*t*)			–2.163***	–1.946***				
			(0.313)	(0.314)				
LGDP_BK_cycle (*t*)					–64.450***	–64.654***		
					(3.555)	(3.455)		
LGDP_HP_cycle (*t*)							–30.016***	–30.543***
							(2.444)	(2.419)
ΔLog(*ToT*)	0.024***	0.024***	0.011***	0.011***	0.017***	0.016***	0.033***	0.031***
	(0.004)	(0.004)	(0.003)	(0.003)	(0.005)	(0.005)	(0.006)	(0.006)
Population growth	0.361***	0.368***	0.249***	0.262***	–0.124	–0.139	0.030	0.030
	(0.128)	(0.130)	(0.082)	(0.083)	(0.148)	(0.144)	(0.132)	(0.135)
Financial account to GDP	0.038***	0.048***	0.034***	0.039***	0.032**	0.038**	0.043**	0.063***
	(0.013)	(0.013)	(0.009)	(0.008)	(0.015)	(0.015)	(0.019)	(0.020)
Trading partners growth	0.121**	0.129**	0.05	0.06	0.008	–0.015	0.150**	0.141*
	(0.052)	(0.054)	(0.032)	(0.034)	(0.059)	(0.059)	(0.074)	(0.074)
Observations/Countries	1298/82	1352/81	1477/82	1548/82	1327/82	1390/82	1498/82	1577/82
R-squared	0.474	0.481	0.602	0.607	0.415	0.401	0.301	0.286
Mean dep. var.	3.329	3.28	3.298	3.246	0.149	0.175	0.323	0.316
St. dev. dep. var.	2.591	2.608	2.001	1.994	3.108	3.114	3.516	3.547

Notes:
$y(t, t + s)$ corresponds to the average over the period t to $t + s$ of the variable y.
Except otherwise indicated, all controls are averages for the period over which the dependent variable is measured.
All regressions included country fixed effects and time dummies.
Robust standard errors in parentheses.
* Significant at 10%; ** significant at 5% *** significant at 1%.

disappointing: intervention is uncorrelated with exports, and positively correlated with import volumes, at odds with the import substitution premise of the mercantilist view.[16] Thus, any direct impact of intervention on trade ratios would be entirely driven by the relative price change due to the real depreciation of the currency.[17]

If it is not an export boom that triggers an increase in output, how can we explain the finding that interventions stimulate growth? Table 5.4 points at one alternative explanation. Here we look at the link between interventions on the one hand, and savings and investment rates on the other. The results are now significant and unambiguous. The savings ratio increases about five percentage points if the reserves-to-M2 ratio doubles (column 2); as can be seen, the result is not driven by external or internal bonanzas, which are captured by the additional controls in the regression. In turn, the investment ratio grows by half that amount (column 4), and interventions are still significant even after controlling for the contemporaneous increase in savings (columns 5 and 6).

5.6 DISSECTING THE EFFECT OF FEAR OF APPRECIATION ON GDP GROWTH

To look at these results from a different perspective, we perform the following simple exercise: based on a commonly used definition of undervaluation, we estimate the contribution of an undervalued currency to output growth and, in turn, to each of the individual output components.

More precisely, we compute an index of overvaluation using data on exchange rates (*XRAT*) and purchasing power parity (PPP) conversion factors (*PPP*) from Penn World Tables 6.2 (Heston et al., 2006) to calculate a 'real' exchange rate (*RER*) defined as:

$$\ln RER_{it} = \ln\left(\frac{XRAT_{it}}{PPP_{it}}\right),$$

where i is an index for countries and t is an index for the time period. *XRAT* and *PPP* are expressed as national currency units per US dollar. When *RER* is greater than one it indicates that the value of the currency is lower (more depreciated) than predicted by purchasing power parity. Next, we account for the Balassa–Samuelson effect (the well-known fact that non-traded goods are cheaper in poorer countries) by regressing *RER* on per capita GDP (*RGDPCH*). More precisely, we run:

$$\ln RER_{it} = \alpha + \beta\frac{\ln RGDPCH_{it}}{\ln RGDPCH_{USt}} + f_i + u_{it} \tag{5.1}$$

Table 5.4 *Intervention, savings and investment rates (sample of 1974–2004, dependent variable: nominal gross domestic savings, real gross capital formation as a share of GDP)*

Variables	Nominal gross domestic savings as % GDP		Real Gross capital formation as % GDP			
	(t + 1)		(t + 1)			
	[1]	[2]	[3]	[4]	[5]	[6]
*Int*1. Index (*t*)	1.058**		1.968***		1.729***	
	(0.477)		(0.264)		(0.258)	
*Int*2. Index (*t*)		5.027***		2.576***		1.566*
		(1.340)		(0.939)		(0.870)
Control variables						
Lagged dep. var			0.641***	0.641***	0.600***	0.597***
			(0.029)	(0.029)	(0.030)	(0.030)
Δ%GDP (*t*)		0.158***	0.162***			
		(0.039)	(0.038)			
Savings/GDP					0.162***	0.168***
					–0.021	–0.021
ΔLog(*ToT*)	0.059***	0.062***	0.00	0.00	–0.01	–0.01
	(0.011)	(0.010)	(0.007)	(0.007)	(0.007)	(0.007)
Population growth	–0.02	0.03	0.01	0.05	0.01	0.04
	(0.187)	(0.183)	(0.134)	(0.142)	(0.150)	(0.157)
Financial account to GDP	–0.171***	–0.142***	0.108***	0.138***	0.156***	0.181***
	(0.036)	(0.033)	(0.025)	(0.025)	(0.028)	(0.028)
Trading partners growth	–0.10	–0.08	0.210**	0.231***	0.246***	0.264***
	(0.137)	(0.132)	(0.085)	(0.087)	(0.084)	(0.086)

Table 5.4 (continued)

Variables	Nominal gross domestic savings as % GDP		Real Gross capital formation as % GDP			
	($t+1$)		($t+1$)			
	[1]	[2]	[3]	[4]	[5]	[6]
Observations/Countries	1467/84	1544/88	1446/81	1525/85	1445/81	1524/85
R-squared	0.805	0.81	0.828	0.82	0.84	0.833
Mean	16.064	16.369	20.95	20.933	20.95	20.933
St. dev.	10.805	10.877	5.988	6.156	5.988	6.156

Notes:
$y(t, t+s)$ corresponds to the average over the period t to $t+s$ of the variable y.
Except otherwise indicated, all controls are averages for the period over which the dependent variable is measured.
All regressions included country fixed effects and Time dummies.
Robust standard errors in parentheses.
* Significant at 10%; ** significant at 5%; *** significant at 1%.

where f_i is a fixed effect for time period and u_{it} is the error term, a regression that yields an estimated $\beta = -0.233$ (with a predictably high t-statistic of around 22).

Finally, we compute the index of undervaluation as the difference between the actual real exchange rate and the Balassa–Samuelson adjusted rate:

$$\ln UNDERVAL_{it} = \ln RER_{it} - \ln \hat{RER}_{it}$$

where $\ln \hat{RER}_{it}$ is the predicted value from equation (5.1). Defined in this way, *UNDERVAL* is comparable across countries and over time. Whenever *UNDERVAL* exceeds unity, it indicates that the exchange rate is such that goods produced at home are cheap in dollar terms: the currency is undervalued. When *UNDERVAL* is below unity, the currency is overvalued.[18]

Next, we run one-year to five-year non-overlapping panels regressions:

$$y_{it} = \alpha + \beta \ln RGDPCH_{it-1} + \delta \ln UNDERVAL_{it} + f_i + f_t + u_{it}$$

where y stands for output growth as well as growth contributions (all expressed in per capita terms and percentage of GDP, and defined as $wdi\_growth\_variable_t = \frac{(variable_t - variable_{t-1})}{wdi\_gdppc\_const\_lcu_{t-1}}$), where *variable* denotes, alternatively, consumption, savings, investment, exports and imports.[19]

Tables 5.5 and 5.6 report the results for five-year non-overlapping panels and different country subsamples. The results, again, show a statistically significant link between an undervalued exchange rate and output growth, that appears to work through an increase in savings and investment – as well as employment – rather than through the external sector.[20]

5.7 FINAL REMARKS: NEW LIGHT ON OLD THEORIES

While our findings (as well as those previously reported in Levy Yeyati and Sturzenegger, 2007) support the claim that undervalued exchange rates foster growth, they cast doubt on the more recent incarnations of export-led strategies such as self-discovery or learning by doing (see Aizenmann and Lee, 2007). Our results also seem at odds with previous findings on the effects of overvaluation on the tradable sector (Rajan and Subramanian, 2006) that, conceivably, may reflect the valuation effect of a change in relative prices on the output of sectors with varying degrees of exchange rate exposure.[21]

Table 5.5 Growth and undervaluation

	Growth, all	Growth, developed	Growth, developing	Growth, developing, 1950–79	Growth, developing, 1980–2004
Growth_lag	–0.031**	–0.034**	–0.039**	–0.052**	–0.029*
	(8.750)	(4.890)	(8.370)	(5.580)	(2.440)
Undervaluation	0.013**	0.023**	0.018**	0.017*	0.029**
	(3.940)	(3.060)	(4.620)	(2.530)	(2.980)
Constant	0.256**	0.329**	0.321**	0.455**	0.288**
	(9.470)	(5.380)	(9.030)	(6.010)	(2.670)
Observations	1270	268	958	241	92
R-squared	0.449	0.591	0.417	0.456	0.637

Notes:
Robust t-statistics in parentheses.
* Significant at 5%; ** significant at 1%.

Instead, the evidence appears to point at a savings channel that has not gone unnoticed in the literature. As early as 1965, Díaz-Alejandro suggested that a devaluation may generate important income distribution effects, shifting resources from workers to firms or agricultural producers. Yet Díaz-Alejandro believed such changes to be contractionary, due to the negative income effect on consumers and the associated slump in domestic absorption.[22] A 'modern' view, in turn, would stress the contractionary effect of balance sheet effects in the presence of financial dollarization. Firms with foreign currency denominated liabilities will find themselves increasingly cash constrained following a sharp devaluation, triggering a potentially large fall in investment.[23]

A consistent story for our findings could be built, however, by combining Díaz-Alejandro's story with the presence of financial constraints. To the extent that a real devaluation reduces labor costs, it contributes internal funds to financially constrained firms, thereby fostering savings and investment. Alternatively, in a financially constrained economy, the implicit transfer from low-income, low-saving-propensity workers to high-income capitalists should boost overall savings, lowering the cost of capital to the same effect.[24] Unlike in the original story, in this version the real devaluation should be expansionary because it relaxes the borrowing constraints that bind the firms (in the first case) of the economy (in the second). Why is this benign effect on financial constraints not outweighed by the adverse balance sheet effects highlighted by the fear of floating argument? Presumably, the policy decision to keep the currency undervalued is

Table 5.6 Undervaluation and output components

Dep. var.: contribution of	Developing countries: coefficient of undervaluation (T = window over which growth rates and contributions are computed)				
	T = 1	T = 2	T = 3	T = 4	T = 5
GDP	0.013**	0.014**	0.011**	0.015**	0.015**
	(4.670)	(4.270)	(2.820)	(3.830)	(3.310)
Consumption	0.006	0.006*	0.005	0.009*	0.007
	(1.910)	(2.000)	(1.280)	(2.490)	(1.770)
Savings	0.005	0.007**	0.007*	0.009**	0.004
	(1.930)	(2.620)	(2.210)	(2.750)	(1.010)
Investment	0.003	0.009**	0.004	0.009**	0.004
	(1.420)	(3.730)	(1.560)	(3.320)	(1.300)
Fixed	0.004	0.009**	0.006*	0.010**	0.006*
Investment	(1.950)	(3.920)	(2.000)	(3.880)	(2.130)
Exports	0.004	0.004	0.004	0.004	0.008*
	(1.890)	(1.330)	(1.480)	(1.160)	(2.240)
Imports	0.000	0.000	–0.003	0.010*	0.009
	(0.020)	(0.030)	(0.560)	(2.150)	(1.540)
Employment	0.008*	0.011**	0.013*	0.012*	0.015*
	(2.470)	(2.840)	(2.390)	(2.380)	(2.260)

Notes:
Robust t-statistics in parentheses.
* Significant at 5%; ** significant at 1%.

not independent of the financial dollarization: fear of appreciation is likely to arise in countries where balance sheet effects are small or nonexistent – an increasingly common case in the 2000s.

The combination of deeper savings and greater internal funds (due to an income transfer to high-income households or to firms, respectively), on the one hand, and financial constraints, on the other, reconciles Díaz-Alejandro's (1965) earlier, contractionary version of the undervalued currency story, with the modern, expansionary view. Díaz-Alejandro's story revolved around the question of how the income transfer from a devaluation was ultimately spent. Because Díaz-Alejandro was thinking of an agricultural society (his 1965 piece was inspired by Argentina), he did not see these increased savings translating into sources of domestic finance but rather he saw them as going abroad in the form of foreign assets; hence, the depressed aggregate demand that explained the drop in output. However, in more developed non-industrial economies it is easy to conceive a simpler story where these funds, which in the earlier version were spent abroad, bring about productive investment previously postponed due to insufficient financing. The empirical characterization of the undervaluation–growth link reported in this chapter provides preliminary support to this version of the story.

NOTES

* The ideas and results discussed in this chapter have been previously presented in Levy-Yeyati and Sturzenegger (2007) and Gluzmann, et al. (2007). We thank Luis Casanova, Pablo Gluzmann, Victoria Coccoz and Ramiro Blázquez for excellent research assistance. The usual disclaimers apply.

1. This does not include the economies of the eurozone, which target inflation jointly but are typically excluded from the float group.
2. See Aizenmann and Lee (2007).
3. The methodology classifies the country year data by the k-means algorithm, through a two-step procedure with five groupings. See Levy-Yeyati and Sturzenegger (2003a, 2003b, 2005) for further reference.
4. See, among others, Reinhart and Rogoff (2004) and Shambaugh (2004).
5. All variables correspond to the end of period for a specific month.
6. To our knowledge, the updated LYS regime classification offers the largest country and year coverage over the post-Bretton Woods period. The data is available online at the authors' web pages.
7. The distributions are based on pooled observations of the variable *R* averaged over the year.
8. This broad distribution masks important differences across groups of countries. For example, Latin American countries seem to have embraced floating arrangements wholeheartedly (mostly in combination with inflation-targeting regimes), with the amount of floats doubling between 2000 and 2004 at the expense of both intermediate and pegged regimes. On the other hand, emerging Asia has preserved its bias toward more rigid arrangements. Interestingly, this evidence is *a* priori at odds with the bipolar view, since currency mismatches in Latin America are large, and certainly larger than in Asia.
9. Alternatively, reserves can increase with broad money due to precautionary motives.
10. See Aizenmann and Lee (2005) and Levy-Yeyati (2005) for evidence on the precautionary motives for reserve accumulation in developing economies.
11. Alternative estimations using the ratio to base money provide the same results and are available upon request.
12. We choose the bilateral over the multilateral exchange rate for these tests because it is the one typically targeted by intervention. However, comparable results are obtained using the IMF's real effective exchange rates.
13. Specifically, we include values of *Int*1 between -150 percent and 150 percent, and values of *Int*2 between -100 percent and 100 percent. Similarly, we restrict our sample to values of the dependent variable within two standard deviations from the mean.
14. While in principle there seems to be no reason why the ratio or reserves over broad money (*Int*2) should increase during economic booms, an argument can be made that in the presence of mean reversing real exchange rate swings, a currency mismatched country should prevent appreciation for fear of an ulterior depreciation (Levy-Yeyati, 2005). See Caballero and Lorenzoni (2006) for an analytical model along these lines.
15. We also tested an alternative measure of past output drops, namely, the current

depth of the recession that measures the vertical distance to the previous local GDP maximum. Results were virtually unchanged and are omitted for brevity.

16. The results are reported and discussed in detail in Levy-Yeyati and Sturzenegger (2007). Note that the mercantilist view presumes that intervention affects trade volumes directly and, in turn, trade has a positive influence on growth. If that is not the case, intervention may still affect trade through its effect on growth, but that will not identify the intervention–growth channel that we are after.
17. Export and import shares are often used in the literature to measure the impact of the exchange rates on trade. However, they suffer from an important drawback in this context because they are bound to reflect changes in the relative price of tradables. In particular, the shares should increase with a real devaluation, thus delivering almost by definition a positive relation between depreciation and their participation in output even if the former has no effect on traded volumes. It is more accurate to look at the growth volume of exports and imports.
18. See Gluzmann et al. (2007) for a detailed analysis.
19. The regressions include a convergence term (initial income level, $RGDPCH_{it-1}$) and a set of country and time period dummies (f_i and f_t) to capture other exogenous time-varying global factors, as well as country-specific characteristics
20. Both in Levy-Yeyati and Sturzenegger (2007) and in Rodrik (2007) there is a discussion on whether this result may occur as a result of reverse causality. This is unlikely because, typically, shocks that depreciate the real exchange rate tend to be negative for growth: reverse causality, if anything, would probably induce, if anything, an underestimation of the effect.
21. Notice that Rajan and Subramanian (2006) use as a dependent variable the annual average rate of growth of value added of industry *i* in country *j* over a ten-year period, obtained by normalizing the growth in nominal value added by the GDP deflator. But this means that a sector that sees its relative price fall with an overvaluation will automatically see a decline in its value added deflated by the GDP deflator, thus producing the results even in the absence of real effects.
22. In fact, his work led to a long debate on whether devaluations were contractionary or expansionary, long before financial dollarization introduced an additional – and often dominating – ingredient into the equation.
23. This is the channel popularized by the 'sudden stop' literature (Krugman, 1999; Chang and Velasco, 2001) that led to the unipolar view of exchange rate policy.
24. The first channel is more likely to apply to small and medium-sized enterprises with limited access to finance; the second, to large companies that fund their investments in capital markets.

REFERENCES

Aizenmann, J. and J. Lee (2007), 'International Reserves: Precautionary Versus Mercantilist Views, Theory and Evidence', *Open Economies Review*, **18** (2), pp. 191–214.

Caballero, R.J. and G. Lorenzoni (2006), 'Persistent Appreciations, Overshooting and Optimal Exchange Rate Intervention,' MIT, Mimeo.

Calvo, G. and C. Reinhart (2002), 'Fear Of Floating', *Quarterly Journal of Economics*, **117** (2), pp. 379–408.

Chang, R. and A. Velasco (2001), 'A Model of Financial Crises in Emerging Markets', *Quarterly Journal of Economics*, **116**, pp. 489–517.

Díaz-Alejandro, C. (1965), 'Exchange Rate Devaluation in a Semi-Industrialized Country', Cambridge, MA: MIT Press.

Gluzmann, P., E. Levy-Yeyati and F. Sturzenegger (2007), 'Exchange Rate Undervaluation and Economic Growth: Díaz Alejandro (1965) Revisited', Mimeo, Universidad Torcuato Di Tella.

Hesten, A., R. Summers and B. Aten (2006), 'Penn World Table Version 6.2', Center for International Comparisons of Production, income and Prices at the University of Pennsylvania, September.

Hausman, R., L. Pritchett and D. Rodrik (2005), 'Growth Accelerations,' *Kennedy School of Government*, Mimeo.

Johnson, S., J. Ostry and A. Subramanian (2006), 'Levers for Growth, Finance and Development', *Finance and Development*, **43** (1), available at: http://www.imf.org/externel/pubs/ft/fandd/2006/03/johnson.htm.

Krugman, P. (1999), 'Balance Sheets, the Transfer Problem, and Financial Crises', *International Tax and Public Finance*, **6** (4), pp. 459–72.

Levy-Yeyati, E. (2005), 'Exchange Rate Regimes in the 2000s: A Latin American Perspective', prepared for the Conference on A New Economic Development Agenda for Latin America, Salamanca, 8–9 October.

Levy-Yeyati, E. and F. Sturzenegger (2001), 'Exchange Rate Regimes and Economic Performance', *IMF Staff Papers*, **47**, pp. 62–98.

Levy-Yeyati, E. and F. Sturzenegger (2003a), 'To Float or to Trail: Evidence on the Impact of Exchange Rate Regimes', *American Economic Review*, **93** (4),

Levy-Yeyati, E. and F. Sturzenegger (2003b), 'A de facto Classification of Exchange Rate Regimes: A Methodological Note', *American Economic Review*, **93** (4), http://www.aeaweb.org/aer/contents/.

Levy-Yeyati, E. and F. Sturzenegger (2005), 'Classifying Exchange Rate Regimes: Deeds vs. Words', *European Economic Review*, **49** (August), pp. 1603–35.

Levy-Yeyati, E. and F. Sturzenegger (2007), 'Fear of Appreciation', Working Paper, JFK School of Government.

Prasad, E., R. Rajan and A. Subramanian (2006), 'Foreign Capital and Economic Growth', Research Department IMF, 30 August.

Rajan, R. and A. Subramanian (2006), 'Aid, Dutch Disease, and Manufacturing Growth', June. Working Paper, Peterson Institute for International Economics, available at http://www.petersoninstitute.org/publications/papers/subramanian0606.pdf.

Reinhart, C. and K. Rogoff (2004), 'The Modern History of Exchange Rate Arrangements: A Reinterpretation', *Quarterly Journal of Economics*, **119** (1), 2004, pp. 1–48.

Rodrik, D. (2007) 'The Real Exchange Rae and Economic Growth: Theory and Evidence', Mimeo, Kennedy School of Government, Harvard University.

Shambaugh, J. (2004), 'The Effect of Fixed Exchange Rates on Monetary Policy', *Quareterly Journal of Economics*, **119**, pp. 300–351.

6. Aid reversals, credibility and macroeconomic policy

Edward Buffie, Christopher Adam, Stephen O'Connell and Catherine Pattillo*

6.1 INTRODUCTION

> To *absorb and spend* the aid would appear to be the appropriate response under 'normal' circumstances. (Berg et al., 2007, p. 19)

> Surprisingly, a full absorb-and-spend response is not observed in any of the sample countries. (Berg et al., 2007, p. 36)

> In all countries, part of the aid increment was lost through reductions in the rate of capital inflow. In Ghana, the deterioration in the non-aid capital account exceeded the entire increment in the aid inflow. In Tanzania and Uganda, the reduction in the rate of non-aid capital inflows was comparable to the aid surge. (Berg et al., 2007, p. 28)

The G8 countries have pledged to increase aid dramatically to sub-Saharan Africa (SSA) in an effort to meet the Millennium Development Goals. It is not clear, however, that a big aid push is realistic. Seven country studies recently completed at the International Monetary Fund (IMF) (Berg et al., 2007) and the Overseas Development Institute (ODI) (Foster and Killick, 2006) found that the current account deficit usually increases by less than half of the rise in aid flows and that aid surges often coincide with large capital outflows. These are disconcerting correlations. If the current account deficit does not increase by the same amount as aid, the transfer of real resources is incomplete. A substantial part of aid ends up financing capital flight or reserve accumulation instead of worthy projects.

The IMF contends that these problems stem from misguided macroeconomic policies. Absorption is too low because central banks are reluctant to sell aid dollars and let the exchange rate appreciate. Indirectly, low absorption is also the source of capital outflows: aid is tied to increases in government spending; but when absorption rises less than the fiscal deficit, the money supply increases and excess liquidity flows out through the capital account.

In this chapter we put forward a different explanation for the stylized facts based on aid volatility and institutional constraints. Although aid reversals are common, political realities limit the use of reserve buffer stocks (Adam and Bevan, 2003; Eifert and Gelb, 2005). (Donors object to aid dollars sitting in a rainy-day fund; they want to see their money spent on doing good.) Consequently, expenditure has to be cut or taxes increased when aid declines to a normal level. This is easier said than done. Typically the ends of resource and aid booms witness large and persistent financing gaps as governments struggle to reverse prior spending commitments. The public has ample grounds therefore to fear that today's aid boom threatens future fiscal stability.

The upshot of these considerations is that policymakers face a potential credibility problem. The Fund's preferred strategy of spending all the aid and floating the exchange rate (the '*absorb-and-spend*' approach) works well when the public believes the aid surge is permanent. It is a recipe for disaster, however, when aid volatility and fiscal inertia undermine credibility. In the numerical simulations we report, the government is committed to a full absorption policy and all extra public sector spending is financed by the sale of aid dollars. Nevertheless, capital flight claims 30–70 percent of the aid inflow and inflation soars from 25 percent to 40–50 percent.

Since *absorb and spend* fails badly, we investigate a variety of other policies. Previewing the bottom line, successful intervention requires a *policy package*. The right strategy combines a critical minimum degree of fiscal restraint with '*reverse sterilization*'. During the low-credibility phase, the government uses part of the aid inflow ($\approx$ 25 percent) to cut the fiscal deficit and pay down the internal debt. Crucially, the reverse sterilization component of the package buys extra time to adjust to future adverse aid shocks. If private sector expectations prove correct and the aid boom subsequently collapses, then the central bank sells the bonds it purchased earlier, maintaining control of money growth and inflation while the fiscal authorities take steps to realign spending with revenue. Thus the fiscal time bomb is no longer an inflation time bomb. The resulting shift from pessimistic to neutral expectations in the private sector repairs much of the damage done by the naive *absorb-and-spend* strategy: inflation stays below its previous level, capital outflows decrease 25–60 percent, and the absorption rate rises 20–30 points. *Temporary fiscal restraint plus reverse sterilization* is not a perfect solution to the credibility problem; it does, however, go a long way toward making the problem manageable.

The rest of the chapter is organized into five sections. In sections 6.2 and 6.3 we develop an optimizing model of a small open economy and calibrate it to the data for Ghana, a country that has long been on the receiving end of volatile aid flows. Section 6.4 demonstrates that the Fund's *absorb-*

and-spend approach is good advice when the aid boom is expected to be permanent but bad advice when it is expected to be temporary. Section 6.5 examines alternative policy responses to the credibility problem and section 6.6 concludes.

6.2 THE BENCHMARK MODEL

We extend the model in Buffie et al. (forthcoming) to allow for temporary aid shocks and fiscal inertia. The specification of the real economy is primitive. Competitive firms produce a non-traded good and a composite traded good. Real output is fixed in both sectors, the exchange rate system is a pure float, and the world price of the traded good equals unity. On the financial side, the private sector divides its wealth between domestic currency M, foreign currency F, and government bonds B. Bonds are indexed to the price level P, so $B = Pb$, where $b \equiv B/P$. Other notational conventions are as follows: C_i and Q_i are consumption and output in sector i; e is the nominal exchange rate; and P_n and E are the relative price of the non-traded good and aggregate real expenditure measured in dollars (that is, units of the traded good).

6.2.1 Preferences and the Private Agent's Optimization Problem

All economic decisions in the private sector are controlled by a representative agent who derives utility from the consumption of traded and non-traded goods and from the liquidity services generated by holdings of domestic and foreign currency. To obtain concrete results, we assume preferences take the form:

$$U = \int_0^\infty \left[\frac{C(C_n, C_T)^{1-1/\tau}}{1 - 1/\tau} + h\frac{\phi(M/P,\, eF/P)^{1-1/\tau}}{1 - 1/\tau} \right] e^{-\rho t} dt, \qquad (6.1)$$

where

$$C(C_n, C_T) = [k_o C_T^{(\beta-1)/\beta} + k_1 C_n^{(\beta-1)/\beta}]^{\beta/(\beta-1)},$$

$$\phi(M/P, eF/P) = [k_2 (M/P)^{(\sigma-1)/\sigma} + k_3 (eF/P)^{(\sigma-1)/\sigma}]^{\sigma/(\sigma-1)},$$

are linearly homogeneous constant elasticity of substitution (CES) aggregator functions; h and $k_o - k_3$ are constants; ρ is the pure time preference rate; τ is the intertemporal elasticity of substitution; β is the elasticity of substitution between traded and non-traded consumer goods; and σ is the elasticity of substitution between domestic and foreign currency.

The private agent solves his optimization problem in two stages. In the first stage, C_n and C_T are chosen to maximize $C(C_n, C_T)$ subject to the constraint $P_nC_n + C_T = E$. The optimal choices $\overline{C}_n$ and $\overline{C}_T$ are subsumed in the indirect utility function:

$$V(P_n, E) = C[\overline{C}_n(P_n, E), \overline{C}_T(P_n, E)] = E/c(P_n),$$

where:

$$c(P_n) = (k_o^\beta + k_1^\beta P_n^{1-\beta})^{1/(1-\beta)}.$$

As a byproduct of optimization, we get the solution for the exact consumer price index:

$$P = ec(P_n). \tag{6.2}$$

For future use, note also that:

$$\pi = \chi + \gamma \dot{P}_n/P_n, \tag{6.3}$$

where $\pi = \dot{P}/P$ is the inflation rate; $\chi = \dot{e}/e$ is the rate of currency depreciation; and $\gamma = k_1^\beta P_n^{1-\beta}/[k_o^\beta + k_1^\beta P_n^{1-\beta}]$ is the consumption share of the non-traded good.

In the second stage of optimization, the private agent chooses asset holdings and expenditure to maximize:

$$U = \int_0^\infty \left[\frac{E^{1-1/\tau}}{1 - 1/\tau} + h\frac{\phi(m, F)^{1-1/\tau}}{1 - 1/\tau}\right] c(P_n)^{(1-\tau)/\tau} e^{-\rho t} dt, \tag{6.4}$$

subject to the budget constraint:

$$\dot{A} = P_nQ_n + Q_T + cg + (r + \pi - \chi)(\underbrace{A - m - F}_{(P/e)b}) - E - \chi m. \tag{6.5}$$

where $m \equiv M/e$ and $A \equiv m + (P/e)b + F$ are real money balances and wealth measured in dollars. In equation (6.5), $(\pi - \chi)(A - m - F)$ is an artificial capital gains term. It shows up because the traded good is the numeraire but bonds are indexed to the price level.

The *Maximum Principle* furnishes the necessary conditions for an optimum. These consist of:

$$E^{-1/\tau}c(P_n)^{(1-\tau)/\tau} = \omega, \tag{6.6}$$

$$h\phi(m,F)^{-1/\tau}\phi_m(m,F) = E^{-1/\tau}(r + \pi), \tag{6.7}$$

$$h\phi(m,F)^{-1/\tau}\phi_F(m,F) = E^{-1/\tau}(r + \pi - \chi), \tag{6.8}$$

$$\dot{\omega} = \omega(\rho + \chi - r - \pi) \tag{6.9}$$

where ω is the multiplier attached to (6.5). Equations (6.6)–(6.8) hold no surprises. As expected, the marginal utility of consumption equals the shadow price of wealth and the marginal rate of substitution between consumption and m or F equals the income foregone from holding that type of money. The co-state equation (6.9) may look less familiar, but it is nothing more than a standard Euler equation. Differentiate (6.6) with respect to time and substitute for $\dot{\omega}$. This gives:

$$\dot{E}/E - \gamma\dot{P}_n/P_n = \tau(r - \rho), \tag{6.10}$$

where the term on the left side is the percentage change in aggregate real consumption.

6.2.2 The Non-Tradables Sector

P_n adjusts to clear the goods market in the non-tradables sector. This requires:

$$C_n = Q_n, \tag{6.11}$$

where C_n is retrieved from the indirect utility function by invoking Roy's Identity:

$$C_n = -\frac{\partial V/\partial P_n}{\partial V/\partial E} = E\frac{k_1^\beta P_n^{-\beta}}{k_o^\beta + k_1^\beta P_n^{1-\beta}}. \tag{6.12}$$

6.2.3 The Public Sector Budget Constraint

Money is injected into the economy when the central bank runs the printing press to finance the fiscal deficit of the central government. For now, we ignore bond sales and open market operations. The consolidated public sector budget constraint is thus:

$$\dot{m} = g + c(P_n)rb - X - \chi m, \tag{6.13}$$

where X is sale of aid dollars net of government imports.

6.2.4 Net Foreign Asset Accumulation

Summing the private and public sector budget constraints produces the accounting identity that foreign asset accumulation equals national saving or the current account surplus:

$$\dot{F} = P_n Q_n + Q_T + X - E. \tag{6.14}$$

In a pure float, the government does not hold foreign exchange reserves. Since the overall balance of payments is zero, the capital account deficit equals the current account surplus inclusive of aid.

6.2.5 Temporary Aid Surges and Fiscal Inertia

Aid flows jump from X_o to X_1 at $t = 0$. The extra money finances an equal increase in transfer payments to the 'poor' (that is, the representative agent):

$$g_1 = g_o + X_1 - X_o. \tag{6.15}$$

The private sector does not believe the aid boom will last. It forecasts a full reversal at year T with probability one:

$$X(t)\Big|_{\substack{\text{private}\\\text{forecast}}} = \begin{cases} X_1 \text{ for } 0 < t < T \\ X_o \text{ for } t > T \end{cases} \tag{6.16}$$

When private expectations prove correct and the aid boom is short-lived, the government must either curtail expenditure or tolerate a higher fiscal deficit and higher inflation. We assume policymakers are averse to higher inflation but find it difficult to dismantle spending programs initiated during the boom phase. After the aid boom collapses, transfer payments decrease at the rate:

$$\dot{g} = v(g_o - g),\ t > T, \tag{6.17}$$

where $v > 0$ determines the degree of fiscal inertia.

In all variants of the model, the government wishes to spend as much of the extra aid as price and exchange rate stability permit. There are two ways to justify this assumption. First, the government may believe donors when they aver that *this time* the jump in aid flows will last forever and that the country should immediately start spending much more on anti-poverty programs.[1] Alternatively, policymakers may harbor the same doubts as the private sector but feel compelled to spend heavily lest donors 'decide to reallocate the aid to a more eager recipient' (Berg et al., 2007, p. 51). The external pressure to spend will usually be reinforced by strong internal pressures – every ministry and department has 'great unmet needs' (Berg et al., 2007).

One final point. We have not taken a position on whether the aid boom is truly permanent because it is not necessary to do so. The path the economy follows in the period $(0, T)$ depends only on private sector beliefs about what will happen at and after T. The private sector may well be too pessimistic: in reality, the aid surge may be permanent or fiscal inertia may be less of a problem than expected. But this is not learned until T arrives. Regardless of what the future brings, the challenge for the government is to find a policy package that allows it to spend a large fraction of the aid without suffering adverse side-effects.

To save space, we proceed directly to calibration of the model. A longer version of the chapter (available upon request) describes the procedure used to solve for the economy's equilibrium path.

6.3 MODEL CALIBRATION

Ghana is a good example of a country that may soon face the problem of managing a non-credible aid boom. Starting in 2008, aid to the country is supposed to double for 15–20 years as part of the campaign to meet the Millenium Development Goals. But it is doubtful that the donors' pledge to sustain a massive increase in aid is credible to the Ghanaian public.[2] For the past 20 years (1987–2007), aid flows have been extremely volatile. As recently as 2002, aid plunged by 8 percent of gross domestic product (GDP).

Table 6.1 lists the parameter values used to calibrate the model. m_o, π_o, b_o, γ_o and X_o are close to the values seen in Ghana in 2003. Data for Ghana also informs our choices (albeit more loosely) for ρ, ψ and F_o, but the values for the deep parameters β, σ and τ are guesses based on econometric estimates for other less developed countries (LDCs). Below we comment briefly on the rationales for the numbers assigned to these parameters and to ρ, ψ and F_o:

- Elasticity of substitution in consumption between traded and non-traded consumer goods (β). Fixing β at 0.50 implies that the compensated elasticity of demand for the non-traded good is 0.25 initially. This agrees with the finding in empirical studies that compensated elasticities of demand tend to be small at high levels of aggregation.
- Elasticity of substitution between domestic and foreign currency (σ). There are no reliable estimates of σ for Ghana or any other country in Africa. For Latin America the numbers range from 1.5 to 7. Not

Table 6.1 Calibration of the model

Parameter/Variable	Assigned Value	Source[1]
Reserve money (m)	10% of GDP[2]	Ghana 2003: 10.2%.
Inflation (π)	25%	Ghana 2003: 23.6 % for Dec.–Dec.; 26.7% = period average
Stock of internal debt (b)	20% of GDP	Ghana 2003: 18.3% of GDP[3]
Consumption share of nontraded good (γ)	50%	Ghana 2003: 50.8% weight in CPI[4]
Aid (X)	10% of GDP	Ghana 2003: 9.44% (World Development Indicators)[5]
Degree of fiscal inertial (v)	1	–
Time preference rate (ρ)	8%	See discussion in text
Foreign currency (*F*)	15% of GDP	See discussion in text
Elasticity of substitution between traded and nontraded consumer goods (β)	0.50	Estimates for other LDCs. See discussion in text
Elasticity of substitution between domestic and foreign currency (σ)	0.30, 0.75, 2	Estimates for other LDCs. See discussion in text
Intertemporal elasticity of substitution (τ)	0.25	Estimates for other LDCs. See discussion in text

Notes:
1. Data for Ghana are from IMF Country Reports 05/286 and 05/292.
2. Average of beginning and end-of-year money stock divided by nominal GDP.
3. Does not include debt of state-owned enterprises.
4. Half of the weight for food plus the weights for rent, fuel and power, medical care and health, transport and communication, and recreation. The guesstimate that half of food consumption is nontradable is based on the findings in Adam and Bevan (2003).
5. Net official development assistance less the estimate of government imports reported in the IMF's Ghana Statistical Appendix 2005.

trusting the high-end estimates (7??), we decided to let σ vary from 0.30 to 2. We include runs for $\sigma = 0.30$ – a value that is probably much too low – to make the point that the results are robust to the diffusion of priors across informed observers.

- Time preference rate (ρ). Across steady states, the real interest rate is fixed by the time preference rate. The value assigned to ρ (8 percent) is slightly less than the average real rate paid by short-term Treasury bills since 1992 (8.25 percent according to IMF, 2003, p. 66).
- Elasticity of intertemporal substitution (τ). Most estimates for LDCs place τ between 0.10 and 0.50 (Agenor and Montiel, 1999,

Table 12.1). Given that Ghana is one of the poorer LDCs, we set τ equal to 0.25.

- Ratio of foreign currency to national income (F_o). Foreign currency deposits in the domestic banking sector are 60 percent of reserve money in Ghana. This suggests $F_o = 0.06$, but the true value is higher because a good deal of foreign currency is held outside of the domestic banking system. We arbitrarily set F_o at 0.15. This is in line with dollarization ratios in other parts of the Third World.
- Degree of fiscal inertia (v). All runs assume $v = 1$. This implies an intermediate degree of fiscal inertia: 87 percent of spending increases introduced during the aid boom are reversed within two years. The results with a low or high degree of fiscal inertia are qualitatively similar. Runs for these cases ($v = 0.50, 2$) are available from the authors upon request.

We chose units so that $P_{no} = E_o = 1$ and carried out simulations for the case where aid inflows increase by 3 percent of national income.

6.4 AID BOOMS WITH AND WITHOUT CREDIBILITY

> Absorption depends on the response of the central bank . . . The combination of absorption and spending chosen by the authorities defines the macroeconomic response to aid. (IMF, 2007, p. 2)

The Fund uses a *spend-and-absorb* framework to classify macroeconomic responses to an aid boom. '*Spend*' is defined to be the increase in the primary fiscal deficit and '*absorb*' the increase in the current account deficit, both measured as a percentage of the increase in aid. The Fund recommends that the central bank sell all the aid dollars and that the central government spend all the counterpart funds (that is, the domestic currency proceeds of the aid).[3] It calls this the '*absorb-and-spend*' approach. '*Absorb*' is treated as a policy variable on the assumption that aggregate absorption is determined by the central bank's willingness to sell aid dollars. This is a considerable stretch, if not altogether wrong. Since the current account depends on how private sector spending responds to the aid inflow, absorption is an endogenous variable, not a policy instrument.[4] At the risk of violating the Fund's property rights, we relabel their approach '*float and full spend*' (FFS hereafter). In this section we conduct a counterfactual exercise to test the sensitivity of the Fund's FFS strategy to credibility of the aid boom. The numerical simulations track the paths of inflation, the real exchange rate ($1/P_n$), the current account surplus inclusive of aid, and private capital flows. Since the goal is to find a policy package that steers the economy safely through the low-credibility period, we report results only up to year T; the period after T is not of interest *per se*.

6.4.1 FFS with Full Credibility

Table 6.2 shows the outcome when the aid boom is permanent. The increase in expenditure raises the demand for non-traded goods and real money balances. Across steady states, this causes the real exchange rate to appreciate 11 percent and the inflation rate to fall 2–3 percentage points.

*Table 6.2 Transition path when the aid boom is permanent**

	$\tau = 0.25$ and $\sigma = 0.30$						
	$t = 0$	$t = 1$	$t = 2$	$t = 3$	$t = 4$	$t = 5$	Long run
π	0.25	0.25	0.24	0.24	0.24	0.24	0.23
RER	0.91	0.90	0.90	0.90	0.89	0.89	0.89
CA	0.006	0.004	0.002	0.001	0.001	0.001	0
F	0	0.005	0.008	0.010	0.011	0.011	0.014
	$\tau = 0.25$ and $\sigma = 0.75$						
	$t = 0$	$t = 1$	$t = 2$	$t = 3$	$t = 4$	$t = 5$	Long run
π	0.24	0.24	0.24	0.24	0.24	0.23	.23
RER	0.90	0.90	0.90	0.89	0.89	0.89	.89
CA	0.004	0.003	0.002	0.001	0.001	0.001	0
F	0	0.003	0.005	0.007	0.008	0.009	0.011
	$\tau = 0.25$ and $\sigma = 2$						
	$t = 0$	$t = 1$	$t = 2$	$t = 3$	$t = 4$	$t = 5$	Long run
π	0.22	0.22	0.22	0.22	0.22	0.22	0.22
RER	0.89	0.89	0.89	0.89	0.89	0.89	0.89
CA	–0.001	0	0	0	0	0	0
F	0	0	–0.001	–0.001	–0.001	–0.001	–0.002

Notes:
* Notation: π, RER, CA and F stand for the inflation rate, the real exchange rate, the current account surplus as a percentage of GNP, and cumulative capital flows as a percentage of GNP.

The initial values for the inflation rate, the real exchange rate, and the current account are 25%, 1 and 0.

Lower inflation and higher expenditure exert conflicting effects on the demand for foreign currency. The two effects cancel out when domestic and foreign currency are close substitutes ($\sigma = 2$). In the other cases, the expenditure effect dominates and capital outflows cumulate to 1.1–1.4 percent of GDP.

Consistent with the Fund view, adjustment is smooth and problem-free in this scenario. The real exchange rate appreciates immediately by 9–11 percent. Aside from this necessary real adjustment, the aid shock is absorbed without macroeconomic volatility. Details differ depending on the value assigned to the currency substitution parameter σ, but the story is essentially the same in each case. At $t = 0$ both the inflation rate and the price level fall, as appreciation of the exchange rate and lower prices for traded goods more than offset upward pressure on non-traded goods prices. Private capital flows are small and the transfer of real resources occurs quickly: in the low currency substitution runs, the absorption rate rises from 84–89 percent in the first year to 90–96 percent in the second and third years; in the high currency substitution run, it is 100 percent from the outset.[5]

6.4.2 FFS without Credibility

> Over the medium and longer term, once a government scales up its expenditure program in response to more foreign aid, it faces the challenge of how to finance these programs if the new aid isn't sustained by donors . . . Such obligations are not easily shed or reduced . . . If governments are not able to reduce expenditures . . . budgetary policy pressures may jeopardize the *macroeconomic* policy framework. (Heller, 2005, p. 12)

Credibility is the Achilles heel of the FFS strategy. In Table 6.3 the aid surge is expected to last three years and retrenchment of spending in the post-boom period takes two years. The public now anticipates an aid collapse and a subsequent transitory phase of high fiscal deficits and high inflation. Naturally, this creates inflationary pressures during the boom period by reducing money demand. In the run for $\sigma = 0.30$, money demand is insensitive to its future return and inflation does not explode until the middle of year three when the aid collapse and fiscal instability are imminent. With a moderate or high degree of currency substitution, inflation increases earlier and much more: in the panel for $\sigma = 2$, inflation is 50–90 percent higher over the entire low-credibility period.[6] Observe also that private capital outflows are very large and that absorption is far less than 100 percent. For $\sigma = 0.30 - 0.75$, the private sector spends only 50–70 percent of aid-generated income; this figure drops to 35 percent when domestic and foreign currency are close substitutes. Disturbingly,

Table 6.3 *Transition path when the aid boom is temporary**

	$\tau = 0.25$ and $\sigma = 0.30$				
	$t = 0$	$t = 1$	$t = 2$	$t = 3$	% change in e, Pn and P at $t = 0$
π	0.24	0.24	0.26	0.41	e = –5.7,
RER	0.93	0.92	0.93	0.94	P_n = 1.9,
CA	0.010	0.008	0.010	0.014	P = –1.9
F	0	0.009	0.018	0.029	
	$\tau = 0.25$ and $\sigma = 0.75$				
	$t = 0$	$t = 1$	$t = 2$	$t = 3$	% change in e, P_n and P at $t = 0$
π	0.28	0.29	0.33	0.44	e = –2.8,
RER	0.94	0.94	0.94	0.95	P_n = 3.5,
CA	0.013	0.013	0.013	0.015	P = .3
F	0	0.013	0.026	0.040	
	$\tau = 0.25$ and $\sigma = 2$				
	$t = 0$	$t = 1$	$t = 2$	$t = 3$	% change in e, P_n and P at $t = 0$
π	0.37	0.38	0.41	0.47	e = 9.4,
RER	0.98	0.96	0.96	0.95	P_n = 12.1,
CA	0.023	0.020	0.018	0.017	P = 10.8
F	0	0.021	0.040	0.058	

Notes:
* 87% of spending increases introduced during the aid boom are reversed within two years.
In the far right column, e, P_n, and P refer to the nominal exchange rate, the nominal price of the non-traded good, and the price level.

in a pure float, the flip side of low absorption and large current account surpluses (inclusive of aid) has to be extensive capital flight. In the worst-case scenario where $\sigma = 2$, 65 percent of aid is wasted in paying for capital flight. Not all of this is the fault of FFS. Some worsening in the capital account is unavoidable because the private sector saves to smooth the impact of the aid shock (perceived as temporary) on consumption. But the pure saving motive accounts for only 36 percent of the outflows.[7] The rest – which *is* the fault of FFS – reflects the public's desire to amass foreign currency as a hedge against inflation.

It would be easy to read these results as supporting the Fund's contention that spending in excess of absorption fuels higher inflation and capital flight.

The right conclusion, however, is quite different. The Fund's conceptual framework and its interpretation of the empirical evidence rest on the dubious premises that: (1) absorption is a policy variable; and (2) the money supply increases *ex ante* when the central bank does not allow absorption to rise by the same amount as the fiscal deficit. Neither premise is valid in our model. There is no increase in the money supply, *ex ante* or *ex post*, and absorption is endogenous because foreign currency is a vehicle for private saving. The government aims for full absorption, but this is not feasible when the private sector fears that the current aid boom portends future fiscal and monetary instability. In Table 6.3, low absorption, capital flight and high inflation are symptoms of an unsolved credibility problem. Bad policy is not to blame.

6.5 POLICY OPTIONS

The default policy, FFS, fares poorly when the aid boom is not credible. This raises the question of whether other policies do better. Accordingly, we move on to examine tight money, temporary fiscal restraint and policy packages that combine modest fiscal restraint with reverse sterilization. This list is not exhaustive but it includes a policy package that wins the battle against weak credibility.[8]

6.5.1 Tight Money

Weak credibility stokes inflationary pressure by depressing money demand. In this section, the central bank reacts by selling securities to reduce money growth:

$$\dot{b} = \alpha[b(t) - b_o], \ \alpha > 0, \ t < T. \tag{6.18}$$

Let $J \equiv b(0) - b_o$ denote bond sales at $t = 0$. The path for b is then:

$$b(t) = b_o + Je^{\alpha t}, \ t < T. \tag{6.19}$$

The values assigned to J and α define the central bank's tight money rule. We search over these two parameters to find the policy rule that delivers the best results. This is not meant to be realistic. It is rather a debating tactic: we want to demonstrate that tight money is the wrong policy even under assumptions favorable to its success.

The introduction of bond sales alters a couple of equations in the model. During the low-credibility period, part of the fiscal deficit is financed by issuing debt. The public sector budget constraint changes to:

$$\dot{m} = g_1 + c(P_n)rb - X_1 - c(P_n)\alpha(b - b_o) - \chi m, \; t < T. \quad (6.20)$$

After aid flows contract at T, bond sales cease and the government reduces expenditure gradually to bring the fiscal deficit and inflation back to their original levels. This requires more fiscal adjustment than in the benchmark model. Transfer payments have to drop below g_o in order to offset higher interest payments on the internal debt:

$$\dot{g} = v(\overline{g} - g), \; v > 0, \quad (6.21)$$

where $\overline{g} = g_o - \rho[b(T) - b_o]$.

Table 6.4 shows the limits of monetary policy acting on its own. Place this table alongside Table 6.3, which provides the relevant counterfactuals. What stands out in the comparison is the remarkable similarity of the paths case-by-case, period-by-period. Tight money, in other words, is almost completely ineffective. There is only one achievement worthy of note. When $\sigma = 2$, the price level in the counterfactual jumps 11 percent at the start of the aid boom. In the run with tight money, the central bank eliminates the nasty spike by selling bonds equal to 1.2 percent of GDP at $t = 0$.

These results are not particularly surprising. Tight money tries to neutralize inflationary pressure and inhibit capital flight by aligning money growth with money demand. This is sensible, intuitive and simplistic. Bond sales imply higher interest payments in the future and even larger fiscal deficits after the aid boom disappears. Viewed from this angle, the tight money strategy is ill-conceived; it slows money growth but exacerbates the credibility and fiscal inertia problem.

6.5.2 Temporary Fiscal Restraint

Under a policy of temporary fiscal restraint, the government spends less than 100 percent of the extra aid while credibility is low. That is:

$$g_1 = g_o + \psi(X_1 - X_o), \; 0 < \psi < 1, \; t < T. \quad (6.22)$$

The primary fiscal deficit decreases by $(1 - \psi)(X_1 - X_o)$, the portion of aid not spent. This reduces money growth without compounding the difficulties of fiscal retrenchment when and if the aid boom collapses. In fact, since spending increases less during the boom phase, adjustment to a future negative aid shock is easier than in the counterfactual scenario.

This sounds nice, but there is a catch. Aid donors want to fund anti-poverty programs; they are not in the business of providing budget

*Table 6.4 Transition path when a tight money policy is followed during the aid boom**

	$t = 0$	$t = 1$	$t = 2$	$t = 3$	% change in e, Pn and P at $t = 0$
			$\tau = 0.25$ and $\sigma = 0.30$		
π	0.23	0.22	0.24	0.41	e = –7.3,
RER	0.93	0.92	0.93	0.94	$P_n = 0.2$,
CA	0.009	0.008	0.010	0.014	P = –3.6
F	0	0.009	0.017	0.029	
			$\tau = 0.25$ and $\sigma = 0.75$		
	$t = 0$	$t = 1$	$t = 2$	$t = 3$	% change in e, P_n and P at $t = 0$
π	0.27	0.28	0.32	0.44	e = –6.2,
RER	0.94	0.94	0.94	0.95	$P_n = -0.1$,
CA	0.013	0.012	0.013	0.015	P = –3.2
F	0	0.013	0.026	0.040	
			$\tau = 0.25$ and $\sigma = 2$		
	$t = 0$	$t = 1$	$t = 2$	$t = 3$	% change in e, P_n and P at $t = 0$
π	0.38	0.39	0.42	0.48	e = –2.5,
RER	0.98	0.96	0.96	0.95	$P_n = -0.3$,
CA	0.023	0.020	0.018	0.017	P = –1.4
F	0	0.022	0.041	0.058	

Note: * Cumulative bond sales are 1% of initial GDP in the first panel, 1.8% in the second panel, and 2.2 % in the third panel.

support. The critical issue therefore is whether temporary fiscal restraint preserves macroeconomic stability when the government spends enough to satisfy the donor community.

The answer in Table 6.5 is discouraging. Fiscal restraint helps, but only for a few years. For $\psi = 0.75$, there is not enough restraint to sustain aborption and inhibit capital outflows after year one or to stop inflation from rising to 34–38 percent in year three. Moreover, temporary control of inflation control is achieved by importing a new problem. Battered by incipient capital inflows, the nominal exchange rate appreciates 13–15 percent at $t = 0$. Consequently, to keep demand equal to supply, the nominal price of the non-traded has to decrease immediately by 5–7

Table 6.5 Transition path when 75% of extra aid is spent

	$t = 0$	$t = 1$	$t = 2$	$t = 3$	% change in e, Pn and P at $t = 0$
			$\tau = 0.25$ and $\sigma = 0.30$		
π	0.16	0.16	0.20	0.34	e = –12.8,
RER	0.92	0.92	0.93	0.94	P_n = –5.5,
CA	0.009	0.008	0.009	0.014	P = –9.2
F	0	0.008	0.017	0.029	
			$\tau = 0.25$ and $\sigma = 0.75$		
	$t = 0$	$t = 1$	$t = 2$	$t = 3$	% change in e, P_n and P at $t = 0$
π	0.18	0.20	0.25	0.36	e = –14.2,
RER	0.92	0.93	0.94	0.95	P_n = –6.8,
CA	0.009	0.010	0.013	0.017	P = –10.5
F	0	0.009	0.021	0.036	
			$\tau = 0.25$ and $\sigma = 2$		
	$t = 0$	$t = 1$	$t = 2$	$t = 3$	% change in e, P_n and P at $t = 0$
π	0.19	0.22	0.28	0.38	e = –14.7,
RER	0.91	0.93	0.95	0.97	P_n = –6.5,
CA	0.006	0.011	0.015	0.021	P = –10.6
F	0	0.008	0.022	0.040	

percent. This is a bit far-fetched. If prices are not exceptionally flexible in the downward direction, adjustment will be accompanied by a demand-switching recession in the non-tradables sector (Buffie et al., 2004). Imposing more fiscal restraint makes the problem even worse. When 50 percent of aid is diverted to budget support, the nominal exchange rate depreciates 20–40 percent and the market-clearing price of the nontraded good declines 13–28 percent at $t = 0$.

6.5.3 Reverse Sterilization plus Temporary Fiscal Restraint

Allocating 25–50 percent of aid flows to budget support causes excessive appreciation of the nominal exchange rate in the short run and fails to prevent higher inflation in the third year. This suggests that fiscal restraint combined with purchases of domestic debt will produce better paths for both the exchange rate and inflation. At $t = 0$, the central bank stabilizes the nominal exchange rate by purchasing bonds and pumping money into the economy. The initial purchase is followed by either further purchases or small sales, so the stock of internal debt is lower at the beginning of year four when all uncertainty is resolved. If aid falls, the central bank sells the bonds it purchased earlier to keep a firm grip on money growth during the difficult period of fiscal retrenchment. The logic behind the strategy is to attack the credibility problem at its source: paying down the internal debt mitigates inflationary pressure during the boom phase by creating the perception that future money growth and inflation will remain low even if current high aid flows prove temporary.

For this variant of the model:

$$g_1 = g_o + \psi(X_1 - X_o),\ 0 < \psi < 1,\ t < T, \tag{6.22}$$

$$\dot{b} = \alpha[b(t) - b_o],\ \alpha > 0,\ t < T, \tag{6.23}$$

$$b(t) = b_o + Je^{\alpha t},\ J < 0,\ t < T, \tag{6.24}$$

$$\dot{m} = g_1 + c(P_n)rb - X_1 - c(P_n)\alpha(b - b_o) - \chi m,\ t < T, \tag{6.25}$$

$$\dot{b} = \delta(b_o - b),\ \delta > 0,\ t > T, \tag{6.26}$$

$$\dot{m} = g + c(P_n)rb - X_o - c(P_n)\delta(b_o - b) - \chi m,\ t > T. \tag{6.27}$$

Reverse sterilization changes J in (6.24) from a positive to a negative number. In equations (6.26) and (6.27), the parameter δ determines how fast the central bank sells bonds in an effort to prevent larger fiscal deficits from increasing money growth during the retrenchment phase. As in the simulations of tight money, the values for α, J and δ were chosen through a trial-and-error search for a good macroeconomic outcome.

This strategy works splendidly. In Table 6.6 the government spends 75 percent of the extra aid and central bank purchases of internal debt range from 1.8–4 percent of GDP. Thanks to the reverse sterilization component, the government can spend more of the aid money – the real objective – without running into macroeconomic problems during the low-credibility phase. Inflation stays below 16 percent, the initial jump in the consumer price index (CPI) is negligible, and appreciation of the nominal exchange rate at $t = 0$ is reduced to 4.2–7.4 percent. Moreover, price and exchange rate stability promote absorption by lessening the incentives for capital flight. This effect is quantitatively substantial, assuming the currency substitution parameter is not unusually small. In the runs for $\sigma = 0.75 - 2$, the average absorption rate is a respectable 67–74

*Table 6.6 Transition path when 75% of extra aid is spent, and the central bank buys back internal debt during the boom**

	$t = 0$	$t = 1$	$t = 2$	$t = 3$	% change in e, Pn and P at $t = 0$
			$\tau = 0.25$ and $\sigma = 0.30$		
π	0.16	0.15	0.14	0.16	e = –4.2
RER	0.92	0.92	0.92	0.94	$P_n = 3.9$
CA	0.009	0.008	0.009	0.015	P = –0.1
F	0	0.008	0.016	0.028	
			$\tau = 0.25$ and $\sigma = 0.75$		
	$t = 0$	$t = 1$	$t = 2$	$t = 3$	% change in e, P_n and P at $t = 0$
π	0.13	0.13	0.14	0.16	e = –5.0,
RER	0.91	0.92	0.93	0.96	$P_n = 4.9$,
CA	0.004	0.007	0.012	0.018	P = 0
F	0	0.006	0.015	0.030	
			$\tau = 0.25$ and $\sigma = 2$		
	$t = 0$	$t = 1$	$t = 2$	$t = 3$	% change in e, P_n and P at $t = 0$
π	0.08	0.09	0.09	0.10	e = –7.4,
RER	0.86	0.90	0.94	0.98	$P_n = 7.4$,
CA	–0.007	0.002	0.012	0.025	P = 0
F	0	–0.003	0.005	0.023	

Note: * Cumulative bond purchases are 1.8% of GDP in the first panel, 2.2% in the second, and 4% in the third. In the second and third panels, all bond purchases are made at $t = 0$.

percent. By contrast, it is only 36–55 percent in the counterfactual (panels for $\sigma = 0.75, 2$ in Table 6.3).

6.6 CONCLUDING REMARKS

Aid flows are highly volatile. This would not be a source of macroeconomic trouble if donors were amenable to full-fledged buffer stock schemes or if African governments could quickly reduce spending when aid flows contract. More often than not, however, donors insist that aid be spent right away. When prior spending commitments are hard to reverse, the recipient country then faces a potentially serious credibility problem. If the public fears that the aid boom might be temporary, it also fears that the future might bring a period of large fiscal deficits and high inflation while the government struggles to curtail expenditure. According to our numerical simulations, the fear of a contingent fiscal time bomb leads to high inflation, capital outflows and current account surpluses (inclusive of aid) during the aid boom. This is consistent with patterns in the data and with the general reluctance of governments in SSA to spend 100 percent of higher aid flows.

We investigated various policy responses to the credibility problem. Tight monetary policy and fiscal restraint are ineffective as they do nothing to counteract the fear that a sudden decline in aid flows will be inflationary. The right strategy is to dedicate a small fraction of aid (20–25 percent) to deficit reduction supported by purchases of internal debt. This policy package creates a financial cushion that enables the government to control money growth when aid flows contract and the fiscal deficit rises. Inflation stays low during the aid boom because the fiscal time bomb is no longer an inflation time bomb.

NOTES

* The views expressed herein are those of the authors and should not be attributed to the International Monetary Fund (IMF), its executive board or its management.

1. African governments are under pressure to act as if they believe that the G8 commitment to double aid flows is firm: 'Countries are being urged to mount ambitious spending programs to achieve the Millennium Development Goals (MDGs), and to be more optimistic with respect to their medium-term spending programs than would seem warranted by immediate aid commitments (given that few donors are able to make long-term aid commitments)' (Heller et al., 2006, pp. 1–2).
2. Foster and Killick (2006, p. 1) observe that: 'The current donor promise to increase aid for the MDGs and sustain it thereafter would, if implemented, represent a sharp break from past experiences.'
3. In high-inflation economies, the Fund also endorses an '*absorb-and-partial-spend*' approach in which part of the extra aid is used to reduce domestic financing of the fiscal deficit.
4. When the exchange rate floats and the capital account is closed, the trade deficit equals sales of foreign exchange by the central bank as assumed in the Fund's '*absorb-and-spend*' framework (Mirzoev, 2007). This is a special and unrealistic case, however.
5. Since the integral of the current account surplus over the year equals the increase in holdings of foreign currency, the annual absorption rate is measured by $1 - [F(t) - F(t-1)]/0.03$. (National income equals unity initially, so the absolute increase in aid is 0.03.)
6. The inflation rate increases much more than 12 percentage points at $t = 0$ because there is a huge spike in the price level at the start of the aid boom. (P jumps 10.8 percent at $t = 0$.)
7. The outflows attributable to the pure saving motive can be approximated by the solution in a run where σ is close to zero. For $\sigma = 0.05$, F increases by 0.0214. This value is 36 percent of the figure for private capital outflows reported in Table 6.3.

8. Heller et al. (2006) recognize the fiscal credibility problem. This section can be viewed as a response to their appeal for analysis of 'self-protection' policies that 'use aid inflows in a way to increase the resilience of the economy in the event of future aid shortfalls' (p. 21).

REFERENCES

Adam, C.S. and D.L. Bevan (2003), 'Aid, Public Expenditure and Dutch Disease', Working Paper No. 2003-02, Centre for the Study of African Economies, University of Oxford.

Agenor, P. and P. Montiel (1999), *Development Macroeconomics*, 2nd edn, Princeton, NJ; Princeton University Press.

Berg, A., S. Aiyar, and M. Hussain (2007), 'Conceptual Framework and Its Application to Five Countries', in A. Berg, S. Aiyar, M. Hussain, S. Roache, T. Mirzoeu and A. Mahone (eds), 'The Macroeconomics of Managing Increased Aid Flows: Lessons from Recent Experiences', IMF Occasional Paper No. 253.

Buffie, E., C. Adam, S. O'Connell and C. Pattillo (2004), 'Exchange Rate Policy and the Management of Official and Private Capital Flows in Africa', *IMF Staff Papers* **51** (Special Issue), pp. 126–60.

Buffie, E., C. Adam, S. O'Connell and C. Pattillo (forthcoming), 'Riding the Wave: Monetary Responses to Aid Surges in Low-Income Countries', *European Economic Review*.

Eifert, B. and A. Gelb (2005), 'Improving the Dynamics of Aid: Toward More Predictable Budget Support', Mimeo, Washington, DC: World Bank.

Foster, M. and T. Killick (2006), 'What Would Doubling Aid Do for Macroeconomic Management in Africa?', Mimeo, London: Overseas Development Institute.

Heller, P. (2005), 'Pity the Finance Minister: Issues in Managing a Substantial Scaling Up of Aid Flows', IMF Working Paper No. 05/180.

Heller, P., M. Katz, I. Adenauer, X. Debrun, A. Fedelino, T. Koranchelian and T. Thomas (2006), 'Managing Fiscal Policy in Low Income Countries: How to Reconcile a Scaling Up of Aid Flows and Debt Relief with Macroeconomic Stability', Mimeo, Washington, DC: Fiscal Affairs Department, International Monetary Fund.

International Monetary Fund (IMF) (2003), 'Ghana: Selected Issues', IMF Country Report, No. 03/134.

International Monetary Fund (IMF) (2007), 'Executive Summary', in A. Berg, S. Aiyar, M. Hussain, S. Roache, T. Mirzoeu and A. Mahone (eds), 'The Macroeconomics of Scaling Up Aid: Lessons from Recent Experiences', IMF Occasional Paper No. 253.

Mirzoev, T. (2007), 'Modeling Aid Inflows in a Small Open Economy', in A. Berg, S. Aiyar, M. Hussain, S. Roache, T. Mirzoeu and A. Mahone (eds), 'The Macroeconomics of Scaling UP Aid: Lesson from Recent Experiences', IMF Occasional Paper No. 253.

PART II

Country Experiences

7. The nexus between monetary and financial stability: the experience of selected Asian economies*

Sukudhew Singh

7.1 INTRODUCTION

The chapter looks at the episodes of monetary and financial instability since the 1980s in five Asian economies – Indonesia, Korea, Malaysia, the Philippines and Thailand – and provides a summary of some of the factors that were important in creating these instabilities. It also attempts to look at common themes across countries as well as the nexus between monetary and financial instability in these countries. A final section looks at the changes in the financial systems of these countries since the Asian financial crisis in 1997 and makes an assessment of their vulnerability to further episodes of instability.

The main finding is that unlike the 1980s, when episodes of monetary and financial instability tended to be largely due to domestic factors, during the 1990s increased financial globalization led to capital flows playing a larger role in generating the imbalances that ultimately resulted in episodes of monetary and financial instability in these countries. A second finding is that monetary instability played an important role in creating the conditions that resulted in financial instability, and once financial instability had set in, it became harder to restore monetary stability. The experience of the Asian financial crisis shows that an approach that coordinates the monetary and financial policy response to such episodes has the greatest likelihood of resolving such problems in the shortest time period and in the least costly manner. A third finding is that despite the improvement in the economic fundamentals, stronger institutions, more robust prudential and supervisory frameworks, and more credible and flexible policies, financial globalization will continue to pose a challenge to the maintenance of monetary and financial stability in these countries.

7.2 EPISODES OF MONETARY AND FINANCIAL INSTABILITY

There is an issue of what constitutes financial instability. Here, I am simply taking periods when these countries experienced significant problems in their banking and financial systems. These problems may or may not have led to crises. In general, what Figure 7.1 shows is that the episodes of banking problems were far more frequent in the 1980s for this group of countries than they were in the 1990s. For some countries, the episodes of financial instability stretched over a number of years, whereas in others they were single-episode events. The 1990s were relatively benign, but all five countries experienced banking problems following the Asian financial crisis in 1997.

As shown in Figure 7.2, the macroeconomic and monetary fundamentals were definitely more distorted during the early 1980s than they were in the mid-1990s for most of these countries. In general, the global macroeconomic fundamentals were less favourable in the early 1980s than they were during the 1990s. Oil prices were high and this not only affected the terms of trade of the oil-importing countries, but also increased the debt service burdens as interest rates in the more developed countries were raised in response to the higher inflation. Economic growth was also weak due to sharp reductions in exports arising from a sharp fall in the growth rates of the developed economies.

Consequently, during the early 1980s, the vulnerabilities were more in the upper right quadrant of Figure 7.2. Inflation was high in most countries, with the possible exception of Malaysia. More importantly, inflation came down sharply in the subsequent period, which coincided with the period when many of these countries had banking problems. All governments were having sustained fiscal deficits, which were particularly large in Malaysia and the Philippines. All countries also had current account deficits.

The one significant vulnerability in the 1990s that does not seem to have existed in the early 1980s is the large-scale capital inflows to these countries following the liberalization of capital accounts. A more benign inflationary environment led to lower interest rates in the developed countries, leading to large capital flows to these Asian countries that generally had higher interest rates. To reduce the pressure on the exchange rate, most countries intervened in the foreign exchange markets, but shallow financial markets and a lack of adequate sterilization capacity led to the build-up of liquidity in the banking system, which then fuelled credit-driven asset price inflation. During the mid-1990s, just before the onset of the Asian financial crisis, the larger vulnerabilities appear to be in the lower left quadrant.

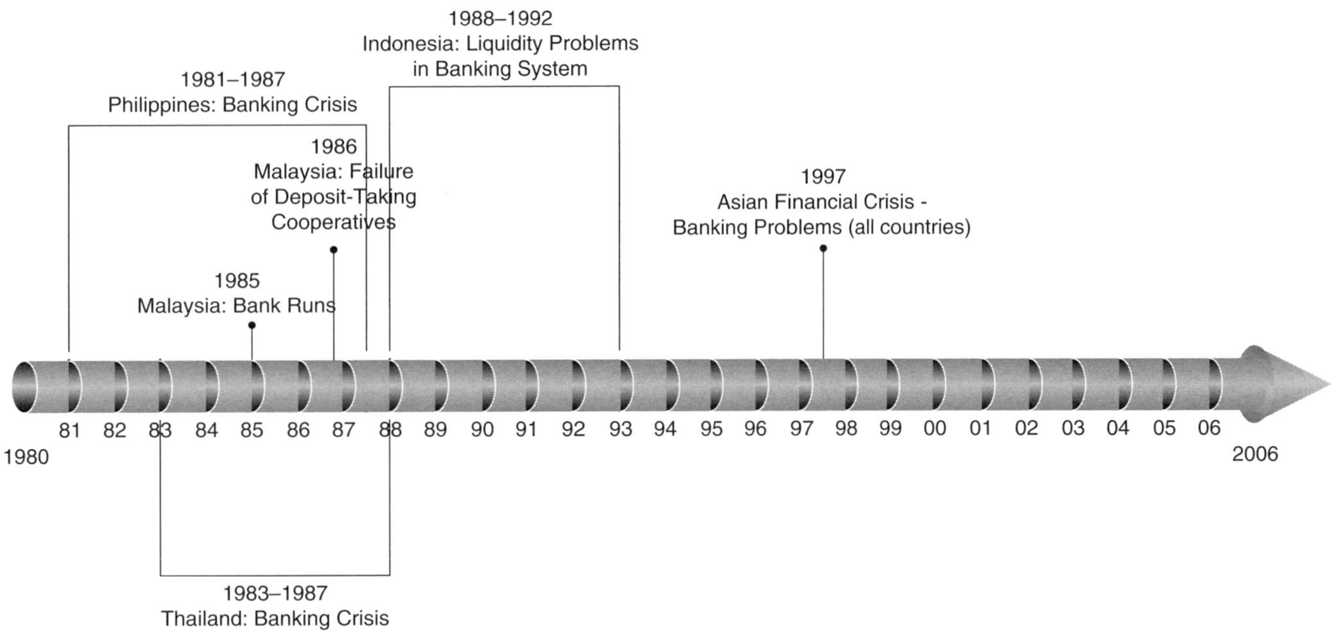

Figure 7.1 Banking Problems in the 1980s and 1990s

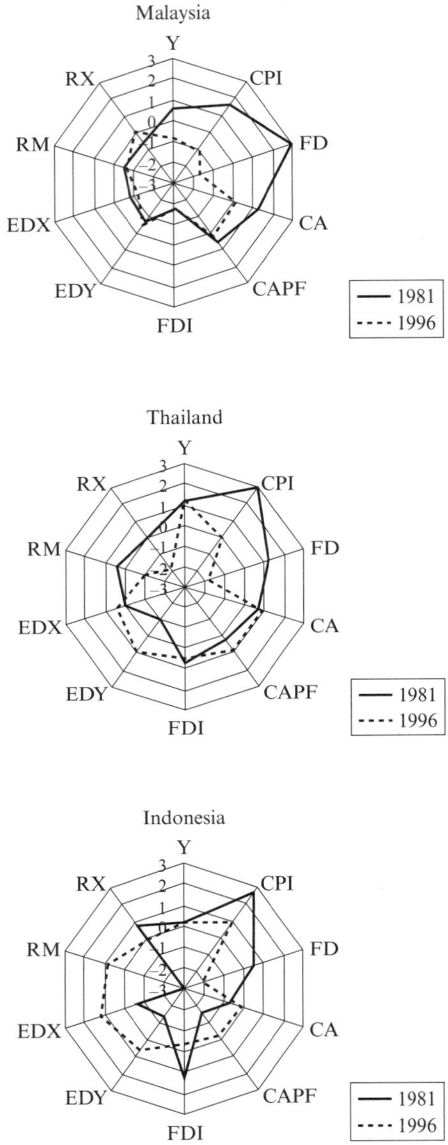

Notes: Y = real GDP growth rate; CPI = inflation; FD = fiscal deficit as % of GDP; CA = current account as % of GDP; CAPF = capital flows as % of GDP; FDI = foreign direct investment as % of GDP; EDX = total external debt as % of export; EDY = total external debt as % of GDP; RM = total reserves as % of broad money; RX = total reserves as % of exports.

Figure 7.2 Macroeconomic fundamentals: 1981 vs. 1996

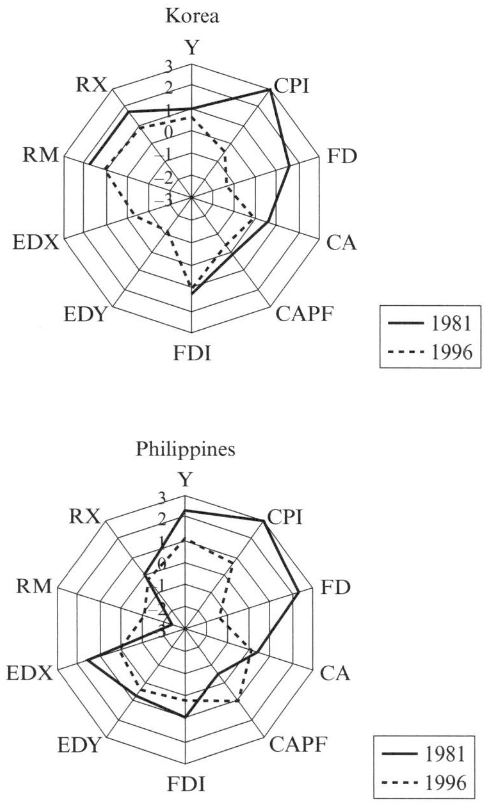

Figure 7.2 (continued)

7.3 INTERACTION BETWEEN MONETARY AND FINANCIAL INSTABILITY

In examining the experiences of these countries with episodes of monetary and financial instability, particularly during the Asian financial crisis, one can pick out a number of factors that appear to have played an important role in instigating or propagating these episodes of instability. As shown in Figure 7.3, there were also factors that are common to both types of instabilities.

Financial stability is central to the conduct of monetary policy, as monetary policy is implemented largely through operations in financial markets and the transmission of monetary policy to the real economy depends crucially on the smooth functioning of key financial institutions

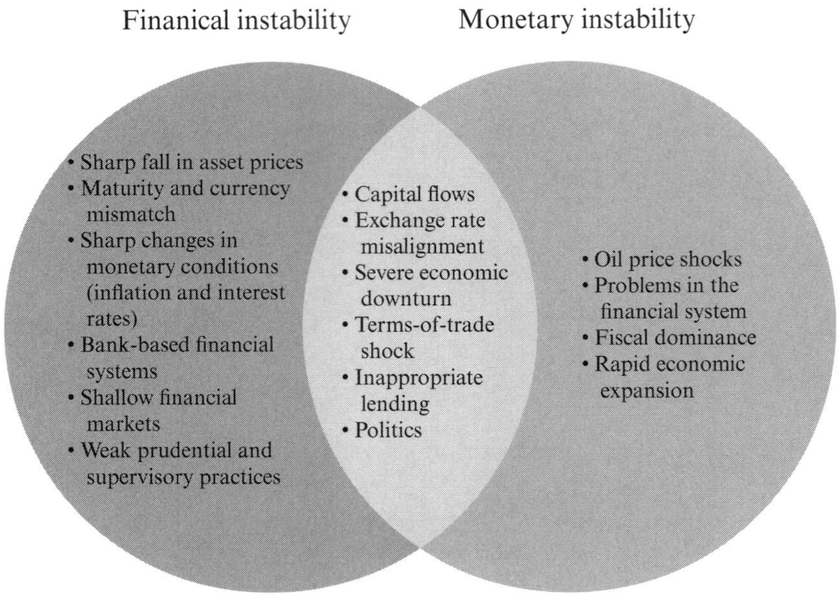

Figure 7.3 Sources of monetary and financial instability

and markets. To illustrate how the different factors played a role in propagating monetary and financial instability, Figure 7.4 draws out the channels of causality. To make the example and lessons more precise, the example focuses on the 1997 Asian financial crisis and also one initial source of vulnerability in the form of large and mainly short-term, capital inflows.[1] In the case of Thailand and Indonesia, the inflows were also the result of the large amount of foreign borrowing by residents.

These large inflows created a dilemma for the central banks of the region. The choice was between allowing the exchange rate to appreciate freely in response to the inflows or to intervene and mitigate the extent of the appreciation of the exchange rate. To not intervene and allow the exchange rate to appreciate sharply would have led to a fall in net exports, slowing economic growth. While this may have helped to lower inflationary pressures, it would have caused the already negative current accounts of these countries to worsen further, raising the possibility of a balance-of-payments (BOP) crisis happening, particularly when the inflows reversed. Appreciating exchange rates also tend to attract additional short-term speculative flows, raising the possibility of exchange rate overshooting.

The other option was to intervene, and that was what all these countries chose to do. However, intervention operations could not be completely

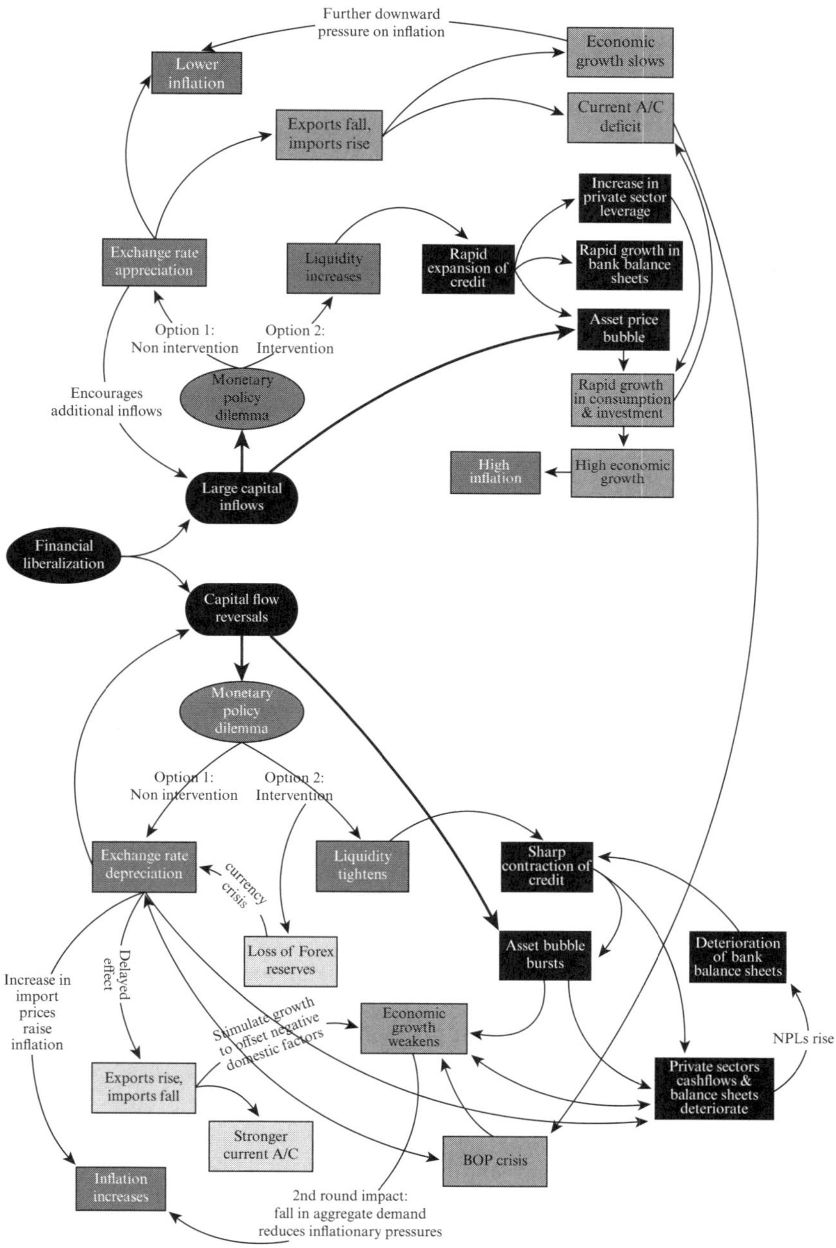

Figure 7.4 Financial globalization and the interaction of monetary and financial instability during the Asian financial crisis of 1997–98

offset by sterilization operations for various reasons such as a lack of instruments or the fiscal costs involved. The outcome was a net accumulation of surplus liquidity in the banking system. This was the failure of monetary policy in that, in the face of capital inflows, it was difficult for central banks to ignore the sharp appreciations of their exchange rates, but in defending those exchange rates, domestic monetary policy was inevitably compromised. It also laid the foundation of the subsequent financial crisis.

In the first instance, the large amounts of liquidity sitting on the balance sheets of banks pressured them to increase their lending, which they did. In the three years leading up to the crisis, claims of the banking system on the private sector were increasing at average annual growth rates of 19 per cent in Korea, 22 per cent in Indonesia, 25 per cent in Malaysia and Thailand, and 40 per cent in the Philippines. In many cases, a substantial portion of the rapid expansion in credit went to the asset markets, fuelling asset price bubbles in markets that were already experiencing buoyant conditions due to the large amount of foreign funds that were already going into these markets. The stock market indices in Indonesia, Malaysia, the Philippines and Thailand experienced average annual growth rates of 13 per cent to 27 per cent over the period 1990–96. There are indications of similar buoyant conditions in the property markets in these four countries. In Malaysia, residential property prices in major Malaysian cities increased by 20–25 per cent during 1994–96, compared with only 4.5–6.4 per cent during 1992–93. In 1996, almost one-half of the banking systems' total outstanding loans were for financing the broad property sector, purchases of stocks and shares, and private consumption.[2] The ready availability of cheap credit led to an increase in the leverage of the private sector. With both the liability and asset sides of the balance sheets of the financial institutions growing rapidly, the quality of lending and credit assessment also probably experienced a decline.

The bottom part of Figure 7.4 shows what happened when the capital flows reversed. The Asian financial crisis in 1997 started with a speculative attack on the Thai baht and then the contagion quickly spread to the other economies. The common feature of the experience of these countries was the large outflows of capital and repeated speculative attacks on their currencies. The choice facing central banks was essentially the same as the one faced when the capital flowed in, but in reverse. This time, intervention resulted in an outflow of foreign exchange reserves, and successful intervention could be made only to the extent that the central bank had an adequate reserves buffer to do so. A significant fall in reserves put further pressure on the currency and made it vulnerable to speculative attacks.

Even if the central bank was successful in managing the outflows, as the central bank took in the domestic currency, liquidity in the banking system would have tightened significantly. On the other hand, the balance sheets of corporates and individuals would have been weakened by the downturn in asset markets affected by the outflows of foreign funds. The resulting rise in non-performing loans eroded the capital of banks, making them more risk averse and less willing to lend. The combination of these factors led to a contraction of aggregate demand and weaker economic growth.

If the intervention was unsuccessful or not undertaken, the exchange rate would have depreciated sharply. In fact, this is what happened in all five countries. In most cases, the exchange rate was allowed to depreciate because the central banks ran down their reserves or needed to preserve the remaining reserves; in other cases, the widespread contagion made such intervention expensive and ineffective. As the exchange rate depreciated it set off further capital outflows, not just of foreign funds but also of resident funds. This exacerbated the downward pressures on the exchange rate and led to sharp depreciations. The exchange rates of the currencies of these countries depreciated by 26 per cent to 70 per cent against the US dollar between the end of June 1996 and the end of December 1998.

When the exchange rate depreciated, it caused the domestic value of external liabilities of the government and the private sector to increase substantially. This magnified the negative wealth effects already being felt from the decline in asset prices due to the outflow of foreign funds. This weakened the cash flows and balance sheets of the private sector, causing an increase in non-performing loans, negatively impacting upon the balance sheets of financial institutions and reducing the availability of credit. If the economy had a current account deficit, the outflow of foreign capital likely caused a balance-of-payment crisis, negatively affecting the economy that was already suffering from a contraction in domestic demand. The economies of Indonesia, Thailand, Malaysia and Korea contracted by 13.7 per cent, 9.4 per cent, 7.5 per cent and 5.8 per cent respectively in 1998. The large depreciations of the exchange rates also caused a sharp increase in the inflation rates in these countries. However, in most cases, the increase in inflation was of a limited duration due to the offsetting effect of slower economic growth in reducing demand pressures. The more problematic policy issue continued to be the way the problems in the banking system and corporate balance sheets exacerbated the downward pressures on growth, which then fed back into the balance sheets of the financial institutions and corporations, in effect setting off a self-feeding vicious cycle, as shown in Figure 7.4.

In attempting to ease the credit crunch, central bank injections of liquidity may have eased the liquidity constraints of the banks, but did not necessarily make them more willing to lend. Effectively, the transmission mechanism of monetary policy had weakened or, in the worst case, become dysfunctional. Financial instability was now hampering the workings of monetary policy. The only way to restore monetary and financial stability was to address the issues weighing down on the balance sheets of the banking institutions. In Malaysia, quick action by the central bank in setting up mechanisms to recapitalize banks, carve out non-performing loans from the books of the banks, and setting up a mechanism to facilitate loan restructuring, was successful in preventing a credit crunch from developing and undermining the effectiveness of monetary policy easing. Nevertheless, the experience during the Asian financial crisis, and also the ongoing subprime crisis-related problems in the developed financial markets, serve to highlight that dealing with large-scale problems in the banking system is often akin to fighting the many-headed Hydra of Greek mythology.

The depreciation of the exchange rates did make exports more competitive, but given the J-curve effect, that advantage is only likely to kick in after some time. Also, during the crisis, there were other factors that prevented the countries from benefiting from their increased price competitiveness. As already mentioned, financing from domestic or external sources was hard to come by. There were also problems with the payment systems as transacting parties worried about the creditworthiness of the other parties. In other cases, there were logistics problems. For example, it was reported that Indonesia's capacity to export was significantly limited by the reduction in ships calling at Indonesian ports due to the crisis-induced contraction in imports.

Figure 7.4 focuses on the large inflows and outflows of short-term capital arising from financial globalization as the starting point of how monetary and financial instability are intertwined, since it largely captures the experience in these five countries during the Asian financial crisis. There are of course other sources of vulnerability, as shown in Figure 7.3.

Table 7.1 summarizes the monetary conditions before, during and after episodes of financial instability in the countries studied here. There is some degree of generalization and all the factors may not apply to every country, but the general pattern seems to be repeated. Essentially, there were signs of monetary instability prior to the episodes of financial instability, manifesting in high and increasing credit growth, appreciating real effective exchange rate (REER), large changes in inflation, and so on. These monetary excesses tended to unwind during the period of financial instability, and monetary normalcy tended to return only after financial instability was restored. At least for this set of countries, monetary instability of some sort seems to have preceded the onset of, and may have very well have contributed to, the episodes of financial instability.

Table 7.1 Monetary conditions before, during and after episodes of financial instability

Signs of monetary instability prior to, and possibly a contributory factor to, financial instability	Monetary excesses tended to unwind during the period of financial instability	Signs of return of monetary stability after financial stability is restored
• High and increasing credit growth • Appreciating REER • High/increasing real interest rates • Current account deficits • Capital inflows • Above average inflation or inflation decreasing from high levels	• Credit growth slowed • REER depreciated • Outflows of capital • But: – Inflation could get worse (esp. when currency depreciated) – Real interest rates could increase sharply as liquidity tightened and risk averseness increases	• Real interest rates came down • Credit started increasing again • Inflation returned to more moderate levels

7.4 PROGRESS OVER THE LAST DECADE

The macroeconomic fundamentals of the five economies have largely remained sound (Figure 7.5). As before the crisis, most traditional factors associated with macroeconomic vulnerabilities remain relatively benign. The areas where the picture possibly appears to be more distorted than before the crisis are the fiscal deficits in Malaysia, the Philippines and Indonesia, as well as higher inflation in Indonesia. Nevertheless, the broad picture is that, by and large, there is an absence of the type of multiple vulnerabilities that can lead to a crisis.

However, the most notable changes have been in the financial systems of these countries. As shown in Figure 7.6, there have been varying degrees of transformation in the financial systems of these countries since the crisis. One development shared by all countries is the reduction in the number of banks. The pace of bank consolidation and mergers picked up substantially in the post-crisis period. At the same time, the balance sheets of these banking institutions have also been improving. Non-performing loans in

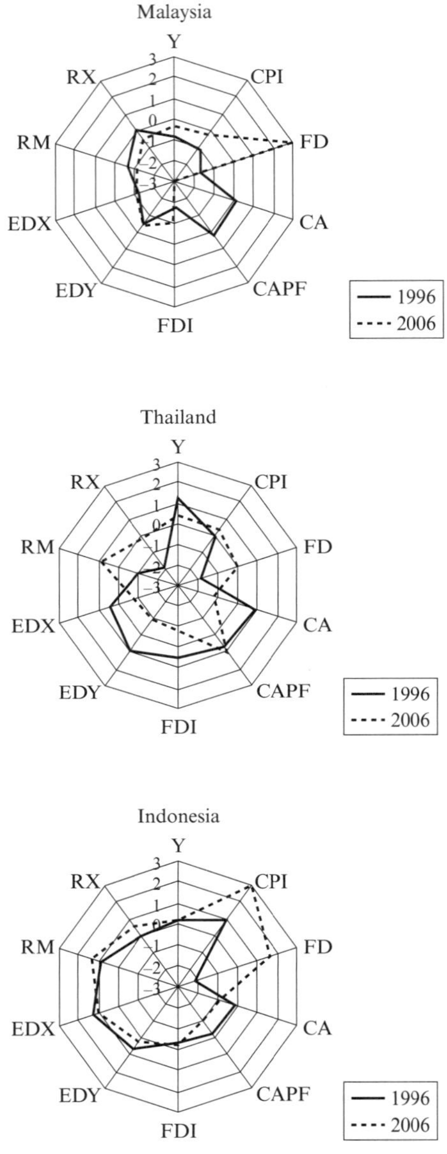

Notes: Y = real GDP growth rate; CPI = inflation; FD = fiscal deficit as % of GDP; CA = current account as % of GDP; CAPF = capital flows as % of GDP; FDI = foreign direct investment as % of GDP; EDX = total external debt as % of export; EDY = total external debt as % of GDP; RM = total reserves as % of broad money; RX = total reserves as % of exports.

Figure 7.5 Macroeconomic fundamentals: pre-crisis vs. 2006

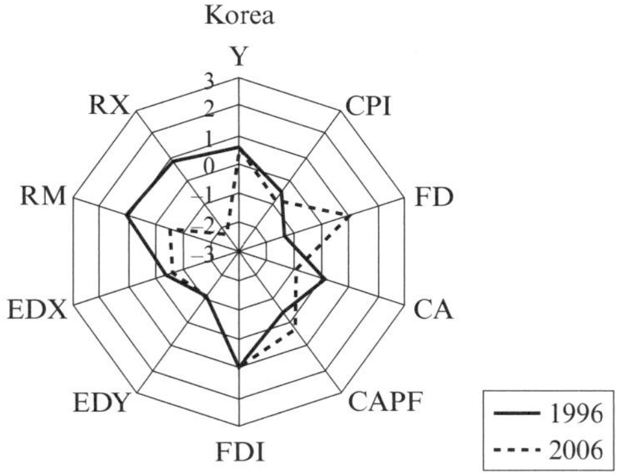

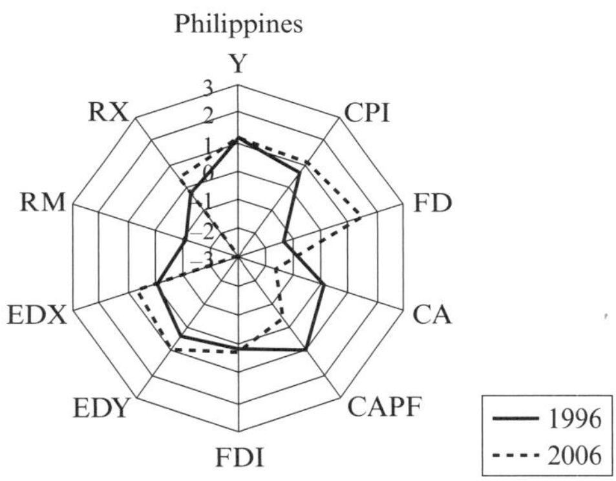

Figure 7.5 (continued)

all countries have fallen significantly compared to the period immediately after the crisis. There is also evidence to suggest that bank lending in the post-crisis period has been less focused on the asset markets. Bank lending to the construction and real estate sectors in Malaysia, Thailand and the Philippines has fallen from double-digit average annual growth rates in the pre-crisis period to single-digit growth rates in 2001–06. Only in Korea has such lending accelerated in the post-crisis period.

The capital markets have also deepened. Across the region, equity markets have grown significantly in terms of market capitalization. Similarly, bond markets have also shown significant growth. This is particularly the case in Malaysia and Korea, where the growth of the capital markets has led to disintermediation of corporate financing from the banks to the bond markets. Consequently, in both countries, households

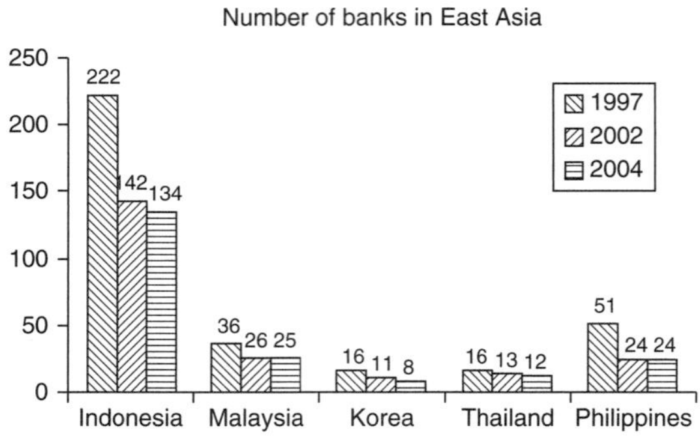

Source: World Bank
Note: Philippines data are for 1999 instead of 1997

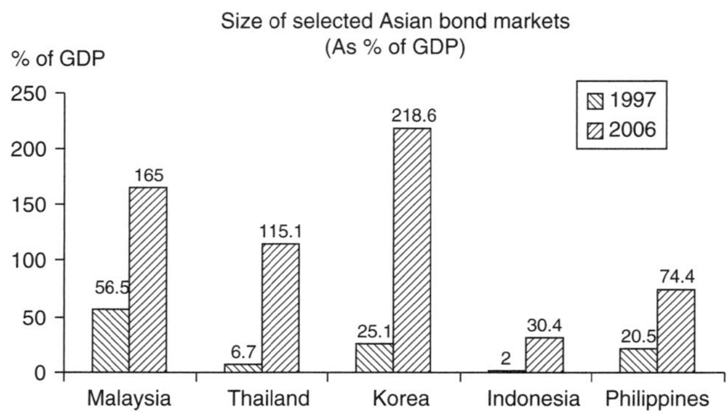

Source: Asian Development Bank (2007).

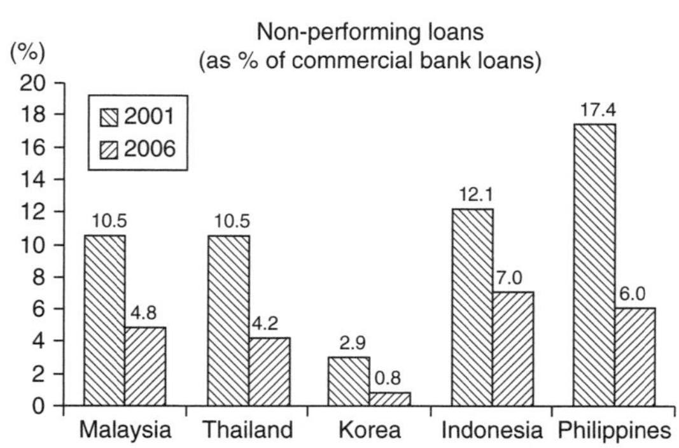

Sources: CEIC data, Bank of Thailand, Bangko Sentral Ng Pilipinas (2007), Bank Indonesia, Bank Negara Malaysia.

Figure 7.6 Improvements in financial systems

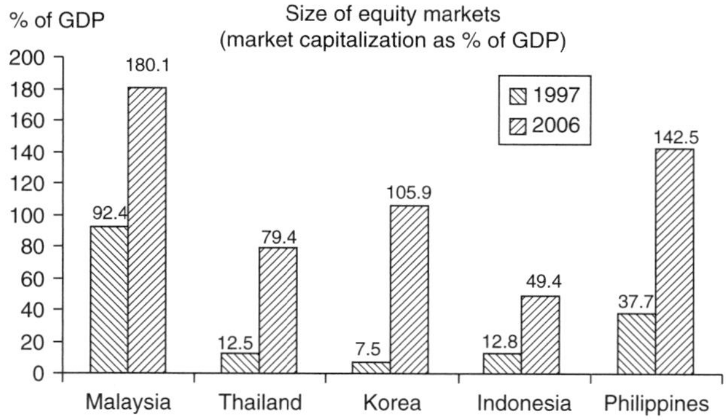

Source: World Federation of Exchange (2007) and International Monetary Fund (2207).

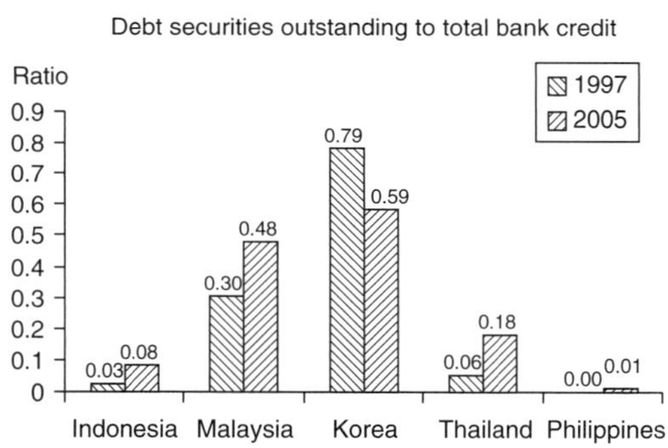

Source: IMF (2007).

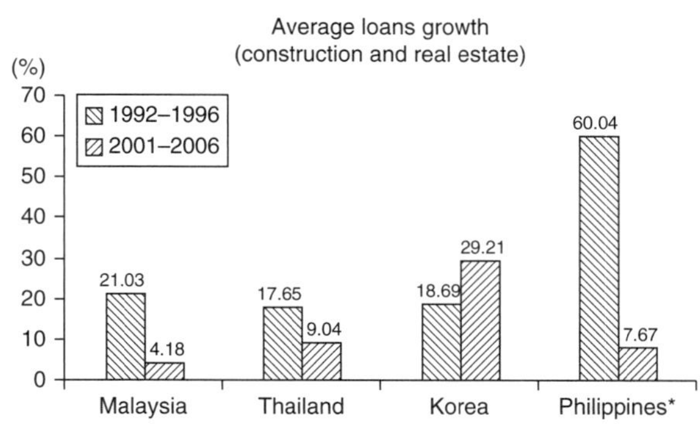

Sources: CEIC data, Bank of Thailand, Bangko Sentral Ng Pilipinas (2007), Bank Indonesia, Bank Negara Malaysia

Figure 7.6 (continued)

now account for a much larger share of overall bank loans as compared to the pre-crisis period. As a percentage of total bank credit, the share of outstanding debt securities was 59 per cent in Korea and 48 per cent in Malaysia. Conversely, while the bond markets in Thailand, Indonesia and the Philippines have also grown since the crisis, the financial systems in these countries continue to be largely bank-based.

In terms of monetary conditions, there is less rigidity in the regional exchange rates now compared to the pre-crisis period. All countries now have a managed float exchange rate system. The monetary policy frameworks in all countries are focused on maintaining price stability and promoting sustainable growth. Both monetary growth and credit growth are more restrained. Real interest rates have also come down significantly. Consequently, monetary and financial conditions appear to have been supporting each other in these countries in recent years. Relative stability of monetary conditions has facilitated the restoration of financial stability, and conversely, the development and improvements in the financial systems have allowed monetary policy to be more effective.

7.5 VULNERABILITIES REMAIN

Although there has been significant progress made with respect to monetary policy and prudential frameworks, there continue to be vulnerabilities relating to both monetary stability and financial stability in these countries (see Figure 7.7). The most important one is that capital flows remain large and have the potential to create the same types of imbalances that occurred before the Asian financial crisis. Although these countries have much larger reserves, the size of these flows can still test the limits of the central banks' tolerance for volatility in financial prices, or in their capacity to intervene and sterilize. In this respect, Thailand had to resort to capital controls in 2006 to manage these flows.

The fact that some countries have significantly deeper and more diversified financial markets, especially Korea and Malaysia, obviously allows for more effective management of capital flows than was previously possible. However, these deeper and more liquid markets may themselves prove to be an attraction for speculative flows since they provide the financial assets and liquidity desired by short-term speculative fund managers.

Consequently, the risk of contagion and asset price bubbles remains a possibility. On the domestic front, it may require central banks to react pre-emptively to emerging imbalances in their financial systems, though not necessarily through changes in interest rates. For central banks that have locked monetary policy into just managing

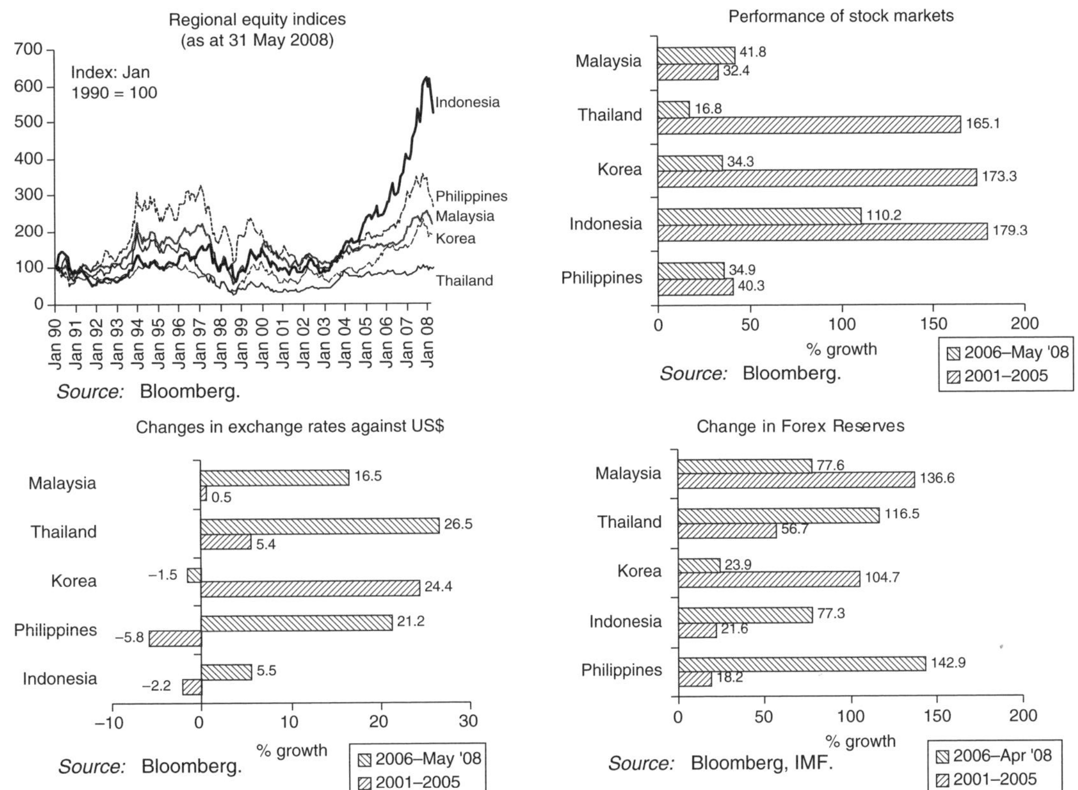

Figure 7.7 New but familiar vulnerabilities

inflation, such pre-emptive moves may be more difficult to undertake. Where the monetary stability and financial stability functions have been separated and put under different institutions, there is a need for enhanced cooperation and information sharing to avoid blind spots in surveillance and policymaking and to ensure coordinated responses to emerging problems. Another key challenge with respect to maintaining financial stability is the capacity of financial regulators and supervisors to keep up with the pace of developments and financial innovations in the financial system. Looking at the ongoing turbulence in the global financial markets, the problems in the subprime mortgage markets have spread to other parts of the financial markets in the developed countries in ways that few would have anticipated. Although their financial systems may have limited direct exposure to the subprime securities, regional regulators and supervisors must nevertheless be wary and vigilant to risks emanating from unexpected sources.

The current environment of rising global inflation with possibly slower growth may also prove to be a test of the robustness of the regional monetary and financial policy frameworks that have been put in place in these countries. In 2007 and into the early part of 2008, all five countries were to varying degrees experiencing higher inflation, capital inflows and appreciating currencies. Since then, in response to the problems in the financial systems of the more developed countries, there have been episodes of reversals of capital flows or greater volatility in such flows, with consequent increased volatility in regional financial markets and exchange rates.

7.6 CONCLUSION

Financial globalization has been a key factor in driving episodes of monetary and financial instability in these countries, at least during the 1990s. Monetary excesses, often instigated by factors like capital inflows, are determined to be at least a contributing factor in the build-up of the types of imbalances which eventually lead to episodes of financial instability. Correspondingly, the onset of financial instability made it more difficult for policymakers to achieve price stability, largely due to volatility of financial prices and the disruption of the transmission mechanism resulting from the problems in the banking systems. Monetary and financial stability is restored only when the excesses have been worked out of the economy and financial system. Furthermore, while significant progress has been achieved in the robustness of policy and prudential frameworks in recent years, it is expected that the large capital flows that accompany financial globalization will continue to challenge policymakers in these relatively open economies.

NOTES

* Paper prepared for the Bank of England/Cornell University Workshop on New Developments in Monetary Policy in Emerging Market Economies, 17–18 July 2007, London. The views expressed are the author's alone and should not be attributed to Bank Negara Malaysia.

1. There were obviously unique factors to the propagation of the financial crisis within the context of individual countries, but all that is attempted here is to highlight some of the common issues and developments, with emphasis on their relevance to monetary and financial stability.
2. Bank Negara Malaysia (1999), p. 167.

REFERENCES

Asian Development Bank (2007), 'Asian Bonds Online', available at: http://asianbondsonline.adb.org/regional/regional.php.

Bank Negara Malaysia, *Annual Reports* (various issues), Kuala Lumpur

Bank Negara Malaysia (1999), 'The Central Bank and the Financial System in Malaysia – A Decade of Change (1989–1999)', Kuala Lumpur.

Bank Negara Malaysia (2007), 'Monthly Statistical Bulletin', available at: http://www.bnm.gov.my/index.php?ch=12.

Bank of Thailand, *Report on Economic and Monetary Conditions* (various issues), Bangkok.

Bank of Thailand (2007), 'Statistics', available at: http://bot.or.th/ENGLISH/STATISTICS/Pages/index1.aspx.

Bangko Sentral Ng Pilipinas (2007), 'Statistic', available at: http://www.bsp.gov.ph/statistics/overview.asp.

International Monetary Fund (IMF) (2007), *International Financial Statistics*, Washington, DC: International Monetary Fund.

World Federation of Exchanges (2007), 'Statistics', available at: http://www.world-exchanges.org/statistics.

8. A framework for independent monetary policy in China

Marvin Goodfriend and Eswar Prasad

8.1 INTRODUCTION AND OVERVIEW

As China's economy develops and becomes more market oriented, and as its integration with the world economy continues, monetary policy will need to shoulder an increasingly large burden in ensuring stable, non-inflationary growth. Rising integration, for instance, implies greater vulnerability to external shocks, and monetary policy is typically the first line of defense against such shocks. Although deeper structural reforms may be the key determinants of long-term growth, monetary policy has an important role to play in creating a stable macroeconomic environment that is essential for those reforms to take root.

Monetary policy in China has in recent years operated under difficult constraints, including a fixed exchange rate regime, an underdeveloped financial system and numerous institutional weaknesses. Having an independent monetary policy is an important policy priority. Maintenance of an exchange rate regime with limited de facto flexibility exposes the economy to significant risks of macroeconomic instability. While capital controls provide some room for maneuver for monetary policy even under such a regime, this room tends to be limited in practice and could result in inadequate control of investment growth and inflationary (or deflationary) pressures. Moreover, the effectiveness of capital controls inevitably erodes over time as domestic and international investors find channels, including rising trade, to evade them.

These considerations have led the authorities to initiate a move towards a more flexible exchange rate regime. On 21 July 2005, the renminbi was revalued by 2.1 percent relative to the US dollar and it was announced that the value of the renminbi would henceforth be set with reference to a basket of currencies rather than having it pegged to the dollar. Since then, the renminbi has been allowed to appreciate by almost 20 percent relative to the US dollar (as of June 2008) but only about 8 percent in real effective terms. This is only a modest appreciation considering that China is running a current account surplus of about 12 percent of gross domestic product (GDP) and also receiving massive capital inflows, indicating limited de facto exchange rate flexibility. Nevertheless, the authorities have clearly stated their intention to allow for greater flexibility over time; recent fluctuations in the exchange value of the renminbi confirm this intention.

An important consequence of the move towards a flexible exchange rate is the need to adopt a new nominal anchor and an associated strategy for monetary policy. In this chapter, we make the case that China should adopt a low inflation objective as the new nominal anchor. Moreover, we conclude that, given the relative merits of an inflation objective and the potential problems associated with maintaining a fixed exchange rate, there are good reasons for China to adopt this new anchor expeditiously.

Theory and experience from around the world – from both advanced industrial economies as well as emerging market economies – suggest that making low inflation the main objective of monetary policy is the most reliable way to enable the People's Bank of China (PBC) to stabilize domestic inflation and employment against macroeconomic shocks. An inflation objective can accommodate fluctuations in productivity growth, and changing relationships between monetary or credit aggregates and inflation, all of which are relevant considerations for a developing economy. It also has the virtue of easy communicability.

We are not advocating a full-fledged inflation-targeting regime, although this could serve as a useful long-term goal. Our approach is more practical for the foreseeable future, and it should deliver most of the benefits of formal inflation targeting. In light of the changing structure of the economy and weaknesses in the monetary transmission mechanism, our framework could accommodate a continued role for the monitoring and management of monetary (and credit) aggregates by the PBC. But money would not constitute a good stand-alone nominal anchor since the changes in China's economic structure and financial markets imply that the rate of money growth consistent with a stable rate of inflation is likely to be highly variable.

Can this framework, which accords primacy to a low-inflation objective, be reconciled with the broader mandate of the PBC? The PBC Law states that: 'Under the guidance of the State Council, the PBC formulates and implements monetary policy, prevents and resolves financial risks, and safeguards financial stability.' And would a low-inflation objective be consistent with promoting sustained high employment growth, a key consideration for Chinese policymakers? Our response is that it is precisely by providing a firm and credible nominal anchor through a low-inflation objective that the PBC can best contribute to overall macroeconomic stability, and best provide for sustained employment growth and financial stability.

Although we are not advocating formal inflation targeting for China, some of the requirements of that regime are important for a low-inflation objective as well. Principal among these is instrument (operational) independence for the central bank. The PBC should have the authority and the capability to use its monetary policy instruments, for example, bank reserves or an interest rate, to anchor inflation credibly and stabilize the macroeconomy in general. We do not believe that broader independence for the PBC is essential, although the PBC must be empowered to build up the institutional capacity necessary to support its monetary policy mission, and be given the financial resources to do so. It is essential, however, that the Chinese government explicitly acknowledges its support for a low-inflation objective as the nominal anchor for monetary policy.

What would it take to put in place a low-inflation objective as an effective nominal anchor? Exchange rate flexibility is of course a prerequisite for an independent monetary policy oriented to domestic objectives. But a move towards greater exchange rate flexibility is hardly the solution by itself. Indeed, enhancing the effectiveness of the monetary transmission mechanism poses difficult challenges independent of the constraints related to the exchange rate regime. Principal among these is the reform of the financial system, since it is through the banking system that monetary policy must influence economic activity.

The Chinese state-owned banking system has long labored under lending directives from the government. Progress has been made since the late 1990s in improving the commercial orientation of the banking sector, and significant strides have been made in improving banking supervision and regulation. But Chinese banks are still far from being robust, commercially driven financial entities. Given the dominance of the banking sector in China's financial landscape, this has important implications for monetary policy transmission.

The essence of the challenge is to transform the banking system from an off-budget arm of fiscal policy – which uses captive savings of households to support state enterprises, whether commercially viable or not – into a banking system that can direct credit prudently to its most valued uses given correct interest rate signals. Even in the best of circumstances, it will take years for China to put in place all of the components of a modern, efficient banking system. This is especially so when one recognizes that the transition process must be supervised and regulated with great care to preserve the public's confidence in the banks and guard against moral hazard problems associated with explicit or implicit deposit insurance provided by the government. The consequences of the legacy of directed lending will also inevitably complicate the transition.

Nevertheless, we believe that it is both feasible and desirable for China to put in place a minimal set of financial sector reforms and regulations that would enable it to adopt an independent monetary policy with low inflation as the nominal anchor. These reforms would be aimed at giving the PBC full control of its balance sheet so that the central bank could manage bank reserves solely for monetary policy purposes. The reforms and regulations would also need to ensure that banks could withstand the financial stress that results from fluctuations in interest rates necessary to stabilize the macroeconomy and maintain price stability. We believe that reforms could be put in place in the next few years to achieve these ends and serve as an adequate foundation for independent monetary policy.

Our proposal has three additional attributes. First, it would allow for continuity in the operational approach to monetary policy. The PBC could continue its current operations and gradually adapt its procedures to the pursuit of independent monetary policy as supporting reforms are put in place. Our proposal would mainly entail a shift in strategic focus to a well-defined inflation anchor. Second, under present circumstances, the shift to an inflation anchor would be seamless since it would involve merely locking in the current low rate of inflation. Third, the adoption of effective independent monetary policy would facilitate various reforms that have intrinsic benefits of their own. For instance, the resulting macroeconomic stability would facilitate the modernization of the financial system. In addition, the new policy regime would necessitate improvements in the statistical base that would enhance public sector transparency and encourage better communication about policy intentions.

Our main goal in this chapter is to make the conceptual case for a low-inflation objective as the nominal anchor for independent monetary policy in China. There are of course a number of important practical details that would need to be worked out, including the appropriate level and width of the target range for the inflation objective, the best method for communicating this objective, the appropriate measure of inflation to be used, and so on. Other than discussing some of these issues from an analytical perspective, we leave the specifics as open questions to be addressed in future work.

8.2 LOW-INFLATION OBJECTIVE AS NOMINAL ANCHOR

An inflation objective – an explicit or implicit long-run range for the inflation rate and an acknowledgement that low inflation is a priority for monetary policy – has emerged as the leading nominal anchor in practice around the world.[1] Numerous major central banks – for example, the

Eurosystem and the Bank of England – now employ an explicit target range for inflation as the nominal anchor for monetary policy. Others, such as the US Federal Reserve, anchor monetary policy with an implicit low-inflation objective. Where central banks have been given the necessary institutional support to stabilize inflation, they have been able to acquire an impressive degree of credibility for low inflation that has anchored inflation expectations firmly and contributed importantly to stabilizing actual inflation (see, for example, Bernanke et al., 1999; Goodfriend, 2005).

Emerging market and developing economies that adopted various forms of inflation targeting have in general had similar positive experiences. As noted by Mishkin (2000), some advantages of inflation targeting are particularly relevant for emerging market economies: (1) a stable relationship between money and inflation is not critical to its success; (2) inflation targeting is easily understood by the public and is transparent; and (3) inflation targeting focuses the political debate on what monetary policy can (and cannot) achieve in the long run, and away from the temptation to use monetary policy to stimulate employment growth in the short run.

Mishkin lists three major potential problems for inflation targeting in emerging markets: (1) inflation may be hard to control because of underdeveloped financial systems; (2) inflation targeting requires fiscal policy to support the inflation target; and (3) the exchange rate flexibility required for inflation targeting might be difficult for policymakers to allow. Based on the experiences of a few inflation-targeting emerging market economies, Mishkin concludes that these problems can be overcome in practice. Moreover, a large and growing empirical literature investigating the macroeconomic performance of emerging market economies under different monetary frameworks finds support for inflation targeting in practice.[2]

8.3 PRINCIPLES OF MONETARY POLICY GEARED TOWARD TARGETING INFLATION

The principle of inflation targeting given above has the important implication that monetary policy geared to targeting inflation yields the best cyclical stabilization of employment (Goodfriend and King, 1997; Woodford, 2003; Goodfriend, 2002 [2004]; Broaddus and Goodfriend, 2004). Thus, even those who care mainly about the stabilization of employment can support a low-inflation objective for monetary policy. But another key implication is that the best that monetary policy can do is to stabilize inflation; it should not be used to try to counteract fluctuations in output and employment that are due to shocks to productivity and other factors affecting aggregate supply.

In addition to the direct benefits of an inflation objective, it can improve macroeconomic performance indirectly by tying down inflation expectations. Imperfect credibility for low and stable inflation makes an economy vulnerable to fluctuating beliefs about inflation or deflation, which in extreme cases can take the form of inflation or deflation scares.[3] On the other hand, if the public believes that the central bank has the power and the scope to use monetary policy to maintain stable inflation, the resulting credibility for low inflation tends to be self-enforcing to a considerable extent. With credible institutional support in place, markets tend to be relatively forgiving of temporary tactical policy mistakes that may be committed by a central bank as it acts to stabilize inflation.

8.4 INSTITUTIONAL SUPPORT FOR INDEPENDENT MONETARY POLICY

A variety of institutional preconditions are needed to support operating procedures to enable a central bank to pursue independent monetary policy with a low-inflation anchor. A central bank must have instrument independence – the authority and will to use its policy instruments to act quickly and decisively in response to incoming data – to maximize the potential for monetary policy to stabilize inflation, inflation expectations and employment, and to ensure financial market stability. In particular, a central bank must be prepared to move short-term interest rates quickly and aggressively over a large range if necessary.

In order for monetary policy consistently to pre-empt fluctuations in inflation around an inflation objective, a central bank must utilize modern statistical techniques together with comprehensive, timely and reasonably accurate statistical indicators of macroeconomic conditions to guide its policy actions. A central bank needs reliable measures of inflation and indicators of the direction of pressures on future inflation. Such indicators could include aggregate price markups, estimates of the gap between actual and potential output, estimates of capacity utilization in the manufacturing sector, measures of employment growth relative to estimated trend labor force growth, and indicators of inflation expectations. In general, it would help to guide monetary policy to keep track of the growth of various financial aggregates such as the monetary base, bank reserves, bank deposits and loans against estimated growth rates believed to be consistent with low inflation. Moreover, a central bank must develop techniques to produce efficient conditional forecasts of inflation and output to inform policy decisions.

Finally, the government should grant the central bank instrument independence with strategic guidance directing monetary policy to be used flexibly to stabilize employment and financial markets, subject to inflation remaining in or near an explicit low-inflation objective. A public understanding of the commitment to low inflation is necessary to assure its credibility. The credibility of that commitment requires central bank instrument independence to achieve it, the government's agreement to support it, and a role for oversight by government and markets to hold the central bank accountable for carrying it out.

As a mechanical matter, monetary policy is implemented by managing the aggregate supply of bank reserves, which are deposits of commercial banks at the central bank. These include required reserves plus any excess reserves beyond those that satisfy reserve requirements. A central bank must have full control of aggregate bank reserves to stabilize inflation expectations credibly. Control of bank reserves is necessary because a central bank must manage aggregate demand over the business cycle by manipulating the supply of bank reserves.

A central bank's control of bank reserves is compromised when it is obliged to acquire or sell assets for reasons other than managing aggregate bank reserves to stabilize inflation. In general, there are three reasons why a central bank might have to do so: (1) it might be directed to buy government debt, that is, to finance a government deficit in whole or in part with newly created bank reserves; (2) it might be directed to lend to banks, non-financial firms or state enterprises; or (3) it might be obliged to buy foreign assets to support a managed or fixed exchange rate. For instance, in order to manage its foreign exchange rate within a tight range, the central bank must accommodate the market's excess demand or supply of foreign exchange at the stabilized exchange rate by creating or draining bank reserves.

It may be possible for the central bank to offset, or sterilize, the effect of the required asset action on aggregate bank reserves by taking an opposite asset action with another asset or liability on its balance sheet. Sterilization of foreign exchange flows, however, does little to mitigate the factors that gave rise to those flows in the first place. Even when supplemented with capital controls, sterilization of inflows leads to rising quasi-fiscal costs or other implicit costs associated with financial repression. And the build-up of foreign exchange reserves exposes the central bank balance sheet to risks of capital losses associated with exchange rate and interest rate fluctuations.

To reiterate, the central bank needs to be free of any significant obligations that compromise its ability to manage aggregate reserves to stabilize inflation. In particular, monetary policy credibly geared toward targeting low inflation must be accompanied by a willingness on the part of the government and the public to allow a substantial degree of flexibility in the foreign exchange rate, so that exchange rate adjustments, and not central bank purchases and sales of foreign assets, can allow the foreign exchange market to clear.

Even if a central bank has full control of aggregate bank reserves, it must be willing to use its control of bank reserves to move short-term interest rates in a relatively wide range, aggressively at times, to sustain credibility for low inflation in order to implement monetary stabilization policy effectively. An inclination to smooth short-term interest rates to cushion the banking system against financial stress would compromise the central bank's ability to manage aggregate demand to sustain low inflation, severely undermine the credibility of its inflation target, and destabilize employment and inflation over the business cycle.

The banking system must be financially robust to fluctuations in short-term interest rates so that the central bank is willing to move short-term interest rates as needed to manage monetary policy effectively. A central bank might be reluctant to make full use of its instrument independence against inflation if raising interest rates triggers cash flow problems for banks, with the potential to precipitate a public sector bailout. Thus, it is essential for the credibility of monetary policy geared to targeting low inflation that financial vulnerabilities of the banking system to high interest rates and to large fluctuations in interest rates be corrected.

Finally, assuming that banks are well capitalized, managed and regulated so that they lend funds prudently, rates on bank deposits and loans as well as non-bank money market instruments should be deregulated and free to reflect the cost of loanable funds in the interbank market. This would broaden the channels by which monetary policy is transmitted to the economy, and minimize disruptions in banking and credit flows that would otherwise occur because rigid interest rates caused disintermediation in certain credit markets.

8.5 THE EXCHANGE RATE REGIME

From 1995 to 2005, the renminbi was maintained at a fixed parity relative to the US dollar. On 21 July 2005, the renminbi was revalued by 2.1 percent relative to the US dollar and the government announced that the external value of the renminbi would henceforth be set with reference to a basket of currencies, although neither the currency composition of the basket nor the basket weights have been publicly disclosed.

Since July 2005, the renminbi has depreciated by about 20 percent relative to the US dollar (Figure 8.1). Given the dollar's sharp depreciation

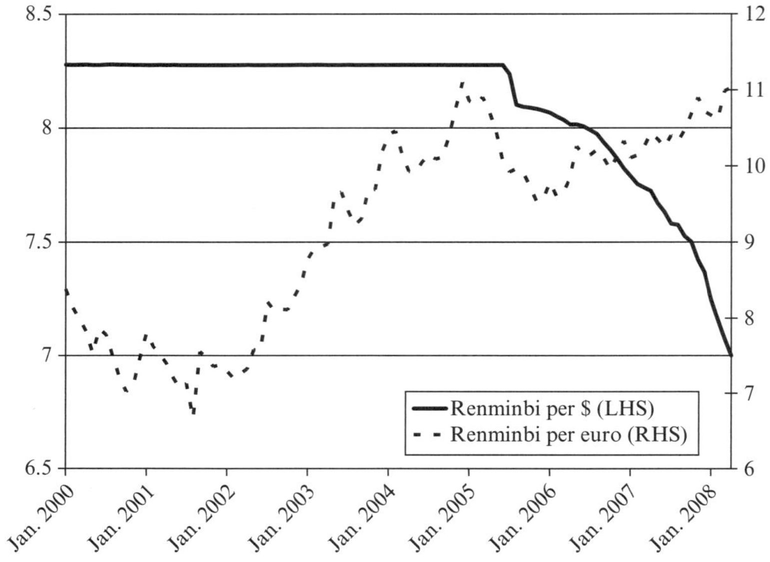

Note: The data in this figure go up to April 2008.

Source: CEIC.

Figure 8.1 Nominal exchange rate

against some major currencies such as the euro, however, the effective appreciation of the renminbi has been only about 7 percent over the same period (Figure 8.2). As a consequence, and especially given its large current account and capital account surpluses, China has continued to accumulate foreign exchange reserves at a hectic pace (Figure 8.3). Clearly, the exchange rate is still being tightly managed.

This rigidity of the exchange rate has constrained monetary policy independence by making it difficult for the PBC to use interest rates as an instrument to meet domestic policy objectives. The existence of capital controls, even though they may not be fully effective, implies some room for monetary policy independence. In practice, however, interest rate changes are tightly restricted by the financial repression and capital controls needed to keep banks solvent.

The lack of exchange rate flexibility also affects banking sector reforms. The inability of the PBC to use interest rates as a primary tool of monetary policy implies that credit growth is often controlled by much blunter and non-market-oriented tools, including non-prudential administrative measures. As argued by Prasad and Rajan (2006), this vitiates the process of

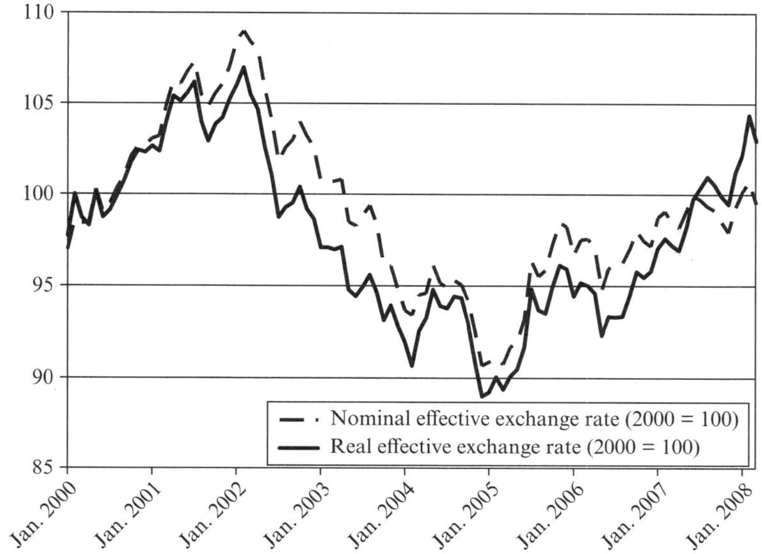

Note: The data in this figure go up to March 2008.

Source: International Monetary Fund's International Financial Statistics Database.

Figure 8.2 Nominal and real effective exchange rates

banking reform by keeping banks' lending growth under the administrative guidance of the PBC rather than letting it be guided by market signals. This constraint has also perpetuated large efficiency costs via provision of cheap subsidized credit to inefficient state enterprises. The incidence of these and other costs of banking system inefficiency are not obvious, but they are probably ultimately borne by depositors in the form of low real returns on their saving (see Prasad, 2008).

8.6 INDEPENDENT MONETARY POLICY FOR CHINA

China's declared intention to adopt a flexible exchange rate necessitates the choice of a new nominal anchor and a new strategy for monetary policy. Employing the principles of monetary policy discussed earlier in light of China's current financial institutions, we present a package of proposals to guide China's new independent monetary policy regime. We recommend a low-inflation nominal anchor, operational independence for the PBC with

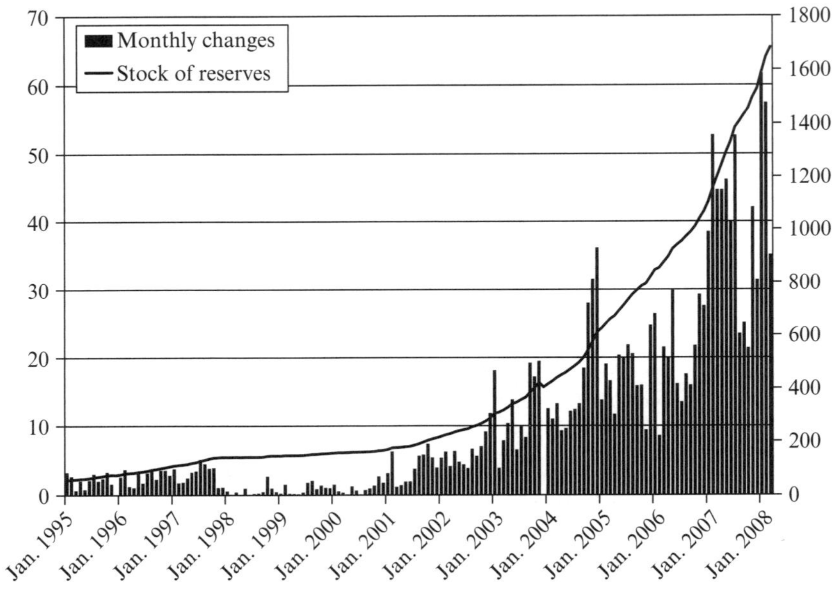

Source: CEIC and author's calculations.

Figure 8.3 Foreign exchange reserves: flows and stocks (in billions of US dollars)

formal strategic guidance from the government, and reforms to make the Chinese banking system robust against interest rate fluctuations.

8.6.1 A Low-Inflation Nominal Anchor

We believe that an explicit, fixed low-inflation objective would be an appropriate nominal anchor for China – it would help to anchor inflation expectations firmly and has many advantages over the alternatives, including the current de facto fixed exchange rate regime. This new nominal anchor could be supplemented, for the foreseeable future, with an operational role for money growth targets to help achieve the announced low-inflation objective. Money growth targets would be of great help in China, which is just beginning to modernize its banking system and to utilize indirect monetary policy instruments in lieu of direct credit controls to implement monetary policy (Yi, 2000). However, we believe that a money growth target would not be a good stand-alone nominal anchor for Chinese monetary policy.

To set in motion the shift to an independent monetary policy framework,

China should announce in the near future its intention to adopt an explicit long-run low-inflation objective in order to lock in the current low inflation rate indefinitely. A qualitative commitment to low inflation might suffice until the details of the explicit inflation objective are worked out. The announcement should explain that monetary policy anchored by a long-run inflation objective would direct the PBC to stabilize employment and financial markets in the short run, subject to a commitment to keep inflation at or near the fixed long-run inflation objective on average over the medium term. Such a statement would be consistent with the broader mandate of the PBC and would enable it to carry out independent monetary policy flexibly. In our view, it is premature and probably unnecessary for China to adopt the formal, elaborate, inflation-targeting procedures advocated by some economists and pursued by some central banks; although more formal inflation-targeting procedures should not be ruled out for the future.

While the shift to independent policy disciplined by a low-inflation anchor is in principle a major undertaking, the PBC would not need to make sharp changes in its operating procedures while supporting reforms for the new framework are put in place. Nevertheless, it is important for China to adopt a low-inflation objective soon so that it is not without a nominal anchor during the transition to a flexible exchange rate regime, which is a stated medium-term objective of the authorities.

Eventually, other choices and decisions about the nature of the inflation objective will need to be addressed – for example, measure of inflation to be targeted; point target versus range; level of the target, and so on. In this chapter, our focus is more on the strategic aspects rather than technical details, so we leave these as open questions for now. What we wish to emphasize here is the principle of transparency in monetary policymaking, which would be embodied in an explicit numerical inflation objective.

8.6.2 Instrument Independence for the PBC with Strategic Guidance from the Government

China has already done much to modernize its banking and financial system. However, it must undertake additional reforms to support an independent monetary policy. The crucial requirement is that the PBC be granted instrument (operational) independence. Operational independence is necessary because the PBC must have the authority to move its policy instruments aggressively on short notice without permission from other government agencies.

In turn, there are two key prerequisites for effective instrument independence: the PBC must be given full control of aggregate bank reserves, and the Chinese banking system must be made financially robust against interest rate fluctuations. We recommend a minimal set of banking reforms below that could provide the requisite financial robustness in a few years. The modernization of the banking system will take much longer, but a fully modern banking system is not essential for monetary policy purposes. In addition, we emphasize that, to make instrument independence fully effective, the PBC will need the discipline and accountability provided by formal strategic guidance from the government.

Full PBC control of bank reserves

China has already put in place some of the institutional arrangements necessary for the PBC to manage aggregate bank reserves effectively in the short run. It has created a deep, liquid market in central bank bills through which the PBC can manage aggregate bank reserves effectively with open market operations. The Chinese have also created an active, liquid repo market that the PBC uses to manage the supply of reserves on a day-to-day basis. The infrastructure for borrowing or lending reserves among banks in the interbank market on the basis of repos or on an uncollateralized basis at the CHIBOR rate is well established. The level of interbank rates is determined flexibly to clear the market for borrowing and lending reserves, and the spread between the rates varies with such things as the nature of collateral backing the loan.

Our positive assessment of certain aspects of the interbank market must, however, be balanced against a number of its unsatisfactory features: its relative thinness and illiquidity, the fact that major players may have excessive market power, and the fact that non-bank participants have the potential to destabilize the market. We believe that the Chinese financial authorities can and will remedy such defects before too long.

At present, the primary threat to the PBC's independent control of bank reserves arises from its responsibility to buy or sell foreign exchange in support of the tightly managed exchange rate. The government, as part of its program to grant the PBC operational independence for monetary policy, should relieve the PBC of the responsibility to support particular exchange rate objectives through its foreign exchange operations. Only then can the PBC manage its balance sheet with full credibility to maximize the power of monetary policy to stabilize the Chinese macroeconomy.

Robust banking against interest rate fluctuations

China has taken a number of steps to modernize its banking system, and has created much of the necessary institutional flexibility for the PBC to transmit monetary policy actions effectively to aggregate demand – through a liquid bank reserves market, with flexible, competitively determined interbank interest rates managed by open market operations. To prepare China for independent monetary policy, it is now essential that Chinese banks be made financially robust to fluctuations in short-term interest rates. This is necessary both for banks to manage lending prudently and for the PBC to allow interbank interest rates to fluctuate as needed to manage independent monetary policy effectively.

The fundamental source of the financial robustness problem in China's banking system is twofold: (1) China's banks have long been a primary means of financing state-owned enterprises (SOEs); and (2) many of China's banks are themselves run by local managers politically motivated (or under pressure of provincial government officials) to direct credit to SOEs. The high rate of saving and the lack of alternative investment opportunities in China provide the banking system with ample loanable funds to finance questionable loans to SOEs. With the government's tacit approval, moreover, banks have an incentive to carry loss-making SOE loans on their books indefinitely.

The problem is that banks whose interest earnings are significantly impaired due to non-performing loans (NPLs) have cash flow sufficient only to pay relatively low interest on loanable funds acquired in the interbank and deposit markets. Higher interbank rates associated with more restrictive monetary policy would put weak banks under stress. Since banks are tightly connected through the payments system and the network of interbank balances, the financial distress would threaten the entire banking system. In short, a financially fragile banking system has the potential to undermine central bank independence by, for instance, making the PBC reluctant to raise interest rates to head off inflationary pressures.

To sum up, the financing of SOEs through the banking system in China impedes the development of banking, fiscal and monetary policies. Chinese banks cannot be governed according to good banking practice, and regulated with the help of good banking policy, unless they are relieved of their responsibility for financing SOEs. The separation of fiscal policy support for SOEs from banking is the key to making Chinese banks financially robust against interest rate fluctuations. The robustness of Chinese banks, in turn, is necessary to provide a sufficient degree of separation of monetary policy from both banking and fiscal policies so that the PBC can conduct monetary operations independently and effectively.

We believe that China could complete the reforms outlined above in a few years, in large part because Chinese financial authorities have been working hard to strengthen the banking system. It will take much longer for Chinese banks to modernize fully, in particular to adopt methods for efficiently pricing loans according to risk. Nevertheless, Chinese monetary policy can be transmitted effectively through a banking system that may be far from the efficient banking frontier, as long as the banking system is financially robust against interest rate fluctuations and the exchange rate regime does not inhibit the PBC from employing the full range of interest rate variability to stabilize inflation and economic activity.

Strategic guidance from the government

We emphasize that instrument independence must be granted in tandem with strategic guidance from the government. The operationally independent PBC should be instructed by the government to pursue the objectives for monetary policy enumerated in the PBC Law, subject to a commitment to keep inflation at or near the fixed long-run inflation objective on average over the business cycle. Government support for operational independence is necessary to encourage the PBC to take potentially difficult monetary policy actions that may be needed on occasion. Explicit government direction must also serve as the basis upon which the PBC can be held accountable in some way for achieving its mandated objectives – perhaps through regular monetary policy oversight hearings. Without such strategic guidance from the government, the PBC would be deprived of the credibility essential to make independent monetary policy work well.

8.7 CONCLUDING REMARKS

A flexible independent monetary policy oriented to domestic objectives is fast becoming indispensable for the effective management of the Chinese economy. We have attempted to provide both motivation and direction for China's transition to an independent monetary policy. Given the current underdeveloped state of the Chinese banking and financial systems, some may think our focus on this issue is premature. We think otherwise. Given China's intention to move to a flexible exchange rate, there are good reasons for China to begin to build the institutional foundations for the transition now. In particular, China must choose a new nominal anchor for monetary policy as it introduces flexibility into its nominal exchange rate.

There is a clear case for making a long-run low-inflation objective that new nominal anchor, and little reason to delay its adoption. It will take many years to modernize China's financial system fully, but we have argued that China could put in place in the next few years a modest package of reforms that would serve as an effective foundation for independent monetary policy anchored by a low-inflation objective.

The key is to grant the PBC operational monetary policy independence, which requires that the PBC be given full control of bank reserves and that the Chinese banking system be made robust against interest rate fluctuations. To satisfy the former requirement, the government must allow a substantial degree of flexibility in the foreign exchange rate, so that exchange rate adjustments, and not PBC purchases and sales of foreign assets, can clear the foreign exchange market. Strengthening of bank balance sheets, including by removal of NPLs, is necessary to satisfy the latter requirement. Bank lending must also be disentangled from the financing of non-viable SOEs, which we proposed could be accomplished by channeling financial support for non-viable SOEs through a separate government agency.

In addition, we emphasized that PBC operational independence must be granted with formal strategic guidance from the government. Without such strategic guidance, monetary policy would lack credibility and the PBC would be deprived of the support needed to take potentially difficult monetary policy actions. Finally, we underscored the need for the PBC to be given financial resources and encouragement by the government to build up the institutional capacity necessary to support its monetary policy mission.

NOTES

1. See Bernanke et al. (1999) for a discussion of inflation targeting around the world, and Goodfriend (2005) on implicit inflation targeting in the United States. Also see Bernanke (2004), Bernanke and Woodford (2005) and Broaddus and Goodfriend (2004).
2. See, for example, Jonas and Mishkin (2005) and Mishkin and Schmidt-Hebbel (2005).
3. See Goodfriend (2002, 2004) and Goodfriend and King (2005).

BIBLIOGRAPHY

Bernanke, Ben (2004), 'Inflation Targeting', *Federal Reserve Bank of S. Louis Review*, July–August, pp. 165–8.

Bernanke, Ben, Thomas Laubach, Fredrick Mishkin and Adam Posen (1999), *Inflation Targeting: Lessons from International Experience*, Princeton, NJ: Princeton University Press.

Bernanke, Ben and Michael Woodford (eds) (2005), *The Inflation Targeting Debate*, Chicago, IL: University of Chicago Press.

Broaddus, J. Alfred and Marvin Goodfriend (2004), 'Sustaining Price Stability', *Economic Quarterly*, Federal Reserve Bank of Richmond, Summer, pp. 3–20.

Goodfriend, Marvin (2002), 'Monetary Policy in the New Neoclassical Synthesis: A Primer', *International Finance*, Summer, pp. 165–92; Reprinted (2004), *Economic Quarterly*, Federal Reserve Bank of Richmond, Summer, pp. 21–45.

Goodfriend, Marvin (2004), 'Understanding the Transmission of Monetary

Policy', manuscript, Federal Reserve Bank of Richmond. Presented at Joint China–IMF High Level Seminar on China's Monetary Policy Transmission Mechanism, Beijing, May.

Goodfriend, Marvin (2005), 'Inflation Targeting in the United States?', in Ben Bernanke and Michael Woodford (eds), *The Inflation Targeting Debate*, Chicago, IL: University of Chicago Press.

Goodfriend, Marvin and Robert King (1997), 'The New Neoclassical Synthesis and the Role of Monetary Policy', in Ben Bernanke and Julio Rotemberg (eds), *NBER Macroeconomics Annual*, Cambridge, MA: MIT Press.

Goodfriend, Marvin and Robert King (2005), 'The Incredible Volcker Disinflation', *Journal of Monetary Economics*, **52** (July), pp. 981–1016.

Jonas, Jiri and Frederic S. Mishkin (2005), 'Inflation Targeting in Transition Countries: Experience and Prospects', in Ben Bernanke and Michael Woodford (eds), *The Inflation Targeting Debate*, Chicago, IL: University of Chicago Press.

Mishkin, Frederic S. (2000), 'Inflation Targeting in Emerging-Market Countries', *American Economic Review, Papers and Proceedings*, **90** (2), pp. 105–9.

Mishkin, Frederic S. and Klaus Schmidt-Hebbel (2005), 'Does Inflation Targeting Make a Difference', manuscript, Columbia University.

Prasad, Eswar (forthcoming), 'Is China's Growth Miracle Built to Last?', *China Economic Review*.

Prasad, Eswar and Raghuram Rajan (2006), 'Modernizing China's Growth Paradigm', *American Economic Review*, **96** (2), pp. 331–6.

Prasad, Eswar and Shang-Jin Wei (2007), 'China's Approach to Capital Inflows: Patterns and Possible Explanations', in Sebastian Edwards (ed.), *Capital Controls and Capital Flows in Emerging Economies: Policies, Practices and Consequences*, Chicago, IL: University of Chicago Press.

Woodford, Michael (2003), *Interest and Prices: Foundations of a Theory of Monetary Policy*, Princeton, NJ: Princeton University Press.

Yi, Gang (2001), 'The Framework of China's Monetary Policy', manuscript, People's Bank of China, Beijing.

9. Monetary policy transmission in India

Rakesh Mohan and Michael Patra*

9.1 INTRODUCTION

Key to the efficient conduct of monetary policy is the condition that it must exert a systematic influence on the economy in a forward-looking sense. A priori economic theory backed by some empirical evidence has identified the main channels through which monetary policy impacts upon its final targets, namely output, employment and inflation. Broadly, the vehicles of monetary transmission can be classified into financial market prices (for example, interest rates, exchange rates, yields, asset prices, equity prices) or financial market quantities (money supply, credit aggregates, supply of government bonds and foreign denominated assets). It is recognized that, whereas these channels are not mutually exclusive, the relative importance of each channel may differ from one economy to another depending on a number of factors including the underlying structural characteristics, the state of development of financial markets, the instruments available to monetary policy, the fiscal stance and the degree of openness.

This chapter focuses on the Indian experience with monetary policy transmission. Section 9.2 sets out an overview of the monetary policy regime in India, covering objectives, framework, operating procedures and instruments, and the evolution of financial markets. Section 9.3 discusses the various monetary policy transmission channels in India – interest rates, bank lending, debt market, exchange rate and communication and expectations. Section 9.4 makes an assessment of monetary transmission in terms of the actual outcomes in the context of the ultimate objectives of price stability and growth. Section 9.5 concludes by providing some suggestions on what is needed to improve monetary transmission and sums up the challenges and dilemmas of monetary policy.

9.2 THE CONDUCT OF MONETARY POLICY IN INDIA

The Reserve Bank of India Act, 1934 sets out the objectives of the Bank: 'to regulate the issue of Bank notes and the keeping of reserves with a view to securing monetary stability in India and generally to operate the currency and credit system of the country to its advantage'.

9.2.1 Objectives

The objectives of monetary policy in India have evolved as: (1) price stability; (2) provision of adequate credit to productive sectors of the economy so as to ensure high and sustained growth; and (3) financial stability consistent with the increasing openness of the Indian economy. Given the overarching consideration for sustained growth in the context of high levels of poverty and inequality, price stability has evolved as the dominant objective of monetary policy. The underlying philosophy is that it is only in a low and stable inflation environment that economic growth can be sustained.

In recent years, financial stability has assumed priority in the conduct of monetary policy in view of the increasing openness of the economy and growing cross border financial integration. Strong synergies and complementarities are observed between price stability and financial stability in India. Accordingly, regulation, supervision and development of the financial system remain within the legitimate ambit of monetary policy, broadly interpreted.

9.2.2 Framework

Prior to the mid-1980s, there was no formal enunciation of monetary policy objectives, instruments and transmission channels in India other than that of administering the supply and allocation of, and demand for, credit in alignment with the needs of a planned economy. Over the period from 1985 to 1997, India followed a monetary policy framework that could broadly be characterized as one of loose and flexible monetary targeting with feedback. Under this approach, growth in broad money supply (M3) was projected in a manner consistent with expected gross domestic product (GDP) growth and a tolerable level of inflation. The M3 growth thus worked out was considered a nominal anchor for policy. Reserve money (RM) was used as the operating target and bank reserves as the operating instrument.

As deregulation increased the role of market forces in the determination of interest rates and the exchange rate, monetary targeting, even in its flexible mode, came under stress. Capital flows increased liquidity exogenously, and put upward pressure on the money supply, prices and the exchange rates, the latter having gained importance vis-à-vis quantity variables. While most studies in India showed that money demand functions had been fairly stable, it was increasingly felt that financial innovations and technology could erode the predictive potential of money demand estimations relative to the past. Interest rates gained relative influence on the decision to hold money. Accordingly, the monetary policy framework was reviewed towards the late 1990s, and the Reserve Bank switched over to a more broad-based multiple indicator approach from 1998–99. In this approach, policy perspectives are obtained by juxtaposing high-frequency information on interest rates and other rates of return in different markets with medium- and low-frequency variables such as currency, credit extended by banks and financial institutions, the fiscal position, trade and capital flows, inflation rate, exchange rate, refinancing and transactions in foreign exchange and output. Monetary aggregates, however, continue to remain important information variables in this framework. For these reasons as well as for simplicity and to facilitate greater understanding, the quarterly policy statements of the Reserve Bank continue to be set in a framework in terms of money, output and prices.

Since the late 1980s, there has been an enhanced emphasis by many central banks on securing operational freedom for monetary policy and investing it with a single goal, best embodied in the growing independence of central banks and inflation targeting as an operational framework for monetary policy, which has important implications for transmission channels. In this context, the specific features of the Indian economy have led to the emergence of a somewhat contrarian view:

> In India, we have not favoured the adoption of inflation targeting, while keeping the attainment of low inflation as a central objective of monetary policy, along with that of high and sustained growth that is so important for a developing economy. Apart from the legitimate concern regarding growth as a key objective, there are other factors that suggest that inflation targeting may not be appropriate for India. First, unlike many other developing countries we have had a record of moderate inflation, with double digit inflation being the exception, and largely socially unacceptable. Second, adoption of inflation targeting requires the existence of an efficient monetary transmission mechanism through the operation of efficient financial markets and absence of interest rate distortions. In India, although the money market, government debt and forex markets have indeed developed in recent years, they still have some way to go, whereas the corporate debt market is still to develop. Though interest rate deregulation has largely been accomplished, some administered interest rates still persist. Third, inflationary pressures still often emanate from significant supply shocks related to the effect of the monsoon on agriculture, where monetary policy action may have little role. Finally, in an economy as large as that of India, with various regional differences, and continued existence of market imperfections in factor and product markets between regions, the choice of a universally acceptable measure of inflation is also difficult. (Mohan, 2006b)

9.2.3 Operating Procedures and Instruments

Short-term interest rates have emerged as the key indicators of the monetary policy stance all over the world. It is also recognized that stability in financial markets is critical for efficient price discovery and meaningful signalling. Since the interest rate and exchange rate are key prices reflecting the cost of money, it is particularly important for efficient functioning of the economy that they be market determined and easily observed.

Central banks follow a variety of operating frameworks and procedures for signaling and implementing the monetary policy stance on a day-to-day basis, with a view to achieving the ultimate objectives – price stability and growth. The choice of policy framework in any economy is always a difficult one and depends on the stage of macroeconomic and financial sector development and is somewhat of an evolutionary process (Mohan, 2006a).

In a market-oriented financial system, central banks typically use instruments that are directly under their control: required reserve ratios, interest charged on borrowed reserves (discount window) provided directly or through rediscounting of financial assets held by depository institutions, open market operations (OMOs) and selective credit controls. These instruments are usually directed at attaining a prescribed value of the operating target, typically bank reserves and/or a very short-term interest rate (usually the overnight interbank rate). The optimal choice between price and quantity targets would depend on the sources of disturbances in the goods and money markets (Poole, 1970).

If money demand is viewed as highly unstable, greater output stability can be attained by stabilizing interest rates. If, however, the main source of short-run instability arises from aggregate spending or unsterilized capital inflows, a policy that stabilizes monetary aggregates could be desirable. In reality, it often becomes difficult to trace the sources of instability. Instead, monetary policy is implemented by fixing, at least over the short-time horizon, the value of an operating target or policy instrument. As additional information about the economy is obtained, the appropriate level at which to fix the policy instrument or target changes.

The operating procedures of monetary policy of most central banks have largely converged to one of the following three variants: (1) a number of central banks, including the US Federal Reserve, estimate the demand for bank reserves and then carry out open market operations to target short-term interest rates; (2) another set of central banks, of which the Bank of Japan used to be one until recently, estimate market liquidity and carry out open market operations to target bank reserves, while allowing interest rates to adjust; and (3) a growing number of central banks, including the European Central Bank and the Bank of England, modulate monetary conditions in terms of both quantum and price of liquidity, through a mix of OMOs, standing facilities and minimum reserve requirement and changes in the policy rate. The operating procedure followed in India presents a fourth variant.

In the context of growing reliance of the monetary policy framework on indirect and market-based instruments, it is important for the central bank to have effective instruments for day-to-day liquidity management at its disposal. Like other central banks, the Reserve Bank too has put in place a liquidity management framework to manage daily liquidity, taking into account the country-specific features as well as the specific challenges posed by large and volatile capital flows. The key features of the current liquidity management framework are set out next.

Liquidity adjustment facility

In the Indian context, reforms in the liquidity management framework which were initiated in the late 1990s crystallized into the Liquidity Adjustment Facility (LAF) in 2000. Under the LAF, the Reserve Bank sets its policy rates, that is, repo and reverse repo rates, and carries out repo and reverse repo operations, thereby providing a corridor for overnight money market rates (Figure 9.1). The LAF avoids targeting a particular level of overnight money market rate in view of exogenous influences impacting upon liquidity at the shorter end, namely, volatile government cash balances and unpredictable foreign exchange flows.

Although repo auctions can be conducted at variable or fixed rates on overnight or longer term, given market preference and the need to transmit interest rate signals quickly, the LAF has settled into a fixed rate overnight auction mode since April 2004. The introduction of the LAF has had several advantages. First, it made possible the transition from direct instruments of monetary control to indirect instruments. Since LAF operations enabled reduction in the cash reserve ratio (CRR) without loss of monetary control, certain dead weight loss for the system was saved. Second, the LAF has provided monetary authorities with greater flexibility in determining both the quantum of adjustment as well as the rates by responding to the needs of the system on a daily basis. Third and most importantly, though there is no formal targeting of a point overnight interest rate, the LAF helped to stabilize overnight call rates within a specified corridor, the difference between the fixed repo and reverse repo rates currently being 150 basis points (as of March 2009). The limit has varied between 100 and 250 basis points at different points in time. It has thus enabled the central bank to affect demand for funds through policy rate changes. In this sense, LAF rates perform the role of nominal anchor effectively (Figure 9.2).

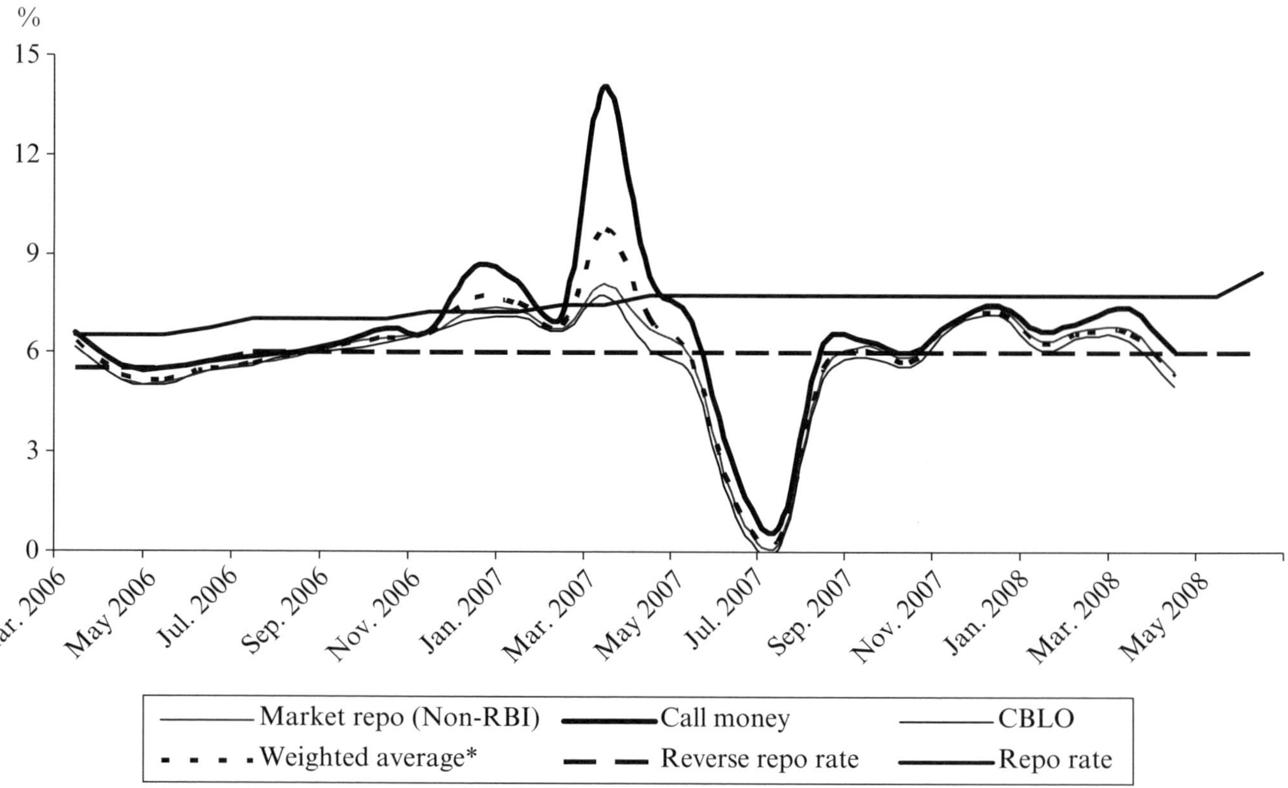

Note: *Weighted average of interest rates in call money, market repo (Non-RBI) and CBLO segments.

Figure 9.1 Policy rates and money market interest rates

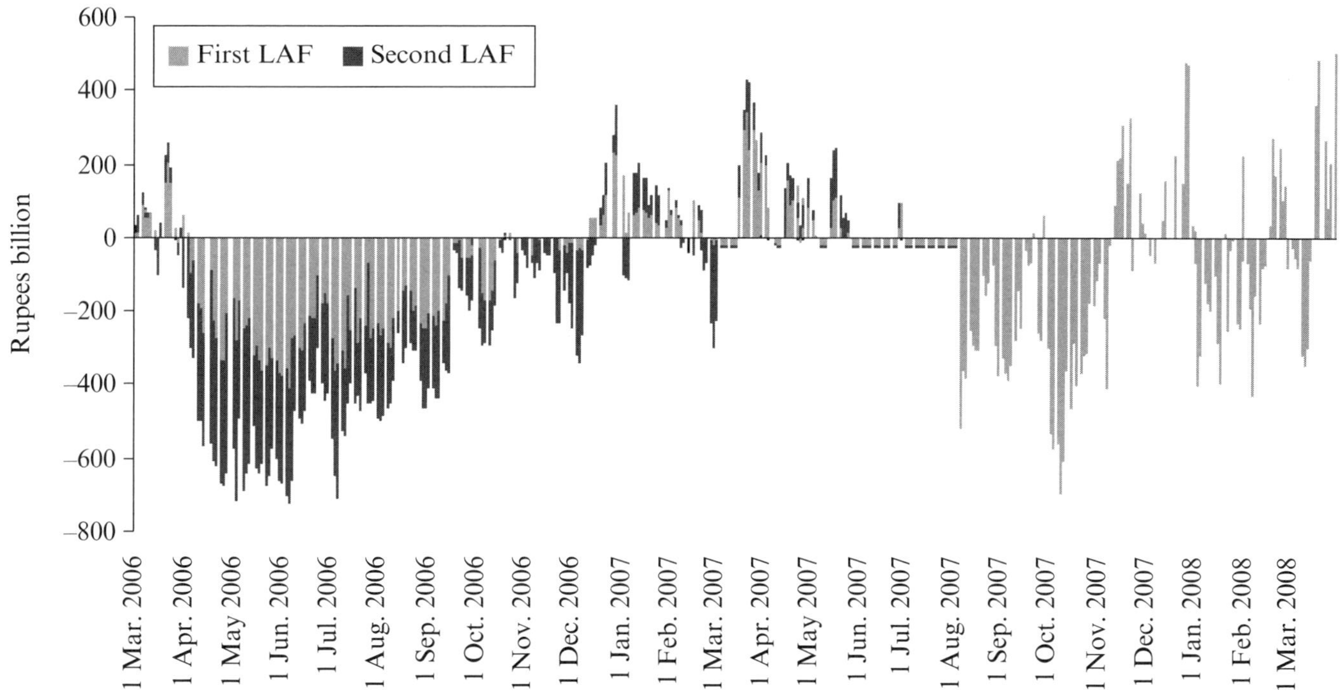

Figure 9.2 *Repo (+)/reverse repo (−) under the LAF*

Interest rates in the collateralized segment of the overnight money market are typically less volatile than the uncollaterized call money segment, thereby strengthening monetary policy transmission and also imparting financial stability.

Market stabilization scheme

In the context of increasing openness of the economy, a market-determined exchange rate and large capital inflows, monetary management may warrant sterilizing foreign exchange market intervention, partly or wholly, so as to retain the intent of monetary policy. The LAF operations, which are essentially designed to take care of frictional daily liquidity, began to bear the burden of stabilization disproportionately during 2001–04 in the face of large capital flows. Initially, the Reserve Bank sterilized capital inflows by way of OMOs. Such sterilization, however, involves cost in terms of lower returns on international assets vis-à-vis domestic assets. The finite stock of government securities with the Reserve Bank also limited its ability to sterilize. The Reserve Bank, therefore, signed in March 2004 a Memorandum of Understanding (MoU) with the Government of India for issuance of Treasury bills and dated government securities under the Market Stabilisation Scheme (MSS), in addition to normal government borrowings. The new instrument empowers the Reserve Bank to absorb liquidity on a more enduring but still temporary basis while leaving the LAF for daily liquidity management and using conventional OMOs on a more enduring basis. The MSS has provided the Reserve Bank with flexibility not only to absorb but also to inject liquidity in times of need by way of unwinding. Therefore, short-term instruments are generally preferred for MSS operations.

Government cash balances with the Reserve Bank often display sizeable volatility, causing unanticipated expansion or contraction of the monetary base and, consequently, money supply and liquidity, which may not necessarily be consistent with the prevailing stance of the monetary policy. In the presence of fluctuating government cash balances, the task of monetary management becomes complicated. Operation of the LAF has also been very effective in counterbalancing this volatility in government cash balances.

Statutory reserve requirements

The relative weights assigned to various channels of transmission of monetary policy in India also reflect a conscious effort to move from direct instruments of monetary control to indirect instruments, albeit with a flexible approach, especially in the context of liquidity conditions engendered by sustained capital inflows. Illustratively, the CRR, which had

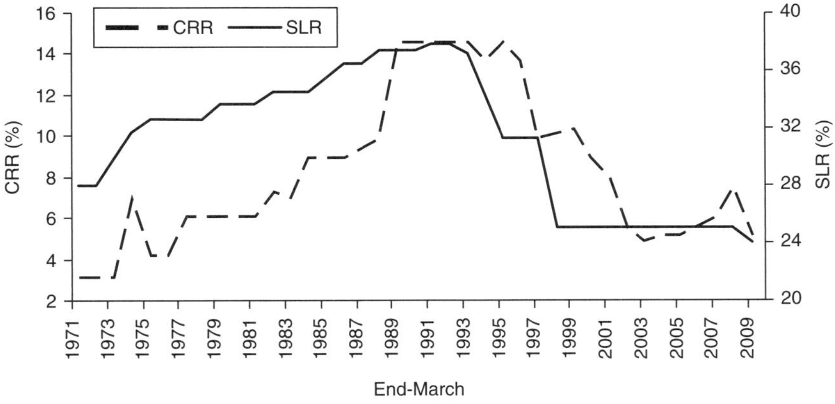

Figure 9.3 *Reserve requirements*

been brought down from a peak of 15 per cent in 1994–95 to 4.5 per cent by June 2003, was raised to 9 per cent in phases by August 2008 with the onset of withdrawal of monetary accommodation in October 2004 (Figure 9.3). The amendment to the Reserve Bank of India (RBI) Act in 2006 strengthens monetary maneuverability since it allows for the removal of the floor of 3 per cent and ceiling of 15 per cent on the CRR. Monetary control is also exercised through the prescription of a statutory liquidity ratio (SLR), which is a variant of the secondary reserve requirement in several countries. It is maintained in the form of specified assets such as cash, gold and 'approved' securities – mainly government securities – as a proportion of net demand and time liabilities (NDTL) of banks. Accordingly, the SLR is also important for prudential purposes, that is, to assure the soundness of the banking system. The pre-emption under the SLR, which had increased to about 38.5 per cent of NDTL in the beginning of the 1990s, was brought to its statutory minimum of 25 per cent by October 1997. Banks, however, continue to hold more government securities than the statutory minimum SLR, reflecting risk perception and portfolio choice. The statutory minimum SLR of 25 per cent has been removed (April 2007) to provide for greater flexibility in the RBI's monetary policy operations. The CRR and the SLR were cut to 5 per cent and 24 per cent by early January 2009, *inter alia* in response to the evolving global financial crisis and its impact on domestic liquidity conditions. The reform of the monetary and financial sectors has, thus, enabled the Reserve Bank to expand the array of instruments at its command and enhanced its ability to respond to evolving circumstances.

The various tools of liquidity management have enabled the Reserve

Bank to maintain liquidity conditions, orderly movement in both exchange rates and interest rates, and conduct monetary policy in accordance with its stated objectives.

9.2.4 Market Development

The success of a framework that relies on indirect instruments of monetary management such as interest rates is contingent upon the extent and speed with which changes in the central bank's policy rate are transmitted to the spectrum of market interest rates and exchange rate in the economy and onward to the real sector. Clearly, monetary transmission cannot take place without efficient price discovery, particularly with respect to interest rates and exchange rates. Therefore, in the efficient functioning of financial markets, the corresponding development of the full financial market spectrum becomes necessary. In addition, the growing integration of the Indian economy with the rest of the world has to be recognized and provided for. Accordingly, reforms focused on improving operational effectiveness of monetary policy have been put in process, while simultaneously strengthening the regulatory role of the Reserve Bank, tightening the prudential and supervisory norms, improving the credit delivery system and developing the technological and institutional framework of the financial sector.

Money markets

Given the pivotal role of the money market in transmission, efforts initiated in the late 1980s were intensified over the full spectrum. Following the withdrawal of the ceiling on interbank money market rates in 1989, several financial innovations in terms of money market instruments such as certificates of deposits (CDs), commercial paper (CP) and money market mutual funds were introduced in phases. Barriers to entry were gradually eased by increasing the number of players and relaxing the issuance and subscription norms in respect of money market instruments, thus fostering better price discovery. Participation in the call money market was widened to cover primary and satellite dealers and corporates (through primary dealers), besides other participants.

In order to improve monetary transmission, as also on prudential considerations, steps were initiated in 1999 to turn the call money market into a pure interbank market and, simultaneously, to develop a repo market outside the official window for providing a stable collateralized funding alternative, particularly to non-banks who were phased out of the call segment, and banks. The Collateralised Borrowing and Lending Obligation (CBLO), a repo instrument developed by the Clearing

Table 9.1 Activity in money market segments (billion rupees)

Year/ month	Average daily turnover (One leg)				Commercial paper (outstand-ing)	Certificates of deposit (outstand-ing)
	Call money market	Market repo	CBLO	Term money market		
1	2	3	4	5	6	7
2003–04	86	26	3	3	78	32
2004–05	71	43	34	3	117	61
2005–06	90	53	100	4	173	273
2006–07	109	84	162	5	213	648
2007–08	107	137	278	4	338	1156

Note: CBLO: Collateralized Borrowing and Lending Obligation.

Source: *Macroeconomic and Monetary Developments*, various issues, RBI.

Corporation of India Limited (CCIL) for its members, with the CCIL acting as a central counter-party for borrowers and lenders, was permitted as a money market instrument in 2002. With the development of market repo and CBLO segments, the call money market has been transformed into a pure interbank market, including primary dealers, from August 2005. A recent noteworthy development is the substantial migration of money market activity from the uncollateralized call money segment to the collateralized market repo and CBLO markets. Thus, uncollateralized overnight transactions are now limited to banks and primary dealers in the interest of financial stability (Table 9.1) (details in Annex II in Mohan, 2008).

Government securities market

The government securities market is important for the entire debt market as it serves as a benchmark for pricing other debt market instruments, thereby aiding the monetary transmission across the yield curve. The key policy development that has enabled a more independent monetary policy environment, as well as the development of the government securities market, was the discontinuation of automatic monetization of the government's fiscal deficit in April 1997 through an agreement between the government and the Reserve Bank of India in September 1994. Subsequently, enactment of the Fiscal Responsibility and Budget Management Act, 2003 has strengthened the institutional mechanism further: from April 2006 onwards, the Reserve Bank is no longer permitted to subscribe to government securities in the primary market. This step completes the transition to a fully market based system for government securities.

Looking ahead, consequent to the recommendations of the Twelfth Finance Commission, the central government has ceased to raise resources on behalf of state governments, which now have to access the market directly. Thus, state government's capability in raising resources is now market determined and based on their own financial health.

Foreign exchange market

In the foreign exchange market, reforms have been focused on market development incorporating prudential safeguards so that the market would not be destabilized in the process. The move towards a market-based exchange rate regime in 1993, the subsequent adoption of current account convertibility and de facto capital account convertibility for select categories of non-residents were the key enabling factors in reforming the Indian foreign exchange market prior to now. India's approach to financial integration has so far been gradual and cautious, guided by signposts and concomitants in terms of improvement in fiscal, inflation and financial sector indicators, *inter alia*. Efforts are currently under way to move towards fuller capital account convertibility even for residents. Over the years, a number of measures have been initiated to integrate the Indian forex market with the global financial system, with increasing freedom given to banks to borrow abroad and fix their own position and gap limits (see Annex III in Mohan, 2008 for details).

The development of the monetary policy framework has also involved a great number of institutional initiatives in the area of trading, payments and settlement systems along with the provision of technological infrastructure. The interaction of technology with deregulation has also contributed to the emergence of a more open, competitive and globalized financial market. While the policy measures in the pre-1990s period were essentially devoted to financial deepening, the focus of reforms in the period since the early 1990s has been engendering greater efficiency and productivity in the banking system. Legislative amendments have also been carried out to strengthen the RBI's regulatory jurisdiction over financial markets, providing greater instrument independence and, hence, ensuring monetary transmission.

9.3 CHANNELS OF TRANSMISSION OF MONETARY POLICY IN INDIA

Traditionally, four key channels of monetary policy transmission are identified, namely, interest rate, credit aggregates, asset prices and exchange rate channels. The interest rate channel emerges as the dominant transmission mechanism of monetary policy. An expansionary monetary policy, for instance, is expected to lead to a lowering of the cost of loanable funds, which in turn raises investment and consumption demand, and should eventually be reflected in aggregate output and prices. Monetary policy also operates on aggregate demand through changes in the availability of loanable funds, that is, the credit channel. It is, however, relevant to note that the 'credit channel' is not a distinct, free-standing alternative to the traditional transmission mechanism, but should rather be seen as a channel that can amplify and propagate conventional interest rate effects (Bernanke and Gertler, 1995). Nevertheless, it is fair to regard the credit channel as running alongside the interest rate channel to produce monetary effects on real activity (RBI, 2002). Changes in interest rates by the monetary authorities also induce movements in asset prices to generate wealth effects in terms of market valuations of financial assets and liabilities. Higher interest rates can induce an appreciation of the domestic currency, which in turn leads to a reduction in net exports and, hence, in aggregate demand and output.

In the recent period, a fifth channel – expectations – has assumed prominence in the conduct of forward-looking monetary policy in view of its influence on the traditional four channels. For example, the link between short- and long-term real rates is widely believed to follow from the expectational hypothesis of the term structure of interest rates. In a generalized context, the expectations channel of monetary policy postulates that the beliefs of economic agents about future shocks to the economy, and also the central bank's reactions, can affect the variables that are determined in a forward-looking manner. Thus, 'open-mouth operation' by the central bank, that is, an announcement of future central bank policy, influences expectations in financial markets and leads to changes in output and inflation. Clearly, the credibility of the monetary authority drives the expectations channel.

9.3.1 Bank Credit and Lending Rate Channels

The monetary policy stance of the Reserve Bank is often articulated as a commitment to ensure that all genuine requirements for bank credit are adequately met in order to support investment and export demand consistent with price stability (see Annex X in Mohan, 2008 for details). Liquidity operations are conducted with a view to ensuring that the demand for reserves is satisfied and credit projections consistent with macroeconomic objectives are achieved. Simultaneously, improvements in the delivery of bank credit are pursued in recognition of the possibility of market failure in efficiently auctioning credit. An integral element of the conduct of monetary policy has, therefore, been the direction of bank credit to certain sectors of priority such as agriculture, exports, small-scale industry, infrastructure, housing, micro-credit institutions and self-help groups. An ongoing policy endeavour is enhancing and simplifying the access to credit with a view to securing the widest inclusion of society in the credit market.

Available empirical evidence covering the period September 1998 – March 2004 suggests that the interest rate pass-through from changes in the policy rate was 0.61 and 0.42 for lending and deposit rates, respectively, that is, a reduction/increase of 100 basis points (bps) in the bank rate led to a reduction/increase of almost 40 bps in the banks' deposit rates and 60 bps in their prime lending rate. Rolling regressions suggest some improvement in pass-through to lending rates and deposits. Thus, though pass-through is less than complete, there are signs of an increase in pass-through over time (RBI, 2004b). The improvement in the pass-through can be attributed to policy efforts to impart greater flexibility to the interest rate structure in the economy through various measures increasing flexibility in interest rates on both the deposit and lending sides. Interest rates have emerged as a more potent instrument than before, with the move towards floating as against fixed-rate products under which the transmission is limited at the margin. Interest rate sensitivity of bank lending could be further enhanced by revamping the current practices on pricing of credit through well-structured, segment-wise analysis of costs at various stages of intermediation in the whole credit cycle.

Available empirical evidence also indicates that prudential norms, as proxied by banks' capital adequacy ratios, exert a significant influence on bank lending (Nag and Das, 2002; Pandit et al., 2006). To enhance monetary policy transmission through the credit demand, Indian monetary policy has often resorted to the use of prudential instruments such as sectoral provisioning and risk weight requirements.

The Indian financial system appears to have responded favourably to reforms initiated in the early 1990s with relatively higher efficiency, competitiveness and resilience. Non-food credit extended by scheduled commercial banks recorded an average annual growth of 24.5 per cent between 2002–03 and 2007–08, notably higher than that of 14.5 per cent recorded during the preceding four-year period (1998–99 to 2001–02) as well as the long-run average of 17.8 per cent (1970–2006). The credit–GDP ratio, after moving in a narrow range of around 30 per cent between mid-1980s and late 1990s, started increasing from 2000–01 onwards to reach 54 per cent by March 2008. The sharp expansion in bank credit also reflects, in part, policy initiatives to improve the flow of credit to sectors like agriculture. The strengthening of the banking system has thus worked towards financial widening and deepening. In the process, greater monetization and financial inclusion are extending the net of the formal financial system and, hence, enhancing the scope of monetary transmission.

The increasing reach of formal finance has gradually expanded to cover larger segments of the population. The 'demographic dividend' of a larger and younger labour force has meant that banks have been able to expand their loan portfolio rapidly, enabling consumers to satisfy their lifestyle aspirations at a relatively young age with an optimal combination of equity and debt to finance consumption and asset creation. In the process, interest rates have begun affecting consumption and investment decisions of the population in a much more rapid fashion than was the case earlier. In view of this growing share of household credit, it is likely that household consumption decisions, in the coming years, may be more strongly influenced by monetary policy decisions with implications for the monetary transmission mechanism. Consequently, the monetary authority may increasingly need to contend with public opinion on monetary management, much more than hitherto in the context of the rising share of personal and household loans. In the context of large-scale public ownership of banks, such pressures of public opinion would also manifest themselves into political pressures.

In brief, while there is increasing evidence that the bank credit and lending rate channels of monetary transmission are gaining in strength, a number of constraints continue to interfere with monetary transmission. First, in recent times, there has been some tendency to widen the net of administered interest rates. In this context, there is a public perception that banks' risk assessment processes are less than appropriate and that there is underpricing of credit for corporates, while there could be overpricing of lending to agriculture and small-scale industry. Furthermore, administered interest rates fixed by the government on a number of small saving schemes and provident funds are of special relevance as they generally offer a rate higher than corresponding instruments available in the market as well as tax incentives (RBI, 2001; RBI, 2004a). As banks have to compete for funds with small saving schemes, the rates offered on long-term deposits mobilized by banks set the floor for lending rates at a level higher than would have obtained under competitive market conditions. In fact, this was observed to be a factor contributing to downward stickiness of lending rates, with implications for the effectiveness of monetary policy (Table 9.2).

Second, the stipulation of priority sector lending of 40 per cent of net bank credit affects flexibility in sectoral credit allocation even though there is no interest rate stipulation for the priority sector.

Table 9.2 Small savings and bank deposits (billion rupees)

Year	Average interest rate on small savings (%)	Small savings outstanding	Average interest rate on banks' term deposits (%)	Bank term deposits outstanding	Small savings as % of banks' term deposits
1	2	3	4	5	6
1991–92	9.95	586	9.1	1322	44.3
1992–93	9.48	609	9.6	1648	37.0
1993–94	12.21	677	8.7	1936	35.0
1994–95	13.20	833	7.0	2225	37.4
1995–96	11.33	937	8.5	2577	36.4
1996–97	13.03	1061	9.4	3085	34.4
1997–98	11.92	1268	8.8	3743	33.9
1998–99	10.34	1553	8.9	4401	35.3
1999–00	11.50	1875	8.6	5162	36.3
2000–01	11.60	2251	8.1	6015	37.4
2001–02	11.61	2629	9.6	7252	36.3
2002–03	11.56	3138	8.7	8180	38.4
2003–04	10.88	3758	6.5	9359	40.2
2004–05	9.37	4577	6.2	10641	43.0
2005–06	8.90	5276	6.5	12464	42.3
2006–07	8.91	5644	8.2	15961	35.4
2007–08	8.33	5532	–		–

Sources: *Annual Report*, *Handbook of Statistics on the Indian Economy and Basic Statistical Returns of Scheduled Commercial Banks in India* (various issues), Reserve Bank of India.

Third, allocational flexibility is further constrained under the prescription of an SLR. Although the relevant Act has now been amended to give the Reserve Bank flexibility to reduce this statutory liquidity ratio, the prevailing high levels of fiscal deficit and public debt may constrain the flexibility to lower the SLR requirements.

Fourth, the system of Benchmark Prime Lending Rate (BPLR) for credit pricing has proved to be relatively sticky downward, and more so for specific sectors like agriculture and small-scale industries. As the BPLR has ceased to be a reference rate, assessment of the efficacy of monetary transmission has become difficult.

Fifth, the Government of India continues to own around 70 per cent of the banking system (by asset ownership across banks). While the government, as a legitimate owner, is entitled to issue direction to public sector banks, such exercise by the government infuses elements of uncertainty and market imperfections, impacting upon monetary transmission.

9.3.2 Debt Market Channel

While government debt management was one of the motivating factors for the setting up of central banks in many countries, currently this function with its focus on lowering the cost of public debt is often looked upon as constraining monetary management, particularly when compulsions of monetary policy amidst inflation expectations may necessitate a tighter monetary policy stance. Therefore, it is now widely believed that the two functions – monetary policy and public debt management – need to be conducted in a manner that ensures transparency and independence in monetary operations. The fuller development of financial markets, reasonable control over the fiscal deficit and necessary legislative changes are regarded as preconditions for the separation of debt management from monetary management. The Reserve Bank currently performs the twin function of public debt and monetary management:

> The logical question that follows is whether the experience of fiscal dominance over monetary policy would have been different if there had been separation of debt management from monetary management in India? Or, were we served better with both the functions residing in the Reserve Bank? What has really happened is that there was a significant change in thinking regarding overall economic policy during the early 1990s, arguing for a reduced direct role of the Government in the economy. A conscious view emerged in favour of fiscal stabilisation and reduction of fiscal deficits aimed at eliminating the dominance of fiscal policy over monetary policy through the prior practice of fiscal deficits being financed by automatic monetization. It is this overall economic policy transformation that has provided greater autonomy to monetary policy making in the 1990s.
>
> The Indian economy has made considerable progress in developing its financial markets, especially the government securities market since 1991. Furthermore, fiscal dominance in monetary policy formulation has significantly reduced in recent years. With the onset of a fiscal consolidation process, withdrawal of the RBI from the primary market of Government securities and expected legislative changes permitting a reduction in the statutory minimum Statutory Liquidity Ratio, fiscal dominance would be further diluted.
>
> All of these changes took place despite the continuation of debt management by the Reserve Bank. Thus, one can argue that effective separation of monetary policy from debt management is more a consequence of overall economic policy thinking rather than adherence to a particular view on institutional arrangements. (Mohan, 2006b)

The Fiscal Responsibility and Budget Management (FRBM) Act, 2003 and similar state-level enactments have set the stage for a fiscal correction path for both the central government and state governments. In preparation, the institutional structures within the Reserve Bank have been modified to strengthen monetary operations with a view to moving towards functional separation between debt management and monetary operations. Accordingly, the Financial Markets Department (FMD) undertakes: (1) monetary operations; (2) regulation and development of money market instruments; and (3) monitoring of money, government securities and foreign exchange markets. The enactment of the FRBM Act has arguably strengthened monetary transmission through the debt market. It has also mitigated the possibility of conflict in monetary policy in order to contain the cost of government borrowing.

The auction-based issue of government debt according to a pre-announced calendar has enabled price discovery and liquidity in the market. A Negotiated Dealing System was introduced in February 2002 to facilitate electronic bidding, secondary market trading and settlement and to disseminate information on trades on a real-time basis. In the context of the Reserve Bank's absence from primary auctions, a 'when, as and if issued' market in government securities has been allowed recently.

Vibrant secondary market trading has helped to develop a yield curve and the term structure of interest rates. This has facilitated the pricing of debt instruments in various market segments and, thereby, monetary transmission across maturity and financial instruments. With the increasing openness of the domestic economy, it appears that international economic developments are set to exert a greater influence on the domestic yield curve than before. Thus, even in the absence of fuller capital account convertibility, monetary transmission may need to contend with impulses that arise from international developments.

While the government securities market is fairly well developed now, the corporate debt market remains to be developed, for facilitating monetary signalling across various market segments. In the absence of a well-developed corporate debt market, the demand for debt instruments has largely concentrated on government securities with the attendant implications for the yield curve and, in turn, for monetary transmission. The secondary market for corporate debt has suffered from a lack of market making resulting in poor liquidity. Corporates continue to prefer private placements to public issues for raising resources in view of the ease of procedures and lower costs. There is a need for the development of mortgage-backed securities, bond insurance institutions for credit enhancement, abridgment of disclosure requirements for listed companies, rating requirements for unlisted companies, real-time reporting of primary and secondary trading, retail access to bond market by non-profit institutions and small corporates, and access to Real-Time Gross Settlement (RTGS). A concerted effort is now being made to set up the institutional and technological structure that would enable the corporate debt market to operate. Furthermore, the ongoing reforms in the area of social security coupled with the emergence of pension and provident funds are expected to increase the demand for long-term debt instruments. In the process, the investor base for government securities would be broadened, extending the monetary transmission across new players and participants.

9.3.3 Exchange Rate Channel

The foreign exchange market in India has acquired increasing depth with the transition to a market-determined exchange rate system in March 1993 and the subsequent gradual but significant liberalization of restrictions on various external transactions. Payments restrictions on all current account transactions have been removed with the acceptance of the obligations of Article VIII of the International Monetary Fund (IMF)'s Articles of Agreement in August 1994. While the rupee remains virtually convertible on the capital account for foreign nationals and non-resident Indians (NRIs), similar moves are on course for the domestic residents. Significant relaxations have been allowed for capital outflows in the form of direct and portfolio investment, non-resident deposits, repatriation of assets and funds held abroad. Indian residents can now open foreign currency accounts with banks in India (Mohan, 2006c).

The annual turnover in the foreign exchange market has increased manifoldly over the past few years: from US$1.4 trillion in 2000–01 to US$12.3 trillion in 2007–08 (Table 9.3). The interbank transactions continue to account for the bulk of the transactions in the forex market, albeit with a declining share over the years. The derivatives segment (swaps plus forward) is also growing at a fast pace. Over the period 2000–2001 to 2007–08, the overall turnover has been almost equally divided between the spot and the derivative segments. Under the market-determined exchange rate regime, the Indian rupee has exhibited two-way movements. The exchange rate policy of the Reserve Bank in recent years has been guided by the broad principles of careful monitoring and management of exchange rates with flexibility, without a fixed target or a preannounced target or a band, coupled with the ability to intervene if and when necessary.

Between April 2004 and April 2007, the increase in foreign exchange market turnover in India was the highest amongst the 54 countries covered in the latest Triennial Central Bank Survey of Foreign Exchange and Derivatives Market Activity conducted by the Bank for International

Table 9.3 Foreign exchange market: activity indicators

Year	Foreign exchange market annual turnover (US$ billion)	Gross volume of BoP transactions (US$ billion)	RBI's foreign currency assets* (US$ billion)	CV of exchange rate of rupee (%)	Col. 2 over Col. 3	Col. 2 over Col. 4
1	2	3	4	5	6	7
2000–01	1434	258	40	2.3	5.6	36
2001–02	1487	237	51	1.4	6.3	29
2002–03	1585	267	72	0.9	5.9	22
2003–04	2141	362	107	1.6	5.9	20
2004–05	2892	481	136	2.3	6.0	21
2005–06	4413	664	145	1.5	6.6	30
2006–07	6571	915	192	1.9	7.2	34
2007–08	12286	1376	299	2.3	8.9	41

Notes: *At end-March.
CV: coefficient of variation; BoP: balance of payments.

Source: Reserve Bank of India.

Settlements (BIS). According to the survey, daily average turnover in India jumped almost fivefold from US$7 billion in April 2004 to US$34 billion in April 2007; global turnover over the same period rose by only 66 per cent from US$2.4 trillion to US$4 trillion. As a result, the share of India in global foreign exchange market turnover trebled from 0.3 per cent in April 2004 to 0.9 per cent in April 2007.

Exchange rate flexibility, coupled with the gradual removal of capital controls, has widened the scope for monetary maneuverability, enabling transmission through exchange rates. However, if large segments of economic agents lack adequate resilience to withstand volatility in currency and money markets, the option of exchange rate adjustments may be muted in its applicability, partially or fully. Therefore, the central bank may need to carry out foreign exchange operations for stabilizing the market. In the Indian context, faced with similar circumstances, sterilization operations are being carried out from 2004 by issuances of government securities under the MSS, as mentioned earlier.

Available evidence suggests that the pass-through of exchange rate changes is around 0.1 in India; that is, a 10 per cent nominal change in the value of the Indian rupee (vis-a-vis the US dollar) would, other things remaining unchanged, change consumer inflation by less than one percentage point (BIS, 2007). There is some evidence of a decline in pass-through during the 1990s, which is consistent with the cross-country evidence. In India, inflation rates have declined significantly since the second half of the 1990s and this could be one explanation for the lower pass-through. Another key factor that could have lowered the pass-through is the phased decline in tariffs as well as non-tariff barriers such as quotas. This steep reduction in tariffs could easily have allowed domestic producers to absorb some part of the exchange rate depreciation without any effect on their profitability.

Another factor that could reduce the pass-through is related to globalization and 'Wal-Martization'. The increased intensity of globalization and the commodification of many goods have perhaps reduced the pricing power of producers, particularly of low-technology goods in developing countries, whereas the pricing power of large retailers like Wal-Mart has risen. The decline in pass-through across a number of countries, as suggested by various studies, has implications for the efficacy of the exchange rate as an adjustment tool. The lower pass-through suggests that, in the new globalized economy, exchange rate adjustments as a means of correction of imbalances may have become less potent; if so, then the swing in exchange rates to correct emerging imbalances will have to be much larger than before, eventually bringing greater instability in their wake (Mohan, 2004).

9.3.4 Communication and Expectations Channel

In a market-oriented economy, well-informed market participants are expected to enable an improved functioning of the markets, and it is held that a central bank is in the best position to provide such useful information to the market participants. Whether providing information would result in shaping and managing expectations, and if so, whether it is desirable, remain unsettled issues. There are several dilemmas faced by central banks while designing an appropriate communications policy. What should be communicated and to what degree of disaggregation? The second set of dilemmas relates to: at what stage of evolution of internal thinking and debate should there be dissemination? The third set relates to the timing of communication with reference to its market impact. The fourth relates to the quality of information and the possible ways in which it could be perceived. It is essential to appreciate that communication policy is not merely about explaining or getting a feedback on policy, but may include elements of influencing the policy direction itself. A central bank does this through several channels, including research publications and speeches (Reddy, 2001, 2006). It is recognized that credible communication and creative engagement with the market and economic agents have emerged as the critical channel of monetary transmission as against the traditional channels. For example, the US Federal Reserve, since 1994, appears to have been providing forward guidance, while the European Central Bank appears to be in the mould of keeping the markets informed rather than guiding them.

With the widening and deepening of interlinkages between various segments of financial markets, the Reserve Bank has adopted a consultative process for policymaking in order to ensure timely and effective implementation of the measures. The Bank has taken a middle path of sharing its analysis in addition to providing information, but in no way guiding the market participants. However, in doing so, the RBI has the benefit of the process of two-way communication, of information as well as perceptions, between the market participants and the RBI. In the process, the Bank's signalling and announcements are increasingly seen to have an influence on expectations formation in the market. The more complex the mandate for the central bank, the greater the necessity for communication (Mohan, 2005). The Reserve Bank of India clearly has complex objectives. Faced with such multiple tasks and such a complex mandate, there is an utmost necessity for clearer communication on the part of the Reserve Bank.

By international standards, the Reserve Bank has a fairly extensive and transparent communication system. Policy statements (quarterly since April 2005 onwards and biannual prior to this period) have traditionally communicated the Reserve Bank's stance on monetary policy in the immediate future of six months to one year. The practice of attaching a review of macroeconomic developments to the quarterly reviews gives an expansive view of how the central bank sees the economy. In the biannual policy meetings with leading bankers, the Governor explains the rationale behind the measures at length. These policy meetings are not one-way traffic. Each banker present in the meeting interacts with the Governor to express his or her reaction to the policy announcement. After the policy announcement is over, the Governor and Deputy Governor in charge of monetary policy have extensive interactions with both print and electronic media.

Communication of policy also takes place through speeches of the Governor and Deputy Governors, and various periodic reports. A significant step towards transparency of monetary policy implementation is the formation of various Technical Advisory Committees (TACs) in the Reserve Bank with representatives from market participants, other regulators and experts. In line with international best practice and with a view to further strengthening the consultative process in monetary policy, the Reserve Bank has (since July 2005; reconstituted and expanded in April 2007) set up a Technical Advisory Committee on Monetary Policy (TACMP) with external experts in the areas of monetary economics, central banking, financial markets and public finance. The committee meets at least once in a quarter, reviews macroeconomic and monetary developments and advises the Reserve Bank on the stance of monetary policy. The committee has contributed to enriching the inputs and processes of monetary policy-setting in India. Recognizing the importance of expectations in the conduct and formulation of monetary policy, the Reserve Bank has recently initiated surveys of business and inflation expectations.

In brief, there has been a noteworthy improvement in the operational efficiency of monetary policy from the early 1990s. Financial sector reforms and the contemporaneous development of the money market, the government securities market and the foreign exchange market have strengthened monetary transmission by enabling more efficient price discovery, and improving allocative efficiency, even as the RBI has undertaken developmental efforts to ensure the stability and smooth functioning of financial markets. The approach has been one of simultaneous movement on several fronts, graduated and calibrated, with an emphasis on institutional and infrastructural development and improvements in market microstructure. The pace of the reform was contingent upon putting in place appropriate systems and procedures, technologies and market practices. There has been close coordination between the government and the RBI, and also between different regulators, which has helped in the orderly and smooth development of the financial markets in India. Markets have now grown in size, depth and activity, paving the way for the flexible use of indirect instruments. The Reserve Bank has also engaged in refining the operating procedures and instruments, as well as risk management systems, income recognition and provisioning norms, disclosure norms, accounting standards and insolvency in line with international best practice with a view to fostering the seamless integration of Indian financial markets with global markets.

9.4 HOW WELL DO MONETARY TRANSMISSION CHANNELS WORK?

Turning to an assessment of monetary policy transmission, it would be reasonable to assert that monetary policy has been largely successful in meeting its key objectives in the post-reforms period. There has been a fall in inflation worldwide since the early 1990s, and in India since the late

Table 9.4 Wholesale price inflation (WPI) and consumer price inflation (CPI) (year-on-year) (%)

Inflation measure	March 2000	March 2001	March 2002	March 2003	March 2004	March 2005	March 2006	March 2007	March 2008
1	2	3	4	5	6	7	8	9	10
WPI Inflation	6.5	5.5	1.6	6.5	4.6	5.1	4.1	5.9	7.8
CPI-IW	4.8	2.5	5.2	4.1	3.5	4.2	4.9	6.7	7.9
CPI-UNME	5.0	5.6	4.8	3.8	3.4	4.0	5.0	7.6	6.0
CPI-AL	3.4	–2.0	3.0	4.9	2.5	2.4	5.3	9.5	7.9
CPI-RL	. . .	–1.6	3.0	4.8	2.5	2.4	5.3	9.2	7.6

Notes: . . .: Not available.
IW: industrial workers; UNME: urban non-manual employees; AL: agricultural labourers; RL: rural labourers.

Source: *Annual Report* and *Handbook of Statistics of Indian Economy*, various issues, Reserve Bank of India.

1990s. Inflation has averaged close to 5 per cent per annum in the period since 1997–98, notably lower than that of 8 per cent in the previous four decades (Table 9.4). More importantly, the regime of low and stable inflation has, in turn, stabilized inflation expectations, and inflation tolerance in the economy has come down. Since inflation expectations are a key determinant of the actual inflation outcome, and given the lags in monetary transmission, the Reserve Bank has been taking pre-emptive measures to keep inflation expectations stable. A number of other factors such as increased competition, productivity gains and strong corporate balance sheets have also contributed to this low and stable inflation environment, but it appears that calibrated monetary measures have had a substantial role to play as well.

In the context of the firming-up of headline inflation during the first half of 2008, primarily on account of higher oil and other commodity prices, issues of the proper measurement of inflation and inflationary pressures have attracted renewed debate. In particular, the debate involves the relevance of core inflation as a guide for the conduct of monetary policy vis-à-vis the use of headline inflation. In India, core inflation is not considered as relevant for several reasons, but especially because the two major sources of supply shock, food and fuel, account for a large share of the index. Further, in the absence of a harmonized consumer price index for India, the use of core inflation based on wholesale prices may not be

Table 9.5 Monetary policy and corporate performance: interest rate-related indicators

Year	Growth rate in interest expenses (%)	Interest expenses to total expenditure	Interest coverage ratio#
1990–91	16.2	5.8	1.9
1991–92	28.7	6.3	1.9
1992–93	21.6	6.8	1.6
1993–94	3.1	6.1	2.0
1994–95	8.1	5.5	2.4
1995–96	25.0	5.4	2.7
1996–97	25.7	6.1	2.1
1997–98	12.5	6.3	1.9
1998–99	11.1	6.5	1.6
1999–2000	6.7	6.2	1.7
2000–01	7.1	6.1	1.7
2001–02	–5.1	6.1	1.7
2002–03	–9.8	5.0	2.1
2003–04	–11.9	3.6	3.3
2004–05	–5.8	2.8	4.6
2005–06	–2.0	2.4	5.5
2006–07	24.9	2.4	6.2

Note: # Represents the ratio of gross profit (that is, earning before interest and taxes) to interest expenses.

Source: Reserve Bank of India.

very meaningful. While the permanent component is judgmental, broad magnitudes could be perceived and articulated. Such an explanatory approach to headline and underlying inflation pressure in monetary policy has added credibility to the policy and influenced and guided the inflation expectations in India.

How did monetary policy support the growth momentum in the economy? As inflation, along with inflation expectations, fell during the period beginning 2000–2001, policy interest rates were also brought down. Consequently, both nominal and real interest rates fell. The growth rate in interest expenses of the corporates decelerated from 1997–98 and even recorded negative growth during the five-year period 2001–02 to 2005–06 (Table 9.5). Such decline in interest costs has been an important factor beyond the significant improvement in the bottom lines of the corporates over the past few years and, in turn, in corporate savings and corporate investment.

9.5 CONCLUDING OBSERVATIONS

This brief survey of monetary policy transmission in India suggests that monetary policy impulses impact upon output and prices through interest rates and exchange rate movements in addition to the traditional monetary and credit aggregates. It is necessary, however, to take note of a few caveats. First, the transmission lags are surrounded by a great deal of uncertainty. In view of the ongoing structural changes in the real sector as well as financial innovations, the precise lags may differ in each business cycle. Second, the period covered in this chapter was also marked by heightened volatility in the international economy, including developments such as the series of financial crises beginning with the Asian crisis. Third, the period under study has been marked by sharp reductions in customs duties and increasing trade openness which could have impacted upon the transmission process. The 1990s were also witness to global disinflation. Overall, the period has been one of substantial ongoing changes in various spheres of the Indian economy as well as in its external environment. Fourth, the period of study has been characterized by significant shifts in the monetary policy operating framework from a monetary-targeting framework to a multiple indicator approach. Fifth, the size of interest rate pass-through has increased in recent years, with implications for transmission.

On the whole, the Indian experience highlights the need for emerging market economies to allow greater flexibility in exchange rates, but the authorities can also benefit from the capacity to intervene in foreign exchange markets in view of the volatility observed in international capital flows. Therefore, there is a need to maintain an adequate level of foreign exchange reserves, and this in turn both enables and constrains the conduct of monetary policy. A key lesson is that flexibility and pragmatism are required in the management of the exchange rate and monetary policy in developing countries, rather than adherence to strict theoretical rules.

NOTE

* The assistance of Sanjay Hansda, Muneesh Kapur and Indranil Bhattacharya in preparing this paper is gratefully acknowledged. This is a revised and abridged version of Rakesh Mohan's paper presented at the BIS and published in the document BIS Papers No. 35, 'Transmission Mechanism for Monetary Policy in Emerging Market Economies', January 2008.

REFERENCES

Bank for International Settlements (BIS) (2007), 'Triennial Central Bank Survey: Foreign Exchange and Derivatives Market Activity in 2007', December.

Bernanke, B. and M. Gertler (1995), 'Inside the Black Box: the Credit Channel of Monetary Policy Transmission', *Journal of Economic Perspectives*, **9** (4), pp. 27–48.

Mohan, Rakesh (2004), 'Orderly Global Economic Recovery: Are Exchange Rate Adjustments Effective Any More?', *Reserve Bank of India Bulletin*, April, pp. 429–32.

Mohan, Rakesh (2005), 'Communications in Central Banks: A Perspective', *Reserve Bank of India Bulletin*, October, pp. 911–19.

Mohan, Rakesh (2006a), 'Coping with Liquidity Management in India: Practitioner's View', *Reserve Bank of India Bulletin*, April, pp. 333–44.

Mohan, Rakesh (2006b), 'Evolution of Central Banking in India', *Reserve Bank of India Bulletin*, June, pp. 127–43.

Mohan, Rakesh (2006c), 'Monetary Policy and Exchange Rate Frameworks: The Indian Experience', *Reserve Bank of India Bulletin*, June, pp. 693–705.

Mohan, Rakesh (2008), 'Monetary Transmission Policy in India', in BIS Papers No. 35, 'Transmisson Mechanism for Monetary Policy in Emerging Market Economies', January, pp. 259–307.

Nag, A. and A. Das (2002), 'Credit Growth and Response to Capital Requirements: Evidence from Indian Public Sector Banks', *Economic and Political Weekly*, 10 August, pp. 3361–8.

Pandit, B.L., A. Mittal, M. Roy and S. Ghosh (2006), 'Transmission of Monetary Policy and the Bank Lending Channel: Analysis and Evidence for India', Development Research Group Study No. 25, Reserve Bank of India.

Poole, W. (1970), 'Optimal Choice of Monetary Policy Instrument in a Simple Stochastic Macro Model', *Quarterly Journal of Economics*, **84** (2), pp. 197–216.

Reddy, Y.V. (2001), 'Communications Policy of the Reserve Bank of India', *Reserve Bank of India Bulletin*, September, pp. 1077–83.

Reddy, Y.V. (2006), 'Central Bank Communications: Some Random Thoughts', *Reserve Bank of India Bulletin*, January, pp. 229–32.

Reserve Bank of India (RBI) (2001), 'Report of the Expert Committee to Review the System of Administered Interest Rates and Other Related Issues', Chairman: Y.V. Reddy, September.

Reserve Bank of India (RBI) (2002), 'Report on Currency and Finance 2000–01', January, Mumbai.

Reserve Bank of India (RBI) (2004a), 'Report of the Advisory Committee to Advise on the Administered Interest Rates and Rationalisation of Saving Instruments', Chairman: Dr Rakesh Mohan, RBI, July.

Reserve Bank of India (RBI) (2004b), *Report on Currency and Finance, 2003–04*, December.

10. Inflation targeting and exchange rate: notes on Brazil's experience

Paulo Vieira da Cunha, Daniela Silva Pires and Wenersamy Ramos de Alcântara

10.1 INTRODUCTION

In 2004, the Central Bank of Brazil (Banco Central do Brasil, henceforth BCB) introduced a program of sterilized interventions in the foreign exchange market, in effect to July 2008. Reserves increased by US$864 million in 2005, US$32.04 billion in 2006, US$94.5 billion in 2007, and US$15.19 billion by July 2008.[1] The primary aim of the program is to accumulate precautionary reserves to buttress the credibility and increase the resilience of the macroeconomic regime. The secondary aim is to reduce exchange rate volatility by acting in anticipation of what the BCB knows to be relatively large and atypical market performance.

The policy of sterilized interventions does not aim to influence the level of the exchange rate. Nevertheless, the build-up of reserves – and the overall steady decrease in net external liabilities of the public sector – reduces the perception of country risk. Thus, indirectly, given the market's positive reaction to strengthened fundamentals, an outcome of the policy has been an increase in foreign investment, notably foreign direct investment (FDI), and greater capital inflows. The BCB's stated goals and practice in its interventions differ markedly from those of other recent intervention experiences, for example China and even Colombia, where there has been an explicit aim to influence the level of the exchange rate. The contrast with Colombia, as examined by Kamil (2008), is illustrative. Undoubtedly, in Brazil as well, the level and trend of the exchange rate affect inflation, both directly and through the channel of expectations. Quite clearly, this influences monetary policy. However, it is not the case that the program of reserves accumulation changed (or responded to) the policies, procedures and day-to-day management of the inflation-targeting regime.

The question remains, however, about the impact of the interventions on the level and trend of the exchange rate. One side of the story is that the

Brazilian real (BRL) appreciated significantly from 2005, not only against the US dollar but also in trade-weighted terms. Moreover, the path of the real's appreciation follows closely that of Brazil's own mix of commodity prices. On the other hand, the very size and velocity of the accumulation process raise doubts about the program's ultimate impact. The fact that the BCB accumulated almost US$200 billion in reserves in the three years to early 2008 has helped the BCB defray political charges of insensitiveness to the effects of the large nominal and real appreciation on the tradable sectors. Causality is difficult to infer. Perhaps the BRL would have appreciated further without the interventions.

In this chapter, we summarize Brazil's inflation-targeting experience and link it to the program of reserves accumulation. Sections 10.2 to 10.4 summarize the experience and sections 10.5 to 10.7 discuss why, in our view, the program of reserves accumulation has not interfered with or affected the working of the inflation-targeting exercise.

10.2 ANTECEDENTS: INFLATION TARGETING WITH EXTERNAL AND FISCAL VULNERABILITIES

Despite the debt crises and the sudden retreat of foreign capital in the early 1980s, the Brazilian government continued its import-substitution policy aiming at increasingly autarkic growth. To maintain the trade surplus needed, the authorities strengthened the permanent daily 'mini-devaluations' regime (a crawling peg) to target a fixed real exchange rate. The initial depreciation of the currency produced a large increase in the value of the external debt in domestic currency and in imports prices, which, together with the destabilization of inflation expectations given the endogenous price of foreign exchange, pressed inflation and generated a widespread backward-looking indexation. In the period between 1981 and 1993, temporary regimes of exchange rate and price controls, including one external and one domestic debt default, unsuccessfully attempted to curb inflation.

In June 1994, the Brazilian government put in place the Real Plan, which brought inflation down to one-digit levels in less than three years. The plan had a critical preadjustment phase, which reduced the short-term fiscal deficit and balanced the budget. Meanwhile, the external tide had turned with the debt rescheduling under the Brady Plan.

In contrast to other critically destabilized economies, in Brazil, indexation substituted for dollarization as the de facto monetary instrument.[2] Thus, to break the inflationary inertia the economy had to be 'de-indexed' without breaking pre-existing contracts, causing an immediate lack of credibility, or freezing the pre-reform pattern of relative prices, engendering an unsustainable set of input–output relations. The plan used a new unit account (URV) to 'liquefy' contractual indexation clauses without violating market mechanisms required for the adjustment in relative prices.[3] Six months before the introduction of the new currency, all prices began to be quoted both in the legal tender and in URVs. The aim was a gradual convergence of contracts and expectations. In July, the URV converted into Real, which began valued at par with the US dollar.

In short, the Real Plan used two overlapping nominal anchors. A monetary program, based on quantitative benchmarks for the expansion of high-powered money, anchored the evolution of aggregate demand. The exchange rate anchored prices through an asymmetric float regime: the real could float downwards against the US currency inside a band where the ceiling was set at parity. In parallel, new measures allowed free convertibility, secured by the BCB's high level of foreign reserves, and further liberalization in trade and capital accounts.

In the event, the external side of the program soon showed signs of misalignment. The reversal in the fiscal regime led to fiscal and external deficits, aggregate demand expansion and an overnight rate increase. The following currency appreciation, together with eschewing unpopular expenditure cuts, drove the authorities[4] first to adopt informal bands in October 1994, maintained through auctions (buying at R$ 0.83/US$ and selling at R$ 0.86 /US$), and then, after the Mexican crisis, in April 1995, to reintroduce the bands formally with an implicit crawling peg. Nevertheless, the regime of bands with implicit crawling peg was equally helpless in promoting external adjustment and, in due time, the regime collapsed.

In retrospect, and with the advantage of hindsight, the fatal flaw in the design seems clear. Confidence in policy, a preannounced crawl, and high interest rates to maintain price stability encouraged external borrowing. Capital inflows with very low inflation and progressively lower activity levels (given tight monetary policy) led to a sustained appreciation of the real exchange rate and to current account deficits. These, in turn, reinforced the option for high interest rates to attract external funding – notwithstanding indications of rapidly diminishing domestic demand and the dangerous impact of the added interest burden on the stock of public debt. The fiscal stance was too loose to anchor expectations of a sustainable path for the debt–GDP ratio. Market assessment of creditworthiness deteriorated; and the result would be, eventually, a new cycle of increases in the interest rate with the attendant negative dynamic.

In the midst of a presidential election, in November 1998, the G7 agreed on a large, although ineffective, emergency funding program. On 13 January 1999, the BCB abandoned the peg and announced a new exchange rate band that proved to be unsustainable. Further defense of the band was by then pointless, and on 18 January the BCB introduced the float.

In March 1999, Armínio Fraga assumed the helm of the BCB and brought to the job much-needed new credibility. On 1 July, he announced the new platform that would govern macroeconomic policy to this date: a nascent yet effective inflation-targeting (IT) regime supported by the float and anchored by a reformulated and credible fiscal rule, a straightforward application of what Taylor has called 'the new Holy Trinity'.[5] Because the economy was in recession and the external support program provided enough ammunition to discourage new speculative attacks (hence, a redoubled overshooting of the currency) inflation did not explode and was soon effectively anchored by the new regime.

In the adopted framework, the National Monetary Committee (CMN) – formed by the Finance Minister, the Planning Minister and the BCB's Governor – sets inflation targets and tolerance intervals. The BCB, as the monetary policy conductor, is accountable for achieving the target. The Monetary Policy Committee (COPOM), whose members are the Governor and Deputy Governors, decides the level of the policy rate (so-called SELIC rate) needed to achieve the target, but additional actions such as changes in the banks' reserve requirements could be taken. The target is met whenever the observed accumulated inflation during each calendar year falls within the tolerance interval. If target is not reached, the Governor has to send an open letter to the Finance Minister with justifications, measures to bring inflation back to the target and the expected timing to do so. The COPOM meets eight times per year to set the policy rate and decisions are announced immediately after the meeting, usually followed by a press release. The committee's minutes are released with an eight-day lag and, additionally, the Inflation Report with the inflation forecasts on different scenarios is published quarterly. (See Bevilaqua et al., 2007; Minella et al., 2002.)

On 6 June, the CMN set targets for inflation in 1999 (8 percent), 2000 (6 percent) and 2001 (4 percent), with a ± 2 percent tolerance interval. The COPOM increased the policy rate by 600 bp (basis points) to 45 percent per year. Meanwhile, to render credible its promises to deliver the primary surplus required and bring down the public debt–GDP ratio, the government imposed new taxes and announced spending cuts. Although the landmark Fiscal Responsibility Law was not approved until January 2000, the government's commitment to this legislation improved the credibility of its fiscal adjustment.

At issue was the threat of fiscal dominance. As in the canonical model, the interaction of three real variables (the real interest rate, the real growth rate and the ratio of debt to GDP) and an important expectations variable (the exchange rate) governed the dynamics of the Brazilian public debt. Given that it had overshot, it was reasonable to expect an appreciation of the exchange rate. The expectations gain would be of short duration, however. Moreover, the real focus was aimed at inflation and thus precluded a stimulus to activity. In this case, the 'heavy lifting' of adjustment had to come from the fiscal side and, in the event, it was so.

Perhaps this helps to explain why, despite widespread uncertainty, the IT framework soon proved effective. On annual basis, consumer price (IPCA) inflation rates declined from 8.6 percent in 1999 to 5.3 percent in 2000. The shift to a float also produced a long-lasting devaluation of the exchange rate and brought back the surplus to the trade account.

In June 2000, the CMN fixed an ambitious target for inflation 30 months ahead, 3.5 percent at end-2002 with a ±2 percent tolerance interval. However, pressures on the exchange rate – driven by a domestic energy shortage, the crisis of Argentina in 2001 (which generated some level of contagion in the confidence of the Brazilian economy and pressures on the exchange rate) and signs of US growth deceleration – and on public and administered prices, led the annual rate to 7.7 percent by the end of 2001.

Monetary policy was set to minimize the secondary effects of these shocks, but was powerless, and did not attempt to eliminate the impact of the shocks. The COPOM interrupted the previously downward trend. Inflation was contained; however, the shocks themselves increased the inflation rate measured at the end of 2001.

In January 2002, the BCB's Governor wrote an open letter to the Finance Ministry to account for the breach in the target. At the time, the COPOM estimated that in the absence of the shocks, 2001 inflation would have measured 4.3 percent. The shocks seemed exceptional and, as the year began in 2002, the COPOM began to implement a measured loosening of policy.

10.3 2002–05: CRISIS, OVERSHOOTING AND REGAINING CREDIBILITY

At the end of the first quarter of 2002, global risk aversion indexes started to deteriorate, prices of emerging market bonds fell, and prices fell even more for Brazilian securities. The underlying reason was the presidential campaign; the market feared that the election of left-wing candidate Luiz

Inácio Lula da Silva would jeopardize the government commitment to the fiscal rule.

In the maelstrom of events in the second half of the year, the monetary policy lost credibility, expectations deteriorated and volatility increased. For the BCB, at issue was the dilemma of what to do to protect the real economy from the transitory effects of the exchange rate volatility. The authorities decided to use the balance sheet to offer a foreign currency hedge to the corporate sector. From April to December 2002, the stock of US dollar-linked debt including swaps increased from 29 percent to 37 percent of the National Treasury and BCB debt.

This strategy had the side-effect of deepening the confidence crisis, putting in motion an explosive dynamic of positive feedbacks between expectations of exchange rate devaluation and increases in the value of public debt, now largely denominated in foreign currency. This threatened the capacity (and the willingness) of the BCB to act with sufficient force to keep inflation under control. Arguably, in those circumstances, increases in the policy rate would destabilize expectations and the stock of public debt even further.

As the confidence in the outturn for 2002 declined, capital inflows stopped and the BCB suffered severe reserve losses, the exchange rates suddenly overshot, and the interbank overnight interest rate market all but collapsed, with annualized rates reaching 30 percent. Nevertheless, the COPOM took extraordinary measures to contain inflation expectations that were deteriorating dangerously, including an unscheduled meeting in October to increase the policy rate to 21 percent. By the year end, inflation reached 12.5 percent.

The fears, though, were unfounded. In November 2002 the new administration acted promptly to establish the basis for sound macro policy and to avoid the hindering of its own political prospects. The new political coalition approved a draconian budget for 2003 and new higher targets for the primary fiscal surplus – 4.25 percent of gross domestic product (GDP) in 2003, 4.5 percent in 2004 and 4.25 percent in 2005.

In due course, the administration would name a powerful and prudent Minister of Finance, a BCB Governor drawn from conservative banking circles, and generally work to re-establish the credibility of the inflation targeting regime.

Since inflation in 2002 breached the band ceiling, the BCB sent another open letter to the Ministry of Finance reaffirming its commitment to IT, and proposed an 'adjusted target' to conduct monetary policy. It asked the CMN for, and received from it, midpoint targets of 8.5 percent for 2003, 5.5 percent for 2004 and 4.5 percent for 2005, with tolerance margins of ±2.5 percent. It is important to note that throughout the political turmoil and transition the BCB's staff and its technical work continued untouched and unchanged, and the integrity of its surveys was never questioned. This continuity and confidence played an important part in restoring the credibility of policy.

Finally by May 2003 inflation expectations started to recede, and continued to converge to targets, allowing the COPOM to ease the cycle. The new administration signaled its approval by supporting a CMN vote for further reductions in the inflation target for 2005: 4.5 percent, with a ±2.5 percent margin. The credentials of the new administration were established. There were new challenges to the IT policy, even though these were not as daunting as the previous ones, but instead of undermining the IT policy, they just managed to reinforce IT credibility.

In 2004, for example, the committee indicated a growing concern with two interrelated trends. First, the inertial elements in inflation would not allow inflation to converge as quickly as expected to the midpoint of the target. Second, the pick-up in domestic demand that began at end-2003 accelerated to a faster pace and had already utilized available excess capacity. Given very low levels of investment, the mismatch between current and envisaged demand threatened future inflation. Accordingly, at a September 2004 meeting, the committee announced that it would pursue informally an 'intermediate' midpoint target set at 5.1 percent in 2005, with more upward space to accommodate inertial inflation, and start to implement a process of interest rate tightening to reduce the pressure on capacity. The policy rate accumulated a total of 475 bp increase until May 2005, reaching 19.75 percent.

It is important to note that by now the monetary policy had become far simpler. It was generally accepted, and transparent to all, that inflation was the single objective of interest rate policy: one objective and one instrument. Changes in the interest rate were aimed at inflation, not the capital account or the exchange rate. At the time, the interest rate increases coincided with a significant appreciation of the exchange rate, partly the expected reversal of overshooting in asset markets, and partly the delayed real response in trade to the previous trend in the exchange rate. There was no contemporaneous cause and effect. The response to monetary policy was a successful retrenchment in inflation expectations back to the midpoint of the target.

Trends in 2004 and 2005 showed that a bounty of international liquidity was a major factor in improving the country's external sustainability. Lower global risk aversion and improving stability led to a quick catch-up in the demand for Brazilian assets. The BCB began to rebuild its reserves and, more importantly, to manage actively its stock of outstanding exchange rate risk hedge instruments to the private sector. The primary aim was to reduce and eventually eliminate all non-real liability exposure, to strengthen its balance sheet and render interest rate policy more effective; and there was also an important secondary aim.

As it is well known, China's entry into the global trading system accelerated the trend of expansion in the volume of global trade. This growth coincided with the end of the very long 'J-curve' effect of trade reforms in the 1990s. Projects long in gestation finally came into fruition, for example the emergence of a powerful agro-business sector and the technological overhaul of important industries such as steel, aviation and high-tech. It also coincided with a significant downward shift in the real exchange rate and, last but not least, with the explosion in commodity prices.

Exports and export revenues surged with the favorable impact of the terms of trade and, combined with the large net inflows in the capital account, produced a surfeit of foreign resources that could easily have overwhelmed the absorptive capacity of the economy at that time, notably in 2004–05, and so policy moved to pre-empt this outcome.

The exchange rate absorbed the price effect of the bounty, as noted. The income effect, however, was largely sterilized. Partial sterilization of the income flows was a deliberate policy: it was the intended outcome. Together with the Treasury, the BCB embarked on a program to use the inflows to reduce the public sector external liabilities, funding it from primary fiscal revenues and by issuing domestic debt to produce the desired debt reduction and currency transformation. The BCB transformed its long real position in the local derivatives markets into a large, long US dollar position (paying the SELIC rate and receiving the variation in the US dollar). It allowed its stock of dollar-denominated domestic debt to mature and helped the Treasury to reduce its own stock of foreign currency-linked domestic debt. The net effect transformed the Brazilian public sector into a net creditor in foreign exchange. The implication is that heretofore a depreciation of the currency produced a capital gain to the balance sheet.

In the 1999, 2001 and 2002 crises many investors were convinced that an external shock would be fatal, eventually, for the incipient IT regime. This could happen thanks to at least two different and potentially explosive positive feedback dynamics: between currency depreciation and reduced creditworthiness of a debtor with foreign indexed debt; and between an increase in interest rates and a decrease of creditworthiness of a debtor with an increasing debt–GDP ratio. In the first case, adverse selection can lead to a sudden stop of capital flows when the country needs them most. In the later case, the so called 'fiscal dominance' can render IT policy useless: higher interest rates, originally intended to control inflation, may in fact cause currency depreciation given an environment of increasing debt–GDP ratio, which in turn can ultimately cause more inflation.

None of this happened in Brazil in 2003, and the probability of happening again became much smaller after 2005, for it became clear thereafter that the external vulnerability was significantly smaller; and there was a correlating improvement in the fiscal position, though not to the same extent or with a corresponding structural change. Driven by large increases in revenues, thus without a reduction in expenditure, the Treasury delivered consistently large primary surpluses that caused the debt–GDP ratio to fall from 46.5 percent in December 2005 to 41.2 percent in April 2008.

In sum, external and fiscal vulnerabilities fell significantly in a period of less than three years. The cumulative effect was strong enough to cut through the destabilizing feedback mechanism between the exchange rate and the public debt. Currently given the public sector's net creditor position in foreign currency, a depreciation of the exchange rate reduces the borrowing requirements and is a net gain for the public sector's balance sheet. In the following years, the continued and consistent reduction in the inflation risk premium allowed bond markets to flourish, maturities to increase and the emergence of a liquid long-term yield curve for fixed-rate papers. This gave the Treasury the possibility of funding itself in domestic currency. Admittedly, in the Brazilian context, the curse of 'original sin' – that is, the lack of confidence in currencies issued by less developed economies, preventing those economies from issuing international debt in local currency – was never quite the specter that it was in smaller economies, 'condemned to borrow in currencies stronger than their own' (Calvo and Reinhart, 2000) (See Figure 10.1.)

10.4 2005–06: REDUCED RISK PREMIA, TERMS OF TRADE AND THE REAL EXCHANGE RATE

By the third quarter of 2005 it was apparent that the combination of the still very favorable external scenario with an increasingly positive domestic scenario built on stronger credibility in policy – monetary policy, in particular – would allow for faster non-inflationary growth. The COPOM voted to start on a cautious path of gradual policy adjustment.

Although the major shift in the currency composition of the liabilities of the public sector took place from 2004 to 2006, BCB's program of reserves accumulation continued through 2007 and to July 2008. Indeed, the pace of reserves accumulation accelerated in 2006 and 2007. Particularly in 2007, a wave of initial public offerings (IPOs) brought in large amounts of foreign investment that underscored the build-up in reserves.

We do not yet understand the consequence of this growth in reserves, its impact on exchange rates and monetary policy. Indeed, it may be too

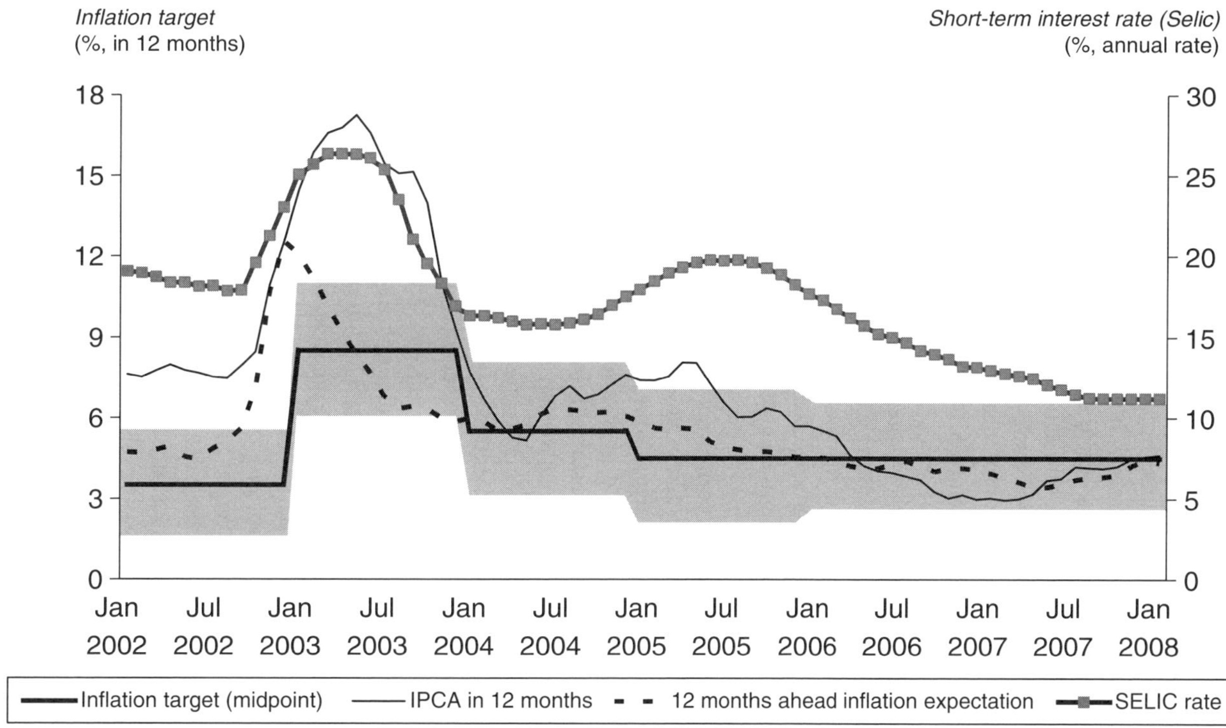

Source: BCB monthly data.

Figure 10.1 Inflation target and interest rate

soon to attempt to try to understand it. However, the simple-minded view that the build-up led to a depreciation of the currency and enfeebled, if not vitiated, monetary policy is incorrect. The BCB did not embark in complicated games to drive up interest rates to attract capital inflows and appreciate the currency to maintain inflation under control, only to then buy reserves to bring the currency down. It did not have a 'fear of floating', nor was it attempting to 'control' the real exchange rate, which would be, anyway, a futile task in a non-indexed economy. Instead, it took the exchange rate to be what it was and set interest rate policy strictly in line with its single-minded aim to steer future inflation close to the midpoint of the target without punishing the economy with unwarranted output volatility.

It is beyond the scope of this chapter to attempt to prove these propositions or even to assemble convincing econometric evidence in that direction. Our aim is to reframe the discussion somewhat by introducing some relevant additional considerations. To begin with, it is useful to understand how the exchange rate market works in Brazil, and how the BCB intervenes.

History imposes a curious contradiction on the institutions that support the foreign exchange regime. Since March 2005, there is a single floating-rate exchange market. However, the laws and regulations governing this market embed mechanisms and procedures designed to protect the level of international reserves and sustain various forms of fixed or quasi-fixed exchange regimes. Much has been done recently to simplify and modernize the system, but important legal and regulatory challenges remain.[6]

An important legacy is segmentation. The regulatory regime discriminates between foreign exchange transactions that affect the balance of payments (the 'primary market') and all other transactions in the market (the 'secondary market') which include, *inter alia*, the interbank market, exchange-traded or over-the-counter (OTC) derivatives, financial operations in national currency but with exchange rate risk,[7] and some government securities. Participation in the interbank market is limited to institutions explicitly authorized by the BCB. Every operation in the primary market must have an authorized financial institution or a broker as one of the counterparts: individuals, corporations and investors, residents or not, cannot transact directly among themselves. Moreover, all onshore spot operations with foreign currency trade through the BCB's proprietary trading platform (SISBACEN).

There are no such limitations in trading US dollar futures on the local derivatives exchange (Brazilian Mercantile and Futures Exchange, BM&F). Thus, while a reduced number of participants in the spot market limit its liquidity, there is usually abundant liquidity in the futures market.

On a typical trading day, the volume in the BM&F is roughly six times larger than in the spot market. According to data provided by the BM&F, the average daily volume of US dollar future contracts traded in 2006 was US$10.4 billion (208 000 contracts), while the volume in the spot market was only US$1.7 billion. In 2007 (first and second quarters) the corresponding numbers were US$16.1 billion (323 000 contracts) and US$2.8 billion, respectively.

Given this staggering difference, it is reasonable to argue that the exchange rate is actually cleared in the futures market, the price then transmitted to the spot. And there are, indeed, several studies that document this link. Garcia and Urban (2005), for example, used Granger causality tests to show that prices in the future market precede prices in the spot market.

Another indication comes from the widely disseminated use of the *casado* (matched, married or covered) contract. A dealer agrees to buy dollars in the spot market and to sell the same amount in dollar futures at the BM&F. The price (quote) of the contract is the difference between the future and spot dollar prices in local currency, usually for the next maturing future contract.

If prices clear in the spot market and there is no arbitrage, the future price of a dollar expressed in reals is:

$$USD_{future} = USD_{spot} \frac{(1 + r_d)^{\frac{T_{business}}{252}}}{\left(1 + r_{f,local} \times \dfrac{T}{360}\right)}$$

where r_d is the domestic interest rate for the period $T_{business}$[8] and $r_{f,local}$ is the foreign interest rate for the period T in 30/360 day count convention. We add the *local* subscript because the onshore funding cost in foreign currency (the local funding cost or *cupom cambial*) is not equal to the foreign interest rate. In addition to the tax wedge between the two markets, local and offshore, there is a cost to the risk of doing the transaction onshore, including the risk of very low liquidity in the local spot market.[9]

Thus:

$$r_{f,local} = r_f + taxes + LP$$

where LP is a liquidity premium[10] and r_f is the foreign interest rate.[11]

Note that the *cupom cambial* is defined in terms of the future dollar price and the corresponding quotation for the *casado* contract:

$$r_{f,local} = \left(\left(\frac{USD_{future} - casado}{USD_{future}} \right) \times (1 + r_d)^{\frac{T_{\text{business}}}{252}} - 1 \right) \times \frac{360}{T}.$$

Since most spot operations are in fact part of a *casado* contract the price that is cleared by the market is the future dollar price USD_{future} with the corresponding *cupom cambial*, $r_{f,local}$.[12] We can express the spot price set in the *casado* market as:[13]

$$USD_{spot} = USD_{future} \frac{\left(1 + r_{f,local} \times \frac{T}{360}\right)}{(1 + r_d)^{\frac{T_{\text{business}}}{252}}}.$$

The expression above defines the contract price for the spot part of the *casado* operation, taking into consideration the value of the USD_{future} quoted in the futures market. Suggestively, market participants call it the 'fair' spot price.

Lack of liquidity in the spot market is the most important reason behind the widespread use of *casado* contracts. In a normal business day, a dealer would be reluctant to buy or sell a large fully hedged dollar position in the interbank market. It may be difficult for him to close the counterpart in the spot market.[14] If he agrees to the deal, he will have to carry the exchange rate risk for as long as it takes to close the position – and the risk may be especially high in volatile markets. Therefore, dealers prefer to do *casado* operations in which they bear only the risk of changes in $r_{f,local}$. This risk is smaller than the risk of changes in USD_{spot}.[15] Purely spot operations are consequently quite small.

In this context, interventions by the BCB help dealers close positions and reduce exchange rate risks and, because they deal in the spot and not in the futures market, it is not clear that they directly influence the trend in the exchange rate.[16] Well-timed interventions play a critical role in reducing volatility in the market. In the period from 2001 to 2004, with hardly any intervention, the exchange rate was quite volatile. There was practically no change in the reserves position. In contrast, during the periods highlighted by the ellipses volatility is lower and reserve accumulation greater. Particularly after 2004, the surpluses in the current account coincide with larger interventions.[17] The pace of interventions followed the rhythm of the current account, smoothing rather than changing the trend in the nominal exchange rate.

Moreover, it may be that the impact of the intervention falls mainly in the *cupom cambial*. If it is true that at the time of the auction the foreign interest rate and the future dollar price are given, and because the BCB will always act to keep the overnight domestic (policy) rate unchanged at the target, the adjusting variable would be the onshore foreign rate; that is, the *cupom cambial*.

Consider that the foreign interest rate is fixed. Since the intervention would normally apply pressure for the future price to drop, but in this case does not, it follows that the onshore foreign rate (the *cupom cambial*) would increase to re-equilibrate the market. If this were the case, the implication would be that rather than inducing depreciation, the intervention could well lead to appreciation. The reason being that a higher onshore rate caused simply by the intervention, thus with all other things unchanged, creates an arbitrage possibility, though not a risk-free one. The inducement is there for dealers to bring capital onshore to arbitrage the difference in rates, overnight. The critical assumption is the dealer's ability to adjust his foreign exchange position as needed the following day. And, indeed, starting at end-2005 interventions have taken place on a daily basis, with few interruptions. (See Figure 10.2.)

10.5 INTERVENTIONS AND EXCHANGE RATE

There is by now an extensive and well-known literature on the effects of sterilized interventions. Most of it pertains to more advanced economies and the results are mixed.[18] Preannounced and coordinated interventions (for example Japan–US) did produce shifts in bilateral exchange rates. However, the impacts were invariably small and ephemeral and, curiously, led to greater exchange rate volatility. Fatum and Hutchison (2005) find an interesting and suggestive result: when the Bank of Japan increased the frequency of unilateral interventions to a daily rate in the first months of 2003, as Brazil did starting in 2006, the JPY–US$ rate actually appreciated further.[19]

Kamil (2008) reviews the evidence for the emerging market economies. Findings from sparse evidence for Chile, the Czech Republic, Mexico and Turkey indicate that interventions usually have no significant effect, and when significant, the impact is unimportant to the exchange rate. His study for Colombia, based on daily data on interventions by the monetary authority, suggests a more nuanced answer. For inflation targeting, the impact of the intervention depends on the business cycle. It may work when the economy is slack, inflation is under control and the monetary authority is reducing the policy rate. However, as the economy approaches full capacity, the commitment to an inflation target limits the scope for lowering interest rates, and low upward exchange rate flexibility provides

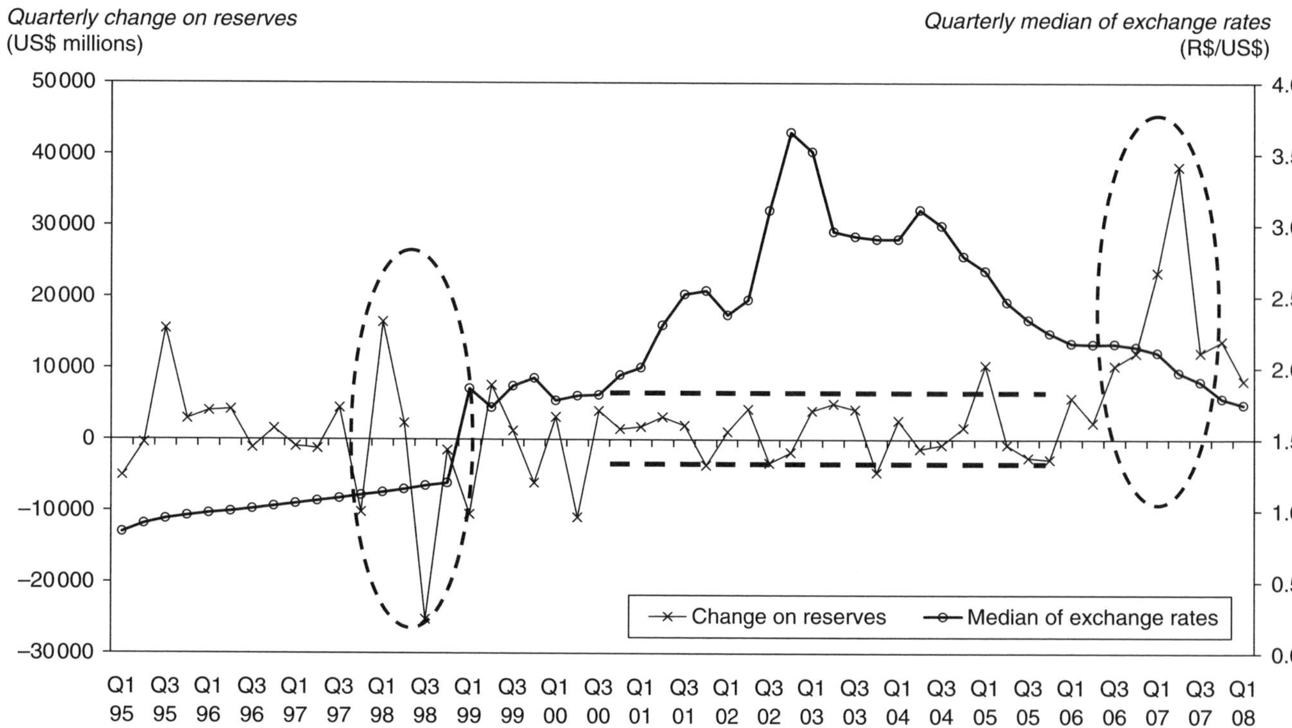

Source: BCB.

Figure 10.2 *Reserves purchases and the exchange rate*

incentives for carry trade and leveraged bets on the currency through derivatives markets. Thus, while a government committed to reducing the value of its currency has, in theory, a large supply of 'ammunition' (that is, printing money to buy reserves), the inflation objective can in practice become a binding constraint that puts a limit on the amount of foreign reserves that a central bank can accumulate.

In the case of the BCB, this dilemma may now be starting, but it was not binding in the period of most intense reserves accumulation (from Q3/2006 to Q4/2007) when the BCB was reducing rates, inflation was below the midpoint of the target, and the economy operated below full capacity. This is a critical point. During the period of its policy-induced build-up of reserves, at least up until July 2008, the BCB did not have to face conflicting objectives between monetary policy and intervention, although this may change in the future. Rather, the BCB remained tightly focused on the inflation objective and did not consider, at any moment, the scope and pace of intervention as a relevant variable in setting the policy rate. We discuss this further in the next section.

10.6 EXCHANGE RATE TRANSMISSION AND MONETARY POLICY

Since their inception in the early 1990s, IT regimes have coexisted with a variety of exchange rate regimes ranging from the 'purest' of floats, as in New Zealand, the UK or more recently Chile, to managed pegs, such as Chile in its transition to the float, to partially dollarized economies such as Peru. The question is not the regime but the peculiarities of the transmission mechanism. Consider the standard small open economy IT model of Ball (1999) or Svensson (2000).

A rise in the domestic interest rate leads in the short term to nominal and real exchange rate appreciation, and this helps reduce inflation. One channel is the favorable impact of a more appreciated exchange rate on tradable prices. Another is the expected (though not always observed) contractionary impact of a more appreciated real exchange rate on demand (a drop in net exports), hence output and prices.

Thus, a key question for an IT central bank is whether to use the exchange rate as an intervening variable for controlling inflation. Does it explicitly attempt to influence the exchange rate? Alternatively, does it target only inflation and allow the nominal exchange rate to adjust to its own expectations influenced, primarily, by the outlook for real variables and capital inflows, given the expected trend of inflation (and the implied expected path of the policy interest rate)?

The latter has been the option espoused by the BCB (except for some short critical periods in 2002 when the confidence crisis destabilized the foreign exchange market). The COPOM works within the framework of a conventional IT regime where the final target is inflation and the operational instrument is the interest rate. In the implicit economic model, the movement in the real exchange rate reflects longer-term expectations about the real economy, country risk and creditworthiness. The movement in the nominal exchange rate reflects, in addition, short-term volatile expectations of capital flows (shocks) and, crucially, the expected path of inflation; hence, implicitly, that of monetary policy.

The pace and extent of intervention does not change the basic operating rule. The exchange rate is the first line of defense against external shocks, and monetary policy addresses their expected impact on inflation. If the shock is thought to be exogenous, monetary policy targets only the secondary (propagating) effects of the spike in the exchange rate. Though there is a concern with the volatility, and how this may influence inflation expectations – quantitatively, the most important variable in the estimated price–price expectations–augmented Phillip's curve – there is no concern with the level of the exchange rate per se.

Of course, expectations about future levels of the exchange rate affect the forecasts of inflation; and they are, in turn, the guideline for policy decisions. However, concerns about the path of inflation reflect on the interest rate decision, not on decisions about the speed and extent of intervention. The COPOM's ability to influence expenditure decisions, and hence market prices, is critically dependent on its ability to influence market expectations regarding the future path of its policy rate, and not merely its current level. To this aim, it focuses on the near future, concentrating on the span of 6–18 months ahead when its actions are likely to have the main effects. The analysis of the recent experience is important, to be sure, but mainly as an indication of possible mistakes made in the forecasting tools. Ultimately, the COPOM responds to changes in inflation expectations, and because its aim is to influence these expectations, it attempts to act pre-emptively, anticipating the market's own change in expectations. The tools are the policy and communication actions. Interventions do not play a role in the IT framework and are quite independent from it.

Having regained its credibility in 2003, and strengthened it further through the tightening episode from September 2004 to May 2005, monetary policy achieved considerable success in the management of expectations. Expectations converged to targets and inflation uncertainty declined in a substantial and seemingly durable way. Anchored inflation expectations freed the COPOM from concerns about the path of the nominal exchange rate, reinforcing the endogenous channel between inflation forecasts and forecasts of the nominal exchange rate, given the expected path of the real exchange rate. The predictions from theory proved to be correct: as credibility increased, the pass-through from the exchange rate to prices decreased (Taylor, 2000).

Correa and Minella (2006) review the empirical evidence and examine some empirical nonlinear mechanisms in the pass-through for the period 1995–2005. They find that the exchange rate pass-through is not statistically different from zero in the regime when the economy is well below its capacity, whereas it is around 9 percent when economic activity is higher. They also find that the pass-through varies with the size of the exchange rate change; quarter-on-quarter changes of 2.1 percent or larger have a significantly larger pass-through, whereas small changes in the exchange rate 'do not have a statistically significant effect' (Correa and Minella, 2006). Finally, they find that in periods of low volatility, as measured by the standard deviation of the exchange rate within each quarter, the estimated pass-through is not statistically significant.

These findings suggest that, during the period of intense reserves accumulation, the link between intervention and inflation was moot if not irrelevant. The economy was operating below capacity; with few exceptions, exchange rate volatility was low by historical standards.[20]

Currency appreciation did play a role in the disinflationary process of 2005–07. Disinflation started with tradable prices and then extended to non-tradables, including services. The expected transmission mechanisms were at work and, undoubtedly, the positive outlook for the nominal exchange rate helped firm up positive inflation expectations. In arguing against the presumed possible role of intervention as an intervening variable in the Brazilian IT regime, we are not trying to reinvent the usual transmission mechanisms. Rather, we are suggesting that, as far as the COPOM was concerned, these effects were perceived as consequences of its policies and, more broadly, of the overall improvement in macroeconomic fundamentals. They were expected and intended results – of the pursuit of a credible inflation target, not of a particular level of the exchange rate.

10.7 SUMMING UP

We have attempted to build two arguments. The first is that reserves accumulation through intervention did not distort the implementation of the IT regime, where the final target is inflation and the operational instrument is the interest rate. The second argument is that intervention may not have changed the longer-term trajectory of the exchange rate. Far from hindering the effectiveness of the transmission mechanisms under IT, exchange rate smoothing through interventions helped reduce the pass-through and make interest rate policy more effective. Moreover, because interventions had a greater impact on liquidity than prices, the structure of the market limited the BCB's ability to influence the level of the exchange rate. Thus, overall, it is more likely that interventions reinforced the trend towards an appreciating currency than otherwise: either through the long-run effects of greater confidence and lower risk that comes with larger reserves or, in the short run, through the incentive for carry trades and/or arbitraging the difference between onshore and offshore dollar interest rates. Our arguments are suggestive and far from definitive. Not being conclusive, they point the way to needed future empirical work.

NOTES

1. On 17 March 2008.
2. Bruno (1993).
3. The scheme was originally proposed by Arida and Resende (1984 [1985]), and nicknamed 'the Larida proposal' by Dornbusch (1985).
4. As this was not a formal policy, no law or regulation was issued by one specific authority. The decision was, though, executed by the Central Bank of Brazil. Nevertheless, monetary and foreign exchange related policies are of the competence of the National Monetary Council, which, by October 1994, included the Ministry of Finance, the Ministry of Planning, Budget and Management, and the President of the Central Bank of Brazil.
5. Taylor (2001).
6. BCB (2008).
7. From the point of view of a resident.
8. In Brazil, domestic interest rates are usually expressed as effective annual interest rates, given a day count convention that considers only business days, assuming that the year has 252 business days.
9. If a bank needs foreign currency for some period, buying and selling it on the spot market may be equivalent to obtaining a local loan in foreign currency, as both selling and buying can be committed together with prices set in advance. If there is some sort of shortage on the spot market, the liquidity premium will sum up to the total cost of obtaining this kind of funding.
10. A credit risk premium could also be considered, but most operations either have some sort of collateral or have the settlement guaranteed by the clearing house of the BM&F. Things could change in the case of distress episodes in the financial system, but for the purposes of this argument the credit risk spread is assumed to be negligible.
11. The usual benchmark is the US dollar LIBOR rate.
12. An informal survey among some of the largest players in the Brazilian interbank market estimated that the share of *casado* operations in the total volume of spot contracts may be as high as 80 percent.
13. As r_f, r_d and presumably USD_{future} are cleared in independent markets, and taxes are known, the *casado* market actually reveals the price of the liquidity premium in the spot market.
14. Even though brokers can intermediate operations, they are not allowed to maintain any position in US dollars.
15. While USD_{spot} embeds the high volatility of international capital flows, the volatility in $r_{f,local}$ is associated with the LIBOR rate volatility and the liquidity premium volatility.

16. The BCB only intervenes through auctions and always fully sterilizes its interventions. It announces and conducts auctions through a proprietary electronic system with 17 authorized dealers chosen on a rotating basis from the list of authorized institutions to deal in foreign exchange. Though sell, buy and spread auctions are possible, since 2004 there have been only buy auctions.
17. Direct and portfolio investments were very important in the reserves growth in 2007, but trade balance surpluses were the determinant factor that allowed for interventions. Although there has been a growth in exports, the domestic demand has fuelled the imports growth. This trend resulted in a current account deficit of $4.4 billion in March 2008 compared with a surplus of $235 million in the same month of 2007, which represents 0.71 percent of GDP in 12 months, still a small and manageable amount.
18. Sarno and Taylor (2001), Dominguez (2006).
19. Fatum and Hutchison (2005) find that Japan's intervention policy in the period 2003–04 had no significant impact on the JPY–US$ exchange rate during the period. They attribute these results to the predictability of intervention and to a high degree of sterilization.
20. Since January 2006, there has been a reduction in the exchange rate historical volatility. The quarter-over-quarter percentage change in the exchange rate was above 2.1 percent in May and July 2006. Further, the quarter-over-quarter change in the exchange rate was above the quarter average change during five months in 2006 (May, July, September, October and November) and three months in 2007 (July, August and December). In 2008, as expected, the quarter-over-quarter change was above the quarter average in January and March.

REFERENCES

Arida, P. and A. Lara Resende (1984), 'Inertial Inflation and Monetary Reform in Brazil', Paper prepared for the conference on Inflation and Indexation of the Institute of International Economics, Washington, DC, 6–8 December; Published as Working Paper No. 85, Department of Economics PUC-RIO (Brazil), January 1985; available at http://ideas.repec.org/p/rio/texdis/85.html.

Ball, L. (1999), 'Aggregate Demand and Long-run Unemployment', in *Brookings Papers on Economic Activity*, **2**, pp. 189–251.

Banco Central do Brasil (BCB) (2008), *Streamlining Foreign Exchange*.

Bevilaqua, A., M. Mesquita and A. Minella (2007), 'Brazil: Taming Inflation Expectations', BCB working paper 129.

Bruno, M. (1993), 'Inflation and Growth in an Integrated Approach', NBER Working Paper 4422, National Bureau of Economic Research.

Calvo, G. and C. Reinhart (2002), 'Fear of Floating', National Bureau of Economic Research, Working Paper No. 7993.

Correa, A. and A. Minella (2006), 'Nonlinear Mechanisms of the Exchange Rate Pass-Through: A Phillips Curve Model with Threshold for Brazil', BCB Working Paper 122.

Dominguez, K. (2006), 'When Do Central Bank Interventions Influence Intra-Daily and Longer-Term Exchange Rate Movements?', *Journal of International Money and Finance*, **25**, pp. 1051–71.

Dornbusch, R. (1984), 'The Larida Proposal: Comment', in J. Williamson (ed.), *Inflation and Indexation*, Washington, DC: Institute of International Economics, pp. 45–55.

Fatum, R., and M. Hutchison (2004), *Foreign Exchange Intervention and Monetary Policy in Japan, 2003–04*, available at SSRN: http://ssrn.com/abstract=642862.
Garcia, M. and F. Urban (2005), 'O mercado interbancário de câmbio no Brasil', in D. Gleizer (ed.), *Aprimorando o mercado de câmbio brasileiro*, São Paolo: Bolsa de Mercadorias & Futuros.
Kamil, H. (2008), 'Is Central Bank Intervention Effective Under Inflation Targeting Regimes? The Case of Colombia', IMF Working Paper 88.
Minella, A., P. Freitas, I. Goldfajn and M. Muinhos (2002), 'Inflation Targeting in Brazil: Lessons and Challenges', BCB Working Paper 53.
Sarno, L. and M. Taylor (2001), 'Official Intervention in the Foreign Exchange Market: Is it Effective and, if so, How Does it Work?', *Journal of Economic Literature*, **39** (3), pp. 839–68.
Svensson, L. (2000), 'Open-Economy Inflation Targeting', NBER Working Paper 6545, National Bureau of Economic Research.
Taylor, John B. (2000), 'Using Monetary Policy Rules in Emerging Market Economies', Stanford University.
Taylor, John B. (2001), 'The Role of Exchange Rates in Monetary Policy Rules', *American Economic Review, Papers and Proceedings*, **91** (2), pp. 263–7.

11. Czech experience with inflation targeting

Luděk Niedermayer

In January 1998, the Czech National Bank (CNB) joined the small club of central banks using inflation targeting as their monetary policy framework.

The main proponents of that regime in the 1990s were the central banks of New Zealand, Canada and the UK. At that time, and even some years later, many academics, central bankers and institutions (including the International Monetary Fund, IMF) were skeptical about how suitable and feasible such a framework was for central banks of emerging or catching-up economies. From that point of view, the decision of the Czech National Bank has provoked many of these concerns, as the adoption of inflation targeting took place after very short preparation, soon after a currency crisis and at a time of big uncertainty about the future path of the economy.

11.1 ECONOMIC SITUATION IN THE EARLY 1990s

Up to November 1989, the former Czechoslovakia was a rigid, centrally planed communist country. In January 1991, liberal economic reform started, with the liberalization of prices, foreign trade and capital flows, privatization and the introduction of a fixed exchange regime. The fixed exchange rate (against a foreign trade weighed basket) was central to monetary policy, despite the formal setting of monetary targets, until the beginning of 1996. In practice, the fixed exchange rate was also the key element of the entire macroeconomic policy, and the nominal anchor of the stabilization process.

In February 1996, after sweeping liberalization of capital flows related to Organisation for Economic Co-operation and Development (OECD) membership and after huge capital inflows as the consequence of positive interest rate differentials and an improvement in the credibility of the country, the fluctuation band around the exchange rate of +/− 7.5 percent was established.

In May 1997, as a result of spillover from the South East Asia currency crises, the Czech currency (koruna – CZK) came under pressure and after a short period of central bank intervention, depreciation from 17 CZK per German Deutschmark (DM) to 19.5 CZK,[1] the fluctuation band was abandoned.[2] The combination of open financial account, fixed exchange rate regime and independent monetary policy proved to be impossible even for the emerging Czech economy.

During the rest of 1997, the main task of the central bank was to stabilize the currency market and avoid a big depreciation of the currency that would cause a jump in inflation. At the same time, a new monetary policy scheme had to be adopted.

11.2 INFLATION TARGETING AS A 'WAY OUT'

The macroeconomic conditions at that time were as follows: the fixed exchange rate regime helped to stabilize prices; inflation was in the high single digits with a relatively substantial proportion of volatile items in the consumer price index (CPI) basket;[3] growth was picking up but there were big concerns about sustainability.[4] Fiscal policy had started to face problems of growing deficits. The financial markets were developing gradually, which allowed the CNB to give up direct instruments of monetary policy for standard, indirect market tools, and there was consensus that open market operations (two-week repo tenders) should be the monetary policy tool.

All possible options were considered. A fixed or semi-fixed currency regime was not a feasible option, as the currency had been forced off its previous peg and such a regime would immediately suffer low credibility.

The monetary targeting option was seriously examined, too. The fact that the Czech koruna was floating in theory made this regime increasingly feasible. Nevertheless, the ability both to meet an intermediate target in the form of money supply growth[5] and to achieve the ultimate target – stability of prices – via fulfilment of this target was far from certain.

Given such a situation, consideration of the inflation-targeting regime not just as the policy choice of an increasing number of central banks but as the explicit resignation of an intermediate target and focus on the ultimate goal of the central banks – price stability – was an attractive option. After intensive discussion at the CNB, inflation targeting finally became its choice at the end of 1997.

11.3 PHASE ONE: EARLY DAYS OF CNB INFLATION TARGETING

In the late 1990s, the attempts of emerging market countries to adopt this regime were just beginning (for example Israel since 1992), and so the

CNB faced many problems related to the implementation of this framework in transforming the economy.

The economy was changing both structurally and institutionally. The availability of short time series of data combined with the fact that they were describing the Czech economy of the past made forecasting inflation, which is the key point of an inflation-targeting regime, a very difficult if not impossible task.

On top of that, the domestic economy, just recovering from the currency crisis in 1997, was facing many uncertainties in monetary policy (whether the currency stabilization would be successful), the real economy (an expected slowdown of growth) and the financial sector (the first clear signs of the banking sector problems).

11.3.1 Inflation Target

In such an environment the CNB had to take two key decisions on its new framework. The first was the choice of the index to be targeted, and the second decision was the level of the target.

One of the key concerns was the unclear impact of the changes in regulated prices and taxes. Prices of some government-regulated commodities were still very low (housing, transport) and an increase in taxes on fuel, alcohol and tobacco was obligatory after entry to the European Union (EU). But strategy of these changes important for inflation was unclear, and was following more political than economic considerations.

So it seemed reasonable to adjust the consumer price index (CPI) for changes in regulated prices or tax changes. A new index, called net inflation (NI), was created and calculated by the Czech Statistical Office.[6]

The CNB was aware of the risk of a lower than desired impact of such an artificial and narrow index on the expectations of economic agents. The issue of the expected difference of the two indices was addressed in the press release announcing the new monetary regime.[7]

Given the very uncertain conditions in the Czech economy at that time, it was decided to go for a target range for inflation for the end of the period one and three years ahead. The size of the range was one percentage point for the short period and two percentage points for the longer one, reflecting the greater uncertainty. The declining slope of the midpoints, 6 percent and 4.5 percent respectively, was a demonstration of the disinflation commitment of the CNB, and its goal to use the inflation-targeting regime to achieve a gradual decline of inflation to low levels.[8]

The history of the inflation targets set by the CNB can be seen in Figure 11.1. The bold black targets refer to NI targets and grey to the CPI targets used later.

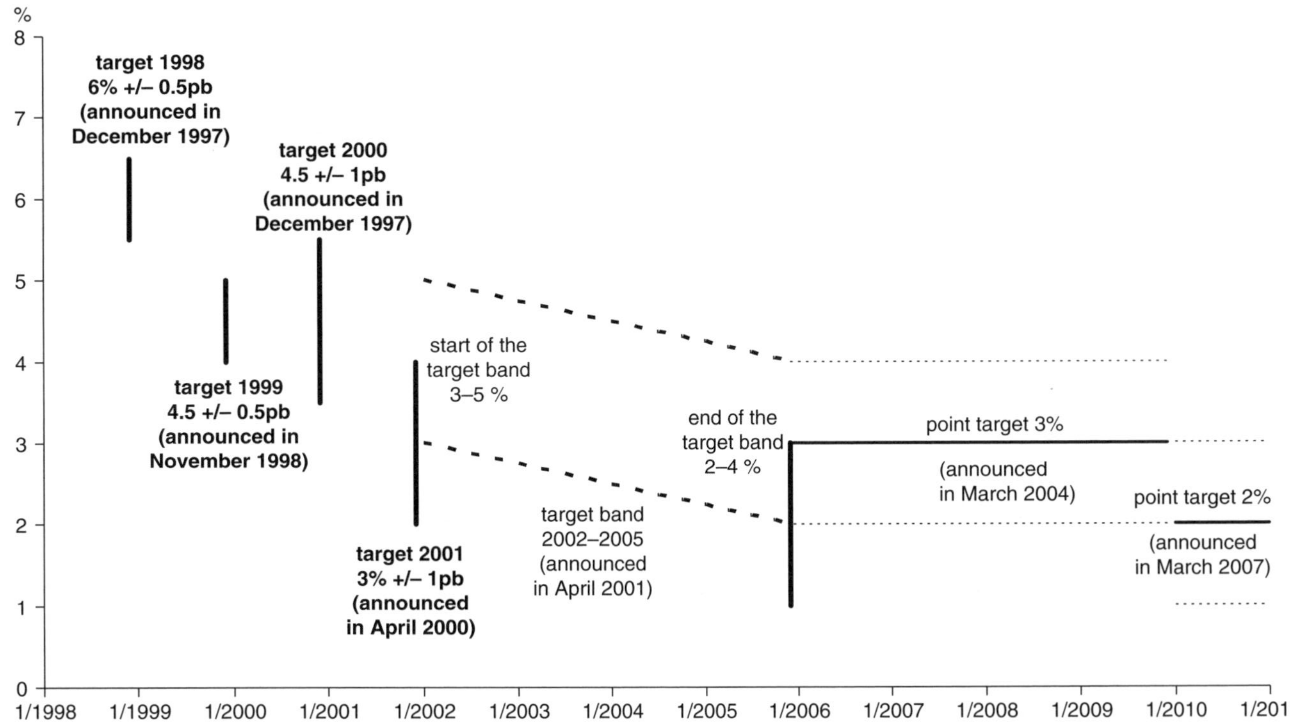

Source: CNB.

Figure 11.1 History of the CNB inflation targets

11.3.2 Communication Issues

Under an inflation-targeting regime, central banks often communicate extensively about their monetary policy in order to influence (in a positive sense) the expectations of agents in the economy and so make the achievement of the target easier and less costly. Expectations in line with central bank targets often allow central banks to use lower interest rates and so, in some circumstances, the loss of output, especially during a reduction in inflation, could be lower.

High transparency was not new to the CNB. Due to the large participation of foreign market players, there was always increased demand for central bank transparency and during the 1990s, the CNB became one of the most open central banks in the region.

With the adoption of the new framework, it was decided to publish quarterly Inflation Reports published always after the board meeting at which the new forecast was approved. The Inflation Report did include a less specific inflation forecast and the report focused on the explanation of the monetary decisions of the CNB in the given quarter.

After each of the 12 monetary meetings held yearly, minutes of the meeting in the form of a relatively detailed description of the discussion were published.[9] It took ten days for the minutes to appear on the CNB website in Czech and English versions, approved by the Bank board. However, neither the individual votes of Bank board members nor the split of their votes were disclosed in that phase.

Internally, monetary policy analyses relied on a rather diversified set of tools including very simple macroeconomic models, or econometric relations only. A lot of expert judgment was used. In the early years of inflation targeting, the forecast was elaborated as 'conditional', assuming no change in interest rates. In practice, as the consequence of the know-how used, the role of monetary policy in the forecast was rather limited.

From 1999, the CNB started to stress 'covenants' in its communications. There were a set of major factors outside the authority of the CNB, external shocks in particular, the impact of which would be that the CNB was likely to miss its inflation target or would not take the necessary action to hit the target in the short horizon. The covenants were made public in January 1999 together with the announcement of the new inflation target for the end of 1999. The set of covenants included, among others, major changes in world prices of raw materials and major deviations of the exchange rate not related to domestic policies.[10]

11.3.3 Challenges to be Coped with in the Early Phase of Inflation Targeting

In practice, the main problem during the early phase of inflation targeting was the state of the economy itself. Inflation, for many years anchored by the fixed exchange rate, was sustained at high single digits.[11] As a consequence of depreciation after the currency crisis, the Czech koruna hit an all-time low against the Deutschmark and inflation expectations rose. At the same time, real economic activity went down significantly, and after 4 percent gross domestic product (GDP) growth in 1996, the economy contracted in the next two years (-0.7 percent and -0.8 percent). The turnaround of the exchange rate (see Appendix 11.2) and the slowdown of the economy, caused mainly by structural problems combined with the decline of some imported prices, caused undershooting of the inflation targets in the first years, despite the gradual easing of monetary policy (see section 11.6).

From many points of view, the Czech economy was at a turning point in 1996–97 and it created a very difficult environment for monetary policymakers, irrespective of their choice of monetary policy framework.

11.4 PHASE TWO: REFINING THE FRAMEWORK OF INFLATION TARGETING

In the following years, CNB had to deal with more standard issues concerning the design of its inflation-targeting framework. These included internal procedures, mainly the technology of inflation forecasting, and improvements in the area of communication.

11.4.1 Inflation Forecasts

The forecasting process in inflation targeting regime is a key part of the monetary policy framework. In that respect, the early system was too fragmented and judgment based. Consequently, it was not able to meet increasing expectations, commensurable to the inflation-targeting frameworks of the developed countries, both from inside and outside the bank.

In the late 1990s the monetary division of the CNB started to work on a small, aggregated macroeconomic model called QPM.[12] It brought many benefits, particularly more transparency, a clear role for monetary policy and extensive possibilities for testing different scenarios.

After several months of using dual forecasts in the CNB internal papers, the Bank board approved a move towards a more model-based forecast in

July 2002. The first three quarters covered in the forecast were still based on the expert forecast, reflecting belief in the dominance of simple, short-term methods and expert judgment in the near term. After that period, the model became the key factor in setting the forecast. Among both groups – the modeling team and the more empirical-based short-term forecasters – there was ongoing discussion about the view on the economy, in order to base the final product – the CNB inflation forecast – on a sound and consistent description of the development of the economy.

The communication of the forecast to the public was also developing. Before 2001, at the end of the inflation report there was always a chapter on 'factors of inflation' followed by a short description of expected net inflation and the CPI. The reports in 2001 included a chart called 'Conditional forecast', showing forecasts of net inflation and the CPI in the following two years on the assumption of no change in interest rates. Later, more information on expected economic activity (GDP) was also provided.

In July 2002, the forecast was changed to an unconditional forecast; that is, with endogenous interest rates. The main reason was to predict 'the most likely development of the economy'. This was made feasible by the shift to the model-based forecast with a role for active monetary via interest rate rule embedded in the model. Publication of unconditional forecasts created demand for disclosure of the interest trajectory consistent with the forecast. In this respect the CNB opted for non-specific verbal descriptions of the direction of interest rates consistent with the forecast.

11.4.2 Adjustment to the Inflation Targets

The most important changes in the inflation-targeting framework took place in April 2001, when the new target was set. Net inflation was replaced by the CPI and the end-of-period target was replaced by the downward-sloping band (see Figure 11.2). In the announcement there was specific reference to the size of expected impact of the price deregulation and of tax changes.[13]

After learning from the not very persuasive experience with the use of the covenants with regard to the fulfilment of the target, there was no rationale for communicating items *ex ante*.

In the course of the first five years of inflation targeting in the Czech Republic, this type of framework gained more popularity among the central bankers from both developed and developing economies.[14] The CNB framework was at that time part of the mainstream approach to implementing inflation targeting, as regards both internal procedures and transparency.

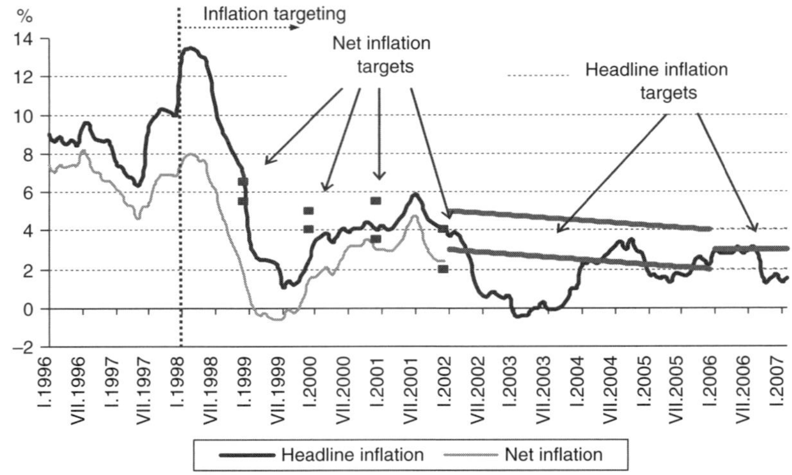

Source: CNB.

Figure 11.2 Inflation targets and actual inflation

11.5 PHASE THREE: CURRENT STAGE OF INFLATION TARGETING

In March 2004, the CNB switched from downward-sloping bands for the inflation target to a horizontal target of 3 percent with a 'tolerance' band of +/−1 percentage point. Following the Bank board decision in March 2007, the level of that target will be lowered to 2 percent, effective from January 2010.

In 2008 CNB also extended its communication on monetary policy decisions. The trajectory of interest rates consistent with the forecast is published in the form of a fan chart. Further, not only the result of voting (introduced in the minutes from 2001), but also the votes of individual board members are provided in the minutes of the meeting and published seven days after the meeting. By taking those two decisions, the CNB further enhanced its position as one of the most open inflation-targeting central banks.

Important changes were taking place in the forecasting technique, too. In January 2004 the expert-based short-term forecast was cut down to only the first quarter, while over the rest of the horizon the QPM model plays the key role. A more substantial change was under way in 2008, with the preparation of a new dynamic stochastic general equilibrium (DSG) model. In early 2008 the DSG model was used just for the shadow forecast, but it is intended to play a key role in future.

11.6 POLICY PROCEDURES AND INVOLVEMENT OF THE MANAGEMENT

When the inflation-targeting framework was approved, it was clear that this choice would have an impact on the CNB's internal procedures and external communications as well. As for internal procedures, there was no change in the structure of the monetary meetings, which were held every month[15] (on the last Thursday). After presentations from the staff, there was internal discussion by the Bank board,[16] followed by voting. A new forecast is presented quarterly and 'intra-meetings' are used to assess whether the developments in the economy are in line with the given forecast.

As the key part of the adopted inflation-targeting regime is the actual inflation forecast, there was a more formalized involvement of the Bank board in the elaboration of the forecast, in particular after the shift towards its more model-based version. A formal schedule of meetings with staff was established in order to promote awareness among board members of the forecast and of its risk. The adoption of the external assumptions (commodity prices and so on) was agreed by the board in advance too, and significant changes to the model, as well as evaluation of the older forecasts were discussed in great detail.

Altogether it takes around one month to prepare a new forecast. There is significant involvement of the Bank board but most of the work is done by the staff. The product is neither a staff forecast nor a Bank board's one. After some discussion, the term 'CNB forecast' was used.

In the course of the inflation-targeting regime, the formalization of the communication policy advanced substantially. Apart from the key publications, that is, minutes of the meeting after each of the monetary meetings and the quarterly Inflation Report, a press conference by the Governor is held after every board monetary meeting[17] and analysts (both domestic and foreign) are addressed at a meeting at the CNB premises in Prague after the release of every Inflation Report. In addition, ad hoc meetings are also organized for the media from time to time.

11.7 RESULTS AND LESSONS LEARNED

Inflation targeting by CNB has brought significant progress towards price stability, though it was less successful with regard to meeting the individual targets. The results can be seen in Figure 11.2.

Several factors contributed to the previously experienced undershooting of the targets:

1. In the period following the currency crisis, the economy slowed down much more than expected and the decline of inflation was fast and deep.
2. After some structural changes materialized within the national economy,[18] its potential growth increased substantially (see Appendix 11.2).
3. Both the CNB and the markets were often surprised by the stronger than expected exchange rate.[19] This development continued when nominal interest rates were lower for the Czech koruna than for most of the world currencies.
4. During the period of fixed exchange rate, prices were at high single digits. Much lower inflation in the later period cannot be attributed only to lower import prices; most likely, stronger competition in the domestic market played its role too.
5. In some periods, the unexpected decline of imported prices of commodities (raw materials, in particular) created downside pressure too.

Figure 11.3 shows the development of the real effective exchange rate. At least two periods of undershooting of the inflation target, in 1998 and 2002, are associated with the substantial appreciation of the currency, not just in absolute terms, but also in the deviation from the trend.

It should be noted that the appreciation of the currency, which in the ten years to 2008 reached around 2.5 percent in real terms annually, does not explain the decline in inflation in comparison with the pre-inflation targeting period of fixed exchange rates, when inflation amounted to around 9 percent per annum in the period 1994–96.

Inflation in the past ten years, which averaged around 3 percent even during times of accelerating growth in the economy, suggests that there were very substantial changes in the economy going on in that period. Despite continuous efforts to calibrate the QPM model better, most forecasts were biased towards higher inflation. Only by 2008 was the calibration leading to more balanced results.

The substantial improvement of CNB know-how allows us to look more closely at its past performance. In 2008, CNB staff prepared several studies assessing performance during the first ten years of inflation targeting. Some of the results can be found in Appendix 11.3.[20]

Given the results, one can argue that while there was significant progress towards price stability, as defined in developed countries, under the inflation-targeting regime in the Czech Republic the outcomes from the point of view of delivering the targeted level of inflation were mixed. From a purely theoretical view, even lower than expected inflation must be considered as failure under this framework.[21]

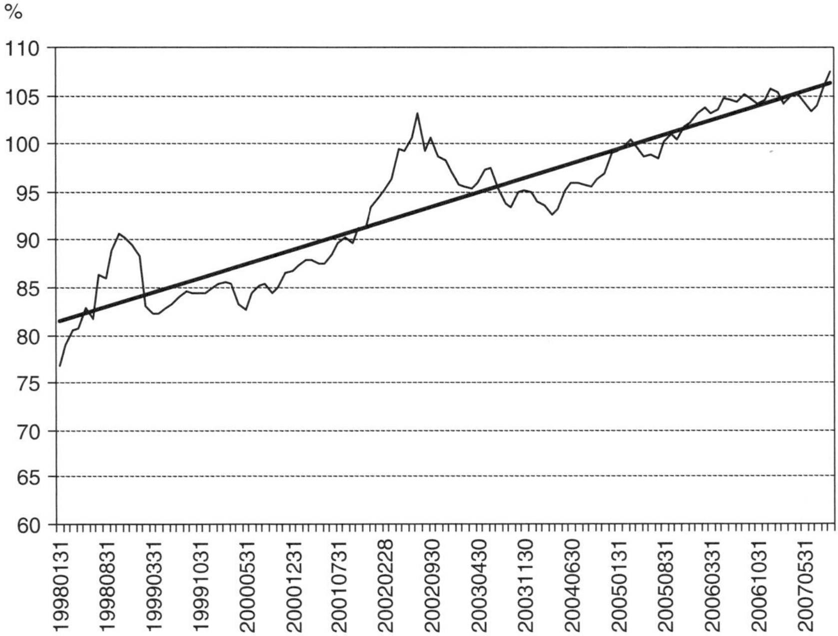

Source: CNB.

Figure 11.3 Real effective exchange rate

One way to assess the negative impact of over-or undershooting is to identify how successful the CNB was from the point of view of influencing inflation expectations, as this channel is one of the key elements of the inflation-targeting framework.

The CNB's regular survey of financial market analysts, firms and households shows that both short- and long-term expectations of analysts are well anchored and partly reflect the undershooting of past inflation targets. Firms' expectations are even less volatile and correspond better to the targets. As for the public, not surprisingly there was always higher volatility, and in 2008 a sharp increase in expectations in reaction to the envisaged price increases due to the approved fiscal reform.[22]

Figure 11.4 shows that both perceived inflation and expected inflation in the Czech Republic, according to the regular European Commission (EC) survey, were low and close to the level achieved by the European Central Bank (ECB) and the Bank of England (BoE).

Despite the difficult and 'non-standard' circumstances surrounding the introduction of an inflation-targeting regime in the Czech Republic, there

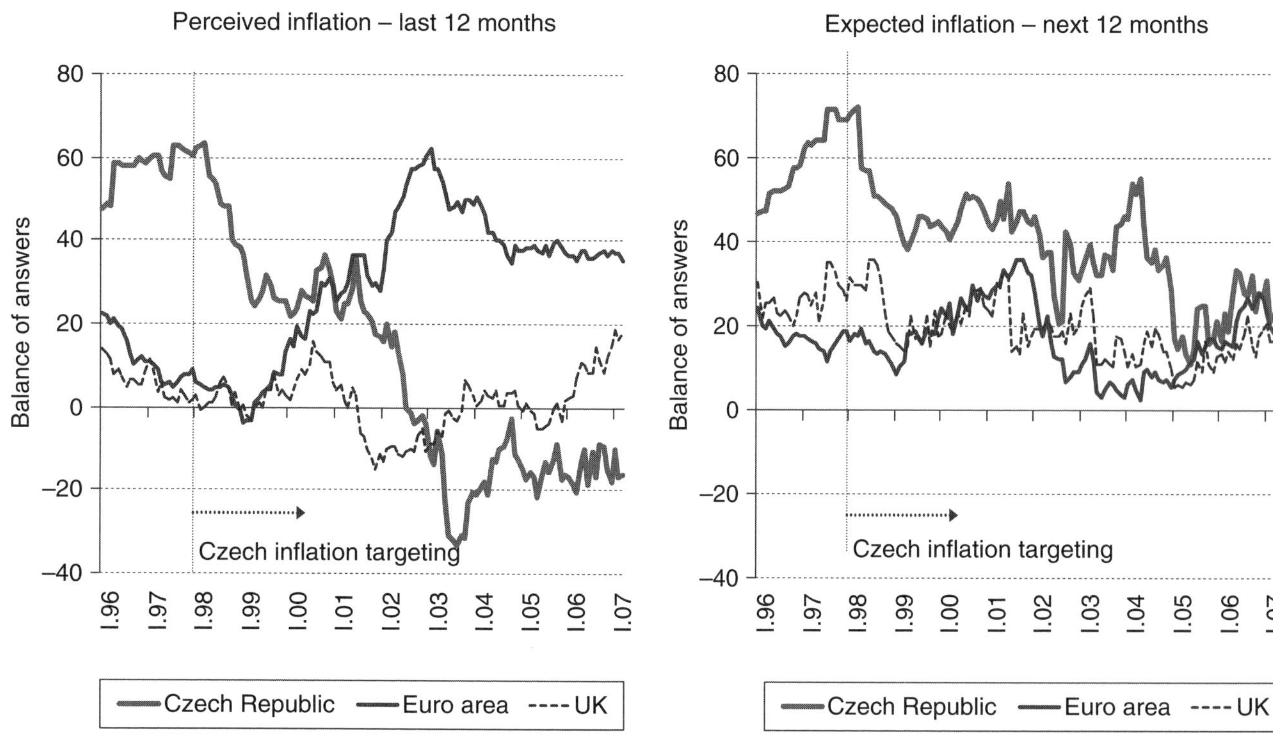

Source: EC survey.

Figure 11.4 Perceived inflation (last 12 months) and Expected inflation (next 12 months)

are undoubtedly positive results from that regime. The main one is the achievement of price stability and inflation levels very similar to developed countries. This allowed the CNB to lower nominal interest rates and thus to contribute to faster growth and the catching-up process of the Czech economy. Internally, there were positive results as well. Transparency of the CNB was further improved and there was substantial progress in internal central bank know-how.

From the point of view of international comparison, the move to inflation targeting was considered to be a risky strategy at the time of the decision. The Czech case showed that inflation targeting is a feasible regime even for developing or transition economies.

APPENDICES

Appendix 11.1: Potential Growth of the Economy

The CNB QPM model is a gap-type model. Consequently, the estimate of the difference between measured GDP growth and potential growth[23] is the key variable for expected inflation. While there are also estimates based on total factor productivity, the main tool for estimations of this parameter is filtering of past data on growth and inflation. That means, with every release of new national accounts, the historical path of the gap, and so potential growth (approximately the difference between change in this gap and actual growth), is recalculated.

Figure 11A.1 shows the assessment in 2008 of the gap for the Czech economy during inflation targeting.

The data show a substantial increase in potential growth mainly since 2003. Its underestimation in the forecasts elaborated at the beginning of the decade could have contributed to the undershooting of the inflation target, as monetary policy was likely more restrictive. Consequently, despite the continuous decline in interest rates, they were still higher than was warranted by the potential growth of the economy, as can be seen in Figure 11A.2.

Appendix 11.2: Exchange Rate under Inflation Targeting

Exchange rate fluctuations have played a very important role both in volatility of output (see Figure 11A.1) and inflation. As well as real effective rate fluctuations there were also very big swings in nominal (and real) exchange rate with respect to the euro (see Figure 11.3). Since the ratio of GDP to export of goods and services in the Czech economy reached

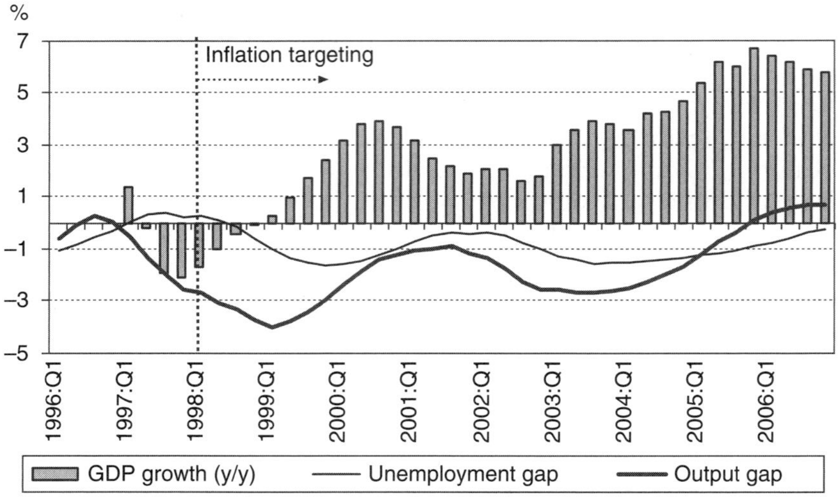

Source: CNB.

Figure 11A.1 Estimated output gap for the Czech economy

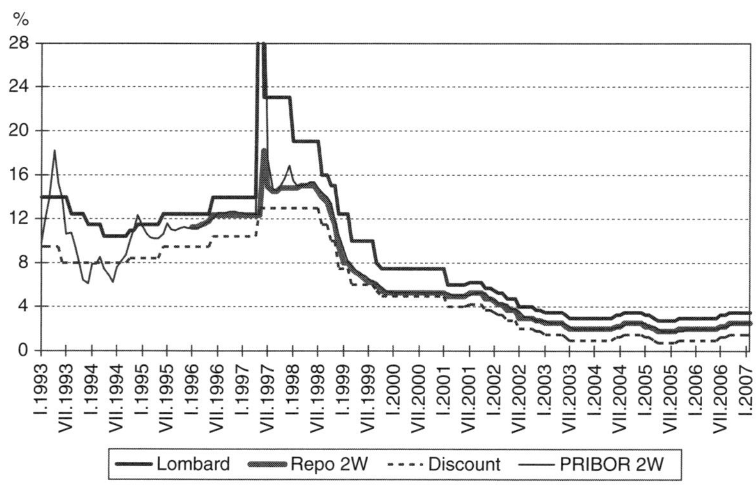

Source: CNB.

Figure 11A.2 Short-term interest rates

65 percent in 2006,[24] those fluctuations have had considerable impact on economic performance. So it is hardly surprising, that in some periods, the CNB has paid great attention to exchange rate movements and has even occasionally intervened in the market.[25]

There were three periods of intervention under the inflation-targeting regime (large in early 1998 and 2002, and smaller between 1999 and 2000). They all took place at times of high volatility and faster-than-trend appreciation of the currency. Nevertheless, the efficiency of the interventions was always difficult to measure and from 2003 onwards the CNB has been in practice skeptical about using this tool.[26] But it does not mean that the CNB would be ready to give it up publicly.

Appendix 11.3: Some Findings on CNB Inflation Targeting Performance

During the first phase of inflation targeting (1998–2001), there was the largest deviation from the target of around 6 pp (percentage points).[27] It took place during the very fast decline in inflation between mid-1998 and 1999. The key reason behind the deviation was an incorrect assessment of the economic conditions prevailing at the beginning of the inflation-targeting regime, when the Czech economy was just recovering from a currency crisis and was heading for a period of long stagnation and substantial structural changes.

Analytically, there were several causes of the undershooting. The dramatic decline of many international prices[28] (oil, food) occurred while the forecasting framework of CNB was too rigid to react early enough to changing conditions in the domestic as well as the world economy.

Later on, the CNB used the faster than originally intended decline of prices for 'opportunistic disinflation', as it would be more costly for the economy to ease monetary conditions first, to get inflation higher and closer to the target and then tighten again, to follow the down-sloping target path.

In the period of 2002–04, the largest target miss dropped down to 4 pp.[29] Again, external prices played a very important role and many other countries with inflation targets also experienced undershooting. However, the episode of fast and unexpected appreciation of the currency played the key role. At the same time, *ex post* analyses show a higher contribution of the overestimation of the inflation from the expert-based forecast, while the model was often correctly warning on undershooting. As the consequence of this observation, the shift was made between the weight of expert-based short-term forecasting and a more model-based approach in favor of the second approach.[30]

The extent of the undershooting dropped further in the next period to a maximum of around 2 pp.[31] A mixture of factors played a role including volatility of food prices, changes of regulated prices and the implied bias towards higher inflation of the model. In most cases higher-than-expected appreciation contributed to the result. That could hardly be explained by interest rate differentials, as the Czech koruna had mostly negative carry against major currencies. Still, despite the inclination of the board towards a lower interest rate path than that implied by the forecast, inflation was most of the time below the midpoint of the target.

To summarize this observation, the CNB was fairly close to other central banks studied in terms of the time spent inside the targeted zone (50 percent). The key difference is that out of the remaining 50 percent, there was no time when inflation was above the targeted zone.

NOTES

1. Since 1993, when the Czech koruna (CZK) was introduced after the split of Czechoslovakia, the Deutschmark was traded between 17 and 18.5 CZK. From this point of view the events of spring 1997 leading to a relatively small loss of reserves and depreciation of 15 percent could hardly be compared with the South-East Asia currency crises.
2. For more information on the 1997 Czech currency crisis see the paper prepared by the CNB staff shortly after the crisis occurred: Šmídková et al. (1998).
3. Food 24.6 percent, fuel 3.8 percent, regulated prices 17.3 percent.
4. From the macro point, the current account deficit of 8.2 percent in 1996 was close to the tolerance level of the financial markets of that time. Other concerns were related to the corporate governance of companies and, particularly, banks. Also the law enforcement and legal systems were areas of concern.
5. An additional problem was the choice of the concrete aggregate, as different aggregates were showing different developments, especially in the short run.
6. At the time of the creation of the NI, it covered 82 percent of the CPI.
7. 'Although various uncertainties exist about the future range and rate of regulated price adjustments, analyses undertaken with respect to the monetary program, based on the presently expected deregulation rate, show that the year-on-year CPI growth rate will be approx. 2.5 percent higher than the NI. After the deregulation measures have faded away, inflation measured by these two indices will be the same' (CNB Press Release, 1997).
8. The quantification of the appropriate level of inflation for the given stage of the Czech economy was one of the key issues at the time of setting the mentioned targets.
9. All the minutes can be viewed on the CNB website www.cnb.cz. Following the decisions of the Bank board, even the staff papers and recommendations, together with more extensive internal records of the meetings, were made available, with a lag of six years.
10. For precise wording see Inflation Report from January 1999 (CNB 1999).
11. Since 1994, average yearly inflation was 10 percent in 1994, 9.1 percent in 1995, and 8.8 percent in 1996.
12. The model was elaborated with the help of IMF experts. Its description was published by the Czech National Bank in Coats et al. (2003).
13. More details can be found in Annex 1 of Inflation Report from April 2001 (CNB 2001).
14. In recent years, the CNB has provided technical assistance in modeling and inflation targeting to a number of central banks in the region.

15. From 2008, the number of meetings has been reduced to eight.
16. The Bank board consists of seven members appointed by the President of the Republic for the term of six years. They are full-time executives responsible for the management of the bank as well as for the execution of monetary policy.
17. Currently with voice record and presentation available on the CNB website (www.cnb.cz)
18. While in the early years of economic transformation there was no preference of foreign capital (and sometimes even active efforts to create 'domestic capitalism'), later there was an active policy of support for foreign investors in almost all areas of the economy
19. For more information on exchange rate management, see Appendix 11.2.
20. The work has been done in the CNB by the Research Department, chaired by Katerina Šmídková.
21. Though it may be difficult to prove that undershooting is as bad as overshooting, there are some costs related to undershooting of the target. One of them might be that real wages could be set higher than intended during collective bargaining, if the inflation was not reaching expected or targeted level.
22. Since January 2008 there has been a VAT increase from 5 percent to 9 percent (lower bracket), the introduction of new fees in the health care services area and so on.
23. The term 'potential growth' in this context does not refer to capacity utilization, but entirely as the non-inflation accelerating growth.
24. Similar ration for the EU-27 is 56 percent Germany itself accounts for 21 percent of exports.
25. There are several methods of 'interventions'. Apart from 'standard' trading, based on the current market conditions, following the decision of the Bank board the CNB also agreed to buy, for a fee, proceeds from privatizations from the government. Recently, in order to limit growth in foreign exchange (FX) reserves, the CNB also started to sell small amounts of reserves daily.
26. CNB researchers have dedicated their attention to studying the experience of the CNB with FX interventions. There are some papers with the following findings:
    - Geršl and Holub (2006): interventions have probably played a minor role in influencing the short-run ER development at best. They contributed to an increased volatility of the ER, but only to a limited extent.
    - Geršl (2006): the results indicate that interventions by the central bank had only a minor, short-term effect on exchange rates and, to a certain extent, contributed to increased conditional and implied volatility.
    - Disyatat and Galati (2005): Intervention had some (weakly) statistically significant impact on the spot rate and the risk reversal but that impact was small. There was no evidence that intervention had an influence on short-term exchange rate volatility.
    - Égert and Komárek (2006): from mid-1998 to 2002, interventions turn out to be (more) successful in reversing the appreciation trend in the short run and in smoothing the exchange rate at longer horizons up to 60 days. The econometric evidence indicates that koruna sales had a positive relationship with the exchange rate from mid-1998 to 2002.
27. Net inflation target at that time was 6 percent.
28. In this period, seven out of ten central banks used as the reference in our comparison undershoot the target. The sample consists of Hungary, Poland, the eurozone, Sweden, the UK, Canada, Chile, New Zealand and Israel.
29. CPI target just below 4 percent.
30. As mentioned in Section 11.5, since 2004 expert-based forecast is capturing only one quarter of the forecasted period. Nevertheless, there is continuing exchange of views on the short-term development between model team and short-term forecasters.
31. CPI target of 3 percent.

REFERENCES

Coats, Warren L., Douglas Laxton and David Rose (eds) (2003), *The Czech National Bank's Forecasting and Policy Analysis System*, Pragne: Czech National Bank.

Czech National Bank (CNB) (1999), *Inflation Report: January 1999*, available at: http://www.cnb.cz/en/monetary_policy/inflation_reports/1999_january/download/ir_january_1999.pdf.

Czech National Bank (CNB) (2001), *Inflation Report: April 2001*, available at: http://www.cnb.cz/m2export/sites/www.cnb.cz/en/monetary_policy/inflation_reports/2001/2001_april/download/ir_april_2001.pdf.

Disyatat, Piti and Gabriele Galati (2005), 'The Effectiveness of Foreign Exchange Intervention in Emerging Maslut Countries: Evidence from the Czech Koruna', *BIS Working Paper No. 172*, Bank for International Settlements.

Égert, Balazs and Lubos Komárek (2006), 'Foreign Exchange Interventions and Interest Rate Policy in the Czech Republic: Hand in Glove?', *Economic Systems*, **30** (2), pp. 121–40.

Geršl, Adam (2005), 'Testing the Effectiveness of the Czech National Bank's Foreign Exchange Interventions', *Czech Journal of Economics and Finance*, **56** (9–10), pp. 398–415.

Geršl, Adam and Tomáš Holub (2006), 'Foreign Exchange Interventions under Inflation Targeting: The Czech Experience', *Contemporary Economic Policy*, **24** (4), pp. 475–91.

Šmídková, K. et al. (1998), 'Koruna Exchange Rate Turbulence in May 1997', Monetary Policy Division Working Paper No. 2–98, CNB, Pragne.

12. Monetary and fiscal policy mix in Serbia: 2002–07

Diana Dragutinovic

12.1 INTRODUCTION

Striking the right balance in the monetary–fiscal policy mix is difficult at the best of times, not least when implementing an inflation-targeting regime in unstable emerging market conditions, such as those prevailing in Serbia. This chapter presents the thoughts of a monetary policymaker on how to strike this balance against the backdrop of the recent experience in monetary and fiscal developments in Serbia.

The National Bank of Serbia (NBS) adopted inflation targeting as its new monetary policy framework in August 2006, facing difficult starting conditions and many challenges. Inflation targeting was born after the failure of the previous regime, which focused on the real exchange rate and involved periodic exchange rate devaluations, resulting in high inflation as well as a high current account deficit. Inflation targeting was chosen as the only reasonable alternative at the time, despite many challenges in terms of low credibility and weak monetary transmission.

The starting conditions for implementing inflation targeting could hardly have been less favorable. Gaining credibility for the new regime required strenuous efforts given the country's turbulent hyperinflation past, high-inflation expectations and less than full institutional independence. Inflation had to be contained despite weaknesses in monetary transmission stemming from fast exchange rate pass-through, a high degree of real and financial euroization, very shallow money and exchange rate markets, and a high share of regulated prices. Moreover, macroeconomic policy options were constrained by a large negative current account deficit.

In addressing these challenges, the NBS has been implementing a number of elements that support inflation targeting. Short-term interest rates became the key monetary policy instrument in achieving the inflation objectives; the role of foreign exchange (FX) intervention was reduced; and the importance of macroeconomic forecasts and analysis in decision-making has increased. The bank's Inflation Report became the main regular communication vehicle, promoting transparency and accountability of the NBS targets and policies.

So far, the new regime has been a success. Following ambitious inflation targets, inflation has fallen to unprecedented levels, while growth has remained strong. Inflation expectations have declined too and appear stable vis-à-vis temporary inflation disturbances. Short-term money market interest rates have been under the control of the NBS. While the NBS has all but withdrawn from the spot FX market, the exchange rate responded well to movements in the NBS rates and its appreciation played a key role in taming inflation and reaching the 2007 core inflation targets.

Reduced inflation was a hard-won success, but the experience has shown that overcoming the difficulties faced by the emerging markets will require endurance and the coordination of wider macroeconomic policies.

In Serbia, the government does not participate in setting core inflation targets. It also put forward a draft NBS Law compromising the NBS independence in several respects.[1] Without explicit government support, institutional independence of the NBS remains weak. The terms of appointment of the Governor's position are not fixed. Moreover there are uncertainties about the procedures involved in recapitalizing NBS losses arising from massive liquidity sterilization.

Furthermore, after two years of near to balanced budgets, the outlook for fiscal policies in 2008 was less favorable, making the disinflation task of monetary policy even harder. Recent experience has shown that monetary policy can deliver low inflation. The question is, though, whether the inflation gains are sustainable without explicit or implicit support from the government and its policies.

Despite the recent success in taming inflation, the options available to the NBS are limited without good coordination with the government. The flexible exchange rate has been a key pillar of the new regime, but exposed the economy's vulnerability to exchange rate movements, exacerbated by the large current account deficit. With the high exchange rate pass-through, exchange rate appreciation has been the main channel of disinflation. However, the alarmingly high current account deficit has raised the question of the sense and sustainability of such a disinflation strategy. With the interest rate transmission weak in a highly dollarized economy, administrative and direct policy measures have been used to prop up the monetary transmission and also to address the external balance problem. However, without the government addressing the current account issue directly, monetary policy cannot bear the burden of so many objectives, especially given the obstacles it faces when using its instruments.

The following sections give more details on these issues. The next section provides a review of the theory of fiscal and monetary policy coordination, followed by empirical assessments of the monetary and fiscal policy stance in Serbia, and their coordination. The final section concludes.

12.2 UNCERTAIN THEORY OF EVERYTHING

Economic theory provides little guidance on how to choose the appropriate fiscal and monetary mix, especially in an emerging market context. The basic questions on how monetary policy should respond to fiscal policy developments, and what the effects on the economy are and how to measure them, remain largely unresolved. Moreover, the theory often lags actual developments and is shaped by empirical experience.

Such a situation naturally leads to policies based on beliefs and 'rules of thumb'. For instance, central bankers 'believe' fiscal expansions tend to be 'bad' and criticize such policies, while welcoming austerity packages. Looser fiscal policy is typically addressed by a monetary tightening. They also tend to believe that capital and especially infrastructure expenditure is 'better' than social spending and that micro-efficiency of spending public money should be improved. They do so, although in many cases they do not have a precise idea even of how to measure the extent of fiscal expansion.

Such beliefs give rise to rules of thumb that guide the behavior of monetary (and other) policymakers. For instance, the 'golden rule' calls for smoothing of public borrowing over the economic cycle. In booms, governments should only borrow to cover capital (but not current) expenditure. The 'sustainable investment rule' says that the public sector net debt as a proportion of gross domestic product (GDP) should be held constant over the economic cycle at a prudently low level. There are various 'golden' numbers attached to it too. For instance, the net debt should be maintained below 40 percent of GDP over the economic cycle. Other examples are the 60 percent debt to GDP ratio and 3 percent deficit to GDP ratio required by the Maastricht Treaty and the Stability and Growth Pact of the European Union.

Such beliefs and rules no doubt have some theoretical foundations, but they are also shaped by experience to a large extent. Over recent decades, the theory of fiscal and monetary policy mix has gone through turbulent changes that do not seem to go away. As a result, the theory is very vague as concerns measurements and predictions of fiscal policy effects and offers few firm recommendations on macroeconomic policy coordination.

12.2.1 Fiscal Policy and Inflation

The flux in the political economy of fiscal policy originates with the post-Keynesian dilemma about whether fiscal and monetary policies are complements in generating growth and inflation. This question was born in the 1960s during the years when governments actively exploited the short-term inflation–output trade-off. Fiscal and monetary policies were believed to generate complementing demand-side stimuli that (depending on the phase of the economic cycle) produced either more inflation (in booms) or more output (in recessions).

Under the post-Keynesian paradigm, disinflationary monetary policy is impossible if the government runs large spending deficits. Indeed, the response to higher inflation is to restrain domestic demand through either fiscal or monetary policies. Such an approach was applied actively in the 1960s and early 1970s, until the experience of stagflation uncovered the weaknesses in the theory.

The realization that output and inflation cannot both be controlled through demand management led to a pure 'monetarist' view of inflation as well as to supply-side fiscal policies. Under the monetary neutrality paradigm, monetary policy cannot affect real variables in the long term, it only determines inflation and other nominal variables. A trade-off between the two is only possible in the short term. In other words, while the short-run Phillips curve is upward-sloping, the long-run Phillips curve is vertical. Perpetual monetary or fiscal stimulus will only result in higher inflation with no gain to output. Output in the long term, on the other hand, is given by economic fundamentals such as productivity, competitiveness or labor supply growth. Focusing on these supply-side characteristics is the only way for fiscal policy to generate more output in the long term.

The separation of roles between monetary and fiscal policies is still behind our behavior today. For instance, the inflation-targeting regimes in Serbia and elsewhere are based on the notion that inflation is a purely monetary phenomenon. Regardless of whether budgets are in deficit or surplus, inflation will be higher with a looser monetary policy and lower with a tighter monetary policy. The most powerful implication of the separation hypothesis is that monetary policy can deliver lower inflation regardless of the fiscal policy stance. In other words, although fiscal policy has an affect on inflation, it is monetary policy that is ultimately in charge. The question, however, is whether monetary policy is indeed in charge in emerging market economies, many of which have a high share of regulated prices and euroization, and a weak monetary transmission. In those countries, monetary policy is much less capable of dealing with fiscal policy idiosyncrasies than elsewhere.

12.2.2 Fiscal Policy and Output

As the predictions about fiscal policy effects on inflation changed, so did the views about fiscal effects on growth and other economic variables. Fiscal expansion, once considered the generator of growth and the business cycle smoothing tool, was found to crowd out private sector activity and cause current account deficits (twin deficits).

Later, it was fiscal contraction (not expansion) that carried the theoretical debate on how to use fiscal policy in stimulating growth. According to this theory, fiscal surpluses are conducive to higher growth by stimulating national savings and suppressing real interest rates. Fiscal consolidation (the theory of expansionary fiscal contraction) makes rational individuals feel wealthier, reduces interest rates and improves private sector balance sheets, spurring growth and reducing current account deficits. At the same time, fiscal surpluses enable easier monetary policy by pressing down long-term real interest rates.

Most recently, fiscal policy is regarded almost as a 'necessary evil' and the focus is on micro-structure and improving the efficiency of fiscal spending and its composition. Promoting capital spending (for example physical and human capital infrastructure) at the expense of current spending is understood as having long-term positive supply-side effects. For instance, the European Union Structural Funds are designed to work along this dimension. There is also a trend of shifting away from income and labor tax to indirect taxation, reducing the tax burden and increasing the efficiency of the tax system. For instance, flat tax rates have become very popular, especially among emerging market economies, although the theory is again not clear-cut on their benefits. The emerging market economies also increasingly use the micro-structure of fiscal policy as a source of competitive advantage against more developed countries with high tax burdens and opaque tax systems.

Indeed, macroeconomic theory struggles to ascribe fiscal demand policies with any short-term output effects whatsoever. Under so-called Riccardian equivalence, fiscal expansion does not affect economic activity, because the economic agents rationally expect the expansion to be offset by later increases in taxes. This prediction is still the cornerstone of many macroeconomic models used today to advise on policymaking.

Yet, practice and overwhelming evidence suggest that fiscal expansion is potent in generating more output, at least in the short term. Indeed, most policymakers have the notion of positive fiscal multipliers (often greater than 1). Theory can be reconciled with this evidence too, for instance by allowing for government access to lower interest rates than private individuals, or supply-side effects of some of the public expenditure, for example on education or physical infrastructure.

There are two other problems with these theories. First is their unclear empirical support. For instance (see Reynolds, 2001), the US federal budget moved from a deficit to a surplus in 2000, while the current account deteriorated, thus defying the twin deficit theory. Japan had the reverse experience over the same period: its budget surplus vanished, yet the current account surplus was high. Similar contradictions can be found for other theoretical predictions. For instance, the theory of expansionary fiscal contraction has only found robust empirical support among industrialized countries with a high and unsustainable level of public debt. Even then, the means of fiscal consolidation are decisive, as higher taxes and cuts in capital spending are more likely to lead to an economic contraction than an expansion.

Even more controversies surround the empirical effects of fiscal policies in emerging market economies. For instance, while it appears that fiscal consolidation is associated with faster growth in less developed economies, it is not so for countries with more macroeconomic stability, such as Macedonia. This seems to be explained by the low efficiency of public spending and poor governance in very low-income countries. Expenditure composition and the method of financing public deficits also seem to matter. Spending on capital has pro-growth effects, unlike public wages. Domestically financed debt is more contractionary than external financing, probably because of the crowding out of the much more efficient private sector.

The second problem with the fiscal theories is the unclear measurement of the theoretical concepts. For instance, fiscal contraction is sometimes measured using a primary surplus, inflation-adjusted primary surplus, cyclically adjusted surplus or cyclically adjusted surplus less capital expenditure. Various measures of the economic cycle (output gap) are used by different studies. Moreover, different concepts often yield different results.

In summary, there is much confusion about both the qualitative and the quantitative effects of fiscal policy on inflation and the economy. There is little theoretical and empirical consensus on how fiscal policy affects these objectives. Fiscal theories say almost anything about macroeconomic impacts, without conclusive empirical backing.

This confusion stands in contrast to the clear predictions of monetary theory. Inflation is a monetary phenomenon. Unless there is fiscal dominance in terms of monetary financed deficits, fiscal effects on inflation are only short term. Monetary policy should exclusively focus on fostering a low-inflation environment, and not attempt to fine-tune real variables. These predictions are well corroborated by empirical evidence, from both industrialized as well as developing countries.

Despite this confusion, the monetary policymaker still needs proper guidance in responding to fiscal policies, especially in the emerging market context. Should he or she always call for public consolidation and fiscal surplus instead of balanced budgets, or should he or she allow room for stabilizing cyclical governmental policies and investment into human and physical infrastructure? If so, how best to measure these concepts?

12.3 MONETARY POLICY IN SERBIA

Following an ambitious disinflationary program, inflation rates fell below 10 percent in 2007. Indeed core inflation was below the inflation target of 4–8 percent for most of 2007, returning to the band in the final quarter (Figure 12.1). The headline inflation rate declined too from more than 16 percent in May 2006 to less than 6 percent in May 2007, but climbed back over 10 percent by the year end following a rise in regulated prices in the second half of 2007. Despite this rise in inflation, these were historically low levels of inflation in Serbia (Figure 12.2).

Inflation was forecast to come back to single digits in the near future, despite a number of recent and anticipated future inflationary shocks. Surveys of private sector inflation expectations showed these were more stable following the price shocks than the inflation rate itself, suggesting that monetary policy was credible.

Indeed, the medium-term factors that were pulling inflation down in 2007 are still present in 2008 and should help reach the core inflation target band of 3–6 percent by the year end. The real exchange rate has appreciated further since the end of summer 2007, bringing down imported

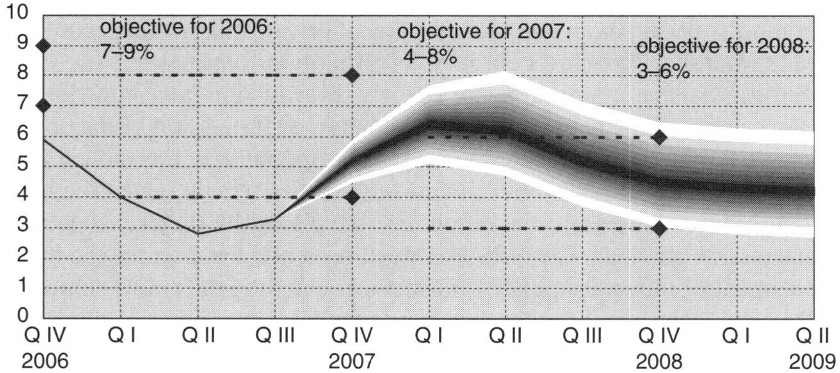

Figure 12.1 Core inflation projections (y-o-y rates %)

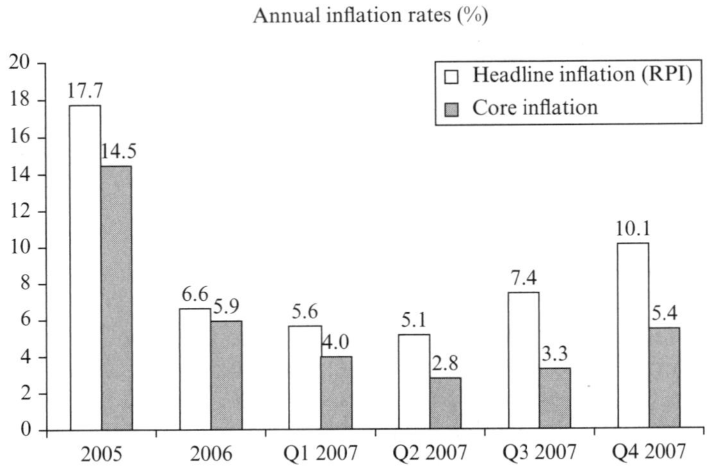

Figure 12.2 Inflation rates

inflation and reducing the costs of domestic production. These effects are clearly seen in the basket decomposition of recent inflation numbers: while items related to agriculture record high growth, prices of imported finished products continue to decline in absolute terms.

Despite strong growth, there are currently no demand pressures on inflation, as output has declined below its potential. Monetary policy remains restrictive and has tightened further since the end of 2007. Moreover, the interest rate outlook is still on the upside, as the NBS has signaled its readiness to increase the rate further should any of the major risk factors materialize, including a stronger fiscal expansion than envisaged in the Budget, higher than expected growth in regulated and world commodity prices, or an unexpected surge of private inflation expectations (see the October 2007 and February 2008 Inflation Reports).

Substantial changes in monetary policy transmission have contributed to the success of the new regime. The monetary transmission of the policy stance has worked reasonably well so far, especially in the money and foreign exchange markets, but obvious difficulties remain, given the high extent of euroization and the dominant role played by the exchange rate transmission channel. The NBS two-week repo rate has become the main instrument of monetary policy transmission signaling the policy stance of NBS, while the role of exchange rate interventions and direct administrative measures has been reduced.

At the start of the monetary policy transmission, short-term money market rates tracked the key policy rate well. Following the introduction

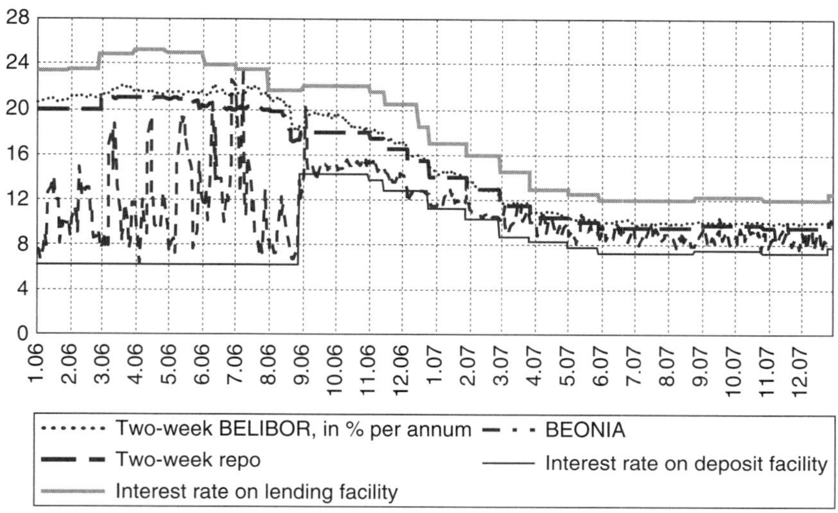

Figure 12.3 Interest rate movements (daily data, annual level, %)

of a new system of the monetary policy implementation based on a key policy rate and a corridor of standing facilities in August 2006, the volatility of short-term money market interest rates has declined and the rates followed the changes in the NBS rates closely (Figure 12.3). Also the overnight rate which previously was well below the key policy rate, gradually moved towards the key policy rate, though it remained below it and was more volatile than expected. The new system of monetary policy implementation facilitated the liquidity management of banks, allowing them to distribute liquidity more freely over the maintenance period. Correspondingly, the key policy rate has become the marginal cost of funds on which the pricing of dinar instruments is based.

The money market yield curve has moved in response to NBS communication about the future changes in its key policy rate. Despite the money market being illiquid at longer maturities, the yield curve still provides useful information on market expectations of short-term rates evolution. Quite surprisingly, the market deposit and lending rates also followed the changes in the key policy rate, irrespective of the currency of denomination. This signals that the interest rate transmission may actually be stronger than initially expected. Although the theoretical explanation for this phenomenon requires further investigation, it appears that the key policy rate helps determine the appropriate spread between the cost of funds from abroad and the return on assets that is passed on to other investments.

Despite the better-than-expected working of the interest rate channel, the exchange rate remained the most important transmission channel. This is illustrated by the strong and fast exchange rate pass-through to prices, with about 30 percent passed within a quarter and a complete pass-through within a year. As Figure 12.4 demonstrates, the strong link between the exchange rate and inflation is a traditional one in Serbia.

The exchange rate channel has however undergone major changes, with the NBS withdrawing from the FX market. The frequency and scale of interventions had been declining since August 2006. In addition, its indirect interventions through the purchase of FX cash from FX bureaus have been partly offset by over-the-counter resales of these proceeds to the interbank market since June 2007.

As the NBS has withdrawn from the FX market, the exchange rate has become more volatile, but has generally responded well to movements and signals in the key policy rate. This strong link between the key policy rate and exchange rate was the backbone of monetary transmission in the period 2006–07 period. The exchange rate appreciation in 2006 helped to bring inflation to record lows, eventually undershooting the inflation targets for 2006. The subsequent depreciation was needed to bring inflation back to targeted levels in 2007.

12.4 FISCAL POLICY AND ITS EFFECTS IN SERBIA

Serbia is a good illustration of the theoretical puzzles introduced above. After years of balanced (or near to balanced) budgets, the fiscal policy outlook in 2008 was uncertain. Moreover, the effects of fiscal deficits and their composition on the real economy and inflation were unclear, also because of measurement and data problems. As a result, a balanced budget or even surplus in one methodology can easily become a deficit of 2–3 percent of GDP in another – something that complicates the conduct of monetary policy enormously.

12.4.1 Measuring Fiscal Policy Stance

Three measures are typically used to assess fiscal policy and its effects on the economy: consolidated fiscal balance, fiscal stance and excess liquidity as a pressure on aggregate demand.

Unfortunately, the results for each fiscal measure depend on measurement conventions and classifications. Although there is a standard

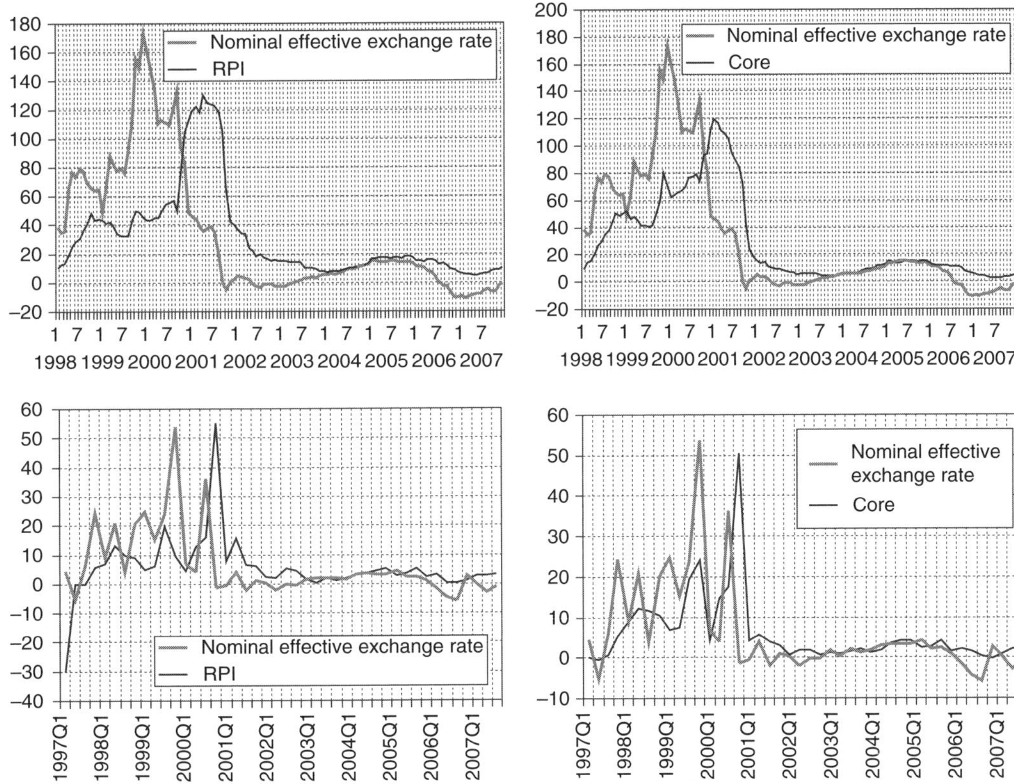

Figure 12.4 *Link between inflation and exchange rate (annual and quarterly growth rates)*

Table 12.1 Consolidated Serbian budget in 2007, in billion dinars (1 EUR ≈ 80 RSD)

Standard revenues	Standard expenditure	Standard fiscal balance
974 543	1 008 343	−33 801
Non-standard revenues (sale of licenses)		Official fiscal balance
25 536		−8 265
	Non-standard expenditure (household sector arrears payments)	True fiscal balance
	31 977	−65 777

approach to these definitions, emerging market realities often find this inadequate, calling for a more imaginative approach. Serbia has many specific factors (such as pension arrears, frozen foreign currency savings, income from privatization and GSM licenses) that are not treated clearly or consistently by the standard methodology (Table 12.1).

For instance, according to the standard methodology, debt repayment is not recorded as an expenditure item, but rather as an outlay (financial operation) decreasing government debt. Similarly, a loan disbursement is not recorded as revenue, but rather as a receipt (financial operation) which increases government debt. However, although a loan disbursement is not revenue, it has the same role because it helps finance outlays; hence, the government may borrow to cover increased spending.

Further, the source of financing should matter for the classification of fiscal policy effects, unlike the standard methodology treatment. When the government borrows in the domestic market, it may spend more because some other sectors like households or enterprises are spending less and/or are saving more, so the overall demand effects are not large. On the other hand, if the government borrows in the foreign market or experiences privatization revenues, demand effects are likely to be larger.

The treatment of fiscal statistics in Serbia illustrates the shortcomings of the standard methodology. The Ministry of Finance (MoF) uses a GFS 1986 methodology creatively, for classification of both revenue and expenditure. Non-standard items (Table 12.1), especially high privatization receipts and high arrears payments, are treated in a way that arguably clouds the overall fiscal position.

As an example, in the official classification the increase in government deposits is interpreted as a prudent behavior mopping up a portion of liquidity that could otherwise induce more demand. Such an interpretation, however, does not make sense in a case when the government uses capital inflows (temporary revenue, for example, for privatization, sale of licenses, grants) to cover outlays which induce growth in spending. In such a case, it is much more important to assess whether government activities induce growth in the overall liquidity of the banking sector.

Similarly, arrears repayments are treated differently from standard loan repayments. They decrease public debt (as do the standard loan repayments), but at the same time have strong demand effects. Direct effects of household sector increasing consumption dominate the indirect effects of the increased savings generating a deposit base for credit extension.

On top of that, there is a methodological dichotomy, as the Ministry of Finance reports on the consolidated budget, while the National Assembly approves only the central government budget, and not the consolidated budget. The National Bank compiles its own estimate of the consolidated budget, and has developed a uniform methodology to prevent ad hoc distortions created by applying different concepts from one period to another.

According to the MoF methodology, the fiscal balance was positive throughout 2004, 2005 and the first half of 2006. Thereafter, it turned slightly negative in the third quarter of 2006 and reached a record low at the end of 2006 (Figure 12.5). However, the methodology applied by the NBS or the International Monetary Fund (IMF) show significantly different results. According to both, the fiscal balance was in substantial deficit in 2006 and 2007 (more so in the NBS methodology). The NBS methodology also shows a fiscal deficit for earlier years (although of a lower magnitude).

The computational difficulties in using the standard methodologies for measuring the fiscal policy effect make a case for an alternative approach using easily observed and accurately measured liquidity data. The liquidity or demand effect of fiscal policy measures the excess liquidity created by government. This concept is not well established, but suffers from fewer methodological issues than other approaches, although it too involves approximations. The monetary effect is approximated by the fiscal balance in dinars, which is only a rough approximation of the liquidity effects of the fiscal policy, as one cannot determine how much of the dinar expenditure leaves the country indirectly.

Despite some ambiguities, the liquidity effect of fiscal policy has some appeal as an indicator from a monetary policy perspective. This methodology takes into consideration all expenditure and outlays the state makes at home, and all the revenues and receipts the state draws at home. The difference between the two is an approximation of the

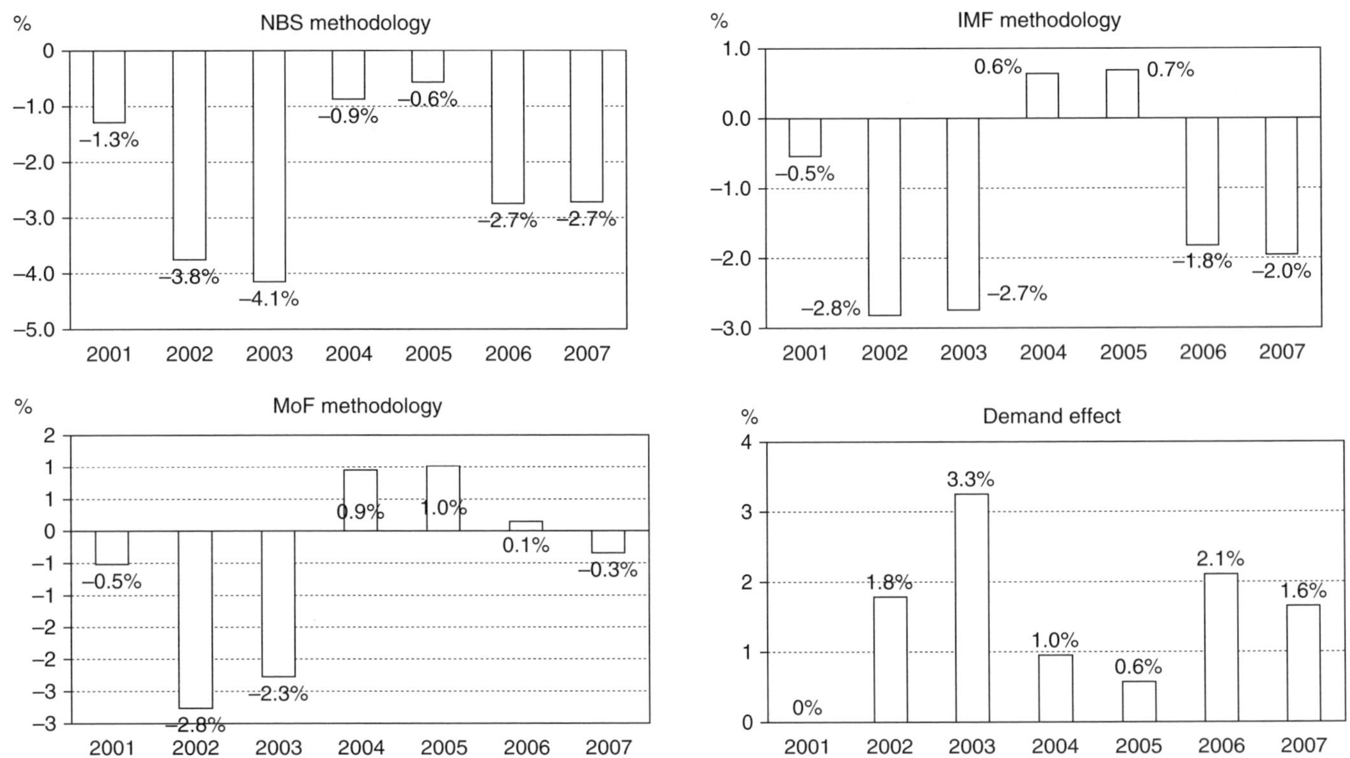

Figure 12.5 Fiscal deficit (%GDP): different methodologies

pressure the budget is exerting on the aggregate demand, if it is assumed that all revenues drawn at home originate at home, and that all the expenditure made at home, stays there. In reality, not all of the fiscal stimulus will result in higher domestic output; some of the fiscal stimulus will feed through to higher prices, and some will result in a larger current account deficit.

Measured by the liquidity effect, the fiscal policy has been expansionary since 2002, more or less. This stands in contrast to the MoF methodology of a fiscal balance that was positive since 2004 until late 2006. It demonstrates the difficulties in understanding the nature and effects of the fiscal policy in Serbia.

Understanding the effects of the fiscal balance on the economy, however, requires further analysis. Typically, such effects are measured by a fiscal stance that adjusts the fiscal balance according to the economic cycle. However, assessment of the business cycle in an emerging market context involves many measurement errors and methodological uncertainties. For instance, GDP statistics are unreliable and often revised.

The NBS methodology for measuring structural fiscal stance adjusts only revenues for the business cycle and assumes expenditure is not cyclical. Currently, the NBS is using model-based Kalman filter estimates of the output gap to measure the economic cycle. However, the estimates are imprecise and are often revised, making the cyclically adjusted fiscal stance an unreliable guide on the fiscal policy effects. As such, it is only used for indicative purposes. These measures show that fiscal policy was expansionary from 2001, except very briefly in the second part of 2005 and first part of 2006.

12.5 MONETARY AND FISCAL POLICY MIX

The above methodologies can be applied to understand the evolution of the monetary and fiscal policy mix in Serbia in the past few years (Figure 12.6).

With fiscal policy loose since 2001, the burden of taming inflation fell on monetary policy. However, monetary policy was expansionary in 2004, as reflected in negative or declining real interest rates and moderately falling average mandatory reserve rates. As a result, inflation rose steadily. The monetary policy stance tightened somewhat in 2005, but not sufficiently to bring inflation down. Average reserve requirements rose, but real interest rates stayed negative. Inflation remained at a high level, but stopped accelerating. Only with a sharp tightening in 2006 did monetary policy bring inflation under control.

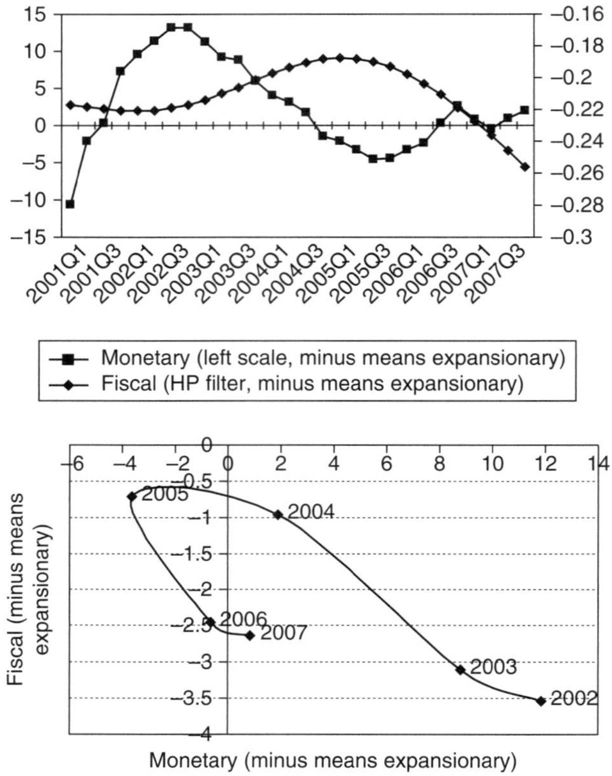

Figure 12.6 Monetary and fiscal policy stance

12.6 CONCLUSIONS

The experience of Serbia demonstrates the importance of and difficulties in understanding the fiscal policy stance and its effect on the economy and inflation. After adjustments to official statistics, the fiscal policy has likely been quite expansionary in recent years, contrary to official estimates. Our analysis has also uncovered how poorly coordinated monetary and fiscal policies have been thus far.

In spite of the poor policy coordination and expansionary fiscal policy, monetary policy has proved capable of taming inflation. The inflation-targeting strategy adopted in August 2006 has shown tangible results, despite many unfavorable predicaments (such as a high exchange rate pass-through, high level of financial dollarization and weak interest rate transmission).

The inflation-targeting regime was chosen as the last resort after earlier attempts at managing the exchange rate failed. We saw in the period of 2003 to 2005 that maintaining a fixed or managed exchange rate can be very difficult and costly in an environment where the real exchange rate has a positive long-term trend. This may explain why more and more emerging market economies prefer a flexible exchange rate regime. The flexible exchange rate allowed Serbia to fight inflation more aggressively.

Though hard-won, the success in taming inflation may be short-lived in the absence of long-term fiscal adjustments. For instance, fiscal adjustments can help reduce the high current account deficit that is imposing a large constraint on monetary maneuvering. Similarly, fiscal adjustments would make room for a more relaxed monetary policy, and thus also help reduce the speed of nominal and real appreciation.

However, in the absence of fiscal adjustment, what is the best reaction of monetary policy? Should it be more restrictive vis-à-vis fiscal uncertainties and take more than a fair share of the stabilization burden? Should the inflation targets be less ambitious given the converging economy, high capital inflows, current account deficits and supply-side inflation shocks? Or should the NBS inflation-targeting framework be modified to account for some local specifics, for example by using less orthodox instruments (such as administrative measures and moral suasion) to overcome the problems in monetary transmission?

Although we do not have answers for these questions today, we hope the monetary policy in Serbia will find the right responses soon.

NOTE

1. The NBS enjoys full *de jure* (that is, legal) and de facto (that is, in practice) independence in using its monetary policy instruments (which probably also means monetary policy regime independence). It also seems to enjoy some form of 'de facto' target independence, although the relationships between NBS core inflation targets, state budget inflation figures, and the program for price deregulations are not clear. It also has full independence in conducting exchange rate policies, but only within a regime agreed upon with the government.

BIBLIOGRAPHY

Baldacci, E., B. Clements and S. Gupta (2003), 'Using Fiscal Policy to Spur Growth', *Finance and Development*, **40** (December), pp. 28–31.

Bezděk, V., K. Dybczak and A. Krejdl (2003), 'Czech Fiscal Policy: Introductory Analysis', Working paper 7/2003, Czech National Bank.

International Monetary Fund (2005), 'Monetary and Fiscal Policy Design Issues in Low-Income Countries', Washington, DC: International Monetary Fund.

International Monetary Fund (2006), 'Fiscal Adjustment For Stability and Growth', Washington, DC: International Monetary Fund.

Kim, J.I. (2007), 'Fiscal Policy and the Exchange Rate–Current Account Nexus', IMF Working Paper No. 07/27.

National Bank of Serbia (2007), *Inflation Report 3rd Quarter 2007*, October, National Bank of Serbia.

National Bank of Serbia (2008), Inflation Report 4th Quarter 2007, February, National Bank of Serbia.

Organisation for Economic Co-operation and Development (OECD) (2004), 'Fiscal Stance Over the Cycle: The Role of Debt, Institutions, and Budget Constraints', *The OECD Economic Outlook, No. 74*, Paris: OECD, Chapter 4.

Reynolds, A. (2001), 'The Fiscal–Monetary Policy Mix', *Cato Journal*, **21** (2), pp. 263–75.

Rothenberg, A.D. (n.d.), 'The Monetary–Fiscal Policy Mix: Empirical Analysis and Theoretical Implications', Unpublished typescript.

13. Aid volatility, monetary policy rules and the capital account in African economies

Christopher Adam,* Stephen O'Connell and Edward Buffie

13.1 INTRODUCTION

The conduct of monetary policy in Africa has undergone significant changes since the mid-1990s. Shifts in the macroeconomic orthodoxy in favour of tighter fiscal control and the emergence of low and stable inflation as a central policy objective of governments across the continent have been reinforced by greater institutional independence of central banks and the removal of administrative controls in foreign exchange and financial markets. Together, these have afforded central banks a degree of protection against excessive fiscal pressures and provided them with the instruments with which to pursue their inflation targets. The removal of exchange controls has reduced exchange rate policy to choices regarding the degree of flexibility of a unified exchange rate, while the shift away from interest rate controls and directed credit has facilitated a move from direct to indirect instruments for controlling overall liquidity, albeit in the context of relatively thin and oligopolistic asset markets.

These institutional changes have occurred against a changing macroeconomic environment across the continent. Many African central banks are currently confronting the challenge of managing rapidly rising primary export prices, often in circumstances where successful adjustment and debt relief programmes have prompted surges in official aid flows. At the same time, and in response to these same developments, short-run private capital inflows have become an important feature of the landscape. In Zambia, for example, foreign investors currently hold around 20 per cent of the stock of domestic government bonds (IMF, 2007a), while in December 2006, over 80 per cent of the subscription to the Government of Ghana's five-year domestic currency bond issue was accounted for by foreign investors (IMF, 2007b). Similar developments are occurring elsewhere across the continent.

With these factors generating substantial upward pressure on nominal and real exchange rates, and given concerns about the possible consequences for external competitiveness, central bankers have been increasingly drawn into attempts to prevent the appreciation of the real exchange rate which, in turn, raises questions about the degree to which intervention should be sterilized and hence the trade-off between exchange rate and interest rate volatility.[1] Central banks are actively seeking feasible monetary rules that provide guidance on how to navigate these concerns about the exchange rate without yielding on their inflation objectives. In particular, they are attempting to determine how aggressively they should seek to manage the path of the nominal exchange rate, if at all; whether there is a role for reserves to smooth the spending response to aid inflows; and whether aid-related liquidity growth should be sterilized through bond sales.

By the end of 2007 only two African countries had sought to resolve these issues by committing themselves to fully fledged inflation targeting: South Africa, which adopted inflation targeting in 2000, and Ghana, which followed suit in May 2007. Elsewhere, however, although many countries are actively considering moves in the same direction, the vast majority maintain what Stone (2003) has labelled 'inflation targeting lite' regimes, typically utilizing a money-based anchor for inflation.

The distinctions between full-fledged and 'lite' regimes are important. The former entails an explicit public commitment to inflation as a nominal anchor, in preference to the exchange rate or some monetary aggregate, and an explicit prioritization of inflation over competing objectives of central bank policy, including output and exchange rate stability. By contrast, although 'inflation targeting lite' regimes also typically announce an inflation target they may retain exchange rate stability and financial stability among their objectives, often reconciled through an International Monetary Fund (IMF)-supported financial programming framework (Porter and Yao, 2005).

Operationally, countries that practice strict inflation targeting almost uniformly employ a short-term interest rate as the primary policy instrument. For this approach to be effective there must be a reliable transmission mechanism from short-term interest rates to expected inflation. But interest rates do not play as central a role in the transmission mechanism in most African economies, consistent with the rudimentary nature of the financial sector. Instead monetary equilibrium tends to play the key role and remains at the core of most programmes of monetary management in sub-Saharan Africa. For a given value of expected inflation, the path of velocity is assumed to be fixed, rather than dependent on a nominal interest rate, so that the path of the price level is then determined endogenously, to equalize the policy-determined path of the nominal money supply with the path of real money demand.

Although the choice of operational target often differs sharply between inflation-targeting central banks and those whose policy is based more loosely on financial programming, it does not constitute an important analytical difference. First of all, unavailability of a policy interest rate does not rule out the setting of available policy instruments to target expected inflation to whatever desired degree of transparency and exclusion of other objectives. Second, even when a policy interest rate is available, the transmission from monetary aggregates to aggregate demand may well be more reliable. Finally, even where a policy interest rate does afford reasonably sensitive control over aggregate demand, a given path for that rate can in principle be accomplished either directly, by controlling the interest rate, or indirectly, by controlling the supply of central bank balances.

The more fundamental difference between these regimes has to do with their choice of nominal anchor and the degree to which they prioritize price stability over other objectives of monetary policy. It is these differences which shape the research programme discussed in this chapter. This research – discussed in Buffie et al. (2004), O'Connell et al. (2007) and Adam et al. (2009) – is fundamentally concerned with integrating these institutional characteristics of African economies into coherent macroeconomic models, with the ultimate objective of building a bridge between the policy frameworks currently in use in most of sub-Saharan Africa and the inflation-targeting frameworks that form the analytical core of monetary policy among emerging market and industrial countries. To date we have framed the policy question rather narrowly in terms of the conduct of monetary policy in the face of volatile but persistent positive shocks to net aid inflows, such as experienced by a number of countries in sub-Saharan Africa since the turn of the twenty-first century. Although it readily extends to the analysis of other shocks and sources of volatility including commodity price shocks, we retain the narrow focus on aid shocks in this chapter.[2]

Our analysis to date suggests that efficient management of aid inflows requires a degree of foreign exchange intervention, particularly when aid is used partly to substitute for domestic deficit financing and where domestic prices are sticky. These results are derived for an environment where countries' integration with global capital markets is rudimentary, so that access to global capital markets has tended to run through official aid channels and processes of currency substitution. One consequence of this is that domestic real interest rates can deviate substantially from world interest-parity conditions for extended periods of time.

Recently, however, as we have noted above, *de jure* capital account openness has become de facto as foreign investors have responded to the compression of risk margins by seeking out ever more exotic markets, including the most underdeveloped African markets. To reflect these recent developments, we modify our basic closed capital account model to allow for capital market integration, albeit limited by considerations of sovereign risk. We show that although an open capital account facilitates smoother adjustment to temporary aid surges when an aid inflow is fully spent, volatility is magnified and the adjustment problems identified in our earlier work are likely to be exacerbated when aid inflows are accompanied by fiscal adjustment. Given this, the case for a managed float in such circumstances is strengthened.

The remainder of the chapter is organized as follows. In section 13.2 we briefly set the scene and discuss the basic structure of the model.[3] Section13. 3 then turns directly to the simulations and a discussion of the results. We start with a review of the principal results reported in Adam et al. (2008) before turning to the contribution of this chapter which is to examine the robustness of our earlier results as foreign participation in domestic debt markets increases. Section13. 4 concludes.

13.2 THE MODEL

13.2.1 Some Background Considerations

We develop a dynamic, stochastic general-equilibrium (DSGE) model whose design is inspired by the structure of low-income African countries, the shocks that preoccupy African central bankers, and the institutional environments they operate within. As a result, our model stands in contrast to the contemporary literature on monetary policy in emerging market economies. In particular, reflecting the nature of the transmission mechanism, there is no policy interest rate in our model. Instead, central banks deploy balance sheet instruments – foreign exchange reserves, base money and bonds.

In this respect, our model shares more with the earlier literature on monetary management in industrial countries (for example, Branson and Henderson, 1985) than with contemporary approaches. However, as Woodford (2003) shows, there exists an isomorphism between a now-conventional AS-IS-IR model (where IR denotes the interest rate rule) and the earlier AS-IS-LM style of model.[4] Thus the choice of model is a matter of taste but typically will turn on a practical matter of institutions (that is, whether a policy interest rate exists).

The simple equivalence is easily derived for a closed economy. To move to an open economy, an equation for exchange rate determination can be added, possibly by assuming uncovered interest parity (UIP) or imperfect asset substitution (Cespedes et al., 2003). These extensions typically entail adding a single equation but two new variables, the exchange rate and reserves. Overwhelmingly, however, the developed-country literature conveniently sidesteps the more subtle issue of the added policy instrument, reserves, by assuming that the authorities pursue a pure float (which implies that the change in the instrument, reserves, is zero throughout).

While this may be an appropriate simplification for full-fledged inflation targeting it is patently not a good approximation of reality in developing countries in general (see for example Edwards, 2007), and for those of sub-Saharan Africa in particular where the authorities often reach for exchange rate intervention as the first instrument of choice. It is for this reason that we include in our model explicit rules for foreign exchange intervention, which represent our first main point of departure from the literature.

A second and related point is that in our model fiscal policy is not innocuous. With only very recent exceptions (for example, Benigno and Woodford, 2007), analytical treatments of inflation targeting tend to assume non-distortionary transfers, so that seigniorage requirements do not complicate the management of monetary policy. In our model, by contrast, the management of seigniorage through the interaction of fiscal policy plays directly on the private sector's portfolio behaviour which in turn shapes the dynamic adjustment to aid (and other) external shocks.

13.2.2 Model Specification

Central to the baseline model is a characterization of households' portfolio choices and the financing options facing government which reflects the 'imperfectly open' capital account structures pervasive in much of sub-Saharan Africa. Formally, we work with a simple optimizing two-sector dependent economy model with currency substitution in which both domestic and foreign currencies deliver liquidity services. The representative private agent consumes traded imports and non-traded final goods and accumulates financial wealth in the form of three assets: domestic currency, foreign currency and government bonds. There are no banks in the model, so that money is base money and foreign currency balances are held in non-interest-bearing forms.

The private agent can accumulate or decumulate foreign currency either via transactions with the central bank or through the current account, depending on the exchange rate regime. The private sector's relative demand for domestic and foreign currencies depends on the liquidity services delivered by each and their opportunity costs relative to holding domestic bonds. This is simply the nominal interest rate for domestic money; for foreign currency, the foregone interest rate is modified by the rate of depreciation, providing for a lower opportunity cost if the exchange rate depreciates. The sensitivity of relative currency demand to these opportunity costs depends on both the elasticity of currency substitution and the elasticity of intertemporal substitution in consumption. The higher the degree of substitutability between currencies, the more private agents will seek to alter their currency portfolio (and hence the greater the pressures on the nominal exchange rate) in response to shocks. A higher value of the intertemporal elasticity of substitution, other things being equal, tends to produce greater volatility in consumption and the current account and less volatility in the real interest rate. The settings adopted in this chapter correspond to mid-range values from the limited empirical evidence on these parameters. When combined with initial steady-state values of inflation and the nominal interest rates, they imply a steady-state inflation elasticity of the demand for base money of around 0.5, consistent with most empirical estimates.[5]

In Adam et al. (2009) we assume that, apart from through this currency substitution channel, neither the private nor the public sector has direct access to world capital markets. Hence domestic government debt is effectively non-traded and domestic interest rates are not tied down by interest parity conditions. Here we nest this as a special case in a more general model which allows for the possibility of foreign portfolio investment in domestic bond markets (although we continue to assume that the government does not issue foreign currency debt instruments). The economy thus faces an upward-sloping foreign supply of funds schedule whose elasticity is determined by the premium over uncovered interest parity demanded by foreign investors to compensate for sovereign risk. The foreign investor is assumed to hold a home bond whose real yield, denominated in units of the tradable good and assumed independent of developments in the local economy, is given by $R^*_t = (1 + r^*_t)$. The foreign supply of funds is defined implicitly by the condition:

$$R_t = R^*_t \left(\frac{e_{t+1}}{e_t} \right)^{-\gamma} \phi \left(\frac{p_t b^f_t}{y_t} \right). \tag{13.1}$$

where e denotes the expected real exchange rate, γ the non-tradable share in the consumer price index (CPI), and $p_t b^f_t / y_t$ the value of domestic debt, in units of gross domestic product (GDP), held by foreign investors. The term $\phi\,(p_t b^f_t / y_t)$ corresponds to the risk premium so that ϕ determines the slope of the supply schedule. As $\phi \rightarrow \infty$ the schedule becomes vertical and the model converges on the 'closed' capital account used in Adam et al. (2009). At the other extreme, as $\phi \rightarrow 0$ the supply schedule becomes horizontal at the UIP interest rate, corresponding to the case of perfect asset substitutability.

The supply side of the model is simple, reflecting our short-run focus. The economy produces exported and non-tradable goods using sector-specific capital and labour, which is intersectorally mobile. The aggregate capital stock is fixed and there is no investment. Non-traded goods prices are sticky so that the output of non-traded goods is demand-determined in the short run. In this case, macroeconomic adjustment can then take place off the production frontier, via booms or recessions in the non-traded goods sector.

The model is completed by defining a stochastic process for the external shocks, and a set of policy rules. In this case we limit the sources of external volatility to stochastic shocks in the net aid inflow which follows a stationary autoregressive order one, AR(1), process around a steady-state mean value equivalent to of 2 per cent of GDP. The autoregressive parameter is 0.50.

Policy rules

We now turn to the macroeconomic policy choices of interest in the analysis of aid shocks. On the fiscal side, our focus is on the financing implications of fiscal policy, and in particular on the consequences of aid-financed deficit reductions. Tax rates are held constant throughout so that aid shocks constitute the only source of revenue volatility. Fiscal behaviour is then governed by the level of spending out of aid.[6] Specifically, a portion δ of aid may be devoted to deficit reduction, substituting for domestic deficit financing. Hence for a given aid surge, denoted $(a_t - \bar{a})$, where $\bar{a}$ denotes the steady-state level of aid, an amount $\delta(a_t - \bar{a})$ is used to substitute for domestic deficit financing and $(1 - \delta)(a_t - \bar{a})$ is spent: in the simulations reported below, we assume $\delta = 0$ or $\delta = 0.25$. Variations in government revenues arising from aid inflows are transferred directly to households by means of variation in transfers.

The instruments of monetary policy are transactions in foreign exchange and government securities with the private sector. To characterize reserve management, we begin with the simplest reaction function that accommodates alternative degrees of commitment to a fixed rate of crawl: $\Delta z_t = -\alpha_1(x_t - \bar{x})$, for $\alpha_1 \geq 0$ and where $\bar{x}$ is the steady-state rate of depreciation. To this we add a fixed long-run reserve target $\bar{z}$, in order to preserve the stationary structure of the analysis. Finally, we allow for a time-varying reserve target tied to the pattern of fiscal spending out of aid. Reserve policy is therefore:

$$\frac{\Delta z_t}{\bar{z}} = -\alpha_1 \frac{x_t - \bar{x}}{\bar{x}} - \alpha_2 \frac{z_{t-1} - \bar{z}}{\bar{z}} + \alpha_3 \frac{(a_t - \bar{a}) - \gamma \cdot (d_t - \bar{d})}{\bar{z}} \qquad (13.2)$$

where $(d_t - \bar{d})$ denotes the deviation of government spending net of taxes from its steady-state level, $\alpha_1 \geq 0$, $\alpha_2 > 0$, $\alpha_3 \in \{0, 1\}$, and $0 \leq \gamma \leq 1$. The parameter α_1 governs the degree of commitment to the steady-state rate of crawl. As $\alpha_1 \rightarrow \infty$ the regime approaches a predetermined crawl in which $x_t = \bar{x}$ on a continuous basis. Lower values of α_1 represent looser commitments to the reference rate of crawl, and for $\alpha_1 = 0$ the exchange rate floats.[7] In the floating case, all foreign exchange available to the economy is immediately priced in a competitive foreign exchange market and either added to private foreign currency holdings or absorbed through an increased current account deficit.

We refer to the combination of $\alpha_1 = 0$ and $\alpha_3 = 0$ as a 'pure float'. The final term in (13.2), however, allows the central bank to tie foreign exchange sales directly to the path of aid-induced government spending. A policy of $\alpha_1 = 0$, $\alpha_3 = 1$ and $\gamma = 1$ corresponds to what we call a 'buffer plus float'. This approach is simple and intuitive: the central bank sells aid dollars in the precise amount required to finance aid-induced spending as it occurs, but floats with respect to all other shocks. In a buffer plus float, any aid that is not spent in the current period is retained as reserves. Of course, if $\delta = 0$ so that aid is always spent immediately, there is no operational difference between a buffer plus float and a pure float. In the presence of deficit-reduction or expenditure-smoothing components, however, a buffer plus float involves a period of potentially substantial reserve accumulation during an aid boom.

Foreign exchange operations are unwound over time, at a rate determined by α_2. Since private foreign currency holdings return to a steady-state level over time, the long-run reserve target implies that aid is ultimately fully absorbed in current account deficits, regardless of the time pattern of aid-induced public spending and the other parameters of the monetary policy reaction functions. In the simulations reported below, we assume a relatively slow rate of adjustment, setting $\alpha_2 = 0.05$ throughout.

The instruments of monetary policy are completed by the rules governing bond operations. A conventional bond reaction function would define bond operations to offset the net impact of domestic credit creation or foreign exchange intervention on the monetary base. In the context of managing liquidity in the face of aid shocks, however, bond operations tend to be geared directly and solely to spending out of aid and actual foreign exchange intervention (rather than to reserve accumulation) to define a bond reaction function of the form:

$$p_t \Delta b_t = \beta_1 (1 - \gamma)(d_t - \bar{d}) - \beta_2 (b_{t-1} - \bar{b}). \qquad (13.3)$$

under this rule, $\beta_2 > 0$ allows for a gradual return of bond holdings to a long-run level.[8] It is useful to consider (13.2) and (13.3) together. In a pure float or buffer plus float, where $\gamma = 1$ in the reserve equation (13.2), the liquidity effect of aid-induced spending is fully offset through the sale of aid dollars. At the other extreme, with $\gamma = 0$ and $\alpha_3 = \beta_1 = 1$, the authorities retain the aid inflow as reserves and sterilize the full aid-spending induced liquidity injection through open market operations. Between these two polar extremes, the same liquidity injection could be absorbed through any combination of foreign exchange and bond sales. For example, in a case we examine below, Berg et al. (2007) advocate a '50–50' approach that allocates half of the task of liquidity management to foreign exchange sales and half to bond sales. In terms of the reaction functions, this entails $\alpha_3 = 1$ and $\gamma = 0.50$.

13.3 RESULTS

We start by briefly reviewing the central results from our earlier work (Adam et al., 2008) in which we focus on the properties of three monetary policy rules under different assumptions about the fiscal response to aid inflows and where government bonds are held exclusively by domestic residents. The first two rules are the polar cases of a pure float (that is, a money anchor) and an exchange rate crawl. In the former case, official foreign exchange reserves are held constant and the growth of the money supply is determined exclusively by the actions of the fiscal authorities. In the latter, the monetary authorities target the nominal exchange rate at the steady-state rate of depreciation, with changes in the money supply arising from intervention potentially being sterilized through bond purchases or sales. The third case, the reserve buffer plus float, entails initially accumulating aid inflows as official foreign exchange reserves and then sterilizing the full domestic currency counterpart of aid-financed non-import spending through foreign exchange sales as it occurs. This rule thus sets a time-varying reserve target corresponding to the unspent component of aid, and allows the exchange rate to float freely once this reserve target is satisfied.

In section 13.3.1 we examine the properties of these rules in circumstances where, initially, the aid inflow is spent as it is received, and then when a portion of the aid inflow is used to substitute for domestic deficit financing. In section 3.2 we re-examine these rules in the presence of an open capital account. Finally, in section 3.3, we explore the characteristics of 'burden-sharing' rules that seek to allocate responsibility for liquidity sterilization between foreign exchange intervention and bond sterilization, under both closed and open capital accounts. Throughout this analysis we eschew any formal welfare comparison, preferring to focus on the positive characteristics of the rules.

13.3.1 Aid Shocks with a Closed Capital Account

Table 13.1 reports the simulated impulse response functions (IRFs) of the key behavioural variables of the model in response to a positive aid shock equivalent to 2 per cent of GDP (around a steady state mean value of 10 per cent of GDP). For convenience we report the IRFs on impact ($t = 0$) and at horizons $t = 1$, $t = 2$ and $t = 15$ only. The final row of each block reports the theoretical standard deviations of the endogenous variables given the stochastic aid process.[9]

When the fiscal authorities spend all the aid inflow as it is received, domestic financing is fully and continuously insulated (panels A and B). In this case, full spending implies there is no distinction between a pure float and a buffer plus float. Both, however, entail a different path for the nominal exchange rate and aggregate prices compared to the crawl, at least in the short run. The aid inflow induces a mild real exchange rate appreciation consistent with a procyclical spending boom, but while an initial inflationary spike is required under the crawl, the initial adjustment is mildly deflationary under a float as the nominal exchange rate appreciates. In neither case, however, are the effects large; macroeconomic adjustment is largely benign. While the crawl delivers marginally less volatility for both inflation and the real exchange rate, and marginally more current account volatility, the differences between these polar approaches to exchange rate policy are second-order, at least for the parameters of the policy rules considered here.

These similarities disappear when aid is used to provide an element of fiscal stabilization (panels C to E). When aid substitutes for seigniorage the monetary authorities are confronted with the explicit challenge of how to manage a first-order alteration to the path of domestic financing. Now, the buffer plus float rule is no longer equivalent to a pure float. The pure float implies that the contraction in the fiscal deficit after net budgetary aid is fully met by a contraction in the government's seigniorage requirement for a given stock of domestic debt. As shown in panel C, the consequences are dramatic: the nominal exchange rate appreciates by more than 13 per cent on impact (compared to an appreciation of around 2 per cent in the corresponding no-deficit reduction case reported in Panel A), and the real rate appreciates by 8 per cent (again compared to 3 per cent). These powerful

Table 13.1 *Impulse response functions for stochastic aid shock: closed capital account*

Time period	Aid shock	Nominal exchange rate	Real exchange rate	Nominal interest rate	Real interest rate	Inflation	Current account balance	Private consump-tion	Demand for non-tradables	Reserve accumu-lation
Panel A										
All aid is spent: pure float [= buffer plus float]										
$t = 0$	2.00	–2.22	–2.94	–0.66	–1.68	–0.60	0.77	1.73	0.55	0.00
$t = 1$	1.00	–1.09	–3.35	–2.80	–1.17	–0.87	0.09	1.08	0.18	0.00
$t = 2$	0.50	–0.80	–2.98	–2.39	–0.69	–1.00	–0.13	0.62	–0.07	0.00
$t = 15$	0.00	0.00	–0.02	–0.01	0.00	–0.01	0.00	0.00	0.00	0.00
Standard deviation	2.32	2.70	6.60	4.50	2.25	1.98	0.82	2.20	0.59	0.00
Panel B										
All aid is spent: exchange rate crawl										
$t = 0$	2.00	0.20	–1.99	1.43	–1.49	1.30	0.88	1.69	0.63	0.00
$t = 1$	1.00	–0.17	–2.57	–1.48	–1.12	0.15	0.14	1.11	0.28	0.00
$t = 2$	0.50	–0.18	–2.39	–1.54	–0.72	–0.28	–0.10	0.68	0.09	0.00
$t = 15$	0.00	–0.02	–0.02	–0.03	0.00	–0.03	0.00	0.00	0.00	0.00
Std. dev	2.32	0.45	5.13	3.09	2.11	1.49	0.91	2.23	0.70	0.00
Panel C										
25% of aid inflow devoted to domestic deficit reduction: pure float										
$t = 0$	2.00	–13.35	–7.75	–10.00	–0.27	–9.09	0.84	0.77	–0.44	0.00
$t = 1$	1.00	–1.30	–5.75	–2.94	–0.60	–2.40	0.09	0.66	–0.28	0.00
$t = 2$	0.50	–1.00	–4.26	–2.68	–0.42	–1.83	–0.14	0.43	–0.24	0.00
$t = 15$	0.00	0.00	–0.02	–0.01	0.00	–0.01	0.00	0.00	0.00	0.00
Std. dev	2.32	13.25	11.66	11.10	0.88	9.73	0.89	1.18	0.65	0.00

Table 13.1 (continued)

Time period	Aid shock	Nominal exchange rate	Real exchange rate	Nominal interest rate	Real interest rate	Inflation	Current account balance	Private consump-tion	Demand for non-tradables	Reserve accumu-lation
Panel D										
25% of aid inflow devoted to domestic deficit reduction: exchange rate crawl										
$t = 0$	2.00	–0.86	–1.89	0.19	–1.22	0.18	1.11	1.29	0.44	0.47
$t = 1$	1.00	–0.54	–2.27	–1.70	–0.84	–0.33	0.33	0.82	0.17	0.27
$t = 2$	0.50	–0.37	–2.04	–1.47	–0.52	–0.50	0.03	0.49	0.03	0.16
$t = 15$	0.00	–0.09	–0.03	–0.11	0.00	–0.10	–0.01	0.00	0.00	0.00
Std. dev	2.32	1.59	4.46	3.06	1.64	1.52	1.16	1.67	0.47	0.59
Panel E										
25% of aid inflow devoted to domestic deficit reduction: buffer plus float										
$t = 0$	2.00	–5.69	–3.95	–3.87	–1.07	–3.51	0.92	1.28	0.22	0.50
$t = 1$	1.00	–1.57	–3.56	–3.14	–0.91	–1.79	0.18	0.87	0.06	0.23
$t = 2$	0.50	–1.51	–2.96	–3.03	–0.55	–1.84	–0.07	0.52	–0.06	0.09
$t = 15$	0.00	–0.49	–0.12	–0.55	0.00	–0.50	–0.02	0.01	–0.01	–0.03
Std. dev	2.32	6.91	7.22	7.66	1.59	5.85	0.96	1.70	0.29	0.57

Notes: The numbers in the table represent percentage point changes for the nominal and real exchange rates, interest rates and inflation. For all other variables the numbers represent percentage points of GDP.
An increase in the nominal and real exchange rate indices denote a depreciation.

price effects induce a contraction in non-tradable output of 0.4 per cent on impact compared to an increase of around the same size in panels A and B. The reason for this outturn is that the reduction in expected inflation as a result of the fiscal adjustment shifts the private sector's asset portfolio decisively in favour of domestic money: given the contraction in the supply of money and the fact that the authorities are not intervening in the foreign exchange market, this requires the nominal exchange rate to overshoot in the short run to restore portfolio equilibrium. Since the nominal appreciation is much larger than the real appreciation required to absorb the aid inflow, non-tradable prices must fall sharply, entailing a sharp recession in the non-tradable goods sector.

Against this counterfactual, strategies that align the absorption of aid more closely to spending and hence smooth the path for seigniorage can substantially close off this source of macroeconomic volatility. Both the crawl (panel D) and a buffer plus float (panel E) do rather well in these circumstances. In both cases, but particularly under the crawl, the disruptive volatility in inflation and the real exchange rate are greatly reduced. The sharp deflationary impact under the pure float is substantially eliminated, with prices falling by 3.5 per cent under the buffer plus float and virtually not at all under the crawl, compared to a 9 per cent fall under the pure float. By the same token, the initial real exchange rate appreciation is pegged back to around 1.9 per cent under the crawl and 4 per cent under the buffer plus float compared to 8 per cent under a pure float, and the strong recessionary pressures on non-traded output are completely avoided.

These latter rules entail substantial reserve accumulation, and although the patterns of accumulation are broadly similar under either rule, as indeed are the real outcomes, the two approaches are not the same. Moreover, the superior performance of the crawl observed here is reinforced if the model is recalibrated to reflect a pre-stabilization situation in which inflation is initially higher and the fiscal authorities are more likely to direct a proportion of aid towards deficit reduction; in such a setting an aggressive crawl is significantly more effective than the buffer plus float strategy.

The reason the crawl contributes to a much smoother adjustment path is that it aligns movements in the nominal exchange rate much more closely to the modest real exchange rate adjustment required to absorb the aid inflow, while the (unsterilized) liquidity injection arising from reserve accumulation forestalls the contraction in the domestic money supply observed under the float. Instead, the increased demand for liquidity as a result of the decline in the seigniorage requirement is accommodated without requiring a sharp price adjustment so that the economy responds to the aid inflow with virtually stable prices. Domestic output is hardly affected, and total private spending follows a smoother path. While the buffer plus float strategy goes some way to delivering this same outcome it does so less efficiently since it involves reserve accumulation with respect to the unspent portion of aid only – thereby serving to efficiently match the supply of domestic money – but does not fully accommodate changes in the demand for domestic money arising from the fall in expected inflation. In the simulations reported in panels D and E, for example, the buffer plus float entails rather more up-front intervention than the crawl but rather less over the remainder of the simulation. As the inflation elasticity of the demand for money rises, this distinction becomes more marked and the buffer plus float does less well in aligning the demand and supply of domestic liquidity compared to the float.

13.3.2 Aid Shocks with an Open Capital Account

These simulations suggest that when deficit-reduction considerations are important, active foreign exchange intervention with little or no sterilization of increases in the monetary base serves to accommodate changes in the increased demand for money associated with declining inflation and delivers a more attractive way of smoothing macroeconomic volatility than relying on a pure float. These results assume, however, that domestic asset markets are fully insulated from the rest of the world. In the next section we consider whether these results remain pertinent as the capital account is liberalized de facto.

Table 13.2 illustrates the impact of incorporating foreign participation in the domestic public debt market. Drawing on the recent experience of countries such as Zambia and Ghana we assume that foreign investors hold 15 per cent of debt in the initial steady state (equivalent to 1 per cent of GDP). We allow for a modest elasticity with respect to the country risk premium by setting $\phi = 0.15$. There are, to the best of our knowledge, no reliable estimates of this parameter, but preliminary sensitivity analysis with our model suggest that the qualitative characteristics of our results are monotonic in ϕ.

In the case where all aid is spent as it is received, integration with world capital markets via foreign bond holders allows for smoother aggregate adjustment to the aid shock than was previously the case. The results are sufficiently similar under a pure float or buffer plus float and the crawl in this case that it suffices to report only the results for the pure float. Relative to the closed capital account case, adjustment entails significantly more muted movements in domestic nominal and relative prices, while the short-run boom in aggregate consumption and non-traded output

Table 13.2 Impulse response functions for stochastic aid shock: open capital account

Time period	Aid shock	Nominal exchange rate	Real exchange rate	Nominal interest rate	Real interest rate	Inflation	Current account balance	Private consump-tion	Demand for non-tradables	Bond accu-mulation (domestic investors)	Bond accu-mulation (foreign investors)	Reserve accumu-lation
Panel A												
All aid is spent with imperfect capital mobility (f = 0.15): pure float												
$t = 0$	2.00	–1.33	–1.96	–0.28	–0.36	–0.25	1.37	0.81	0.20	1.14	–1.14	0.00
$t = 1$	1.00	–0.12	–2.28	–0.34	–0.26	0.05	0.53	0.67	0.10	1.58	–1.58	0.00
$t = 2$	0.50	–0.09	–2.30	–0.37	–0.20	–0.07	0.13	0.57	0.04	1.68	–1.68	0.00
$t = 15$	0.00	–0.01	–0.55	–0.09	–0.03	–0.05	–0.07	0.11	0.00	0.42	–0.42	0.00
Standard deviation	2.32	1.32	6.61	1.08	0.61	0.49	1.53	1.67	0.23	4.84	4.84	0.00
Panel B												
All aid is spent with imperfect capital mobility (f = 0.001): pure float												
$t = 0$	2.00	–1.06	–1.26	–0.41	–0.09	–0.37	1.67	0.39	0.06	1.60	–1.60	0.00
$t = 1$	1.00	–0.04	–1.43	–0.05	–0.04	0.05	0.83	0.35	0.03	2.40	–2.40	0.00
$t = 2$	0.50	–0.01	–1.49	–0.01	–0.02	0.03	0.41	0.34	0.01	2.80	–2.80	0.00
$t = 15$	0.00	0.01	–1.50	0.01	0.00	0.01	–0.01	0.32	0.00	3.12	–3.12	0.00
Std. dev	2.32	1.06	19.89	0.43	0.11	0.40	1.93	4.24	0.07	41.24	41.24	0.00
Panel C												
25% of aid inflow devoted to domestic deficit reduction with imperfect capital mobility (f = 0.15): pure float												
$t = 0$	2.00	–12.47	–6.74	–9.64	0.95	–8.77	1.44	–0.15	–0.79	1.12	–1.12	0.00
$t = 1$	1.00	–0.41	–4.67	–0.65	0.37	–1.54	0.53	0.22	–0.39	1.61	–1.61	0.00
$t = 2$	0.50	–0.24	–3.53	–0.56	0.10	–0.87	0.12	0.36	–0.20	1.73	–1.73	0.00
$t = 15$	0.00	–0.01	–0.56	–0.10	–0.03	–0.05	–0.07	0.11	0.00	0.42	–0.42	0.00
Std. dev	2.32	12.21	10.95	9.57	1.04	8.88	1.60	1.14	0.91	4.93	4.93	0.00

Table 13.2 (continued)

Time period	Aid shock	Nominal exchange rate	Real exchange rate	Nominal interest rate	Real interest rate	Inflation	Current account balance	Private consump- tion	Demand for non– tradables	Bond accu- mulation (domestic investors)	Bond accu- mulation (foreign investors)	Reserve accumu- lation
Panel D												
25% of aid inflow devoted to domestic deficit reduction with imperfect capital mobility (f = 0.15): crawl												
$t = 0$	2.00	–1.10	–1.44	–0.34	–0.35	–0.31	1.51	0.64	0.17	0.91	–0.91	0.60
$t = 1$	1.00	–0.43	–1.79	–0.63	–0.21	–0.23	0.64	0.51	0.06	1.20	–1.20	0.20
$t = 2$	0.50	–0.25	–1.82	–0.50	–0.15	–0.24	0.21	0.43	0.02	1.27	–1.27	0.10
$t = 15$	0.00	–0.08	–0.42	–0.16	–0.03	–0.11	–0.05	0.09	0.00	0.31	–0.31	0.00
Std. dev	2.32	1.58	5.11	1.72	0.51	1.23	1.68	1.27	0.18	3.64	3.64	0.64
Panel E												
25% of aid inflow devoted to domestic deficit reduction with imperfect capital mobility (f= 0.15): buffer plus float												
$t = 0$	2.00	–4.90	–3.08	–3.53	0.09	–3.21	1.44	0.47	–0.09	1.00	–1.00	0.50
$t = 1$	1.00	–0.73	–2.62	–0.98	–0.08	–0.98	0.57	0.51	–0.02	1.40	–1.40	0.23
$t = 2$	0.50	–0.87	–2.35	–1.21	–0.13	–1.01	0.15	0.48	–0.01	1.48	–1.48	0.09
$t = 15$	0.00	–0.49	–0.58	–0.62	–0.03	–0.53	–0.07	0.10	–0.01	0.37	–0.37	–0.03
Std. dev	2.32	5.82	7.12	5.55	0.34	4.83	1.61	1.32	0.11	4.24	4.24	0.57

Notes: See Table 13.1.

is substantially eliminated. These smoother paths for consumption and production are facilitated by larger current account adjustments. With an open capital account, the private sector's consumption is less procyclical as it can now smooth more efficiently over the temporary aid flow by indirectly accumulating net foreign assets via the bond market.[10] In the limiting case shown in panel B of Table 13.2, where we allow $\phi \rightarrow 0$, so that the economy's financial terms of trade are invariant to the shock, the economy follows a textbook adjustment to a temporary income shock (recalling that the data-generating process for the aid shock is known to the private sector). The real interest rate does not move and consumption adjusts rapidly and permanently to the annuity value of the increase to aggregate wealth represented by the temporary aid shock.[11]

The results in panels A and B give the impression that greater capital account openness creates an important additional degree of freedom for efficient adjustment to external shocks and that this necessarily smoothes the adjustment path for the economy. As the results in panels C to E suggest, however, this is false when some fraction of the aid inflow is used for deficit reduction purposes: if anything, the open capital account raises the stakes. In this case the open capital account exacerbates the adjustment problem under the float (panel C) and accentuates the wedge between the float on the one hand and the crawl (panel D) and buffer plus crawl (panel E) on the other. This is seen most clearly if we focus on the costs of the real exchange rate appreciation for the non-traded sector. Previously, the limited capacity of the private sector to acquire foreign assets ensured that aggregate consumption was quite strongly procyclical, and this in turn limited the contractionary effects of real exchange rate appreciation on the non-traded sector. With a more open capital account, however, the private sector is better placed to smooth aggregate consumption with the result that aggregate demand effects provide less support to the non-traded sector, exposing it to a much sharper contraction than before.

By contrast, the properties of the crawl and buffer plus float strategies, in which reserve accumulation serves to avoid nominal and real exchange rate overshooting, change relatively little when we allow for foreign participation in domestic debt markets. As such, the relative benefits from pursing these strategies over the pure float, in terms of facilitating a smooth macroeconomic adjustment to deficit-reducing aid shocks, are further enhanced in the presence of a more open capital account. The central insights from our earlier work are preserved and even reinforced when the capital account is open: when aid is used to substitute for seigniorage the incipient portfolio adjustment by the private sector in response to changes in expected inflation will dominate macroeconomic dynamics and ensure that efficient adjustment to temporary aid surges entails a fairly heavy degree of unsterilized foreign exchange intervention, either under an explicit exchange rate crawl or through the operation of a buffer plus float rule. This result is not surprising. The fundamental factor underpinning the volatility observed when the domestic government debt market is closed is the domestic private sector's incipient portfolio adjustment, between domestic and foreign currency. Opening the domestic debt market serves to anchor the real return on debt, which may have important implications for interest-sensitive expenditure in the public and private sectors, but given that bonds do not generate liquidity services (or, in an alternative set-up, satisfy cash-in-advance constraints) the open capital account by itself does not eliminate the domestic agent's portfolio problem.

13.3.3 Burden-Sharing and Bond Sterilization

The discussion so far has focused on monetary policy from the perspective of alternative degrees of commitment to a floating exchange rate. In doing so, we have seen how the crawl and buffer plus float each end up allocating 100 per cent of the burden of liquidity control to foreign exchange sales. Macroeconomic adjustment is smooth, suggesting that there is no obvious case for shifting any of the burden to bond operations. In practice, however, central banks in Africa often feel compelled to adhere to strict monetary targets and match intervention with active bond sterilization. This is particularly so in the context of the IMF-supported financial programmes, most of which are predicated on the assumption of a constant velocity of circulation over the short to medium term. Table13.3 illustrates the case where the domestic currency value of aid spending is exactly matched by sales of foreign exchange and government securities in the share $[\gamma, 1 - \gamma]$. In the case of 'full bond sterilization', $\gamma = 0$ and for the '50–50' rule $\gamma = 0.5$.

In either case, these sterilization rules are decisively dominated by the buffer plus float and crawl which rely on foreign exchange sales alone to manage domestic liquidity growth for aid-funded spending. Panels A and B of Table 13.3 illustrate the case in which aid is fully spent – so that seigniorage requirements are stationary. In this case, bond sterilization, whether partial or full, merely imparts a substantial dose of conventional 'unpleasant arithmetic', with higher domestic debt service costs contributing to persistent domestic inflation over the horizon and a steady depreciation in the nominal exchange rate. Moreover, as the memorandum items indicate, the real interest rate (*RIR*) and the budget deficit (*def*) under bond sterilization are both substantially higher than under the comparable buffer plus float run reported in Table 13.1.

Table 13.3 Impulse response functions for stochastic aid shock: bond sterilization

Time period	Aid shock	Nominal exchange rate	Real exchange rate	Nominal interest rate	Real interest rate	Inflation	Current account balance	Private consumption	Demand for non-tradables	Total bond sales	Bond accumulation (domestic investors)	Bond accumulation (foreign investors)	Reserve accumulation	Budget deficit before aid
Panel A														
All aid is spent with closed capital account: pure float with full bond sterilization														
$t = 0$	2.00	31.48	–12.95	26.79	–1.10	24.36	3.13	0.20	1.48	2.00	2.00	0.00	2.00	2.05
$t = 1$	1.00	6.44	–7.21	9.35	0.55	9.60	1.81	–0.22	0.65	0.90	0.90	0.00	0.90	1.71
$t = 2$	0.50	7.63	–4.34	10.74	0.47	9.21	0.92	–0.01	0.46	0.36	0.36	0.00	0.36	1.18
$t = 15$	0.00	3.91	0.65	4.24	–0.03	3.89	–0.21	0.27	0.07	–0.10	–0.10	0.00	–0.10	0.17
Standard deviation	2.32	40.70	16.23	41.21	1.32	37.45	3.93	1.47	1.82	2.29	2.29	0.00	2.29	3.35
Panel B														
All aid is spent with closed capital account: pure float with 50:50 bond and foreign exchange sterilization														
$t = 0$	2.00	14.63	–5.01	13.07	–1.39	11.88	1.95	0.96	1.01	1.00	1.00	0.00	1.00	2.02
$t = 1$	1.00	2.67	–1.93	3.27	–0.31	4.37	0.95	0.43	0.42	0.45	0.45	0.00	0.45	1.21
$t = 2$	0.50	3.42	–0.68	4.18	–0.11	4.11	0.40	0.31	0.23	0.18	0.18	0.00	0.18	0.71
$t = 15$	0.00	1.95	0.33	2.12	–0.02	1.94	–0.11	0.14	0.03	–0.05	–0.05	0.00	–0.05	0.08
Std. dev	2.32	19.23	5.67	19.21	1.42	17.97	2.28	1.38	1.15	1.14	1.14	0.00	1.14	2.59

Table 13.3 (continued)

Time period	Aid shock	Nominal exchange rate	Real exchange rate	Nominal interest rate	Real interest rate	Infla-tion	Current account balance	Private consump-tion	Demand for non-tradables	Total bond sales	Bond accumu-lation (domestic investors)	Bond acc-umulation (foreign investors)	Reserve accumu-lation	Budget deficit before aid
Panel C														
All aid is spent with imperfectly open capital account: pure float with 50:50 bond and foreign exchange sterilization														
$t = 0$	2.00	14.43	–4.83	12.95	–1.65	11.77	1.83	1.15	1.09	1.00	0.77	0.23	1.00	2.24
$t = 1$	1.00	2.47	–1.76	2.76	–0.60	4.15	0.88	0.51	0.44	0.45	0.39	0.10	0.45	1.09
$t = 2$	0.50	3.18	–0.57	3.56	–0.21	3.84	0.37	0.28	0.20	0.18	0.21	–0.03	0.18	0.53
$t = 15$	0.00	1.96	0.32	2.14	–0.01	1.96	–0.10	0.13	0.03	0.00	0.00	0.00	–0.05	–0.02
Std. dev	2.32	18.99	5.43	18.87	1.76	17.75	2.14	1.48	1.21	1.14	6.32	0.80	1.14	2.57
Memo Item														
All aid is spent with closed capital account: pure float [Table 13.1 Panel A]														
$t = 0$	2.00				–1.68									1.86
$t = 1$	1.00				–1.17									0.84
$t = 2$	0.50				–0.69									0.35
$t = 15$	0.00				0.00									0.00
Std. dev	2.32				2.25									2.07

Notes: See Table 13.1.

Opening the capital account does little to alter this picture. As the comparison of panels B and C indicates, the adjustment path for the economy is virtually unchanged beyond the change in the composition of debt holdings arising from the sterilization rule. The path for the real interest rate is pegged slightly tighter to the foreign bond rate (adjusted for the expected real exchange rate appreciation), debt service costs are consequently marginally lower across the response horizon and the paths for inflation and the real exchange rate are very slightly smoother. But overall, these differences are nugatory. Moreover, the results do not change substantially as the elasticity of the foreign bond supply increases: even with a perfectly open capital account the same outcomes prevail for this particular shock and response. The reason is that the sterilization rule in operation here – where the bond issue is conditioned directly and exclusively on the fiscal response to the aid shock – is invariant to the evolution of the intermediate target such as reserve money or indeed to the evolution of inflation. As such, the chosen volume of sterilization is independent of capital market conditions so that the fiscal burden of sterilization varies only in terms of the variations in the real interest rate which, as noted, changes relatively little with changes in the elasticity of foreign bond supply. Indeed, as the results presented in Table 13.3 show, this particular rule does not do a particularly good job in controlling inflation. To understand fully the consequences of capital account liberalization on the properties of sterilization rules, including the implications for the offset between bond sterilization and the path of reserves, requires an examination of a wider range of settings for the intervention and bond reaction functions, a task beyond the scope of this chapter.

13.4 CONCLUSIONS

We argued at the beginning of this chapter that central bankers in Africa face substantial problems in managing aid surges. In practice, many appear to have adopted strategies involving substantial intervention and reserve accumulation in response to aid surges, accompanied in many cases by fairly aggressive bond sterilization. Our simulations suggest that when currency substitution is active, this pattern is consistent with an efficient monetary policy response to an aid surge, and particularly so when a portion of the aid will be used for inflation stabilization. Conditional on these portfolio effects, however, there is essentially no role for bond sterilization during an aid surge, at least when the capital account is closed. Moreover, we find that the relative properties of the alternative rules are robust to relaxing the assumption that the domestic bond market is entirely closed to external influences. We show that while foreign participation in the domestic bond market allows for more efficient adjustment when aid flows are fully spent, this does not carry over to the case in which aid alters the trajectory for domestic deficit financing. In the latter case, foreign bondholders exacerbate the short-run trade-offs facing the monetary authority and strengthen the appeal of temporary reserve accumulation.

Monetary policy has a complex mandate in sub-Saharan Africa, where conventional objectives of macroeconomic stability coexist with an interest in facilitating the development of financial markets. While we have emphasized the appeal of temporary reserve accumulation in the face of an aid surge, there is a sharp divergence between how this is accomplished under a crawl and a buffer plus float. In a crawl, the monetary authority targets the exchange rate, while in a buffer plus float intervention coincides with aid-financed spending in a version of reserve-money targeting. The two approaches have widely divergent implications for how the exchange rate responds to other shocks, and therefore for the patterns of volatility facing portfolio holders (and their assumptions regarding the nominal anchor). Our current DSGE model treats the parameters of portfolio behavior as exogenous to these variations in monetary policy behaviour. We are therefore ignoring any impact of alternative rules on the trajectory of financial market development. This is an important area for further work.

NOTES

* Christopher Adam acknowledges the support of Economic and Social Research Council (ESRC) World Economy and Finance Programme (RES-156-25-0001 Managing Macroeconomic Risks in Developing Countries: Policies and Institutions).

1. A second concern is that volatile external flows, particularly aid flows, threaten fiscal destabilization as aid inflows induce difficult-to-reverse public spending commitments, raising the risk that the fiscal authorities will fall back on deficit financing when aid inflows recede (see Buffie et al., Chapter 6 in this volume).
2. The short-run management of aid surges has become a central policy issue amongst donors and the international financial institutions, particularly when set against the background of commitments on the part of some donors to scale up aid flows to some of the world's lowest-income countries; see Berg et al. (2007).
3. We do not present the model in this chapter. An extended version of the chapter which includes the full model specification can be found at http://www.worldeconomyandfinance.org/working_papers_publications/working_papers.html.
4. This is achieved by including the first-order condition for money (that is, the money demand equation), which adds one equation and one variable (money) to the model.
5. The sensitivity of our central results to variations in these elasticities is discussed in Adam et al. (2009) and O'Connell et al. (2007).
6. In principle, given this planned level of spending out of aid, the fiscal authorities may

choose also to smooth the path of spending relative to that of the aid inflow. Smoothing rules are discussed in Adam et al. (2009).

7. Equation (13.2) can be adapted to accommodate a real rather than a nominal exchange rate target by replacing the exchange rate term $(x_t - \bar{x})$ with $(e_t - \bar{e})$, where e denotes the real exchange rate.
8. Ensuring that bonds held by the private sector return to their steady-state level means in turn that interest payments and the fiscal deficit are unchanged in the long run. This is required by consistency with the long-run inflation target.
9. The simulations are generated by the Dynare-Matlab routines (Julliard, 1996) using a first-order Taylor approximation to the nonlinear model around the non-stochastic steady state.
10. In terms of the model, and given that total bonds are fixed in supply, the private sector accumulates claims on government which in turn amortizes an equivalent volume of bonds held by the foreign investor.
11. The one-period aid shock is equivalent to 2 per cent of GDP and has an autoregressive parameter of 0.5 implying a present value of 4 per cent of GDP which, at the steady-state real interest rate of 10 per cent, corresponds to an annuity value of 0.364.

REFERENCES

Adam, Christopher, Stephen O'Connell, Edward Buffie and Catherine Pattillo (2009) 'Monetary Policy Rules for Managing Aid Surges in Africa', *Review of Development Economics*, DOI: 10.1111/j.1467-9361.2009.00502.x, available at: http://www3.interscience.wiley.com/journal/120124989/issue.

Benigno, Pierpaolo and Michael Woodford (2007), 'Optimal Inflation Targeting Under Alternative Fiscal Regimes', in Frederic Mishkin and Klaus Schmidt-Hebbel (eds), *Monetary Policy under Inflation Targeting*, Santiago: Central Bank of Chile.

Berg, Andrew, Shekhar Aiyar, Mumtaz Hussein, Shaun Roache, Tokhir Mirzoev and Amber Mahone (2007), 'The Macroeconomics of Scaling Up Aid: Lessons from Recent Experience', IMF Occasional Paper 235.

Branson, William and Dale Henderson (1985) 'The Specification and Influence of Asset Markets' in Robert Jones and Peter Kenen (eds), *Handbook of International Economics*, Vol. 2, Amsterdam and Oxford: Elsevier, North-Holland.

Buffie, Edward, Christopher Adam, Stephen O'Connell and Catherine Pattillo (2004), 'Exchange Rate Policy and the Management of Official and Private Capital Inflows in Africa', *IMF Staff Papers*, **51** (Special Issue), pp. 126–60.

Cespedes, Luis Felipe, Roberto Chang and Andres Velasco (2003), 'IS-LM-BP in the Pampas', *IMF Staff Papers*, **50**, Special Issue, pp. 143–56.

Edwards, Sebastian (2007), 'The Relationship between Exchange Rates and Inflation Targeting Revisited', in Frederic Mishkin and Klaus Schmidt-Hebbel (eds) *Monetary Policy under Inflation Targeting*, Santiago: Central Bank of Chile.

IMF (2007a), 'Zambia: 5th and 6th Reviews of Poverty Reduction and Growth Facility', IMF Country Report CR 07/209.

IMF (2007b), 'Ghana: Selected Issues and Statistical Appendix', IMF Country Report CR 07/208.

Julliard, Michel (1996), 'Dynare: A Program for the Resolution and Simulation of Dynamic Models With Forward Variables Through the Use of a Relaxation Algorithm', CEPREMAP Working Paper 9602.

O'Connell, Stephen A., Christopher S. Adam, Edward Buffie and Catherine Pattillo (2007), 'Managing External Volatility: Central Bank Options in Low-Income Countries', in Nicoletta Batini ed. *Monetary Policy in Emerging Market and Other Developing Countries*, New York: Nova Science Books and Journals.
Porter, Nathan and James Yudong Yao (2005), '"Inflation Targeting Lite" in Small Open Economies: The Case of Mauritius', IMF Working Paper WP/05/172, August.
Stone, Mark R. (2003), 'Inflation Targeting Lite', IMF Working Paper WP/03/12.
Woodford, Michael (2003), *Interest and Prices: Foundations of a Theory of Monetary Policy*, Princeton, NJ: Princeton University Press.

14. Regional asymmetries in the impact of monetary policy on prices: evidence from Africa

David Fielding

14.1 INTRODUCTION

It is known that there are substantial deviations from the Law of One Price across regions or cities within Organisation for Economic Co-operation and Development (OECD) countries (Parsley and Wei, 1996; Engel and Rogers, 2001; Ceglowski, 2003). Although deviations in the prices of specific consumer goods at the barcode level may be small, regional variations in consumption patterns lead to much larger deviations at higher levels of aggregation, for example at the level of a US Bureau of Labor Statistics (BLS) expenditure category. Moreover, deviations in regional services prices can be substantial. Convergence towards intra-national purchasing power parity happens very slowly; the half-life of deviations from the Law of One Price across US cities is estimated to be about nine years (Cecchetti et al., 2002).

These deviations may be caused partly by factors entirely outside the control of any policymaker, for example by asymmetric regional supply shocks, and may not represent any particular economic inefficiency. However, there is also evidence that regional deviations from the Law of One Price are partly caused by asymmetric responses to federal monetary policy. Clausen (2001), Fountas and Papagapitos (2001) and Putkuri (2003) among others discuss regional asymmetries in monetary transmission in euroland; Fielding and Shields (2007) discuss similar asymmetries in the US. Such asymmetries have important consequences for monetary policy design, and substantial welfare losses can arise if policy is based only on aggregate data (De Grauwe, 2000; Gros and Hefeker, 2002; Nolan, 2002; De Grauwe and Sénégas, 2006).

These issues are likely to be at least as important in developing and transitional economies as they are in the OECD. The underdevelopment of transport and communication networks is likely to raise intra-national transportation costs, and regional markets are likely to be less well integrated than elsewhere. In this chapter we will illustrate the magnitude of the problem using data from two African countries, Cameroon and South Africa. Given data limitations in these two countries, our statistical analysis will be less extensive than previous work on US and EU data. Nevertheless, the OECD experience can still provide us with clues about the potential policy implications for the African monetary authorities.

14.2 REGIONAL PRICE DEVIATIONS IN CAMEROON AND SOUTH AFRICA AS COMPARED WITH THE US

In order to illustrate the magnitude of intra-national variations in relative prices in Cameroon and South Africa, we focus on aggregate quarterly consumer price indices in the five main metropolitan areas in each country. The Cameroonian data are taken from the National Institute of Statistics (www.statistics-cameroon.org) and the South African data from Statistics South Africa (www.statssa.gov.za).

The location of the metropolitan areas is indicated in Figures 14.1–14.2. In Cameroon the largest cities, Yaoundé and Douala, are located in the more populous south-western part of the country. The smaller cities further north, Bamenda and Bafoussam, lie in a slightly more isolated area. In the far north lies Garoua, the centre of a much more isolated and arid area of low population density. In South Africa the area of highest population density is in Gauteng, containing both Pretoria and Witwatersrand (that is, the greater Johannesburg region), which is the largest metropolitan statistical area. The other large metropolitan statistical areas are spread out across the country: Durban in KwaZulu-Natal, Bloemfontein in the Free State and the Cape Peninsula (that is, the greater Cape Town region) on the south coast.

Figure 14.3 illustrates the characteristics of relative prices in Cameroon and Figure 14.4 the characteristics of relative prices in South Africa. Each line in each figure plots the evolution of the quarterly relative price index for a particular metropolitan area. In Figure 14.3, each series represents the log of the consumer price index in one of the five largest metropolitan areas relative to the price index for all metropolitan areas in Cameroon. In Figure 14.4, each series represents the log of the consumer price index in one of the five largest metropolitan areas relative to the price index for all metropolitan areas in South Africa. The base period in both figures is 1996Q1.

The two figures share a number of common features. There are large and

Figure 14.1 Map of Cameroon

persistent movements in relative prices in most metropolitan areas. Shocks to relative prices are substantial and are not quickly dissipated. The relative price series in the two figures do not show any marked tendency to revert back to a fixed level. Statistical analysis of monthly Cameroonian price data does indicate some evidence of eventual mean reversion in all metropolitan areas except Bamenda, but there is no such evidence in South Africa (see Appendix 14.1). While prices in one or two metropolitan areas seem to track the national average quite closely (Douala in Cameroon, Witwatersrand in South Africa), others often exhibit increases or decreases of 2 or 3 percent within the space of a year. The extreme case is Bamenda, where relative prices fell by over 12 percent between 1999 and 2004. These movements are substantial relative to average nationwide

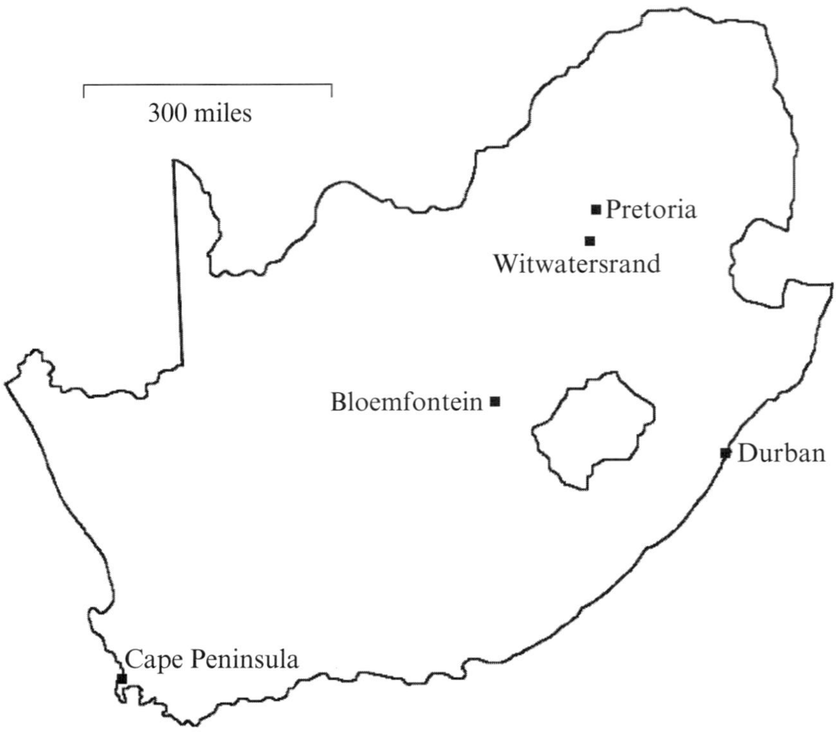

Figure 14.2 Map of South Africa

inflation rates in this period: 3.2 percent per annum in Cameroon and 5.5 percent per annum in South Africa. Moreover, there appears to be no obvious correlation of the distance between two metropolitan areas with the size of the movements in their relative prices. Prices in Bamenda relative to prices in Bafoussam (less than 50 miles away) fell by over 15 percent between 1999 and 2004. Prices in Pretoria are no more closely tied to prices in Witwatersrand than those of any other major South African metropolitan area.

These characteristics are shared by many OECD countries. Figure 14.5 depicts the evolution of relative prices in the five largest metropolitan areas in the US, measured in the same way as relative prices in Cameroon and South Africa but using BLS data. The magnitude of relative price movements in the US metropolitan areas is similar to that in South Africa, and to that in Cameroon apart from Bamenda. The relative price series in the US also exhibit a high degree of persistence. Given these basic relative price data, it seems quite likely that the discussions about

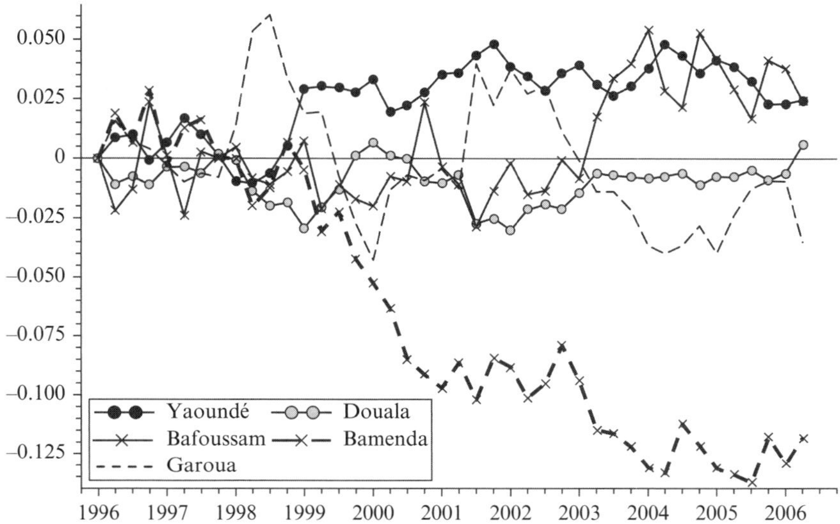

Figure 14.3 *The log of consumer prices in five major metropolitan areas relative to the national average (Cameroon)*

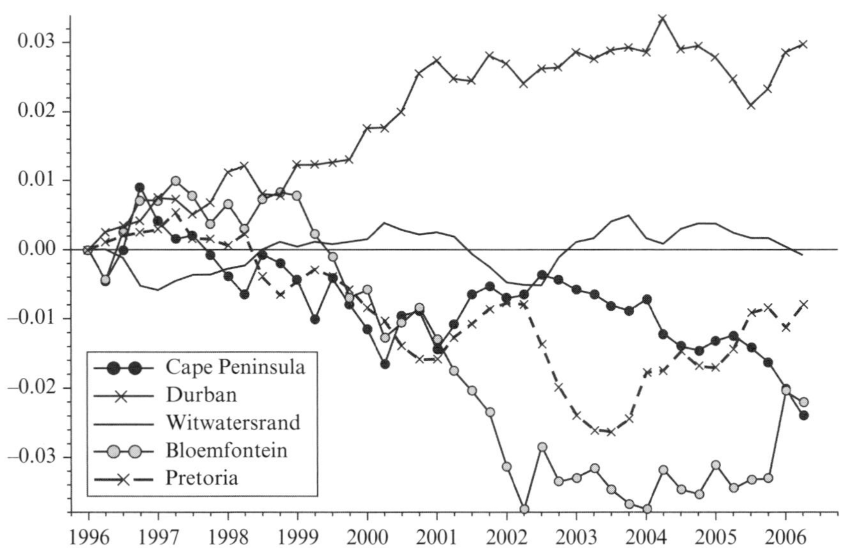

Figure 14.4 *The log of consumer prices in five major metropolitan areas relative to the national average (South Africa)*

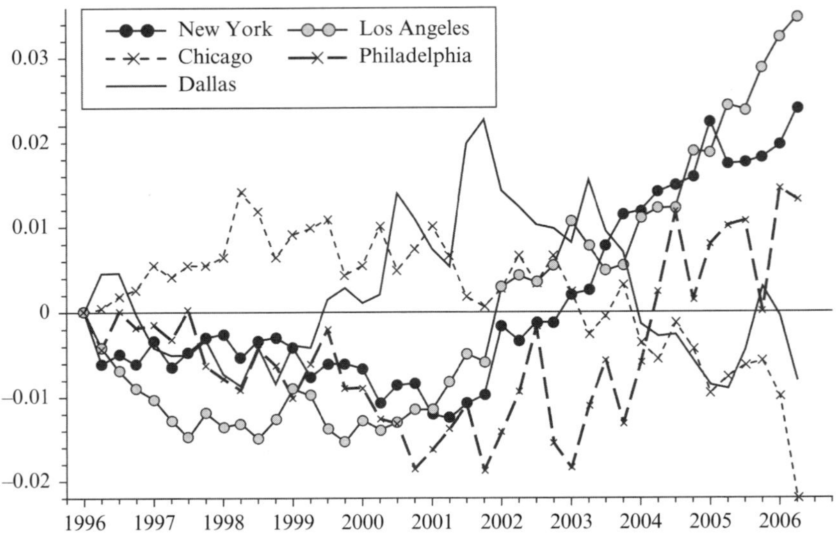

Figure 14.5 The log of consumer prices in five major metropolitan areas relative to the national average (USA)

the importance of regional asymmetries with regard to federal monetary policy in the US and the EU are equally relevant to monetary policy in Africa. Macroeconomic data are generally more limited in Africa than in the OECD, which constrains the extent to which we can gather empirical evidence on the magnitude of regional asymmetries in monetary transmission in Africa. Nevertheless, there are enough data in Cameroon and South Africa to conduct some basic statistical analysis, which is discussed in the following section.

14.3 THE IMPACT OF MONETARY POLICY ON REGIONAL PRICES IN CAMEROON AND SOUTH AFRICA

Both Cameroon and South Africa have relatively stable monetary policy environments. Cameroon is a member of the Central African Economic and Monetary Community, a monetary union that includes most of Cameroon's neighbors: the Central African Republic, Chad, the Congo Republic, Equatorial Guinea and Gabon. The single currency (the central African CFA franc) is pegged to the euro, and the current constitution of the union guarantees a stable, credible fixed peg underwritten by the

Table 14.1 Effect on relative prices in five major metropolitan areas of an interest rate increase in Cameroon

	Effect at three months		Eventual effect	
	Semi-elasticity	Std. err.	Semi-elasticity	Std. err.
Yaoundé	**–0.411**	**0.179**	**–1.575**	**0.649**
Douala	0.082	0.136	0.304	0.500
Bafoussam	**–0.404**	**0.233**	**–1.421**	**0.806**
Bamenda	**1.905**	**0.377**	**7.699**	**1.011**
Garoua	0.148	0.290	0.545	1.069

French Treasury. The central bank, the BEAC, based in Yaoundé, enacts a single monetary policy for all member states. Many of the local capital markets are very thin, so the central bank uses a number of monetary instruments, including a liquidity ratio for clearing banks and quantitative limits on the rediscount facilities, in addition to adjustment of the rediscount rate. There is no explicit inflation target, but policy is designed to ensure that the fixed peg remains credible.

In South Africa, Reserve Bank policy is also ultimately designed to stabilize the exchange rate. Since 2000, this objective has been pursued through an explicit inflation target: 'The primary objective of monetary policy is to protect the value of the currency in order to obtain balanced and sustainable economic growth in the country . . . It requires the achievement of financial stability, i.e. price stability as well as stable conditions in the financial sector as a whole.'[1] Current Reserve Bank monetary policy is based on adjustment of the interest rate on its repurchase transactions, although in the recent past it has made reference to a wider range of policy instruments.

Tables 14.1–14.3 provide some evidence on the impact of monetary policy on regional prices in the two countries. The statistical model on which these tables are based is discussed in Appendix 14.2. The tables show how each of the price series depicted in Figures 14.3–14.4 can be expected to change, on average, after there is a change in monetary policy. We make a distinction between the immediate movement in relative prices (within the first quarter) and the eventual movement in prices that can be expected, on average, after a change in policy. The price data used in the analysis underlying the tables are the same as in Figures 14.3–14.4, but measured at the monthly rather than the quarterly frequency. The monthly data on monetary policy variables are taken from the BEAC (www.beac.int) and the South African Reserve Bank (www.reservebank.co.za).

Since the BEAC uses several monetary policy instruments in addition to

Table 14.2 Effect on relative prices in five major metropolitan areas of increased monetary growth in Cameroon

	Effect at three months		Eventual effect	
	Elasticity	Std. err.	Elasticity	Std. err.
Yaoundé	**0.105**	**0.035**	**0.712**	**0.257**
Douala	**–0.072**	**0.028**	**–0.431**	**0.176**
Bafoussam	0.014	0.047	0.076	0.268
Bamenda	**–0.096**	**0.051**	**–0.781**	**0.439**
Garoua	0.015	0.054	0.093	0.326

Table 14.3 Effect on relative prices in five major metropolitan areas of an interest rate increase in South Africa

	Effect at three months		Eventual effect	
	Semi-elasticity	Std. err.	Semi-elasticity	Std. err.
Cape Peninsula	0.016	0.026	–	–
Bloemfontein	**0.080**	**0.029**	–	–
Durban	–0.013	0.024	–	–
Pretoria	**–0.047**	**0.024**	–	–
Witwatersrand	0.005	0.011	–	–

an interest rate, we measure monetary policy in Cameroon in two alternative ways. First of all, we look at one specific direct policy instrument, the monthly value of the annualized BEAC rediscount rate. Secondly, we look at the monthly rate of growth of the nominal M2 money stock. This stock is not under the direct control of the central bank, but it is an intermediate target variable that can be influenced by all of the different instruments under direct BEAC control.

Table 14.1 deals with the movement in relative prices that can be expected after a change in the rediscount rate. For each metropolitan area, the figures in the first column show the percentage change in prices relative to the national average that can be expected three months after a percentage point increase in the (annualized) rediscount rate; the next column shows the standard error associated with this point estimate. The third and fourth columns show corresponding figures for the eventual total change in relative prices, were the increase in the rediscount rate to be permanent. For two out of the five metropolitan areas, Yaoundé and Bafoussam, the figures are negative and statistically significant: that is, an increase in the rediscount rate is followed by a significant reduction in prices in these areas relative to the national average. Since an increase in the rediscount rate will be generally deflationary, the negative figures indicate a relatively large sensitivity of prices in Yaoundé and Bafoussam. By contrast, the figures in Bamenda are positive and statistically significant, indicating a relatively low sensitivity of prices. (Once again, the geographical proximity of Bamenda and Bafoussam does not preclude highly asymmetric price behavior.) Were the rise in the rediscount rate to persist for several years, the consequent movements in relative prices would be substantial. Prices in Yaoundé and Bafoussam would drop by around 1.5 percent relative to the national average; prices in Bamenda would rise by about 7.7 percent relative to the national average.

In Table 14.2 we report another set of relative price responses for Cameroon, now using the rate of growth of the money supply instead of the rediscount rate. For each metropolitan area, the figures in the first column show the percentage change in prices relative to the national average that can be expected three months after a 1 percent increase in the monthly rate of growth of the money supply; the next column shows the standard error associated with this point estimate. It can be seen that the statistically significant figures in the first column have the opposite sign to the equivalent figures in Table 14.1, as one would expect: an increase in the rediscount rate constitutes a monetary contraction, whereas in Table 14.2 we are considering a monetary expansion. With a 1 percent increase in the money supply, we can expect an increase in relative prices in Yaoundé of about 0.1 percent after three months; if the increase were permanent, this figure would eventually rise to about 0.7 percent. As we would expect from Table 14.1, the effect on relative prices in Bafoussam is also positive, although it is no longer statistically significant. The same monetary expansion can be expected to lower relative prices in Bamenda by about 0.1 percent after three months, and eventually by about 0.8 percent if the expansion were sustained. There is also a similar though slightly smaller effect on relative prices in Douala.

Finally, Table 14.3 presents results concerning the response of relative prices following an increase in the South African Reserve Bank's repurchase rate. The short-run effects in South Africa are generally smaller than those in Cameroon, and all of the long-run effects are statistically insignificant. A percentage point increase in the (annualized) repurchase rate can be expected to raise relative prices in Bloemfontein by around 0.08 percent within three months and lower relative prices in Pretoria by around 0.05 percent; the effects in other metropolitan areas are statistically insignificant.

These results are based on a statistical model that is less elaborate than those used to model regional prices in OECD economies. In particular, the results in Tables 14.1–14.3 do not identify a particular causal channel through which a change in monetary policy affects relative prices. The results in Tables 14.1–14.3 do not establish conclusively that the change in monetary policy is the direct cause of relative price movements.[2] Nevertheless, the fact that relative price changes follow a change in monetary policy is consistent with results from OECD countries with more extensive data, where a direct causal connection has been established. In the next section, we review evidence from the US that can inform monetary policy in African countries with regional price asymmetries.

14.4 LESSONS FROM THE US

Fielding and Shields (2007) analyze the impact of innovations in monetary policy on relative prices for the aggregate Consumer Price Index (CPI) and 43 CPI components in 29 US metropolitan areas. Monetary policy innovations are found to have a substantial and persistent impact on relative prices for many metropolitan areas and many goods and services. These direct causal effects are not confined to any one particular type of good or service. Given the high level of transport and communications infrastructure development in the US, it is unlikely that poor infrastructure is the main cause of asymmetries in monetary transmission in Africa. Improvements in infrastructure may help to mitigate asymmetries, but will by no means eradicate them entirely.

One characteristic of the US results is also suggested in Tables 14.1–14.3: that is, relative prices in some metropolitan areas are much more sensitive to monetary policy than others, either because monetary policy has a particularly large effect on inflation in a certain area, or because it has a particularly small effect. With data from only five metropolitan areas in Cameroon and South Africa, it is not possible to perform any statistical analysis of the characteristics of an area that lead to especially high or low sensitivity. However, such statistical analysis is possible with the US data, and the US results suggest possible avenues of future research into relative prices in Africa.

In the US, inflation is particularly sensitive to monetary policy innovations in areas in which commerce makes up a relatively large part of local economic activity. It is also particularly sensitive in areas with high property values: households with more valuable property find it relatively easy to refinance their mortgages to take advantage of a fall in interest rates. On the other hand, inflation is less sensitive to monetary policy innovations in areas with a relatively large child population: consumer demand is less interest-elastic when a large proportion of consumer goods are regarded as necessities, because they represent expenditure on children. There is also less sensitivity of prices to monetary policy in areas where financial institutions are relatively large and more able to absorb changes in reserve bank rates, so interest rate pass-through is lower, at least in the short run.

Some of these characteristics reflect a relatively high level of economic development that is not currently directly relevant to countries like Cameroon, and only partially relevant to countries like South Africa. Nevertheless, they provide a framework for interpreting African data. Some characteristics of relatively large financial centers (such as a large amount of commerce and higher property values) tend to lead to higher sensitivity of prices to monetary policy. Others (such as relatively large financial institutions) tend to lead to lower sensitivity. The largest Cameroonian financial center and national capital, Yaoundé, exhibits the highest sensitivity of any metropolitan area. Possibly this is because in a country with very thin and imperfectly competitive capital markets the size of financial institutions makes little difference to monetary transmission, so the commerce effect dominates. South Africa represents a higher level of financial development, and financial and commercial activity there is geographically dispersed. Nevertheless, it is again the country's capital, Pretoria, which exhibits the highest sensitivity to monetary policy.

The fact that the sensitivity of regional prices to monetary policy in the US depends on a wide range of economic, financial and demographic factors suggests that the degree of sensitivity is not a fixed characteristic, but one which can change over time. In a developing country, these factors are likely to be even more fluid, so the results in Tables 14.1–14.3 should not be regarded as permanent, but rather as a snapshot of regional asymmetries in monetary transmission at a particular point in time and at a particular stage of economic development.

APPENDICES

Appendix 14.1: Tests for the Stationarity of the Relative Price Series

In order to test the stationarity of the relative price series, we conduct standard Augmented Dickey–Fuller (ADF) tests. The test results are reported in Table 14A.1. The results for Cameroonian metropolitan areas are shown on the left-hand side of the table; the results for the South African metropolitan areas are shown on the right-hand side. The sample period in Cameroon (after taking lags) is May 1994 to March 2007; the sample period for South Africa is May 1996 to June 2006. All of the ADF regressions include an intercept but no trend. For each metropolitan area, we report the lag order of the ADF regression and the ADF t-statistic.

Table 14A.1 ADF test statistics

Cameroon	ADF t ratio	Lag order	South Africa	ADF t ratio	Lag order
Yaoundé	–2.74	1	Cape Pen.	–1.11	0
Douala	–4.10	0	Bloemfontein	–0.92	0
Bafoussam	–3.53	0	Durban	–1.63	3
Bamenda	–0.81	3	Pretoria	–1.49	0
Garoua	–4.09	0	Witwatersrand	–2.33	3

For three Cameroonian metropolitan areas (Douala, Bafoussam and Garoua), the null hypothesis that the series are difference-stationary can be rejected against the alternative that they are stationary in levels at the 5 percent level. For one area (Yaoundé), the null can be rejected at the 10 percent level. In only one case (Bamenda) is it impossible to reject the null. We conclude that relative price series in Cameroon are generally mean-reverting. Prices in Bamenda may be an exception, and therefore the standard errors associated with the elasticities for Bamenda in Tables 14.1–14.2 should be treated with some caution. However, the price dynamics for Bamenda in Table 14A.2 are very similar to the dynamics for other metropolitan areas, so the ADF test result may be an anomaly.

None of the South African relative price series exhibits any sign of stationarity in levels. In no case can the null of difference-stationarity be rejected at any conventional confidence interval.

Appendix 14.2: Modelling the Response of Relative Prices to Monetary Policy

The results in Tables 14.1–14.3 are based on the following statistical model. For Cameroon, we fit the following set of regression equations:

$$\ln(p_{it}) = \alpha_0 + \alpha_1 \cdot \ln(p_{it-1}) + \alpha_2 \cdot r_{t-3} + u_{it} \qquad (14A.1)$$

$$\ln(p_{it}) = \alpha_0 + \alpha_1 \cdot \ln(p_{it-1}) + \alpha_2 \cdot m_{t-3} + u_{it} \qquad (14A.2)$$

where p_{it} is the price index in metropolitan area i relative to the national average in month t, r_t is the BEAC rediscount rate in month t and m_t is the rate of growth of Cameroonian M2 in month t. u_{it} is a regression residual. In each case there are five regressions, one for each metropolitan area. The regression equations are stacked and the parameters fitted simultaneously using a maximum likelihood estimator. The α_2 parameters provide the

Table 14A.2 Regression coefficients for Cameroon

	Model with r		Model with m	
	Coefficient	s.e.	Coefficient	s.e.
Yaoundé				
α_0	0.036	0.013	0.002	0.001
α_1	0.739	0.033	0.853	0.024
α_2	–0.411	0.179	0.105	0.035
σ	0.010		0.010	
Douala				
α_0	–0.016	0.010	–0.006	0.001
α_1	0.731	0.033	0.834	0.025
α_2	0.082	0.136	–0.072	0.028
σ	0.008		0.008	
Bafoussam				
α_0	0.035	0.017	0.003	0.001
α_1	0.716	0.036	0.823	0.028
α_2	–0.404	0.233	0.014	0.047
σ	0.013		0.014	
Bamenda				
α_0	–0.132	0.026	0.003	0.002
α_1	0.753	0.037	0.877	0.024
α_2	1.905	0.377	–0.096	0.051
σ	0.014		0.015	
Garoua				
α_0	–0.002	0.021	0.005	0.002
α_1	0.728	0.033	0.834	0.025
α_2	0.148	0.290	0.015	0.054
σ	0.016		0.016	

figures for the three-month effects in Tables 14.1–14.2, while the long-run effects in the tables are calculated as $\alpha_2/[1 - \alpha_1]$. In no case is any other lag of r_t or m_t is statistically significant. The full set of regression results is reported in Table 14A.2.

In South Africa the relative price series are non-stationary, and there is no evidence of cointegration between the relative price and repurchase rate series. We therefore fit a set of regression equations in differences:[3]

$$\Delta \ln(p_{it}) = \beta_0 + \beta_1 \cdot \Delta r_{t-3} + u_{it} \qquad (14A.3)$$

The three-month effects reported in Table 14.3 are based on the β_1 coefficients. Again, no other lag of Δr_t is statistically significant.

NOTES

1. Appendix to the Statement of the Monetary Policy Committee (6 April 2000).
2. This is because the statistical framework described in Appendix 14.2 does not incorporate a model monetary policy, so the results in Tables 14.1–14.3 show the average response of relative prices whenever there is a change in policy (for whatever reason). If policy responds systematically to other macroeconomic events, these events may be part of the explanation for the relative price movements.
3. In the case of South Africa, there is a deterministic seasonal pattern in relative price movements, so the equation is fitted with a different intercept for each month of the year.

REFERENCES

Cecchetti, S., N. Mark and R. Sonora (2002), 'Price Index Convergence among United States Cities', *International Economic Review*, **43**, pp.1081–99.

Ceglowski, J. (2003), 'The Law of One Price: Intra-national Evidence for Canada', *Canadian Journal of Economics*, **36**, pp.373–400.

Clausen, V. (2001), *Asymmetric Monetary Transmission in Europe*, Heidelberg: Springer Verlag.

De Grauwe, P. (2000), 'Monetary Policies in the Presence of Asymmetries', *Journal of Common Market Studies*, **38**, pp.593–612.

De Grauwe, P. and M.-A. Sénégas (2006), 'Monetary Policy Design and Transmission Asymmetry in EMU: Does Uncertainty Matter?', *European Journal of Political Economy*, **22**, pp.787–808.

Engel, C. and J. Rogers (2001), 'Violating the Law of One Price: Should We Make a Federal Case Out of It?', *Journal of Money, Credit, and Banking*, **33**, pp.1–15.

Fielding, D. and K. Shields (2007), 'Regional Asymmetries in the Impact of Monetary Policy Shocks on Prices: Evidence from US Cities', paper presented to the Bank of England/Cornell University Workshop on New Developments in Monetary Policy in Emerging Economies, Bank of England, 17–18 July.

Fountas, S. and A. Papagapitos (2001), 'The Monetary Transmission Mechanism: Evidence and Implications for European Monetary Union', *Economics Letters*, **70**, pp.397–404.

Gros, D. and C. Hefeker (2002), 'One Size must Fit All: National Divergences in a Monetary Union', *German Economic Review*, **3**, pp.247–62.

Nolan, C. (2002), 'Monetary Stabilisation Policy in a Monetary Union: Some Simple Analytics', *Scottish Journal of Political Economy*, **49**, pp.196–215.

Parsley, D. and S.-J. Wei (1996), 'Convergence to the Law of One Price without Trade Barriers or Currency Fluctuations', *Quarterly Journal of Economics*, **111**, pp.1211–36.

Putkuri, H. (2003), 'Cross-Country Asymmetries in Euro Area Monetary Transmission: The Role of National Financial Systems', Bank of Finland Discussion Paper 15/2003.

15. Monetary policy and inflation modeling in a more open economy in South Africa

Janine Aron and John Muellbauer*

15.1 INTRODUCTION

South Africa (SA) in the 1990s became globally more integrated after years of isolation through trade and financial sanctions, prohibitive trade policies and a mainly closed capital account. The cessation of sanctions beginning in the early 1990s with an improved political dispensation in prospect, the gradual opening of the trade and capital accounts and the concomitant emergence of SA as a desirable emerging market destination for investors, gave impetus to a monetary policy regime change to inflation targeting from early 2000. The preceding monetary regime in the 1990s was founded on outmoded and dysfunctional monetary targeting, and was hampered by unclear policy objectives and poor policy transparency. With the opening of the economy, conflicting policy goals led to costly monetary mismanagement, hampering growth. The adoption of an inflation-targeting regime in a more open economy aimed to enhance policy transparency, accountability and predictability, and align monetary policy more closely with widespread international practice. The inflation-targeting regime (supported by fiscal policy) has successfully enhanced the credibility and effectiveness of monetary policy, achieving greater macro-stability and reducing inflation (Aron and Muellbauer, 2005, 2007a, 2008). SA's international economic standing has consequently improved, evidenced by reduced sovereign risk spreads and improved debt ratings, while investment and growth have risen.

However, changes in openness can disrupt the inflation forecasting on which targeting monetary policies depend. Since lowering import barriers typically exerts downward pressure on prices, evolving openness represents a structural break from the inflation forecasting perspective. Omitting this factor can confuse modellers studying the determinants of inflation and output. For instance, a greater degree of openness due to trade liberalization is likely to lower the rate of inflation and may alter the influence of the real exchange rate on growth, via the impact on the demand for exports and leakage of demand into imports. Unfortunately, attempts to measure trade policy are fraught with measurement problems for observable components (such as tariffs), and by the presence of difficult-to-quantify components of policy, such as quotas and other non-tariff barriers (see the empirical survey of trade policy measures in Aron and Muellbauer, 2007b).

We demonstrate the importance of accounting for this structural change in modelling SA inflation, using innovative time-series openness measures that address some of the shortcomings of existing measures. Including the openness measures in the central bank's own inflation model produces more stable equations, and stable over longer periods. It also allows a role for the level of the output gap rather than only its change, with policy implications relevant to current debate.

This chapter first summarizes the trade liberalization from 1990 and the freeing of the capital account, suggesting the challenges posed for monetary policy of greater trade and capital account openness. In section 15.3, we explain the derivation of innovative measures capturing greater openness (details in Aron and Muellbauer, 2007b), and in section 15.4, show improved results in various dimensions for the wholesale price inflation model of the South African Reserve Bank (SARB) when these openness measures are included. Further improvements in the model result when the real exchange rate, the international interest rate differential and food prices are introduced, as suggested by our previous work (Aron et al., 2003; Aron and Muellbauer, 2007b).

15.2 GREATER ECONOMIC OPENNESS AND THE IMPACT ON MONETARY POLICY

SA's trade was heavily protected from before the 1960s. There have been extensive changes in SA trade policy especially since the early 1990s, and a greater openness to capital inflows from 1995. Externally imposed trade and financial sanctions, first applied after 1976, were also lifted in the 1990s, mainly after the democratic elections. This structural change – the greater openness associated with the international reintegration of the democratic SA – has significantly influenced the conduct and design of monetary policy in SA.

15.2.1 Greater Openness in the Current and Capital Accounts

SA's extensive trade liberalization since 1990 is outlined in Edwards et al. (2009).[1] Conventional measures of openness based on real trade ratios and price ratios (Aron and Muellbauer, 2007b) suggest that the most trade-restrictive period was 1980–85, followed by a substantial liberalization from the early 1990s with the removal of remaining quotas and a decline in tariffs. From 1983, quotas were replaced by equivalent import tariffs with the share of imports subject to quotas falling to below 15 per cent by 1992. However, tariffs were flexible upwards in replacing quotas and their coverage was pervasive. The liberalizing effect of dismantling quotas was also partly offset by the imposition of periodic import surcharges. Particularly after the 1985 debt crisis, the government ensured current account surpluses through import surcharges to help meet foreign debt repayments. These were eventually abolished in 1994–95. SA's reintegration with international and regional communities after the democratic elections heralded several multilateral and bilateral trade agreements that instituted tariff reduction for the first time, beginning with the General Agreement on Tariffs and Trade (GATT) Uruguay Round of 1994. Quotas and export subsidies were also eventually largely phased out by 1997.

The question as to whether these tariff reforms achieved a reduction in effective rates of protection of industry has been contentious; see Edwards (2005). Using a consistent set of tariff data for 1988–2004, Edwards finds significant reductions in protection during the 1990s, both in terms of average nominal protection and effective protection in manufacturing, including the import surcharges but excluding non-tariff barriers (through lack of *ad valorem* equivalents for these). Reductions in protection occurred in almost all traded sectors.

The impact on monetary policy of the rapid opening of the current account from 1990, and the virtual cessation by 1995 of sanctions, was twofold. The key effects of tariff reduction and other aspects of opening the economy to trade would be expected to be seen in improved productivity figures for traded sectors under competition, and also in the impact on inflation. Indeed, the surge in labour productivity in the manufacturing sector coincided with greater trade openness. It seems likely too that greater trade openness could cause a shift in the relative importance of the different channels by which monetary policy operates, for example the real exchange rate channel. There is evidence for an increase in the role of the real exchange rate in influencing the growth of gross domestic product (GDP), Aron and Muellbauer (2002a).

SA's capital account had been subject to controls from before the 1960s. From the second quarter of 1979, a dual-currency exchange rate regime with commercial and financial rand exchange rates[2] was adopted, with a brief abortive period of unification in 1983 to 1985 (details in Aron et al., 2000). There was little access to international finance in the sanctions era after 1976, especially after 1985, with the exception of some trade finance.

However, from the 1994 elections, capital flows increased strongly. Flows, and particularly portfolio equity and bond flows, further accelerated with the effective lifting of exchange controls on non-residents in March 1995, when the dual exchange rate regime was finally successfully unified to a managed float. The change from negligible capital inflows to a substantial positive net inflow after 1994 reflected SA's status as a leading emerging market. This structural shift in the size of sustainable flows required adjustment via a 'permanently' more appreciated real exchange rate (unless offset by liberalization of exchange controls on residents).

By contrast with the sudden lifting of controls on non-resident flows, controls on residents were only gradually liberalized under the democratic government, and some controls remain. Chronological details can be found in Leape and Thomas (2009), who characterize the process as avoiding large and potentially destabilizing capital flight in a transitional period. Greater reform has occurred in periods of capital inflows, but has moderated during periods of instability and capital outflows. The pace of reform has been influenced by the continuing need for effective regulatory instruments for macroeconomic risk management, especially concerning SA's large institutional investors.

The monetary implications of the more open capital account depend on the monetary rule followed, and the sequencing of the lifting of domestic exchange controls. One impact on monetary policy of the sudden liberalization of non-resident capital controls should arise from a dramatic readjustment of the sustainable level of inflows with upward pressure on the exchange rate. On the other hand, a liberalization of the pervasive exchange controls on residents would be expected to have the opposite effect on the exchange rate. If the rule was to stabilize inflation and the exchange rate floated freely and appreciated, the deflationary effect would give the opportunity to reduce domestic interest rates and perhaps moderate the inflows. Clear prioritization of monetary policy objectives is important because, for instance, with an open capital account and persistent capital outflows, an adverse trade-off can arise where sustaining an exchange rate 'target' occurs at the expense of higher inflation, higher interest rates and eventually reduced output (for example Obstfeld, 1996).

15.2.2 SA Monetary Regimes and their Evolution with Greater Openness

In Table 15.1, we summarize the key features of the two consecutive monetary policy regimes coinciding with the period of greater openness in SA from 1990.[3] The table contrasts, *inter alia*, the transparency and accountability of the two frameworks. There were costly consequences from the

Table 15.1 Comparative design, transparency and accountability features of monetary regimes from 1990

Characteristics	Money targeting regime under Governor Stals 1986–98 (Stals' term began in 1989Q2)	Inflation targeting regime under Governor Mboweni 2000Q1 onwards (Mboweni's term began in 1999Q3)
Objective(s) and explicit prioritization of monetary policy	*Objective:* Under Stals, an initial mission statement, published in 1990, entrusted the protection of the domestic and external value of the rand to the Bank. This was carried through to the Interim Constitution (late April, 1994): 'The primary objectives of the South African Reserve Bank shall be to protect the internal *and* external value of the currency in the interest of balanced and sustainable economic growth in the Republic.' (Italics added) *Priority:* This can be interpreted as having both a price and an exchange rate target in mind, without explicit prioritization. The objective was clarified in late 1996 – see next column.	*Objective:* The Constitution Act of the Republic of South Africa, No 8 of 1996 (section 224) and the amended South African Reserve Bank Act, No 90 of 1989 (section 3 substituted by section 2 of Act 2 of 1996): 'The primary objective of monetary policy is to protect the value of the currency in order to obtain balanced and sustainable economic growth in the country.' *Priority:* Appendix to the Statement of the Monetary Policy Committee (MPC) – 6 April 2000: 'A New Monetary Policy Framework', Statement issued by Mr T.T. Mboweni, Governor of the SARB: 'The new inflation-targeting monetary policy framework is primarily concerned with one element of financial stability, i.e. price stability.' (http://www.reservebank.co.3a/)
Appointment and tenure of Governor	The President of South Africa appoints the Governor and three Deputy Governors for terms of five years, after consultation with the Minister of Finance and the board (see below). Parliament does not have the power to veto the appointment of the Governor. The Finance Minister may dismiss governors but, under current law, only for malfeasance or incapacity.	

Table 15.1 (continued)

Characteristics	Money targeting regime under Governor Stals 1986–98 (Stals' term began in 1989Q2)	Inflation targeting regime under Governor Mboweni 2000Q1 onwards (Mboweni's term began in 1999Q3)
Accountability to Parliament	The number of appearances before Parliament, made by central bank officials is decided by statute and a parliamentary committee.[1] The objective is to account for monetary policy decisions. Parliamentary scrutiny of the SARB is provided for in the Reserve Bank Act. Monthly statements of assets and liabilities, annual financial statements and an audit report have to be submitted to the Department of Finance, that later are tabled in Parliament by the Minister of Finance (Section 32). The Governor is also required by the Act to submit an annual report to the Minister on the implementation of monetary policy. Periodically, the Governor and senior staff appear before the Parliamentary Portfolio Standing Committee on Finance to account for monetary policy (now televised). Under the Reserve Bank Act, the Ministry of Finance has recourse to the Supreme Court should it judge the SARB as having deviated from its mandate, where it has not appropriately responded to written instructions from the Ministry to rectify matters (Section 37).	
Accountability to shareholders	The Reserve Bank is unusual in being one of only three central banks that is still privately owned. The SARB is internally governed by a board of 14 directors, seven appointed by the President (of whom one is the Governor and three are Deputy Governors) and seven by public shareholders. The Annual Report and accounts are approved by shareholders in annual meetings. The South African Reserve Bank Act stipulates conditions for tenure of Bank directors (including the Bank's Governor), but it does not explicitly give criteria for the removal of directors from office. The Minister of Finance has powers of regulation in relation to good governance by the board (Section 35).	

Explicit contract between the monetary authorities and the government	Operational responsibility was described by the South African Reserve Bank Act (No 90 of 1989). But before the Interim Constitution was adopted there were no explicit arrangements or contracts between the government and the SARB on instrument independence. The Interim Constitution (Act 200, 1993, assented to on 25 January 1994, commencing on 27 April 1994) states it shall perform its functions independently.	Constitutional independence of the SARB was enacted in 1996: Section 224 (2) of the Constitution states: 'The SARB, in pursuit of its primary object must perform its functions independently and without fear, favour or prejudice, but there must be regular consultation between the Bank and the Cabinet member responsible for national financial matters.' Operational independence was achieved initially through an exchange of letters between government and Bank.
Nature of target	Rate of increase in M3: a broad definition of money including notes and coins held by the public and all types of deposits of the domestic private sector with domestic banking institutions.	Rate of increase in CPIX: the overall consumer price index, excluding the mortgage interest cost. From January 2009 a new consumer price index was introduced including owner-equivalent rent, and was adopted as the targeted inflation measure.
Setting of the target	Set by the National Treasury after consultation with the SARB.	Set by the National Treasury after consultation with the SARB, ratified by the Cabinet.
Range and horizon of target	Annual target ranges were set using a three-month moving average of broad money growth (M3), and announced in the March Budget to cover the year from the preceding fourth quarter to the current fourth quarter.	The inflation target announced in February 2000 was specified as an average rate of increase in CPIX of 3–6 per cent per annum for the calendar year 2002. This was revised in October 2001 to 3–6 per cent for 2003 and 3–5 per cent for 2004 and 2005; in October 2002, to 3–6 per cent for 2004 and 3–5 per cent for 2005; and in February 2003 the target range for 2005 was increased from 3–5 per cent to 3–6 per cent. Since then, the inflation target aims to achieve a rate of increase in CPIX of between

Table 15.1 (continued)

Characteristics	Money targeting regime under Governor Stals 1986–98 (Stals' term began in 1989Q2)	Inflation targeting regime under Governor Mboweni 2000Q1 onwards (Mboweni's term began in 1999Q3)
		3 and 6 per cent per year. The unfortunate requirement that CPIX be within the target range on average over the calendar year was altered only in November 2003, to a continuous target of 3–6 per cent beyond 2006.
Breach of target/ escape clause/ explanation clause	There was discretion without penalty to breach targets, for instance in the face of external trade and financial shocks, but there was no formally required public explanation (Gidlow, 1995a, 1995b).	A letter to the Governor from the Minister of Finance at the inception of inflation targeting (letter released in June 2001), contained an 'escape clause'; there was an 'escape clause' in the inflation-targeting statement in the appendix to the MPC statement, 6 April 2000; and a clause in the Medium Term Budget Policy Statement, October 2001. Detailed statements can be found in Aron and Muellbauer (2007a). In November 2003, the SARB in consultation with the National Treasury revised earlier clauses into a forward-looking 'explanation clause' (Medium Term Budget Policy Statement, November 2003, http://www.finance.gov.3a/): 'When the economy is buffeted by a supply side shock similar to those envisaged by the original escape clause that will take inflation outside the target range (e.g. an oil price shock, a drought, a natural disaster, or financial contagion affecting the currency), at the subsequent meeting of the Monetary Policy Committee, the SARB will fully inform the public of the

		nature of the "shock", the anticipated impact on CPIX inflation and the monetary policy response to ensure that inflation returns to the target and the time frame over which this will occur.'
Explicit policy rule or strategy in monetary policy framework	In 1994 under Stals, the monetary policy targets were supplemented by a range of indicators (*Quarterly Bulletin*, October 1997). There was no explicit rule and policy was thus opaque (see Aron and Muellbauer, 2002b).	Inflation targeting with an explicit target was adopted in 2000, see Appendix to the Statement of the Monetary Policy Committee – 6 April 2000: 'A New Monetary Policy Framework', Statement issued by Mr. T.T. Mboweni, Governor, SARB, http://www.reservebank.co.3a/
MPC and meetings	By the South African Reserve Bank Act (No. 90 of 1989, and subsequent amendments), only the Governor and Deputy Governors can vote on monetary policy matters. Dates of meetings were not publicized. The Minister of Finance could also be consulted, but policy could be altered without his/her approval, and minutes of meetings with the SARB were not required to be published. There was no MPC: decisions were made by the Governor, after consultation with the Deputy Governors.	Interest rate decisions are reached by the Monetary Policy Committee (initially 15 and now nine members). By the South African Reserve Bank Act (No. 90 of 1989, and subsequent amendments), only the Governor and Deputy Governors can vote on monetary policy matters; however, in practice, decisions are made by 'consensus'. Since late 1999, the Governor appoints members to the MPC (there is no provision in the Reserve Bank Act for the composition of the committee). The MPC has no external members. The structure of the MPC has changed since its formation in October 1999, as have the frequency of its meetings. In 2007, it comprised seven SARB officials, chaired by the Governor, and meeting six times per year as of 2004. Dates of meetings are published in advance on the website.
Minutes of meetings	Minutes of these meetings were not published	Minutes of these meetings are not published.

Table 15.1 (continued)

Characteristics	Money targeting regime under Governor Stals 1986–98 (Stals' term began in 1989Q2)	Inflation targeting regime under Governor Mboweni 2000Q1 onwards (Mboweni's term began in 1999Q3)
Voting records	No voting records.	No voting is carried out in the MPC.
Announcement of policy decisions	There were sometimes press announcements about rate changes, but not every time the rate changed.	Policy decision changes are currently announced on the last day of the three-day MPC meeting, at 3 p.m. There is a press release and the announcement is televised.
Explanation of policy decisions	Explanations were given on those occasions when there were press statements. There were no announcements or explanations when it was decided to maintain interest rates.	An explanation is given in the MPC statement directly after every MPC meeting, both when interest rates change and when they do not.
Explicit policy inclination after policy meetings	Explicit inclinations were not given after every announcement of interest rate changes.	No explicit policy inclination is given after policy meetings, though the MPC statement as of about 2006 refers to the MPC's perception of the balance of risks with respect to the forecast.
Publication of macroeconomic model used for policy analysis	Prior to inflation targeting, various *Quarterly Bulletin* articles revealed parts of the SARB's large (400-equation) model, but it was never published as a whole.	The SARB model has been reconstructed since about 1999 with assistance from the Bank of England and others. It is still under development, and one working paper has been published with the core model. The actual series employed in the equations are not given.
Publication of macroeconomic forecasts	No forecasts were published in the Stals era.	The *Monetary Policy Review* is published twice annually, and contains an inflation forecast up to two years ahead in the form of a fan chart. No detail

		is given on the underlying assumptions, except that the repo rate is assumed unchanged for the forecast period. There are no forecasts for output.
Evaluation of forecasts	There was a quarterly analysis of current macro-economic developments and disturbances in the *Quarterly Bulletin*, but no forecasts were published.	There is a quarterly analysis of current macroeconomic developments and disturbances in the *Quarterly Bulletin*. The forecast errors up to 2005 were discussed in a recent SARB working paper, but they are not annually evaluated.
Evaluation of the policy outcome given macroeconomic objectives	Governor Stals gave extensive speeches and explanations, which were available on the web (no longer) covering some aspects of discrepancies between the policy outcome and target.	The *Monetary Policy Review* discusses discrepancies between the policy outcome and the target.

Notes:
1. Applying the survey of Sterne and Lepper (2002) on parliamentary accountability, there were three parliamentary hearings in 2006, all attended by the Governor, with one or two officials, relating to anything published in the *Quarterly Bulletin*. Currently there are 13 members of the Portfolio Standing Committee on Finance; on average ten members attend and eight members have academic training (at different levels). There are two full-time staff members. The committee receives no technical or analytical support, and has no part-time external advisors. One-off briefings are sometimes given to the committee on chosen topics by external economists, though after the address of the Governor to the committee.

Sources: Aron and Muellbauer (2002b, 2005, 2007a, 2008, 2009), Gidlow (1995a, 1995b).

comparatively poor monetary policy transparency and accountability under the first framework, in the transition to a more open economy. We argue that these encouraged the adoption of an inflation-targeting regime from 2000, to enhance monetary policy transparency, accountability and predictability.

Since 1986 there have been two monetary policy regimes in SA.[4] Monetary target ranges, by then already effectively abandoned by the UK and the US, were announced annually from 1986 to 1998. Any usefulness of these targets had been sharply diminished by extensive domestic financial liberalization beginning in the 1980s (Aron and Muellbauer, 2002b) and the later resurgence of capital inflows. From 1990, the monetary guidelines were supplemented by an eclectic set of indicators, including the exchange rate, asset prices, output gap, balance of payments, wage settlements, total credit extension and the fiscal stance (Stals, 1997). The policy rule under money targeting was thus not transparent, with a range of potential indicators influencing policy in addition to money targets, but without known weights.[5] This diminished the accountability of the SARB.

By contrast with the detailed fiscal policy objectives toward greater transparency and accountability in the government's RDP and GEAR plans,[6] rather cursory treatment was given to monetary policy. The plans and the Interim and Final Constitutions[7] expressed the monetary policy objectives differently, and until mid-1996 there was no clear prioritization amongst the objectives (see Table 15.1). There was also a lack of transparency about the extent of forward foreign exchange market intervention (in the absence of significant reserves).

Policy actions during 1994 to 1998 were often highly questionable. Aron and Muellbauer (2007a) argue that Governor Stals had dual and conflicting objectives for monetary policy objectives from April 1994, and despite official claims that the exchange rate was freely floating, engaged in heavy intervention in the period of resumption of capital inflows to restrain appreciation, and again to stem depreciation in the currency crises of 1996–98. Most intervention occurred via forward foreign exchange contracts (Kahn and Leape, 1996), ultimately proving extremely costly to the fiscal authority. The high levels of policy interest rates severely damaged economic growth and curtailed investment. With growth falling to 0.5 per cent in real terms during 1998, this monetary policy was hardly compatible with the official objective of 'balanced and sustainable economic growth' (Table 15.1).

With the advent of inflation targeting, introduced in February 2000 under a new Governor, Tito Mboweni, the constitutional primary objective for monetary policy was formalized through an announced, credible target range for inflation. The exchange rate was deemed to float freely, and mechanisms were instituted for a high level of policy transparency (Table 15.1). There are no conflicting policy goals under this arrangement. The SARB can accumulate foreign currency reserves and may at times intervene in the market to stabilize short-term fluctuation in the currency. However, it cannot under this mandate intervene for long periods to influence the currency in a particular direction without jeopardizing its target.

Since its adoption, the inflation-targeting regime has seen several improvements with an evolving institutional design (Table 15.1), and has significantly raised monetary policy transparency.[8] Interest rate policy is determined by a Monetary Policy Committee (MPC), in practice by consensus. The process of interest rate setting[9] can now broadly be described by Svensson's recommended moderate policy of flexible and forward-looking inflation targeting (Svensson et al., 2002), thus coping reasonably well with supply shocks. Inflation is not controlled at the shortest possible horizon by aggressive and volatile policy, with often volatile interest rates, but rather at a longer horizon of two to three years. The flexible approach aims also to stabilize the business cycle and hence the output gap. In the short term, inflation may well deviate, and sometimes significantly, from the target. Monetary policy decisions taken in response to sizeable external and domestic shocks under inflation targeting have significantly improved relative to the preceding framework, despite some data constraints (Aron and Muellbauer, 2007a, 2009). In particular, the steady handling of the 2001 exchange rate shock under inflation targeting can be contrasted with the policy mistakes during the 1998 exchange rate shock. The elimination by 2004 of the net open foreign currency position[10] accumulated under previous monetary policy regimes is an important achievement that has reduced sovereign risk. It has allowed the accumulation of foreign exchange reserves for reducing short-term exchange rate instability, and thus inflation and interest rate volatility.

15.3 MEASURING OPENNESS

Trade openness depends on several factors. These include trade policy via tariffs and non-tariff barriers (including quotas and licences, inspection standards, local content requirements and the like), externally imposed barriers to trade such as trade and financial sanctions, and domestic and external capital controls operating via legislation, taxation or multiple exchange rate regimes. The most important of these is likely to be trade policy. Unfortunately, attempts to measure the trade policy component of openness are fraught by measurement problems for observable components (such as tariffs), and by the presence of difficult-to-quantify components of policy (such as quotas and a range of other non-tariff barriers). A comprehensive literature survey of available empirical measures for trade openness in Aron and Muellbauer (2007b) suggests considerable controversy over the validity of trade policy measures commonly used, for instance, in the growth literature.

For SA, there is no index of effective protection combining the effects of surcharges, tariffs and quotas (these last being important in SA trade policy until the mid-1990s). The annual measures of effective protection of Edwards (2005) date only from 1988, too brief a series for robust modelling and forecasting. These measures also do not take account of mismeasured official trade policy, non-tariff barriers, the effects of sanctions being lifted or greater access to international finance through a more open capital account.

Our own innovative measure of trade openness overcomes many of the shortcomings of existing measures, and encompasses both observable and unobservable trade policy (details in Aron and Muellbauer, 2007b). The time series measure from 1971 to 2005 is based on modelling the ratio of manufacturing imports to home demand for manufactures, a variable likely to be strongly influenced by trade openness. This is purged of other determinants by including in the model GDP growth, the terms of trade and the real exchange rate or relative import prices. We measure observable trade policy in the model with trade-weighted tariffs. The unobservable trade policy component (non-tariff barriers and mismeasurement of tariffs) is captured in the model by a smooth, non-linear stochastic trend.[11] Our openness measure is constructed as a weighted combination of known trade policy and the stochastic trend, with weights from the regression coefficients in the model. In application to SA, the shape of the trend is likely also to reflect such factors as the lifting of capital controls and unification of dual exchange rates in the 1990s (as often used in composite trade policy measures), and the lifting of externally imposed trade sanctions. Our measure thus captures a broader sense of 'openness' than is due only to trade policy. It is shown in Figure 15.1 and corresponds well with the known phases of liberalization.

In practice, when modelling SA inflation, Aron and Muellbauer (2007b) separate the observable trade policy component measure into its subcomponents, customs duties, *CUSTOM*, and temporary surcharges, *SURCHARGE*, and find the former are significant and the latter are not, probably because of their temporary nature. Moreover, the relative weight on the stochastic trend proxying *NTBs* differs from that found in the import share equation. Thus, *CUSTOM* as a long moving average and

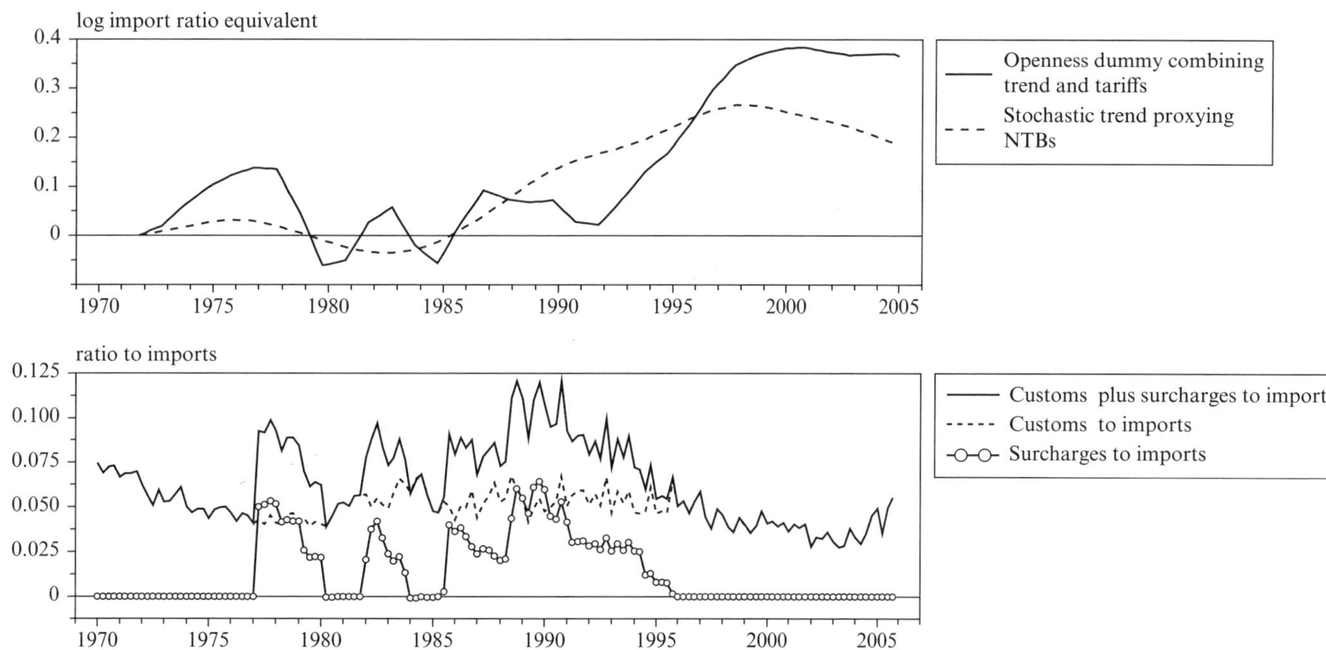

Source: SARB *Quarterly Bulletin* and Aron and Muellbauer (2007b).

Figure 15.1 Openness measure and stochastic trend, plus the tariff ratios for South Africa

the stochastic trend proxying *NTBs* are included separately in our models below.

More conventional measures, real and nominal trade and imported trade volume measures for SA are shown in Figure 15.2. This nicely illustrates that nominal trade ratios can be misleading where there are large terms of trade shocks, as the value of exports is sensitive to terms-of-trade fluctuations for primary exporters. The real and nominal import ratios and the real total trade ratios have all risen from the early 1990s. The real total trade ratio rose more with the rand depreciation from the mid-1990s, which depressed imports but had less of an effect on total trade. The growth in real imports since 1990 (and especially since 1994), appears to correlate with the removal of the remaining quotas, and the sharp reduction in tariffs from 1994. However, business cycle effects and volatility in the real exchange rate are conflated with these effects, and one cannot interpret individual parts of the graph for imports.

15.4 EXPLORING THE IMPLICATIONS OF CHANGING OPENNESS USING THE SARB'S INFLATION MODEL

In this section we demonstrate how the SARB's equation for producer price inflation in its core model, with long-run and short-run homogeneity restrictions, can be improved. By adding a measure for structural change from greater openness, and variables that capture the foreign exchange monetary transmission channel, the fit is better and the model is stable for a decade longer than the SARB model. The new equations are easy to implement and attractive for policymakers, as we suggest below. We focus here on the SARB's own equation, using its own choice of variables and its definition of long-run costs.[12]

The SARB models overall producer prices including imports (*WPI*) as a mark-up over costs, using a weighted combination of unit labour costs for the whole economy (*ULC*) and import prices (*IMPP*) to capture the overall costs. They employ a quarterly error correction model for 1990–2005, and the long-run log cost component applies a weight of 27 per cent to log import prices, which is its recent weight in the WPI index, and a weight of 73 per cent to log unit labour costs. This imposes long-run homogeneity, in that a doubling of unit labour costs and import prices implies that the level of producer prices will also double in the long run. The modellers also impose short-run price homogeneity[13] on the dynamic terms in import prices, unit labour costs and the lagged dependent variable. Figure 15.3 plots these price data. The only other variable in the model, apart from

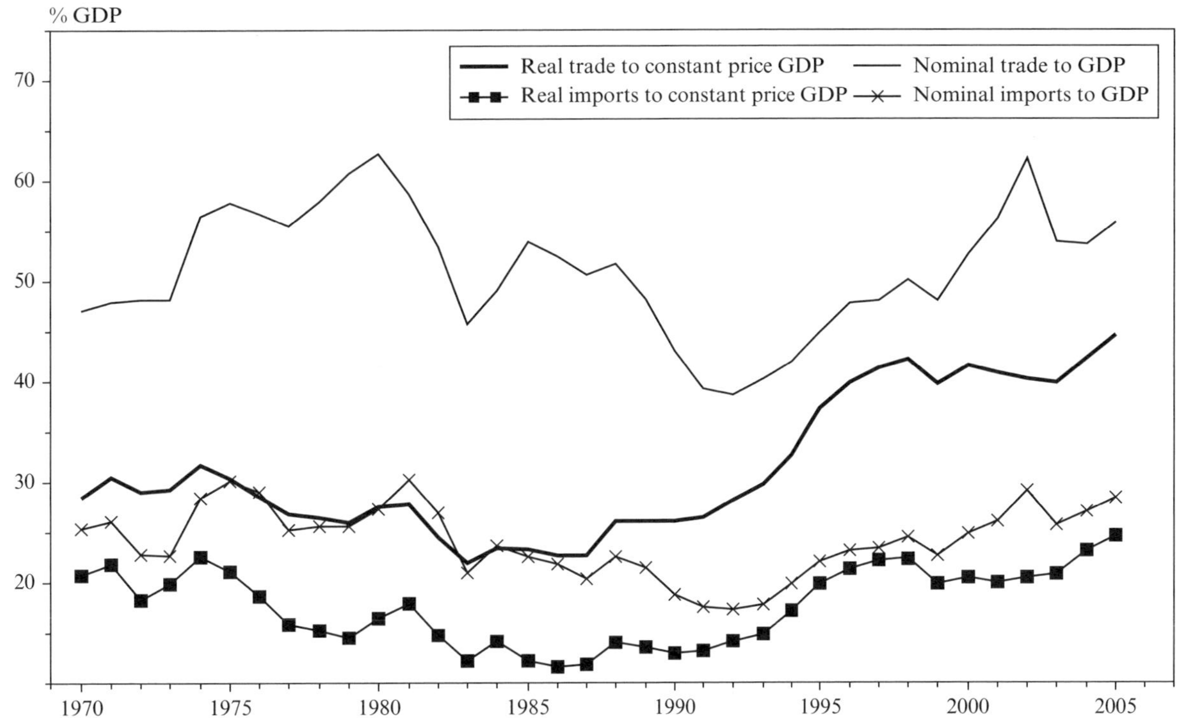

Source: SARB *Quarterly Bulletin.*

Figure 15.2 Real and nominal trade and imported trade volume measures for SA

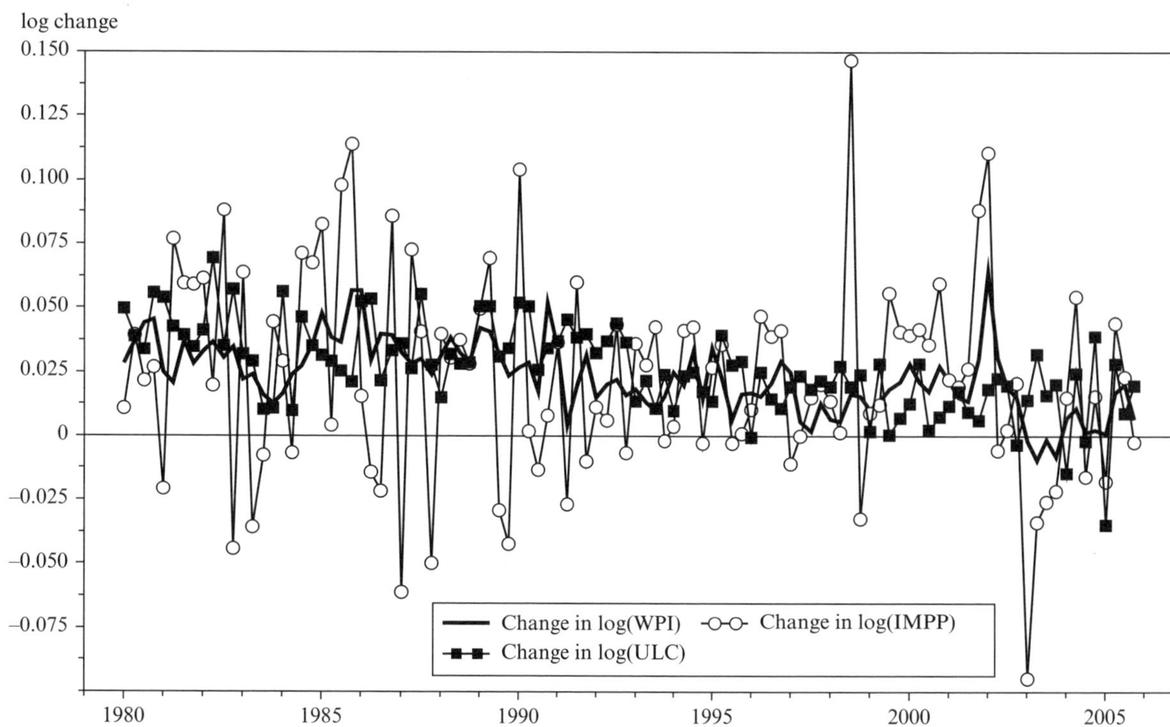

Source: SARB *Quarterly Bulletin* (definitions in Table 15.2).

Figure 15.3 Log changes in wholesale and import prices and unit labour costs

two dummies, is the output gap, but this enters only in the short run (that is, as ΔGAP). The dummies capture outliers in 1990Q4 and 2002Q1.

The model[14] is shown below:

$$\Delta\ln(WPI)_t = 0.0347 + 0.0371DUM90Q4 + 0.0260DUM02Q1$$

$$(3.11) \qquad (5.27) \qquad (3.58)$$

$$-\ 0.0632[(\ln WPI - 0.73\ln(ULC) - 0.27\ln(IMPP)]_{t-1}$$

$$(3.36)$$

$$0.3360\ \Delta\ln(WPI)_{t-1} + 0.1454\ \Delta\ln(IMPP)_t \qquad (15.1)$$

$$(4.37) \qquad (5.91)$$

$$+\ 0.3162\ \Delta\ln(ULC)_t + (1 - 0.3162 - 0.3360 - 0.1454)\Delta\ln(ULC)_{t-1}$$

$$(4.74)$$

$$+\ 0.0059\ \Delta(GAP)_{t-1}$$

$$(3.22)$$

We were able to reproduce this equation from vintage data provided by the Reserve Bank.[15] The data now on the website differ in that post-2000 data have been somewhat revised. However, the vintage data on the producer price index WPI provided by the SARB differ from current data on the Reserve Bank's website all the way back to the mid-1970s. Figure 15.4 shows the log ratio of the data currently on the website to the vintage data for 1979 to 2005: it is clear that the seasonal pattern is quite different, though both series are meant to be seasonally adjusted. By including seasonal dummies, we were able to get results quite close to equation (15.1) using data available on the website at the end of 2007. Variables are defined with basic statistics in Table 15.2, and these results are shown in column 1 of Table 15.3a. The estimated speed of adjustment is there 0.054 compared to the 0.063 shown in equation (15.1), but the fit and estimated dynamics are very similar.

However, it is desirable to estimate over longer samples than from 1990. Avoiding the period of fixed exchange rates in SA (see Aron et al., 2000), the longest sample would be from after 1979Q2, exceeding the SARB

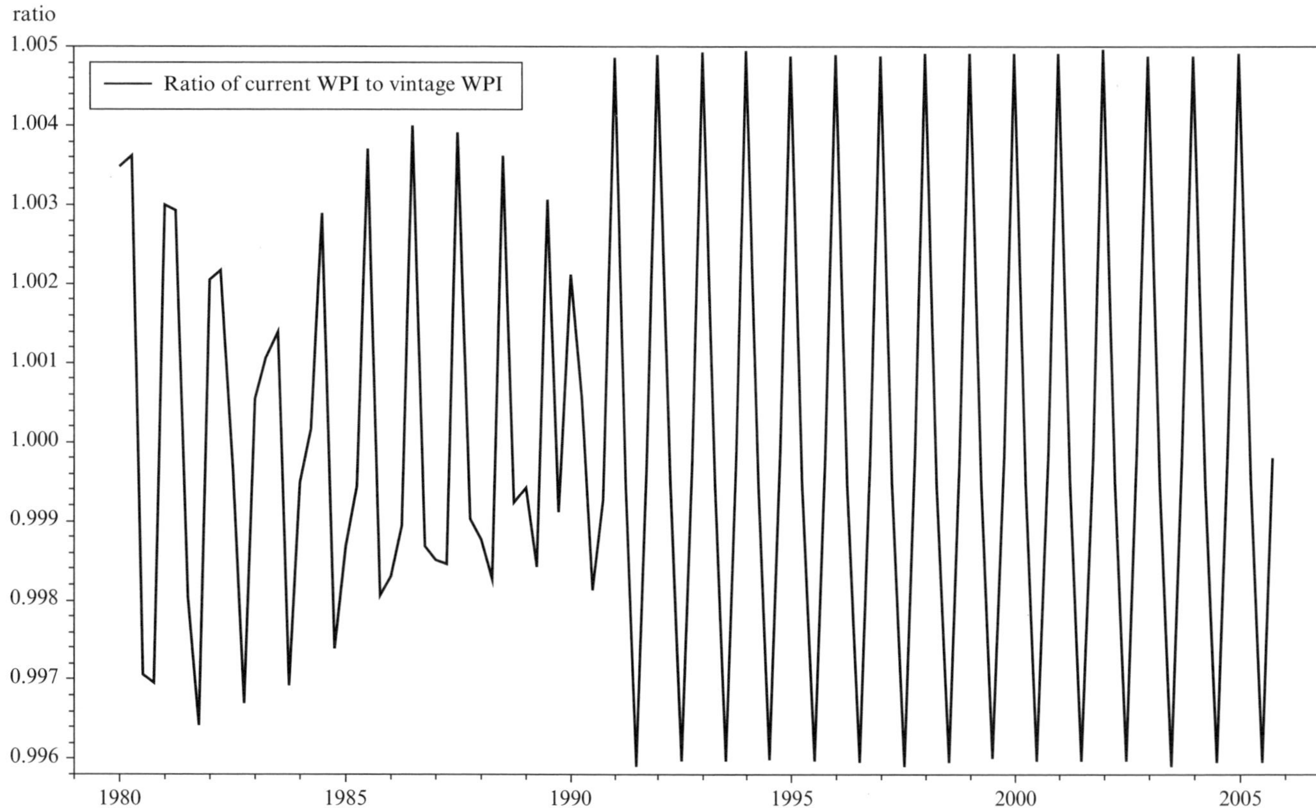

Figure 15.4 Log ratio of current WPI data to the vintage data used in the SARB's model

Table 15.2 Variable definitions for parsimonious equations

Variable name	Variable definition	Mean	Standard deviation	I(1)	I(2)
log(*WPI*)	Log of overall producer price index including imports	–0.665	0.715	–2.61	–3.83*
log(*ULC*)	Unit labour costs measured as: log of National Accounts labour compensation to real GDP	–1.52	0.814	–0.0513	–11.7**
log (*IMPP*)	Import prices measured as: log of National Accounts total imports deflator	–0.739	0.718	–1.75	–10.9**
(log(*WPI*) −0.73log(*ULC*) −0.27log(*IMPP*))	The SARB model's long-run cost component measured as: log(WPI) minus the weighted sum of log unit labour costs, ULC, and the log import price, IMPP	0.643	0.0793	–1.84	–3.98**
log(*REER*)	Log of real effective exchange rate; a rise is appreciation	4.75	0.148	–3.22	–4.87**
USSPREAD	Spread between the SA prime rate and US government Treasury bill rate	0.108	0.0466	–3.39*	–7.00**
log(*FOODP*)	Log of the raw price of food, from the agricultural food component of the CPI	4.08	0.613	–2.32	–5.62**
ASYMFOOD	Asymmetric effect of food price changes: Δlog(*FOODP*) if Δlog(*FOODP*) > 0, and zero otherwise	0.0519	0.0564	–7.25**	–12.2**
GAP	The output gap measured as: log real GDP adjusted with a Hodrick–Prescott filter (lambda = 1600) for potential GDP (× 100)	0.114	1.67	–4.22**	–5.70**
RCUSTMA8	Tariff measure: ratio of customs earnings to merchandise imports, 8-quarter moving average	0.049	0.00783	–2.77	–3.00*
MA4TRVOL	Conventional trade policy measure in real terms: ratio of real exports plus real imports to real GDP, 4-quarter moving average	32.0	7.69	–2.44	–3.01*
MA4TREND	Non-tariff barrier measure: quarternalized stochastic trend, 4-quarter moving average, from Aron and Muellbauer (2007b)	0.139	0.107		

Table 15.2 (continued)

Variable name	Variable definition	Mean	Standard deviation	I(1)	I(2)
DUM90Q4	Impulse dummy for 1990Q4				
DUM02Q1	Impulse dummy for 2002Q1				
DUM05Q4	Impulse dummy for 2005Q4				
DUM2000	Step dummy, 0 up to 1999Q4, 1 from 2000Q1				

Notes: Statistics are rounded to three significant figures. The augmented Dickey–Fuller test statistics are based on specifications including a linear trend where this is significant, and lag lengths are based on the longest significant lag. The log(*ULC*) test statistic is based on the inclusion of a time trend, though this is not strictly significant. If the trend is excluded, the test would suggest that log(*ULC*) is *I*(0) but with an implausibly low speed of adjustment. * and ** denote rejection at 5 per cent and 1 per cent critical values.

Source: All variables from the *Quarterly Bulletin*, South African Reserve Bank, except the US Treasury bill and SA prime rates (from IFS, International Monetary Fund). Derivation and motivation for *MA4TREND* is given in Aron and Muellbauer (2007b). Critical values are obtained from MacKinnon (1991).

model's sample by a decade. When we estimate this model for the longer sample 1980Q1 to 2005Q4, we find that the speed of adjustment and the significance of the long-run cost component falls sharply, the fit of the model deteriorates and there is first-order residual autocorrelation; see column 2. We are able to improve on this model by introducing openness indicators capturing the significant structural change from opening the trade and capital accounts in stages. Accounting for this important structural shift restores the estimated speed of adjustment and the significance of the long-run cost component, and improves the fit and stability of the model for 1980 to 2005; see column 3. With an alternative indicator of trade openness defined as the four-quarter moving average of real exports plus real imports divided by real GDP, all measured in constant prices, we can achieve a similar effect, though with a somewhat worse fit; see column 4.

Imposing short-run homogeneity is not desirable because it fails to account for plausible temporary inflation misperceptions by economic agents. Relaxing the assumption of short-run homogeneity in the longer sample and allowing the dynamics to be estimated freely improves the fit, implying that the hypothesis of short-run homogeneity is rejected; see column 5 (the probability of acceptance is 0.001). However, the speed of adjustment is now effectively zero so that the model implies no long-run adjustment of producer prices to import prices and unit labour costs. This

Table 15.3a The SARB's producer price inflation model enhanced with openness measures over longer samples

Dependent variable Δlog (WPI)	1		2		3		4		5	
	1990Q1–2005Q4		1980Q1–2005Q4		1980Q1–005Q4		1980Q1–2005Q4		1980Q1–2005Q4	
	Coeff	*t*	Coeff	*t*	Coeff	*t*	Coeff	*t*	Coeff	*t*
Long-run terms and dummies										
Constant	0.027	2.31	0.006	0.96	0.041	2.85	0.042	2.56	0.006	0.37
Q1 seasonal	0.0071	3.10	0.0036	1.84	0.0037	2.00	0.0036	1.91	0.0028	1.60
Q4 seasonal	0.0051	2.38	0.0044	2.30	0.0040	2.19	0.0043	2.30	0.0022	1.28
DUM90Q4	0.037	5.14	0.033	4.09	0.035	4.51	0.0317	4.03	0.0354	4.91
DUM02Q1	0.025	3.34	0.028	3.38	0.029	3.64	0.0287	3.54	0.0276	3.63
(log(*WPI*) −0.73log(*ULC*) −0.27log(*IMPP*))(-1)	–0.054	2.80	–0.016	–1.54	–0.068	–3.53	–0.0502	–2.84	–0.004	–0.17
Dynamic and asymmetric terms										
Δlog(*IMPP*)	0.154	6.29	0.122	6.30	0.114	6.04	0.122	6.42	0.111	6.00
Δlog(*IMPP*) (-1)	–		–		–		–		0.074	3.40
Δlog(*WPI*) (-1)	0.422	5.70	0.587	9.10	0.553	8.81	0.568	8.97	0.391	5.58
Δlog(*ULC*)	0.233	3.57	0.139	2.62	0.174	3.33	0.160	3.04	0.009	0.14
Δlog(*ULC*) (-1)	0.191 (restrict)		0.152 (restrict)		0.159 (restrict)		0.150 (restrict)		0.024	0.39
Δ*GAP*(-1)	0.0053	2.94	0.0034	3.34	0.0041	4.01	0.0037	3.67	0.0024	1.89
Trade policy measures										
RCUSTMA8(-1)	–		–		0.083	0.76	–		0.152	1.42
MA4TREND(-4)	–		–		–0.039	–2.91	–		–0.0297	–2.33
MA4TRVOL(-1)	–		–		–		–0.0424	–2.36	–	

Table 15.3a (continued)

Dependent variable Δlog (WPI)	1	2	3	4	5
	1990Q1–2005Q4	1980Q1–2005Q4	1980Q1–005Q4	1980Q1–2005Q4	1980Q1–2005Q4
Diagnostics					
Equation std. error	0.0675	0.00784	0.0753	0.00766	0.00696
Adjusted R^2	0.879	0.825	0.839	0.833	0.742
DW	2.37	2.31	2.29	2.32	2.00
Chow (mid-sample)	p = 0.66	0.10	0.43	0.39	0.51
Normality test	p = 0.90	0.59	0.62	0.69	0.97
AR/MA1- test (Breusch–Godfrey)	p = 0.044	0.039	0.056	0.045	0.87
AR/MA4-test (Breusch–Godfrey)	p = 0.20	0.18	0.087	0.106	0.20
Hetero test (Breusch–Pagan)	p = 0.84	0.047	0.053	0.056	0.051

seems highly implausible, suggesting a possible misspecification because of omitted relevant determinants of wholesale price inflation.

In Aron and Muellbauer (2007b), we argued that the markup of producer prices on unit labour costs and import prices was likely to be affected by the real exchange rate: the more appreciated the real exchange rate, the greater is likely to be foreign competitive pressure on domestic price setters. We suggested that inflationary expectations were likely to be influenced by the monetary policy stance as reflected in the short-term interest rate differential between SA and the world (proxied by the SA prime rate of interest minus the US Treasury bill rate). Indeed, in Aron et al. (2003), the connection is demonstrated between the interest rate differential and the exchange rate, suggesting that the foreign exchange channel is an important link between monetary policy and inflation in SA. In both papers we argued that prices of unprocessed foodstuffs were likely to be an important part of inflation dynamics, in a country where food is a large component in the budgets of the mass of households. We found evidence there that there is a short-run asymmetry in the inflation process, in that a rise in the price of food has a larger effect on producer price inflation than a fall (measured as the log change in raw food prices if this is positive and zero if the log change is negative, or *ASYMFOOD*).

We thus augment the specification shown in column 5 by including the above determinants: the lagged values of the log real exchange rate and its change, the interest rate differential and its change, the current and lagged values of *ASYMFOOD*, and the level of the lagged output gap. We call this the 'simple GUM' (general unrestricted model). Eliminating individually insignificant variables sequentially, or using the Autometrics software (Doornik, 2009), results in the parsimonious model shown in Table 15.3b, column 6. This fits dramatically better than previous specifications shown in Table 15.3 and supports the claims made by Aron and Muellbauer (2007b). The influence of the long-run cost component is restored, and the real exchange rate, the interest rate spread and (asymmetric) raw food price inflation all have highly significant coefficients. Furthermore, the level of the output gap rather than the change in the output gap is now significant. Parameter stability is satisfactory by the CHOW test. If the alternative openness measure based on real trade volumes is used, again very similar results but with a slightly worse fit are obtained; see column 7.

There are major advantages for policymakers from the equations shown in columns 6 and 7 in Table 15.3b, compared to the SARB's estimated equation. They capture in two ways the important foreign exchange channel, so relevant in open economies, in the transmission from interest rates to inflation: firstly, directly, through the interest rate differential; and secondly, through the real exchange rate, on which monetary policy

Table 15.3b *The SARB's producer price inflation model enhanced with openness measures and other variables*

Dependent variable Δlog (WPI)	6		7		8		9		10	
	1980:1–2005:4		1980:1–1999:4		1980:1–2005:4		1980:1–2005:4		1980:1–1999:4	
	Coeff	*t*	Coeff	*t*	Coeff	*t*	Coeff	*t*	Coeff	*t*
Long-run terms and dummies										
Constant	0.257	8.87	0.272	9.27	0.272	9.40	0.325	9.26	0.294	10.11
Q1 seasonal	0.0028	2.55	0.0034	2.81	0.0028	2.71	0.0030	2.55	0.0036	3.14
DUM90Q4	0.036	7.47	0.036	7.53	0.035	7.33	0.028	5.29	0.035	7.71
DUM02Q1	0.020	3.90	–		0.020	3.89	0.020	3.50	–	
DUM05Q4	–0.018	–3.51	–		–0.017	–3.38	–		–	
DUM2000	–0.0053	–2.25	–		–0.0046	–2.00	–0.0084	–4.15	–	
(log(*WPI*) −0.73log(*ULC*) −0.27log(*IMPP*))(-1)	–0.047	–2.77	–0.052	–2.73	–0.070	–3.66	–0.098	–4.05	–0.089	–3.96
log(*REER*)(-1)	–0.048	–10.03	–0.051	–10.01	–0.049	–10.46	–0.041	–8.33	–0.052	–10.78
USSPREAD(-1)	–0.102	–5.48	–0.101	–4.05	–0.114	–6.06	–0.107	–5.55	–0.133	–5.03
GAP(-1)	0.0012	3.42	0.0013	3.94	0.0011	3.54	0.0021	4.74	0.0014	4.31
Dynamic and asymmetric terms										
Δlog(*IMPP*)	0.071	5.32	0.059	4.20	0.072	5.51	0.095	6.79	0.063	4.68
Δlog(*IMPP*) (-1)	0.075	5.34	0.069	4.55	0.071	5.14	0.090	6.04	0.066	4.56
Δ4log(*ULC*)	–		–		0.049	2.38	0.050	2.20	0.059	2.80
ASYMFOOD	0.069	7.55	0.083	7.90	0.069	7.76	0.063	6.57	0.087	8.58
Trade policy measures										
RCUSTMA8(-1)	0.74	5.50	0.77	4.37	0.74	5.70	–		0.89	5.15
MA4TREND(-4)	–0.063	–6.35	–0.066	–6.58	–0.061	–6.23	–		–0.061	–6.25
MA4TRVOL(-1)	–		–		–		–0.0138	–7.60	–	

Diagnostics					
Equation std. error	0.00523	0.00454	0.00457	0.00511	0.00433
Adjusted R^2	0.855	0.857	0.889	0.861	0.870
DW	1.97	1.98	1.98	1.73	2.06
Chow (mid-sample)	$p = 0.35$	0.09	0.49	0.83	0.16
Normality test	$p = 0.64$	0.78	0.57	0.77	0.97
AR/MA1- test Breusch–Godfrey	$p = 0.83$	0.96	0.95	0.23	0.77
AR/MA4-test Breusch–Godfrey	$p = 0.45$	0.15	0.42	0.32	0.14
Hetero test (Breusch–Pagan)	$p = 0.61$	0.43	0.31	0.58	0.33

is generally believed to have influence. Moreover, since the real exchange rate is affected by the terms of trade, the impact of such shocks on inflation is therefore implicit in the model. The important role of food price inflation in the SA inflation process was also confirmed, highly relevant given the record rises in world food prices experienced in 2008. Finally, because the output gap appears as a significant level effect, the model counters a potential criticism often levelled at inflation targeting: that it focuses on inflation at the expense of concerns about stabilizing economic activity. The model clearly indicates a connection between the output gap and inflation. Other things being equal, forward-looking inflation-targeting policy will therefore tend to raise interest rates to reduce high output gaps (actual log real output minus trend log real output), and lower rates to increase low or negative output gaps. Thus, inflation targeting will tend also to stabilize economic activity.

We also checked the specifications in columns 6 and 7 against an 'extended GUM' in which somewhat longer lags are added to the 'simple GUM' discussed above. These take the form of four-quarter log changes in import prices, unit labour costs, raw food prices, and in last quarter's producer prices, real exchange rate and the interest rate differential (this last not in logs). Furthermore, other lags in the two components of openness are introduced, and a dummy for the introduction of inflation targeting, *DUM2000*, which is zero up to 1999Q4 and 1 from 2000Q1 onwards. We also allow detection of outliers in Autometrics, where it adds impulse dummies where residuals exceed three times the equation's standard error.

The parsimonious equation now selected, when *DUM2000* is forced to be retained,[16] is shown in column 8. Apart from the impulse dummy for 2005Q4 and *DUM2000*, only one new variable appears: the annual log change in unit labour costs. Given the primacy of unit labour costs in the long run solution, it seems quite plausible to find this additional dynamic role. (Without the outlier correction for 2005Q4, the same specification is chosen, with parameter estimates still very close to those shown in column 8.) The coefficient on *DUM2000* is -0.005 and its t-ratio is -2.1. This suggests that inflation targeting may have helped reduce producer price inflation by half a percentage point per annum on top of whatever influence it might have had on the other variables in the model, including unit labour costs, the interest rate differential and the real exchange rate. However, the effect is only marginally significant, and would not have been retained under the automatic model selection run by Autometrics. Again, using the trade volume-based measure of openness gives broadly similar results but a slightly worse fit, seen in column 9. *DUM2000* is more significant than before, while the four-quarter change in unit labour costs is now of marginal significance and the 2005Q4 impulse dummy becomes insignificant.

The reason for the last of these seems to be that this measure of trade openness rose quite sharply in 2005, so helping to explain the low producer price inflation rate in the last quarter.

We test the model for robustness from 1980 over a shorter sample. Interestingly, when applying Autometrics, the same model would have been selected for the 1980Q1 to 1999Q4 sample, but obviously excluding *DUM2000* and the impulse dummies for 2002Q1 and 2005Q4. These estimates are shown in the final column, column 10.

Three of the right-hand side variables shown in the last three columns are potentially endogenous. However, when these are instrumented, using 'intelligent' instrumenting equations based on import price, unit labour cost and food price equations from Aron et al. (2003), the results are hardly affected, apart from a marginal drop in the coefficient for the current inflation rate for imports.

Further evidence in favour of this model for WPI inflation comes from a cointegration analysis (see Johansen, 1988; Johansen and Juselius, 1990), based on the version of the model shown in column 9 of Table 15.3b. Here the openness indicator is a moving average of real imports plus exports relative to real GDP. The results of unit root tests are given in Table 15.2. We consider a set of five endogenous $I(1)$ variables: log (*WPI*), log import prices, log unit labour costs, log real exchange rate and the interest rate spread. We treat the openness indicator like an exogenous trend, and together with the step dummy, *DUM2000*, it is included as part of the cointegration space. The output gap and *ASYMFOOD* are both $I(0)$ variables and are assumed to be weakly exogenous (subsequently tested for). Together with the two impulse dummies, they enter the system in an unrestricted form. The information criteria suggest a lag length of 2. Thus, the unrestricted Vector Autoregressive (VAR) models consist of five equations in the endogenous variables, with openness, the dummies, *ASYMFOOD* and the lagged output gap appearing in every equation. Using *PCGIVE*, we find that the data support a rank of 4 for this system of equations. The following restrictions were imposed on the beta matrix of the system:

1. Four normalizing restrictions in the four cointegrating vectors, for example a coefficient of 1 on log(*WPI*) in the first vector.
2. A restriction of −0.73 and −0.27 on the coefficients respectively of log(*ULC*) and log(*IMPP*) in the first cointegrating vector (that is, imposing long-run homogeneity).
3. Three further homogeneity restrictions in the remaining cointegrating vectors, on the logs of WPI, import prices and unit labour costs in each, requiring the sum of their coefficients to add to 0.

These are acceptable restrictions in terms of a likelihood ratio test. However, with four cointegrating vectors, finding an economic interpretation of each is not straightforward. We successfully tested for the restriction that the alpha coefficients (speeds of adjustment) for the first equation (that is, for log(*WPI*)) are zero, except for the first cointegrating vector. In other words, we can accept the hypothesis that the other three cointegrating vectors do not appear in an equation for the change in log(*WPI*).[17] The p-value for the chi-squared test for the full set of restrictions, including homogeneity, is 0.06. As a final check, we confirmed the weak exogeneity of the output gap and of *ASYMFOOD* by regressing them on the lagged value of the equilibrium correction term implied by the cointegrating vector, and on the *I*(0) variables appearing in the VAR: the equilibrium correction term proved insignificant in both equations.

Thus, the cointegration analysis confirms the key findings of the single-equation model for producer price inflation. However, instrumenting current import price inflation in single-equation modelling is desirable, given the endogeneity of import prices.

15.5 CONCLUSION

We have outlined the changing openness of the SA economy particularly since the early 1990s, with the liberalization of the trade and capital accounts, and the greater acceptability of SA as a trading partner and investment destination under a new democratic government since 1994. Systematic risk was lowered by the post-1994 political dispensation, by the fiscal policies adopted since 1994 and by monetary policies, primarily since 1999. Conducting monetary policy with outdated monetary targets, and without clear policy priorities and policy transparency in a more globalized economy between 1994 and 1999, saw large fiscal losses and highly volatile interest rate policy during mismanaged currency crises, particularly in 1998. This led to the adoption of a more transparent and effective regime of inflation targeting from 2000. The fiscal–monetary policy mix since 2000 has stabilized the macroeconomy, lowering sovereign risk, uncertainty and the real (tax-adjusted) user cost of capital.

We have argued that modelling and forecasting inflation, a key ingredient of policymaking under inflation targeting, needs to take account of the structural breaks due to changing openness, in order to produce stable and well-fitting models over longer samples. We have demonstrated the improvements when including our indicators for openness in the SARB's own inflation model for wholesale price inflation. We also confirmed the strong influence on producer price inflation, found in our earlier work, of the real exchange rate and the international interest rate differential. This makes explicit the foreign exchange channel of monetary transmission on inflation, important in open economies. The role of food price inflation in the SA inflation process was also confirmed. This is highly relevant, given the record rises in world food prices experienced in 2008. The result is a model for producer price inflation with a greatly improved fit and stability over longer samples, and a role for the level of the output gap rather than simply a short-run effect, as in the SARB's model. This helps mitigate the arguments against inflation targeting regarding its apparent unconcern for stabilizing output. Given the important role for the output gap in the inflation model, inflation targeting automatically tends also to stabilize output. Finally, it is worth noting the easy-to-implement and constructive nature of our improvements to the SARB producer price inflation model: essentially we add five new regressors to its model and relax a restriction on the short-term dynamics.

The technique we have used to capture increased openness is potentially of use to other emerging market countries. In the case of SA, we also showed that a cruder measure of trade openness based on real import plus export volumes relative to real GDP, does almost as well in the inflation model as our more sophisticated measures. It seems that this volume measure compensates quite well for real exchange rate and terms of trade shocks which are liable to bias measures based on nominal data or on import data alone (see section 15.3).

Many analysts believe that the use of inflation targeting will spread. This makes it even more important for economists to develop a better understanding of the determinants of inflation in the short and medium run in increasingly open economies. Failing to do so may lead central bank modellers to forecast from misspecified models that omit the structural breaks of past trade liberalization, and may lead to the choice of inappropriate monetary policy.

NOTES

* The authors acknowledge funding support from the Economic and Social Research Council, UK (grant RES-000-22-2066). We are grateful for advice from Brian Kahn (South African Reserve Bank), Gavin Keeton (Anglo American), Andre Hermans (South African Parliament) and Bent Nielsen (Nuffield College, Oxford).

1. For a description of earlier trade liberalizing episodes, see also Edwards (2005).
2. The financial rand applied to most non-resident portfolio flows and direct investment. The intended impact of the financial rand was to break the direct link between domestic and foreign interest rates, as well as to insulate the capital account from certain categories of capital flows.

3. This section draws on a few of our recent papers: Aron and Muellbauer (2002b, 2005, 2007a, 2008, 2009).
4. For earlier regimes, see Gidlow (1995a, 1995b) and Aron and Muellbauer (2002b).
5. Aron and Muellbauer (2002b) apply an extension of the Taylor rule model (Taylor, 1993) to try to estimate the weights applied to different policy objectives in the interest rate rule during 1986–97.
6. Following elections in April 1994, the initial objectives of macroeconomic policy were contained in two highly publicized macro-policy plans The broad goals of the Reconstruction and Development Programme (RDP) launched in January 1994, were reinforced by the government's Growth, Employment and Redistribution strategy (GEAR), announced in June 1996. These plans are available on the web (http://www.info/gov.3a/view/DownloadFileAction?id=70507 for GEAR; http://www.anc.org.3a/rdp/rdp.html for RDP), and see also Hirsch (2005) and Nowak and Ricci (2005).
7. An Interim Constitution was adopted in 1994 and the Final Constitution in December 1996.
8. The regime is evaluated in Aron and Muellbauer (2005, 2007a, 2008, 2009). Other studies describing this regime include Arora (2008), du Plessis (2002, 2003, 2005a, 2005b), Mboweni (1999) and Van der Merwe (2004).
9. In operational terms, the repurchase or 'repo' interest rate is market-determined in tenders of liquidity through repurchase transactions.
10. The net open foreign currency position (NOFP) refers to the accumulation by the SARB of foreign currency obligations through forward market intervention that were far in excess of its net international foreign currency reserves. At its worst, the NOFP exceeded (minus) US$23 billion (in 1998), implying a large negative net international reserve position, with substantial costs accruing to the fiscal authority.
11. In a model that captures known influences on the import ratio, any unexplained variance (apart from white noise error) is then represented by the stochastic trend (estimated using Koopman et al., 2000).
12. This differs from our previous work, upon which we draw to improve this equation (Aron and Muellbauer, 2007b).
13. Short-run homogeneity in equation (15.1) below implies that the sum of the coefficients on the quarterly inflation rates of import prices, unit labour costs and lagged producer prices on the right-hand side of the equation add up to 1. This has the implication that doubling these inflation rates would immediately double the inflation rate of producer prices.
14. The model has a standard error of 0.00678 and an adjusted R-squared of 0.85 and passes the Breusch–Godfrey serial correlation test with test statistic 0.11620(4). For details see Smal et al. (2007).
15. The documentation concerning variables used was insufficiently precise in Smal et al. (2007) to be able to get close without extensive advice. These are the actual variables they used: import prices and unit labour costs are measured using seasonally adjusted series from the National Accounts, respectively as the total imports deflator (SARB codes: KBP6014LK/KBP6014DK) and compensation series relative to real GDP (KBP6000LK/KBP6006DK); overall producer prices including imports (KBP7050N); and log real GDP adjusted with a Hodrick–Prescott filter for potential GDP (KBP6006DK).
16. Autometrics gives the option to force a regressor to be in the final model.
17. To overcome a convergence problem which can arise when restrictions on the beta and alpha coefficients are imposed at the same time, we used a grid method on the log(*REER*) coefficient to obtain the optimal values of the parameters. We then find the following cointegrating vector: (log(*WPI*) − 0.73log(*ULC*) − 0.27log(*IMPP*) + 0.27log (*REER*) +1.08 *USSPREAD* +0.0149 *MA4TRVOL*(−1) +0.085 *DUM2000*). This is similar to the long-run solution implied by the single equation estimate in Table 15.3b, column 9, though the weight on log (*REER*) is a little lower than in Table 15.3b. The speed of adjustment, at 0.098, is identical to the single-equation estimate. We are grateful to Bent Nielsen for advice on using the grid method.

REFERENCES

Aron, Janine, Ibrahim Elbadawi and Brian Kahn (2000), 'Real and Monetary Determinants of the Real Exchange Rate in South Africa', in Ibrahim Elbadawi and Trudy Hartzenberg (eds), *Development Issues in South Africa*, London: Macmillan.

Aron, J. and J. Muellbauer (2002a), 'Interest Rate Effects on Output: Evidence from a GDP Forecasting Model for South Africa', *IMF Staff Papers*, **49** (IMF Annual Research Conference), pp. 185–213.

Aron, J. and J. Muellbauer (2002b), 'Estimating Monetary Policy Rules for South Africa', in Norman Loayza and Klaus Schmidt-Hebbel (eds), *Monetary Policy: Rules and Transmission Mechanisms*, Series on Central Banking, Analysis and Economic Policies, Vol. 4, Central Bank of Chile, pages 427–75, http://www.bcentral.cl/eng/studies/central-banking/v4.htm.

Aron, J. and J. Muellbauer (2005), 'Monetary Policy, Macro-Stability and Growth: South Africa's Recent Experience and Lessons', *World Economics*, **6** (4), pp. 123–47.

Aron, J. and J. Muellbauer (2007a), 'Review of Monetary Policy in South Africa since 1994', in J. Aron and G. Kingdon (eds), Special issue on 'South African Economic Policy under Democracy', *Journal of African Economies*, **16** (5), pp. 705–44.

Aron, J. and J. Muellbauer (2007b), 'Inflation Dynamics and Trade Openness', Centre for Economic Policy Research, London, Working Paper Series no. 6346, http://www.cepr.org.

Aron, J. and J. Muellbauer (2008), 'Transparency, Credibility and Predictability of Monetary Policy under Inflation Targeting in South Africa', 23rd Meeting of the European Economic Association, Milan, Italy, 27–31 August.

Aron, J. and J. Muellbauer (2009), 'The Development of Transparent and Effective Monetary and Exchange Rate Policy', in J. Aron, B. Kahn and G. Kingdon (eds) *South African Economic Policy Under Democracy*, Oxford University Press, pp. 58–91.

Aron, J., J. Muellbauer and B. Smit (2003), 'Understanding the Inflation Process in South Africa', Keynote Address, 8th Annual Conference on Econometric Modelling for Africa, Stellenbosch University, South Africa, July, http://www.csae.ox.ac.uk/, 'The SA Macroeconomic Research Programme'.

Arora, V. (2008), 'Monetary Policy Transparency and Financial Market Forecasts in South Africa', *Journal of Economic and Financial Sciences*, **2** (1), pp. 31–56.

Doornik, J.A. (2009), 'Autometrics', in J.L. Castle and N. Shephard (eds), *The Methodology and Practice of Econometrics: A Festschrift in Honour of David F. Hendry*, Oxford: Oxford University Press.

du Plessis, S.A. (2002), 'Evaluating the SARB's Inflation Target', *South African Journal of Economics*, **70** (6), pp. 982–1007.

du Plessis, S.A. (2003), 'Much Ado About Nothing: A Note on the Modified Inflation Target', *South African Journal of Economics*, **71** (2), pp. 407–13.

du Plessis, S.A. (2005a), 'The Democratic Deficit and Inflation Targeting', *South African Journal of Economics*, **73** (1), pp. 93–104.

du Plessis, S.A. (2005b), 'Proposals for Strengthening the SARB's Inflation Targeting Regime', *South African Journal of Economics*, **73** (2), pp. 337–54.

Edwards, Lawrence (2005), 'Has South Africa Liberalised its Trade?', *South African Journal of Economics*, **73** (4), pp. 754–75.

Edwards, L., R. Cassim and D.E. van Seventer (2009), 'Trade Policy since Democracy', in J. Aron, B. Kahn and G. Kingdon (eds) *South African Economic Policy Under Democracy*, Oxford: Oxford University Press, pp. 151–81.

Gidlow, R.M. (1995a), *South African Reserve Bank Monetary Policies under Dr T.W. de Jongh, 1967–80*, Pretonia: South African Reserve Bank.

Gidlow, R.M. (1995b), *South African Reserve Bank Monetary Policies under Dr Gerhard de Kock, 1981–89*, Pretonia: South African Reserve Bank.

Hirsch, A. (2005), *Season of Hope: Economic Reform under Mandela and Mbeki*, Scottsville, South Africa and Ottawa: University of KwaZulu-Natal Press and International Development Research Center (IDRC).

Johansen, S. (1988), 'Statistical Analysis of Cointegration Vectors', *Journal of Economic Dynamics and Control*, **12**, pp. 231–54.

Johansen, S. and K. Juselius (1990), 'Maximum Likelihood Estimation and Inference on Cointegration – with Applications to the Demand for Money', *Oxford Bulletin of Economics and Statistics*, **52** (2), pp. 169–210.

Kahn, B. and J. Leape (1996), 'Managing the Rand's Depreciation: The Role of Intervention', *Quarterly Review*, Centre for Research into Economics and Finance in Southern Africa, London School of Economics, April, pp. 2–13.

Koopman, Siem J., Andrew C. Harvey, Jurgen A. Doornik and Neil Shephard (2000), *STAMP: Structural Time Series Analyser, Modeller and Predictor*, London: Timberlake Consultants Press.

Leape, J. and L. Thomas (2009), 'Capital Flows and the External Balance Sheet', in J. Aron, B. Kahn and G. Kingdon (eds) *South African Economic Policy Under Democracy*, Oxford University Press, pp. 118–50.

MacKinnon, J. G. (1991), 'Critical Values for Cointegration Tests', in Robert Engle and Clive Granger (eds), *Long-Run Economic Relationships: Readings in Cointegration*, Oxford: Oxford University Press, pp. 267–76.

Mboweni, T.T. (1999), 'Inflation Targeting in South Africa', *South African Journal of Economics*, **67** (4), pp. 221–5.

Nowak, N. and L. Ricci (eds) (2005), *Post-Apartheid South Africa*, Washington, DC: International Monetary Fund.

Obstfeld, M. (1996), 'Models of Currency Crises with Self-fulfilling Features', *European Economic Review*, **40**, pp. 1037–47.

Smal, M.M., C. Pretorius and N. Ehlers (2007), 'The Core Forecasting Model of the South African Reserve Bank', Working Paper WP/07/02, June.

Stals, C. (1997), 'Effect of the Changing Financial Environment on Monetary Policy in South Africa', Address to the Annual Dinner of the Economic Society of South Africa, Pretoria Branch, 15 May.

Sterne, Gabriel and Jonathan Lepper (2002), 'Parliamentary Scrutiny of Central Banks in the United Kingdom and Overseas', *Bank of England Quarterly Bulletin*, Autumn, pp. 274–84.

Svensson, L., K. Houg, A. Berg, H. Solheim and E. Steigum (2002), 'An Independent Review of Monetary Policy and Institutions in Norway', Norges Bank Watch, Centre for Monetary Economics, BI Norwegian School of Management, September.

Taylor, J. (1993), 'Discretion versus Policy Rules in Practice', *Carnegie-Rochester Conference on Public Policy*, **39**, pp. 195–214.

Van der Merwe, E. (2004), 'Inflation Targeting in South Africa', Occasional Paper No. 19, July, South African Reserve Bank.

16. Inflation management and monetary policy formulation in Ghana

Nii Kwaku Sowa and Philip Abradu-Otoo*

16.1 INTRODUCTION

In spite of the apparent weaknesses inherent in the notion of the Wicksellian classical dichotomy, strong sentiments still persist in establishing a divide between 'real' and 'nominal' variables. This dichotomy is sometimes used to assign operational domains for institutions as well. Thus, a number of people, including economists, see central bank actions as those intended to affect, in the main, the nominal side of the economy. Thus, in this era of 'inflation targeting' central banks are generally accused of sacrificing growth, in particular, to meet their inflation targets.[1]

Economic policy management in Ghana has gone through several phases since independence. Until the 1980s, economic management of the early years of independence was dictated by the political ideology of sitting governments rather than ideas reflecting national consensus. Thus, as the regimes vary from *dirigiste* socialist regimes to quasi-capitalist regimes economic policy management was swayed between planned direct-control systems through to near laissez-faire systems. The general objective of policy has, however, always been the improvement in the living standard of the Ghanaian, with increased output and stable prices as the main goals.

Monetary management by the central bank as a major arm of economic policy management in Ghana has, by law and practice, often focused on price stability. Yet, over the years, high rates of inflation – soaring into triple digits at the close of the 1980s – have undermined economic performance in Ghana. Even the strict monitoring of fiscal and monetary aggregates under the International Monetary Fund and World Bank-sponsored Structural Adjustment Programme (SAP) could only yield an average inflation rate of about 25 per cent per annum between 1986 and 2000. Inflation, however, has been in continuous decline since 2001. Significantly, output growth has also been rising over the same period.

It is significant to note that since 2001 the main policy rate of the Bank of Ghana – the prime rate – has generally followed a downward trend, indicative of an expansionary monetary policy. This chapter seeks to explain why in the face of falling rates of interest the Ghanaian central bank still achieves its desired objective of lowering the rate of inflation.

The chapter continues in the next section with a review of processes of monetary management in Ghana and the outcomes. Monetary policy in the pre- and post- Monetary Policy Committee (MPC) eras is examined to amplify changes that may have occurred during the latter period. Section 16.3 models and estimates the reaction function for the Bank of Ghana. An analysis of the outcome of monetary policy in the MPC-era is carried out in section 16.4. Policy recommendations and a summary are drawn up in the last section to conclude the chapter.

16.2 MONETARY MANAGEMENT IN GHANA

On the eve of independence in 1957, Ghana weaned itself off the West African Currency Board and established its own central bank – the Bank of Ghana. The 1957 Ordinance which established the Bank of Ghana stipulated that its principal objectives were: 'to issue and redeem bank notes and coin; to keep and use reserves and to influence the credit situation with a view to maintaining monetary stability in Ghana and the external value of the Ghana pound; and to act as banker and financial adviser to the Government'.[2] As the Bank developed, the 1957 Ordinance was replaced by a consolidating law, namely the Bank of Ghana Act (1963). This Act spelt out clearly some of the Bank's developmental goals which had been conspicuously omitted in the 1957 Ordinance: the 1963 Act enjoined the Bank of Ghana 'to propose to the Government measures which are likely to have a favourable effect on the balance of payments, movements of prices, the state of public finance and the general development of the national economy and monetary stability'.[3] This broad mandate placed the Bank of Ghana under the Ministry of Finance as one of the government's development apparatus. The Bank thus found itself engaged in a number of non-monetary management ventures including the establishment of a brick and tile factory as well as a cattle ranch.

In 2002, a new Bank of Ghana Act (Act 612) was enacted which sought to give more operational independence to the central bank. As part of the process for the establishment of this operational independence, the Bank of Ghana had to establish a Monetary Policy Committee (MPC) as the main policymaking body within the central bank. The committee was made up of seven individuals, two of whom were external to the central bank. In this section, we will review the process of monetary management in Ghana before and after the establishment of the MPC.

16.2.1 Monetary Management: Pre-MPC Era

Monetary management in Ghana prior to the establishment of the MPC can be categorized into two main distinct phases: the period associated with direct monetary controls and the period of financial sector liberalization.

Direct controls

The direct monetary control is based on an International Monetary Fund (IMF) monetary programming model, which assumes that some broad monetary aggregate (M2 or M3) is the 'intermediate target variable' for monetary control, and that this in turn is connected in some reasonably predictable way with the 'ultimate policy targets' such as inflation and real output.[4]

The basis of the simple direct approach to monetary control is an estimate of the public's demand to hold money (currency in circulation plus bank deposits), which in turn requires specific targets and forecasts for two of the main determinants of that money demand, namely the future rate of inflation and the growth rate of real output. This approach is very straightforward and reliable if:

1. there is a very stable or predictable link between money demand on the one hand and prices and real output growth on the other (that is, a stable money demand equation involving those two variables); and
2. the authorities can directly control the supply of money.

In these cases, any ultimate package of targets and forecasts for the two variables, namely real income growth and inflation, can be achieved by setting and effectively controlling the aggregate money supply. More typically, where the external component of the total money supply is not under direct government control,[5] this element (represented by net foreign assets – NFA – in the central bank balance sheet) can be added as a third target of policy. This was the case in Ghana as the country was under a fixed exchange rate regime in which the central bank occasionally intervened to defend the exchange rate. In this case, the controllable part of the total money supply (Ms) is indicated by total domestic credit (DC) – to both private and public sectors – and from both the central bank and the commercial banks. This is shown by the simple formula derived from the consolidation and simplification of commercial bank and central bank balance sheets, namely:

$$Ms = DC + NFA \quad or \quad DC = Ms - NFA \qquad (16.1)$$

Putting this in first difference form, we have:

$$\delta Ms = \delta DC + \delta NFA \quad or \quad \delta DC = \delta Ms - \delta NFA \qquad (16.2)$$

where δ is the difference operator.

It follows from equation (16.2) that efforts to control changes in the money supply in order to achieve some ultimate forecast values of, or targets for, real income growth and inflation will be achievable through the direct control of domestic credit only if a consistent target for NFA is also specified. This being done, an aggregate target for domestic credit expansion is readily set. The operational aspects of control are then managed in most cases by assigning particular targets or shares of the aggregate δDC to each bank and/or specific sectors. The above simplified outline of an IMF monetary programming model formed the basis of monetary management in Ghana for a period of about three decades. Up until 1972, and with the exception of 1964, growth of money supply in Ghana hardly exceeded the 15 per cent mark set out in the Bank of Ghana Act (1963). The 1964 lunge of 39 per cent in monetary growth made inflation surge into the double digits from that year on. But the distinct era of monetary indiscipline was the 1972–82 period in which money supply grew at an average of about 40 per cent per annum. An examination of the sources of growth in money shows that a lot of it came from domestic credit creation: basically, the government was just printing money.

The successful outcomes seen in Table 16.1 were part of the general success produced by the Economic Recovery Programme (ERP) which was initiated in 1983. Growth in output which had been negative at the beginning of the 1980s was reversed, and the high rates of inflation were slowed down. These results were achieved in spite of the persistent high rates of growth in the stock of money. It is important to note that the source of monetary growth got switched between the pre- and the

Table 16.1 Some economic outcomes under the system of direct monetary control (%)

	1981	1982	1983	1984	1985	1986	1987	1988	1989	1990
Real GDP	–3.2	–5.9	–3.9	8.5	5.1	5.2	4.8	5.6	5.1	3.3
Inflation	100.4	16.7	142.4	6.0	19.5	33.3	34.2	26.6	30.5	35.9
Money (M2)	38.2	23.4	64.5	44.7	59.5	53.5	53.0	43.1	26.9	18.0
Interest rates	19.5	10.5	14.5	18.0	18.5	20.5	23.5	26.0	26.0	33.0

Source: Bank of Ghana.

post-ERP periods, from net domestic assets (NDA) to net foreign assets (NFA), as the country received substantial capital inflow in the form of balance of payments and budgetary support loans and grants under the ERP. These external inflows augmented the country's reserves position and, thus, its capacity to increase domestic liquidity. A substantial portion of the inflows resulted in direct cedi-counterpart payments to domestic entities (government, public and private organizations, individuals) leading directly to enlargement of domestic liquidity.

Thus, except for the ERP period there was no strong evidence of success with the direct method of control by the monetary authorities. In addition, other issues arising from high administrative costs and allocative efficiency considerations suggested a more market-based form of monetary management.

The market-based system

The liberalization process entailed progressive deregulatory measures, culminating in the institutionalization of a market-based system of monetary management in early 1992 and focused largely on the use of indirect market-based instruments in the conduct of monetary policy. This brought into focus a new dimension to the way monetary management was designed and implemented. The basic underlying model remained the IMF's financial programming model.

Under this framework, the central bank relied on open market operations as the major tool in regulating the net domestic assets of the banking system. Thus, the central bank released or redeemed bills on the market as appropriate to keep growth in the money stock in check. Monetary outcome under the regime of market-based monetary management appeared better than in the controlled regime. Growth in the stock of money slowed down, although not significantly from the earlier years of direct control except for 1998 and 1999.

Inflation appeared to have been contained under the market-based monetary management system. Except for the spike in 1995 (see Table 16.2), inflation was for most the period very moderate. One distinct feature of the period of the market-based monetary control was the high rates of interest that prevailed in the country. This was not unexpected of a developing country like Ghana. Firstly, with an underdeveloped financial system and a state confronted with structural fiscal deficits, government was not discouraged by high rates in borrowing from the money market. Secondly, as argued by Roe and Sowa (1997):

> if most banks were liquid, few of them would be encouraged to take the significant position necessary to get an active money market up and running. Hence

Table 16.2 Some economic outcomes under the system of market-based monetary control (%)

	1991	1992	1993	1994	1995	1996	1997	1998	1999	2000	2001
Real GDP	5.3	3.9	5.0	3.8	4.5	5.2	5.1	4.7	4.4	3.7	4.2
Inflation	10.3	13.3	27.7	34.2	70.8	32.7	20.8	15.7	13.8	40.5	21.3
Money (M2)	15.0	59.4	27.4	46.2	37.4	34.2	45.1	28.2	19.8	33.8	47.9
Interest rates	20.0	30.0	35.0	25.0	45.0	45.0	45.0	37.0	27.0	27.0	27.0

Source: Bank of Ghana.

> in the early days of indirect monetary controls, the central bank's efforts to influence bank lending indirectly by engineering small percentage changes in the availability of, or interest rates on, reserve assets, was unlikely to have much effect. Either the indirect monetary controls would prove ineffective or they would need to achieve their targets by accepting very large movements of interest rates to alert the banks to the pressures for a change in lending.

It is noteworthy that growth performance under the market-based system of monetary control was not significantly different from that under the direct controlled system.

16.2.2 Monetary Management: The MPC Era

To refocus the central bank for more effective discharge of its core functions and to assert its independence, Parliament enacted the new Bank of Ghana Act (Act 612) in 2002. Section 27 of the new act required the establishment of a Monetary Policy Committee (MPC). This Act also enjoins the central bank to:

(i) Formulate and implement policy in the areas of money, banking and credit with the main aim of maintaining stable prices conducive to balanced and stable economic growth;
(ii) Promote and preserve monetary stability.

The MPC was launched on 9 September 2002 and has since been meeting every other month. The main policy tool of the MPC is the prime rate – an indicative interest rate around which all other rates operate. As an indicative rate the positioning of the prime rate sends signals to all economic agents on the tempo of economic activity and its expected impact on the rate of inflation in the immediate future. In this sense the prime rate does not carry the same interpretation as the erstwhile bank rate which was the rate at which the central bank extended advances to the commercial bank as 'lender of last resort'. Under the new monetary management the role of the central bank as 'lender of last resort' is rendered superfluous. Instead, banks are encouraged to trade more among themselves using the interbank market. For monetary management purposes the central bank uses open market tools as well as repurchase agreements (repo) and reverse repo.

The policy framework

Unlike many central banks in the vogue of operational independence, the Bank of Ghana did not adopt an explicit 'inflation targeting' framework at the inception of the MPC. Instead, the MPC adopted a framework which mimicked an inflation-targeting regime, whereby economic evaluation and analysis is conducted based on information on all aspects of the economy, and the prime rate is appropriately placed to influence inflationary expectations. Inflation targets are set jointly by the central bank and the Ministry of Finance and Economic Planning, and presented annually as a year-end target during the presentation of the government's Budget and Statement of Economic Programme for the fiscal year. Since 2001, one of the medium-term objectives of economic policy has been the drive towards a single-digit inflation target.

As mentioned above, in setting the prime rate, the MPC evaluates developments in the macroeconomy and the threats these developments may pose to macroeconomic stability and consequently inflation. This generally involves a thorough review of fiscal, monetary, financial market, external, real sector and price developments since the previous meeting of the MPC.

Real sector issues

Of particular interest in the process leading to decision-making by the MPC is the review of the real sector. This is quite an innovation in monetary management in Ghana. This nevertheless underlies the fact that the new monetary framework ensures that all information on the economy is allowed to feed into the monetary management decision-making process.

As with most developing countries, statistics on Ghana's GDP are woefully inadequate and where they exist carry a one-year lag. The Bank of Ghana, at the inception of the MPC process, designed three ways to solicit information to give an indication of real sector activity. The first is the survey of business confidence – involving the administration of questionnaires to cross-sections of businesses on conditions and expectations on employment, output, sales, cost and the general economy. Data from this survey are complemented with data from the second methodology which is the computation of a Composite Index of Economic Activity (CIEA)[6] (as is done in most industrialized countries). A third methodology comes in the form of a consumer confidence survey, which attempts to gauge consumer confidence in the economy and expectations on prices and the performance of the economy. Indices are constructed out of these surveys in order to get an idea of real sector performance. As can be expected these indices do not always move in the same direction and pose challenges to the decision-making process.

Inflation and risk analysis

A critical element in the analyses leading to the decision-making by the MPC is a review of the inflationary process in the country. The Inflation Report includes the following basic elements:

1. An analysis of the current inflation situation and the main factors driving prices in the economy.
2. An exploration of possible threats from monetary, fiscal, financial sector, real sector, and external sector developments.
3. A forward-looking view of inflation along with associated uncertainties. Forecasts are generated using simple vector error correction models. The central path is then embodied in the form of fan charts with the upside factors and downside risks critically assessed.
4. The construction of a matrix of risk assessment using the available information on all aspects of the economy; and an inflation risk measure is derived from the matrix. An assessment of whether inflationary risks are rising or diminishing based on the movement of this index is made.

At the end of the review of developments in the economy, decisions on setting the prime rate are arrived at by consensus. When there are strong disagreements, the committee goes over the critical issues several times until a consensus is reached. The outcome is announced in a press conference.

Figure 16.1 shows decisions at the MPC given an assessment of perceived inflationary risk. An upward movement in the inflationary risk index signifies potential increases in inflationary pressures and vice versa. The key policy rate, the prime rate has dropped by as much as 12 percentage points, moving from 24.5 per cent in November 2002 to 12.5 per cent by the end of March 2007, as a result of easing of inflationary risks over the years.

Economic outcomes under the MPC

Since 2001 most economic indices in Ghana have shown positive signs, indicative of robust economic fundamentals. These include:

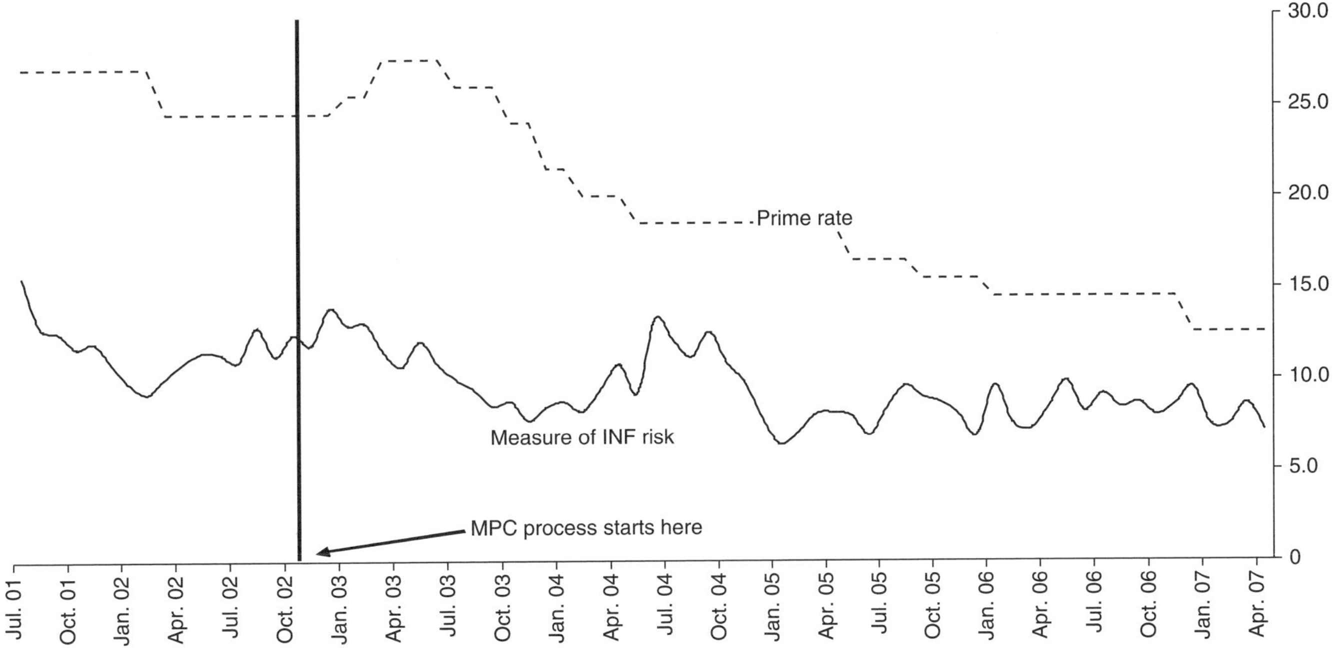

Figure 16.1 *Measure of inflationary risks: derived from matrix of risk assessment*

Table 16.3 Economic performance in the MPC era (2000–06, end-year data, %)

	GDP growth rate	Rate of inflation	Treasury bill rate	Ave. lending rate	Repo rate	Reverse repo rate
2000	3.74	40.5	38.0	47.0	27.0	26.0
2001	4.20	21.3	27.6	43.8	27.0	26.0
2002	4.50	15.2	26.6	38.5	24.5	21.0
2003	5.20	23.6	18.7	32.8	21.5	20.5
2004	5.80	11.8	17.1	28.8	18.5	17.5
2005	5.80	14.8	11.5	26.0	15.5	14.5
2006	6.20	10.5	9.6	23.8	12.5	10.5

Source: Bank of Ghana, Research Department; Government of Ghana, *Budget Statements*; and Ghana Statistical Service, various, *CPI Newsletters*.

- sustained increases rate of growth in output;
- drastic slowdown in the rate of inflation;
- falling rates of interest;
- increasing inflow of private remittances; and
- stability in the exchange rate.

Output growth has improved tremendously over the years while inflation has, within a six-year span, dropped to about a quarter of its level at the close of the millennium (see Table 16.3). Ironically, these positive outturns were achieved under expansionary monetary policies.

16.3 POLICY RULES

16.3.1 Theory

The monetary policy decision-making process has been the subject of intense debate for a long time. In the main, the debate has centred on whether monetary policy should rely more on rules or discretion. In his original seminal paper, Taylor (1993) argues that in positioning its policy instrument, the central bank does so keeping in mind two basic objectives: either to improve on output performance or to enhance price stability, or both. Specifically, Taylor (1993) argued that using historical data to analyse decisions of the Federal Reserve Bank one observes that the Bank positions its rate such that deviations of the policy rate from the long-term market rate can be explained by an inflation gap and/or an output gap. Thus, the Taylor rule prescribes how a central bank should adjust its interest rate policy instrument in a systematic manner in response to developments in inflation and macroeconomic activity. The rule provides a useful framework for the analysis of historical policy and for the econometric evaluation of specific alternative strategies that a central bank can use as the basis for its interest rate decisions.

Since the initial Taylor Rule, there have been variants in the literature depending on specific peculiarities of the countries concerned. Rules 1–7 show the various types of rules that could exist in practice:

- Rule 1: nominal income level
  $i_t = \bar{r} + \pi_{t-1} + \gamma(py_{t-1} - py^T_{t-1})$
- Rule 2: nominal income growth rule
  $i_t = \bar{r} + \pi_{t-1} + \gamma(\Delta py_{t-1} - \Delta py^T_{t-1})$
- Rule 3: price level rule
  $i_t = \bar{r} + \pi_{t-1} + \gamma(p_{t-1} - p^T_{t-1})$
- Rule 4: Taylor rule
  $i_t = \bar{r} + \pi_{t-1} + \gamma_1(\pi_{t-1} - \pi^T) + \gamma_2(y_{t-1} - \bar{y}_{t-1})$
- Rule 5: Inflation-only rule
  $i_t = \bar{r} + \pi_{t-1} + \gamma_1(\pi_{t-1} - \pi^T)$
- Rule 6: change rule
  $i_t = \bar{r} + \pi_{t-1} + \gamma_1(\pi_{t-1} - \pi^T) + \gamma_2(y_{t-1} - \bar{y}_{t-1})$
- Rule 7: constant real interest rate rule
  $i_t = c + \pi_{t-1}$

where i_t denotes the nominal interest rate at the time t, r the neutral real interest rate, π the inflation rate over the past year, py the nominal income, the superscript T being a target, p the price level, y the real income, $\bar{y}$ potential output, c an unspecified constant real interest rate, and γ a reaction parameter.

For instance if one assumes that the gap in inflation does not really matter for purposes of policy then rules 1 and 2 will apply. Rules 1 and 2 respectively tie the interest rate to deviations of nominal income from a target level or target growth rate. These rules both yield the same forecasts for nominal income, but the outcomes can be quite different since a growth rule allows levels drift, in the sense that past shocks to growth are bygones once growth is back on track.

Rule 3 is a variant of rule 1, by which policy is changed when the price level deviates from the target price level.

Rule 4 is a hybrid nominal income rule by which policy is tightened when inflation is above target and output above potential. In contrast to the nominal income growth rule, it is the output gap rather than output growth that enters the reaction function. This rule is widely acknowledged to describe the variables that are of most concern to central banks

Rule 5 is an inflation-only rule, a special case of the Taylor rule when policy is designed and made to respond only to deviations of inflation from target. Both the Taylor rule and the inflation rule are tied to the inflation target but the Taylor rule also responds to the output gap.

Rule 6 is a variant of the Taylor rule by which the nominal rate is changed when inflation deviates from target and output deviates from potential. This rule reacts to the same target variables as a Taylor rule but is not explicitly grounded to the neutral or equilibrium real interest rate.

Rules 1–5 also include two other variables, the neutral real interest rate and the prevailing inflation rate. This means that if the reaction variables – nominal income, the price level, inflation or output – are at their target value, then the nominal interest rate equals the neutral real interest rate plus the inflation rate. The economy is in equilibrium, and so policy remains neutral.

Rule 7 states that the real interest rate should be kept constant. This rule has been proposed, for example, on the view that fiscal policy should stabilize output, while monetary policy should stabilize the intertemporal price of consumption (Quiggin, 1997)

16.3.2 The Bank of Ghana's Reaction Function

In this section we employ an econometric model to analyse the historical outcomes of the Bank of Ghana's policy decisions since 2000. The specification used in analysing the reaction function of the Bank of Ghana is informed by two main considerations: what literature suggests and what actually pertains by way of decision-making by the main policy body. The model adapted in this chapter is a variant of the Taylor (1993) paper which was used by Beenstock and Ilek (2005) to test the dichotomy between the natural rate of interest and the policy rate set by the Central Bank of Israel within a policy rule framework. The policy variable in that paper was defined as a function of the lagged policy rate (to capture elements of persistence), a natural rate of interest, the deviation of inflation from target and the deviation of output from potential.

Our specification of the policy rule in equation (16.3) is also informed largely by the actual internal workings of the Monetary Policy Committee. In arriving at its key policy decision, a whole set of information is made available to the committee. The important variables to which the Bank of Ghana's Monetary Policy Committee reacts to include information on the current output conditions in the economy (the output gap), the Bank of Ghana's composite index of economic activity (known as the CIEA), current inflationary conditions, short-term inflation expectations (derived mainly from surveys normally extending for a period of six months to one year) and information from the money market used in capturing long-term market rate of interest.

Algebraically, we specify the functional form of the central bank's reaction function as follows:

$$pr_t = \alpha_1 + \left(\beta_k \sum_{k=1}^{4} r_{t-k}\right) + \gamma_1(\pi_t - \pi^*) + \gamma_2(y_t - \hat{y}_t) \qquad (16.3)$$

where pr_t is the key policy rate of the central bank, the prime rate; r_t is the market rate of interest; π_t is the rate of inflation and π^* is the target rate of inflation; y_t is the output level while $\hat{y}$ represents potential output. α_1, β_k, γ_1 and γ_2 are parameter constants.

Note that the second term in equation (16.3) that defines an autoregressive (AR) process of the short-term market rate of interest defines the long-term market rate of interest. For the short-term market interest rates we selected the rate on the 91-day Treasury bill.

The term $[\pi_t - \pi^*]$ is the inflation gap. π^*, the target rate of inflation, for purposes of this study was kept at 8 per cent over the entire sample period. Since 2001, repeated statements of government policy have specified the attainment of a single-digit rate of inflation as the prime monetary objective. We have conservatively placed this single-digit figure at 8 per cent.

The expression $[y_t - \hat{y}]$ defines the output gap. The potential output, $\hat{y}$, can be obtained either by simply passing actual output through the Hodrick–Prescott (HP) filtering technique or through an autoregressive process.

In Table (16.4) we produce full estimates of equation (16.3), using ordinary least squares (OLS) techniques. The time series properties[7] of the variables show that they are all of unit roots. The OLS estimation of equation (16.3) reported in Table 16.4 shows that about 85 per cent of variations in the dependent variable are explained by variations in the independent variables, with most of the parameter estimates statistically significant.

The results also show that the weight on the inflation gap ($\gamma_1 = 0.14$) was far less than the weight on the output gap ($\gamma_2 = 2.45$). This suggests that, historically, monetary policy in Ghana has aimed at closing the output gap at a greater speed than the inflation gap.

Although the policy rate implied by the estimated Taylor rule moves very much in tandem with the actual policy rate (Figure 16.2), it appears that there are more variations in the former than the latter.

Table 16.4 Estimated Reaction Function of the Bank of Ghana

Variable	Coefficient	Std. Error	*t*-statistic	Prob.
C	0.415260	0.234223	1.772928	0.0815
R(−1)	0.755256	0.160698	4.69984	0.0000
R(−2)	−0.162718	0.240814	−0.675702	0.5019
R(−3)	−0.204077	0.242374	−0.841992	0.4033
R(−4)	0.457467	0.165212	2.768972	0.0075
INFGAP8	0.145859	0.054338	2.684265	0.0095
YGAP	2.452678	0.916025	2.677523	0.0096
R-squared	0.853604	Mean dependent var		3.32312
Adjusted R-squared	0.838460	S.D. dependent var		0.36285
S.E. of regression	0.145836	Akaike info criterion		−0.91123
Sum squared resid	1.233546	Schwarz criterion		−0.67707
Log likelihood	36.615060	F-statistic		56.36437
Durbin-Watson stat	0.905008	Prob (F-statistic)		0.00000

Notes:
Dependent Variable: PR.
Method: Least Squares.
Date: 07/15/07; time: 19:16.
Sample (adjusted), 1991Q1 2007Q1.
Included observations: 65 after adjustments.

A different kind of estimation was carried out using an AR process to derive the potential output. This appears to be a poor fit with some of the parameter estimates wrongly signed and was therefore relegated.

16.4 ANALYSIS OF THE ECONOMIC OUTTURNS IN THE MPC ERA

16.4.1 Democracy Dividend

Economic management in Ghana has in the past witnessed spectacular episodes of inflation control. For instance, the authorities managed to bring down inflation from the triple-digit level of 123 per cent to 10.3 per cent between 1983 and 1985. However, it is clear that more subdued inflationary outturns have been sustained over a longer term in the MPC era than under any other policy regime in Ghana since independence. In addition, output performance has been very encouraging over the same period. Care, however, has to be exercised in adducing causality.

Signs of positive changes in the economy of Ghana were observed in

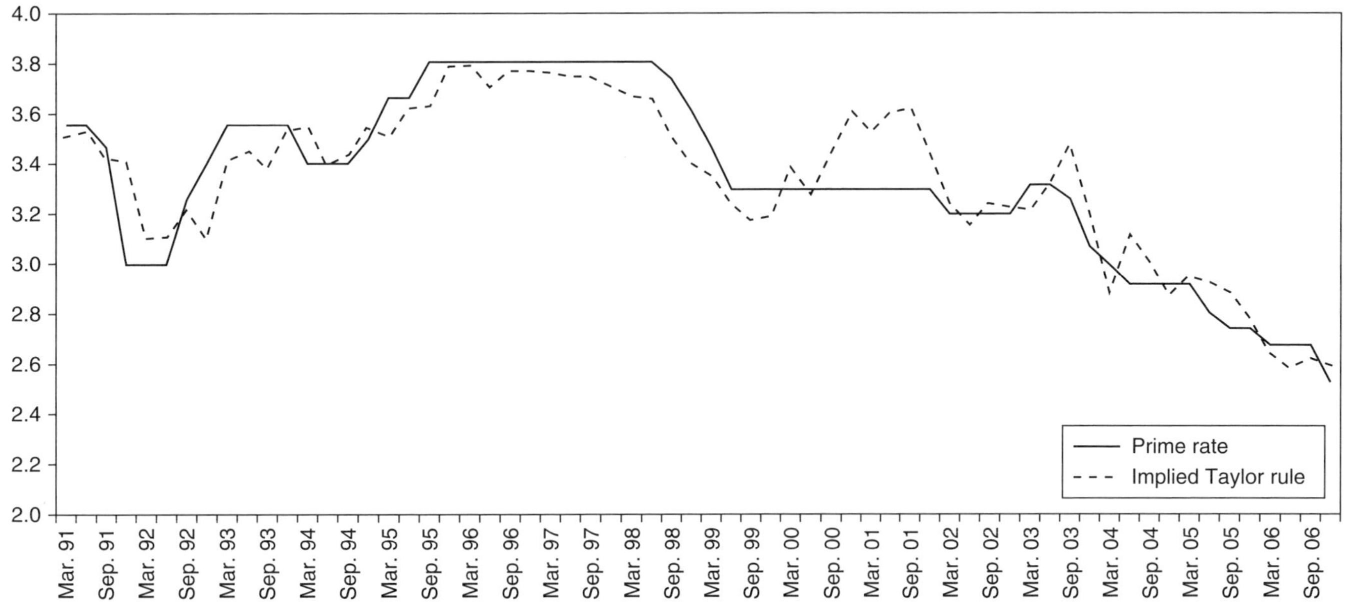

Figure 16.2 *BOG estimated reaction function (with lags on market rate of interest)*

2001, a year before the institution of the Monetary Policy Committee. In 2001, for the first time since the country's independence in 1957, political power changed hands other than through the barrel of the gun. It has been estimated that the elections which took place yielded a 'democracy dividend' equivalent to about 10 per cent of GDP: this is made up of about 8.3 per cent GDP of 'exceptional financing' support from the international donor community and 1.7 per cent GDP of private transfers and tourism receipts. The 'democracy dividend' facilitated the macro stabilization process by:

- calming down inflationary expectations;
- stabilizing the exchange rate;
- halving the rate of inflation;
- sharply reducing the nominal rate of interest; and
- achieving a modest rebuilding of the nation's international reserves.

It is quite obvious that while the so-called 'democracy dividend' could have initiated the initial outcomes in 2001, the developments in the latter years were the result of other policies. The totality of economic management by the government of the National Patriotic Party under President John Kufuor, including bold decisions in taking the country under the Heavily Indebted Poor Countries (HIPC) initiative as a way of managing the country's debt, yielded the positive outcomes witnessed over the years.

The rest of this section is devoted to explaining the mystery behind the policy success of the Bank of Ghana at disinflation, particularly when to all intents and purposes the policy decisions have been expansionary. The argument is based on two principles: first, part of the process of disinflation Ghana has witnessed since 2001 can be explained by policy credibility gained through the central bank being granted operational independence; and second, inflation in Ghana is significantly influenced by output and structural factors, the easing of which confers benefits on the disinflation process.

16.4.2 Policy Credibility and Inflation

Recent developments in monetary theory have shown the importance of credibility in the achievement of the objectives of the central bank.[8] The theory on policy credibility started in the 1970s when Calvo (1978) and Kydland and Prescott (1977) independently demonstrated the implications of the then novel hypothesis of rational expectations for the credibility of macroeconomic policy in general, and monetary policy in particular. The basic underlying principle of their argument was set within a game-theoretic model of dynamic inconsistency.

Government generally has several objectives it may wish to achieve. For example, in addition to the desire to have stable prices, policy may also be directed at closing a fiscal gap, lowering the rate of unemployment or increasing output. Thus, at a particular time, while government may have convinced all economic agents that policy is working towards lower rates of inflation, it may suddenly initiate surprise inflation in order to achieve another objective, say close a fiscal gap. This is the time-inconsistency problem. In other words government is likely to sacrifice one objective for another and hence loses credibility in the eyes of the general public in the implementation of macroeconomic policy geared toward the achievement of certain objectives.

The solution to this time-inconsistency problem lies in having a credible independent agency with the sole objective of implementing policies aimed at achieving the particular objective. Rogoff (1985) argued that the inflation bias arising from the time-inconsistency problem may be eliminated by the appointment of a 'conservative' central banker with the sole mandate of achieving stable prices – hence, central bank independence.

The conferment of operational independence of the Bank of Ghana, and the establishment of the Monetary Policy Committee in November 2002, exploited and extended the 'democracy dividends' of the year before. Central bank independence (CBI) as introduced in Ghana in 2002 has all the trappings of a typical textbook case. An index of CBI, created by Cukierman (1992, Chapter 19) specifies the conditions to be met as follows:

- The appointment, dismissal and legal term of office of the Governor of the central bank (CB).
- The institutional location of the final authority of monetary policy, and procedures for the resolution of conflicts between government and the Bank.
- The importance of price stability in comparison to other objectives like high employment and financial stability.
- The stringency and universality of limitations on the ability of government to borrow from the CB, at market or at subsidized rates, or to instruct the CB to lend to third parties.

While the Governor of the Bank of Ghana has the same four-year term of office as the elected government, because he is not likely to have been appointed at the inauguration of a new government he invariably outlasts the government, as his dismissal cannot be arbitrary. In this particular instance, a rare opportunity was offered the country when the term of Dr Kwabena Duffuor as Governor ended in September 2001 just before the enactment of the law that gave operational independence to the central bank. Thus, the appointment of Dr Paul Acquah, from an institution most averse to inflation – the IMF – was most opportune. Whether by design or fortuity, he fits very much into the model of Rogoff's 'conservative central banker'.

The other conditions satisfying CBI are clearly spelt out in the Bank of Ghana Act, 2002 (Act 612). The establishment of the MPC, for example, ensured that the Bank of Ghana has the final authority on monetary policy. Further, the law also limits the amount of public sector borrowing from the central bank to 10 per cent of the revenue collected for the period. Above all, the law makes it clear that the main object of the Bank of Ghana is to maintain stable prices.

It is clear from the foregoing that policy credibility was greatly enhanced by the granting of operational independence to the Bank of Ghana, the appointment of a 'conservative' Governor, and the establishment of the MPC as the sole monetary policy authority with the sole aim of keeping prices stable. It is important to note that since the commencement of sitting of the MPC, all business and consumer surveys attest to the confidence economic agents have in the management of the macroeconomy. It is not for naught that the economic scene in the country is usually apprehensive when the MPC sits. It is our submission that this credibility in policy helps lower inflationary expectation and hence has been partly responsible for the fall in inflation rates since 2002.

16.4.3 Output Growth and Inflation

The fall in the rates of inflation and the renewed faith in macroeconomic performance had positive feedback on other economic indices. In particular, private remittances increased substantially, exchange rates stabilized and interest rates began to fall. Between 2000 and 2006, the average lending rate of commercial banks fell by more than 2000 basis points from about 47 per cent to about 24 per cent over the seven years. In addition to the likely improvement in the credit situation for businesses as a result of the drop in interest rates, other supportive fiscal programmes of government and inflow of resources from donors as well as Ghanaians resident abroad led to a boost in growth of the Ghanaian economy.

Studies have shown that inflation in Ghana, especially in the short run, is affected largely by structural factors including production and distribution bottlenecks. Non-parametric analysis usually points to the composition of the basket of goods and services used in the construction of the consumer price index and also the share of food in the expenditure of the average Ghanaian.[9] Econometric analyses of inflation in Ghana have pointed to strong evidence from the real sector as the major cause (Sowa and Kwakye, 1993; Sowa, 1994). Thus, the improvement in growth performance over the years has greatly helped in subduing the inflationary pressures in the country.

16.5 CONCLUSION

Monetary policy formulation and inflation management in Ghana has changed drastically since 2002. Institutional restructuring of the central bank, which conferred on it operational independence, has not only asserted its position as the ultimate body in terms of monetary policy formulation and implementation, but has also imbued it with a measure of credibility which has led to the attainment of positive outcomes. In particular, there has been steady decline in the rate of inflation, while output performance has also been impressive. Estimation results of the central bank's reaction function also confirm the fact that policy is indeed geared at closing an inflation gap as well as an output gap, albeit that the policies appear to be closing the latter faster than the former.

The mystery of the achievement of the double desirable objective of improved output performance and falling rates of inflation is explained by the benefits of 'policy credibility' as a result of central bank independence as well as the feedback of improved output performance on the disinflation process. In sum, the conferment of operational independence on the central bank led to policy credibility which calmed inflationary expectations and set off the disinflationary process. The consequent fall in interest rates, coupled with improvements in macroeconomic management, helped to increase output growth. Because of the influence of output in the inflationary process in Ghana, an improvement in growth performance leads to further disinflation.

It is important to note that monetary policy cannot afford to be expansionary and maintain its credibility. As soon as inflation is allowed to take off, credibility will be lost; and once lost, it will be difficult to build up again.

NOTES

* The views expressed in this chapter are those of the authors and do not necessarily reflect the views or policies of their respective institutions.

1. The Former Bank of New Zealand Governor decried his being accused of holding back on output growth to protect inflation; and in fact claimed that he resigned because output was not growing fast enough.

2. Section (5) of the 1957 Ordinance.
3. Section 3(e) of the Bank of Ghana Act (1963).
4. A more complete discussion of this model and the IMF financial programming methodology is provided in Khan et al. (1990).
5. Because this lack of control over NFA arises most commonly in situations where the government is committed to controlling a fixed exchange rate, the use of credit rather than monetary targets is more commonly advocated for fixed or managed exchange rate systems.
6. The CIEA captures key important economic variables such as industrial electricity consumption, levels of exports, level of imports, sales of selected key 'blue-chip' companies in the formal and informal sectors of the economy, tourist arrivals, sales of selected key companies involved in the construction sectors of the economy, commercial banks' credit to the private sector and a measure of aggregate demand pressures (proxied by VAT collections).
7. The data and tests for its properties can be obtained from the authors. Suffice it to mention that the univariate time series properties confirmed that all the variables had unit roots. The first difference of all the series therefore induced stationarity, as confirmed by the augmented Dickey–Fuller and Phillips–Perron tests. Further, the trace and maximal eigenvalue suggested the existence of cointegrated relationships among the variables. A structural restriction imposed on the cointegrating space also confirmed that indeed the variables did cointegrate. The implication of all these tests indicated that using the ordinary least squares estimation technique would yield 'super-consistent' estimates.
8. 'Credibility' in this context means that the public believes that policymakers will keep their promises, even if they face incentives to renege; Bernanke (2004).
9. The 1999–2000 Ghana Living Standards Survey estimates that about 65 per cent of the average Ghanaian's expenditure is on food. The CPI basket itself allocates about half of its weight to food.

REFERENCES

Beenstock, M. and A. Ilek (2005), 'Wicksell's Classical Dichotomy: Is the Natural Rate of Interest Independent of the Money Rate of Interest?', Bank of Israel Working Paper Series, 780.

Bernanke, Ben (2004), 'Remarks by Governor Ben S. Bernanke to the Conference on Reflections on Monetary Policy 25 years After October 1979', Federal Reserve Bank of St Louis, St Louis, Missouri, October.

Calvo, Guillermo A. (1978), 'On the Time Consistency of Optimal Policy in a Monetary Economy', *Econometrica*, **46** (November), pp. 1411–28.

Cukierman, Alex (1992), *Central Bank Strategy, Credibility, and Independence: Theory and Evidence*, Cambridge, MA: MIT Press.

Khan, Mohsin S., Peter Montiel and Nadeem U. Haque (1990), 'Adjustment with Growth: Relating the Analytical Approaches of the IMF and the World Bank', *Journal of Development Economics*, **32** (1), pp. 155–79.

Kydland, Finn E. and Edward C. Prescott (1977), 'Rules Rather Than Discretion: The Inconsistency of Optimal Plans', *Journal of Political Economy*, **85** (3), pp. 473–91.

Quiggin, J. (1997), 'The Welfare Effects of Alternative Choices of Instruments and Targets for Macroeconomic Stabilisation Policy', Reserve Bank of Australia 1997 Conference.

Roe, Alan and Nii K. Sowa (1997), 'From Direct to Indirect Monetary Control in Africa', *Journal of African Economies*, **6** (1), pp. 212–64.

Rogoff, Kenneth (1985), 'The Optimal Degree of Commitment to an Intermediate Monetary Target', *Quarterly Journal of Economics*, **100** (November), pp. 1169–89.
Sowa, N.K. (1994), 'Fiscal Deficits, Output Growth and Inflation Targets in Ghana', *World Development*, **22** (8), pp. 1105–17.
Sowa, N.K. and J.K. Kwakye (1993), 'Inflationary Trends and Control in Ghana', AERC Research Paper, No. 22.
Taylor, J.B. (1993), 'Discretion versus Policy Rules in Practice', *Carnegie Rochester Series on Public Policy*, **29**, pp. 195–214.

17. Monetary policy in Zambia: experience and challenges

Denny H. Kalyalya*

17.1 INTRODUCTION

Since liberalization of the economy in 1991, the formulation and implementation of monetary policy in Zambia have been focused on correcting the macroeconomic imbalances that characterized the economy over the previous two decades. The period after 1991 has therefore witnessed a transformation of the economy through a series of reforms, including the move towards market-based instruments of monetary policy.

Prior to 1991 monetary policy had multiple objectives without clearly defined targets and largely employed direct instruments for monetary control. The latter included interest rate and credit allocation controls, high core liquid assets and statutory reserve requirements. The national budget was predominantly financed through borrowing from the central bank. In other words, the fiscal budget deficits were being monetized, particularly after experiencing significant loss of government revenue from the mining industry following the slump in copper prices. As a result, the economy experienced fundamental internal and external imbalances as well as structural and institutional deficiencies (Kalyalya, 2001). In the period that followed, there was a general movement of the economy towards market-based structures and systems which included the deregulation of prices of real and financial assets alongside the introduction of market-based instruments of monetary policy.

This chapter highlights major changes that have taken place in respect of monetary policy formulation and implementation following liberalization of the Zambian economy in 1991. The rest of the chapter is organized as follows: section 17.2 highlights the nature of monetary policy and the major changes in monetary policy from 1991 to date. This is followed in section 17.3 by a discussion on the performance of monetary policy in Zambia since 1991. Section 17.4 outlines some major challenges to monetary policy going forward. Finally, section 17.5 provides a conclusion.

17.2 MAJOR CHANGES IN MONETARY POLICY, 1992–2006

Since 1991 monetary policy in Zambia has been directed at reducing and stabilizing inflation. This has been supported by efforts aimed at maintaining a stable financial environment conducive to financial deepening and economic expansion. The thrust of monetary and financial policies, therefore, have been to achieve price stability (that is, low inflation), financial system stability and stability in the foreign exchange market (underpinned by a relatively stable exchange rate of the kwacha against major currencies).

In its conduct of monetary policy, the Bank of Zambia has increasingly placed greater reliance on indirect than direct instruments. The shift to indirect instruments is in line with the government policy of economic liberalization and the current global trends in the conduct of monetary policy. Indirect instruments are considered to be more efficient in resource allocation than direct instruments (Alexander et al., 1995, pp. 3–6). In addition, indirect instruments are preferred as they are believed to enhance the effectiveness of monetary policy in reducing and stabilizing the growth of money supply and subsequently inflation, both in the short and the long run. Further, efficient financial intermediation, which enhances the efficiency of money and capital markets, is encouraged. In contrast, direct instruments are only effective in the short run, as in the long run commercial banks (or other agents for that matter) devise ways to circumvent regulation, such as creating non-bank subsidiaries through which credit and transactions with financial institutions are channelled without being subjected to direct controls. Moreover, direct instruments prevent banks from making optimal decisions about the structure of interest rates and balance sheets and thus discourage competition. This in turn results in inefficient money and capital markets.

It was precisely for the above reasons that the monetary policy framework in Zambia was transformed from one dominated by indirect policy instruments to one reliant on market-based instruments. The market-based instruments have included open market-type operations (Treasury bills, short-term credit and term deposits). However, direct instruments, such as reserve requirements (core liquid assets and statutory reserves) and the discount policy (quantitative limits and penalty rate) continued, to a limited extent, to complement the indirect instruments.

Reserve money or liquidity programming has been at the centre of monetary policy implementation since 1991. This approach takes reserve money as the operating target, on the assumption that the money multiplier is known and stable. Broad money is the intermediate target,

Table 17.1 Zambia's reserve money framework

Sources (Supply = 1 + 2)	Uses (Demand = 3 + 4 + 5 + 6)
1. Net foreign assets (i − ii)	3. Currency in circulation
(i) BoZ foreign assets	4. Commercial bank's deposits
(ii) Foreign liabilities	5. Statutory reserves
2. Net domestic assets (iii + iv)	6. Other deposits
(iii) Net claims on government (a − b)	
(a) BoZ claims on government (loans, securities)	
(b) Govt assets with BoZ (deposits)	
(iv) Claims on others (loans and bank overdrafts)	

while low and stable consumer price inflation is the ultimate target. The approach has been employed under the three economic reform programmes that Zambia has undertaken since 1992 with the support of the Benton Wood Institutions and other development partners. The programming framework is presented in Table 17.1.

To forecast reserve money, on a daily basis, the Bank assesses the liquidity position of all deposit money banks, which in effect represents the central bank's net foreign assets (NFA) and net domestic assets (NDA) position. The other component of reserve money supply is the net claims on government (NCG). This is forecast on the basis of government revenue to be collected and deposited at the Bank of Zambia and the anticipated government expenditure. Treasury bills and bond transactions and their rediscounts are also considered. Claims on commercial banks are projected through open market operations and the overdraft facility with the deposit money banks' aggregate current account position projecting the overdrafts to commercial banks. On the demand side, reserve money is the sum total of currency in circulation, statutory required reserves, commercial banks' positive current account balances and other deposits.

The reform programme, between 1991 and 1996, also entailed that legal reforms were undertaken to update and modernize the central bank and commercial banking laws. To this end, a new banking law, the Banking and Financial Services Act (BFSA), was enacted by Parliament in 1994 (and further amendments were made in 2000 and 2005 to, among other things, expand the Bank of Zambia's supervisory mandate to include supervision of non-bank financial institutions). Further, a new Bank of

Zambia Act was enacted in 1996, which incorporated international best practice, notably focusing the primary objectives of the Bank to price and financial system stability as opposed to multiple objectives, as was the case in the repealed Bank of Zambia Act.

17.3 PERFORMANCE OF MONETARY POLICY UNDER VARIOUS ECONOMIC REFORM PROGRAMMES

17.3.1 Monetary Policy under the Rights Accumulation Programme (RAP), 1992–95

In 1991, Zambia held multiparty elections and a new administration was ushered into office. Given the state of the economy at the time, the new government quickly had to undertake major economic reforms. To this end, and in a bid to normalize relations with the international community, which had been severed since 1987, the government embarked on the Rights Accumulation Programme (RAP), covering the period 1992–95. The focus of monetary policy under this programme was to reduce high growth rates of domestic credit and money supply, which had resulted in persistently high inflation. This was expected to put the economy on a recovery path and achieve sustainable economic growth with low inflation and thus contribute to the fight against widespread poverty. These objectives were to be achieved through: stabilization of the macroeconomic environment; promotion of free market principles in the formulation and implementation of economic policies and private sector development through privatization; and achievement of a sustainable external position. Specifically, a policy matrix was designed and implemented in all sectors of the economy with liberalization as the anchor (see Table 17.2).

The implementation of these policies resulted in a number of initiatives in various areas of reform. In the monetary sector, a primary Treasury bill auction was introduced in 1993 to enhance monetary policy and government debt management. Following the liberalization of interest rates, by abolishing interest rate ceilings, initially sharp rises in interest rates and money supply were experienced but these receded by the end of the programme period. The lending rate fell to 45.5 per cent in 1995 from 55.8 per cent in 1992 while broad money growth slowed to 54.9 per cent from 73.3 per cent, over the same period.

Consistent with the objectives of the programme, government introduced the cash budget system in 1993. The principal aim of the system was to curtail unnecessary expenditure by ensuring that only collected revenues

Table 17.2 Policy matrix under the Rights Accumulation Programme, 1992–95

Policy area	Policy
Monetary	Limit money supply growth by mopping up liquidity from the financial system
Fiscal	Restore fiscal prudence by reducing fiscal deficit through reduction and control of expenditure and improving revenue collection
External	• Stable and competitive exchange rate through a liberalized regime • Liberalize trade • Move towards export-based industrialization • Seek relief from heavy external debt burden.
Structural and institutional	• Privatize state-owned enterprises • Promote economy based on free market principles • Reverse infrastructure decay • Reduce public sector size and improve efficiency

could be spent, to control expenditure and reduce the fiscal budget deficit. In addition, to improve efficiency in revenue collection, during the same year the government transformed the Customs and Excise Department in the Ministry of Finance into an autonomous Zambia Revenue Authority. Further, the Income Tax Act was amended to widen taxable income (for example cash benefits under Pay As You Earn – PAYE; dividends) and a mechanism for routinely adjusting fees, fines, and so on when necessary as changes in inflation took place was established. These fiscal measures reduced the overall fiscal deficit in 1992 although it deteriorated again in 1993 and 1994 at the height of inflation before improving in 1995. However, poor expenditure control (largely as result of arrears accumulation) despite introduction of the cash-budget system, continued to be a major budget weakness.

To support the monetary and fiscal measures, in the external sector, the government in 1992 abolished quantitative imports and exports controls, unified and liberalized exchange rates and legalized a private bureau de change system of buying and selling foreign exchange. Another noteworthy development in the external sector was the liberalization of both the current and capital accounts as the Exchange Control Act was suspended in 1994. Other structural and institutional policies implemented between 1992 and 1995 included: liberalization of all markets, including pricing and marketing of agricultural inputs and goods; removal of all subsidies; establishment of the Zambia Privatisation Agency (ZPA) in 1992 to manage the privatization programme which started in earnest; and the commencement of a programme to rehabilitate the rundown social and physical infrastructure.

Although the external sector showed some signs of improvement it was considered to be still highly fragile. Nonetheless, the current account deficit narrowed to 2.1 per cent of gross domestic product (GDP) in 1995 from 7.4 per cent in 1992. Similarly, the overall balance-of-payments position improved to minus 1.6 per cent from minus 6.3 per cent, over the same period. The exchange rate of the kwacha against major currencies, while continuing to depreciate over the Rights Accumulation Programme (RAP) period, depreciated at a slower rate. Further, re-emerging confidence in the Zambian economy resulted in the restoration of multilateral and bilateral balance-of-payments support and project capital inflows.

With regard to inflation, the tight monetary and fiscal policies, coupled with some positive developments in other sectors of the economy, culminated in a reduction in consumer price inflation. Initially, inflation rose sharply, mainly due to the inevitable correction to market conditions that occurred, budget overruns in 1993 and 1994, and high credit and money supply growth between 1992 and 1994. However, by the end of the RAP, inflation declined significantly from three- to two-digit rates, to 46 per cent in 1995 from 180.7 per cent in 1992. Appendix 17.1 has details on developments in inflation and other indicators over the RAP period.

17.3.2 Monetary Policy under the Enhanced Structural Adjustment Facility Arrangement, 1996–99

After successful completion of the RAP, the country, with the continued support of the International Monetary Fund (IMF), embarked on another reform programme, under the Enhanced Structural Adjustment Facility (ESAF) arrangement. The ESAF later changed to the Poverty Reduction and Growth Facility (PRGF) arrangement. The major aim of the programme was to promote economic growth and attain positive per capita income growth, so as to reduce poverty and improve people's living standards, and move the economy towards a sustainable balance-of-payments position.

In particular, the programme sought to reduce inflation to 4 per cent and raise GDP growth to 3–4 per cent by end-1998. To support these objectives monetary growth needed to be contained to appropriate levels and consistent with a reasonable expansion in private sector credit. At the same time, following the failure of the Meridien BIAO bank in 1995 and other small banks in its aftermath, authorities needed to undertake measures that would bring about banking system stability.

Reserve money programming and credit and deposit auctions introduced in 1995 continued under the ESAF arrangement. Monetary policy was tightened towards end-1996 and the first half of 1997 by increasing the core liquid assets and statutory reserve ratios. However, from end-1997 to 1999 monetary policy eased, as evidenced by reductions in the core liquid assets ratio and the accommodation of fiscal deficits. This was occasioned by severe pressure to stimulate growth, especially after the partial drought of the 1997–98 farming season.

The tightening of monetary policy during 1996–97 resulted in a steady contraction of broad money supply growth to 22.6 per cent in 1998 from 54.9 per cent in 1995. This however was reversed with the easing of monetary policy between 1997 and 1999. Broad money growth rose to 29.2 per cent in 1999 from 22.6 per cent in 1998.

With regard to fiscal policy, the programme aimed at attaining a surplus of 1 per cent of GDP in the period 1996–98, by: increasing government savings and reducing domestic debt stock; creating an efficient and broad-based tax system that would maintain tax revenues above 17 per cent of GDP; restricting expenditure to no more than 25 per cent of GDP by 1998; improving the effectiveness of tax policy and administration; and supplementing the cash-budget system with an operational mechanism for controlling expenditure commitments. Thus, in 1996 and 1997, the overall fiscal deficit decreased to 3.9 per cent and 2.4 per cent of GDP, respectively, before increasing to 6.9 per cent in 1998. The increase in the deficit was brought about by a decline in revenues accompanied by increased expenditure. As a result, and similar to what happened under RAP, the accumulation of domestic arrears due to poor controls continued, thereby undermining the achievement of the fiscal targets.

External sector policies under the ESAF continued to focus on enhancing free market determination of the exchange rate and allocation of foreign exchange, and deepening and modernization of the foreign exchange market. In this regard, the Bank of Zambia continued to pursue a policy of not targeting the exchange rate, but intervening in the foreign exchange market to smoothe temporary fluctuations to ensure a stable and competitive rate. The other key element of external sector policies was the need to accumulate international reserves. Above all, the country was to seek effective resolution of the debilitating external debt problem, including through concessionary rescheduling from the Paris Club.

However, the outturn over the programme period was a steady deterioration in the overall balance-of-payments position, from a surplus of 1.6 per cent of GDP in 1995 to a deficit of 3.9 per cent in 1998. This was largely driven by the worsening of the current account deficit, which increased to 12.8 per cent in 1998 from 2.1 per cent of GDP in 1995. The major explanatory factors for this outturn included poor performance in both traditional and non-traditional export sectors, on account of the fall in global demand due to international financial crisis, regional conflicts and internal operational problems.

The external debt burden increased from 202 per cent of GDP in 1995 to 255 per cent in 1998, as debt servicing became difficult with reduced export earnings and the withholding of balance-of-payments support by cooperating partners. The resulting chronic foreign exchange shortages in the period 1997–98 induced a sharp depreciation of the kwacha (72.8 per cent) during 1998. This was compounded by the easing of monetary policy, referred to earlier, and the loss of consumer and business confidence.

In terms of structural and institutional reforms, the thrust of the ESAF included: increasing public sector efficiency by reducing the size of the civil service and using the financial savings so generated to enhance the remuneration of the remaining civil servants; improving the efficiency of the economy by privatizing or liquidating parastatal companies (which were performing poorly); developing efficient financial markets; implementing a partial freeze on hiring, and developing a competitive salary structure for the civil service; and coming up with a plan to deal with retrenchment costs.

More specifically, to address the protracted issue of civil service reform the government adopted a medium-term public sector reform programme (PSRP). One principal objective of the PSRP was to reduce the number of non-military public service employees from 136 775 to 80 000 by end-1999. However, the programme got off to a slow start, as by 1998, only 13 400 civil servants had been retrenched.

In the financial sector, supervision of banks was strengthened through the introduction of enhanced on-site inspection methods and gazetting of amended regulations on large loan exposure, insider lending and provisioning for bad loans. The strengthening of supervision and regulation resulted in the placing into receivership of four insolvent banks.

In spite of the above measures, the programme fell short of meeting its major objective: finalization of the privatization of the Zambia Consolidated Copper Mines (ZCCM). This remained outstanding following the withdrawal of a worthy prospective international consortium from the negotiations. Ultimately, the failure to meet the 1998 program structural benchmarks, in particular the firming up of the survival financial plan for ZCCM, resulted in the withholding of IMF financial support that subsequently led to the withholding of balance-of-payments support from other multilateral and bilateral partners. These developments in turn undermined the credibility of government commitment to the program, and subsequently led to a general loss of business and consumer confidence. It was not until 2000 that the major assets of ZCCM were privatized. This resulted in improved investor confidence in the economy almost instantaneously.

Meanwhile, the combined effect of the developments in the monetary, fiscal, external and structural and institutional reforms was a sharp decline in inflation, which fell to 18.6 per cent in 1997 from 35.2 per cent in 1996. Clearly, the tightening of monetary policy during the mid-1996 to end-1997 period also played a significant role in this inflation outturn. It is therefore not surprising that when there was a loosening of monetary policy in the subsequent period, inflation was back on the upward trend, surging to 30.6 per cent in 1998. However, inflation slowed down to 20.6 per cent in 1999 (see Appendix 17.1).

17.3.3 Monetary Policy under the ESAF/PRGF Arrangement, 1999–2007

The main macroeconomic objectives under the ESAF/PRGF (Poverty Reduction and Growth Facility) arrangement, 1999–2007, were to achieve average economic growth of about 5 per cent a year, further reduce inflation, and strengthen the external position. These objectives were to be achieved through prudent financial policies, complemented by structural reforms.

Specific macroeconomic targets included: an average annual inflation rate of 4 per cent; an international reserves build-up equivalent to 2.5 months of import cover in 2001, from the equivalent of two weeks at end-1998; and reducing the overall fiscal deficit to less than 1 per cent of GDP in 2001 while generating an annual average domestic fiscal surplus of 1.3 per cent of GDP. The latter was to be achieved through the broadening of the tax base and raising the revenue–GDP ratio by 1.5 per cent during the period 1999–2001 through improvements in customs administration, unification of the corporate tax structure and tax compliance, and exercising greater budget control and cash management, as well as eliminating domestic payment arrears and the accumulation of new arrears.

The outturn for 1999 and 2000 indicated underperformance. Overall fiscal deficits of 4 per cent and 7.8 per cent of GDP were registered, compared to the targets of 3.2 per cent and 5.6 per cent, respectively. The deterioration in the budget deficit arose from shortfalls in revenue collection and the easing of fiscal policy to fund arrears. There was also a marked increase in arrears due to continued weaknesses in controlling expenditure commitments.

In the external sector, the government sought to achieve an efficient mechanism for foreign exchange allocation, a competitive tradables sector and to reduce the external debt burden. Accordingly, the overall balance-of-payments position improved to a deficit of 0.3 per cent of GDP from a deficit of 3.9 per cent, largely due to an increase in the capital account position. The kwacha depreciated against major currencies, on account of persistent foreign exchange shortages and increased domestic absorption. In December 2000, Zambia accessed the enhanced Heavily Indebted Poor Countries (HIPC) initiative. This was a major boost to the economy, as it provided the country with the long-sought-after opportunity to receive significant debt relief, estimated at US$3.8 billion.

A notable development in the structural programme was the introduction of an electronic clearing-house in 1999. This was expected to improve the safety and efficiency of the commercial banks' payments and settlement system.

For the programme period to end-2000, good progress was made with regard to inflation and the stimulation of real sector activities. Inflation decreased further from 30.6 per cent in 1998 to 20.6 per cent in 1999, before rising to 30.1 per cent in 2000. The rise in consumer prices in 2000 was mainly attributed to the increase in oil prices on the international market. Economic growth recovered in 1999 and 2000, growing by 2.4 per cent and 3.5 per cent, respectively, compared to the 1.8 per cent decline in 1998, largely due to a good agricultural crop harvest in 1999 and growth in the manufacturing sector following the privatization of ZCCM, which was a major consumer of manufactured products on the Copperbelt. Additionally, the government made some payments towards the arrears of ZCCM trade creditors. This was part of the government's commitment to the privatization process and private sector development.

However, the mining and quarrying sector continued to be a drag on the economy for the third consecutive year. Operational problems at the mines, arising from many years of low capital investment and the use of obsolete equipment prior to the privatization of ZCCM, contributed to the decline in the performance of the mining sector. Nevertheless, it is important to note that although mining sector output declined by 5 per cent in 2000, it was an improvement compared to a decrease of 25 per cent in 1999. This improvement was mainly attributed to improved management and recapitalization of the mines following privatization.

In 2003, Zambia however went off-track with respect to the IMF-supported PRGF arrangement and was put on a staff-monitored program (SMP). This followed fiscal slippages owing to larger-than-budgeted increases in emoluments to public service workers. Thus, the incoming administration had to take urgent measures to bring the programme back on track. Indeed, due to the consistent implementation of prudent macroeconomic policies, the country was able to get back to the PRGF arrangement in 2004.

Accordingly, in June 2004 the IMF board approved a three-year PRGF arrangement in the amount of SDR 220.1 million (45 per cent of quota), of which SDR 192.6 million was disbursed. This set the stage for Zambia to reach the Completion Point under the enhanced HIPC initiative, which it did in April 2005 and received SDR 508.3 million in total debt relief from the IMF. As it turned out, by reaching the Completion Point Zambia also became eligible to receive further debt relief under the Multilateral Debt Relief Initiative, which the G8 established in July 2005.

In January 2006 Zambia received its share of the MDRI in respect of its eligible debt to the IMF amounting to SDR 402.6 million. As a result, Zambia's external debt declined substantially (see Appendix Table 17A.1). With these savings, the country has been provided the much-sought-after opportunity for the government to increase its funding to the social sector and private sector development so as to stimulate sustainable growth and hence poverty reduction.

Since 1999, monetary policy performance has improved. This is reflected in the fall in inflation to single digits in 2006, the first time in over 30 years, ending 2006 at 8.2 per cent compared to 30.1 per cent in 2000. At end-2007 it was at 8.9 per cent. Similarly, GDP growth remained consistently positive throughout the period 2000–07. As a matter of fact, in 2002 to 2007 GDP growth averaged about 5 per cent per year. GDP per capita also showed improvements after 2000 (see Appendix 17.1).

17.3.4 Volatility of Inflation and Broad Money, 1992–2007

To get a sense of the volatility of inflation and broad money over the reform period, 1992–2007, standard deviations of the variables were calculated. The results, as depicted in Figure 17.1, show some contrasting behaviour.

The volatility of inflation increased shortly after the implementation of the economic reforms to a peak of 31.9 in 1994, but declined sharply three years later. Since then, it assumed a downward trend, averaging 3 as the reforms got entrenched. The increase in volatility in the period 1992 to 1994 can be attributed to the decontrol of prices of goods and services as well as the removal of subsidies, especially on consumption. Needless to say, these were the factors that made inflation appear artificially low. As economic agents recognized that the government was committed to economic reforms, as seen from the monetary policy regime being pursued by the Bank of Zambia, inflation expectations appear to have adjusted well. The volatility of inflation reduced substantially, especially in the period 2003–07, averaging 1.4.

The volatility of broad money, on the other hand, has been increasing

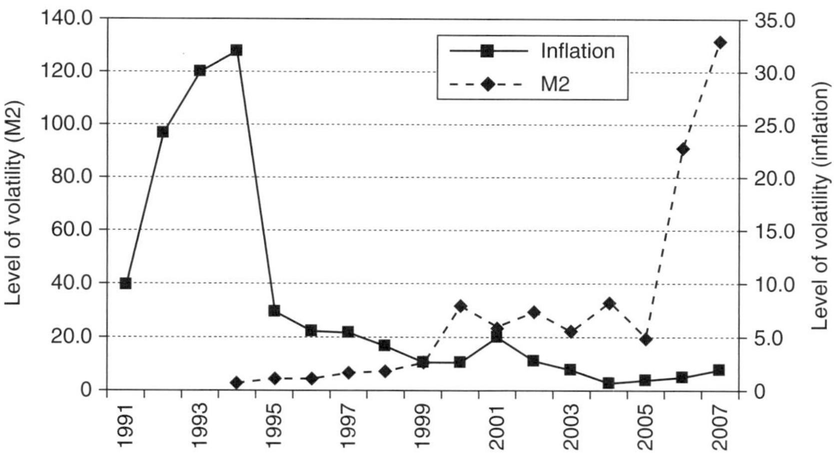

Figure 17.1 Volatility of inflation and broad money

since the implementation of the economic reforms, with the period between 2006 and 2007 being the most volatile. During the period 1994–98 the volatility of broad money was relatively low, with its standard deviation averaging 5.1. This increased later to an average of 24.1 in the period between 1999 and 2005, largely due to fiscal slippages. Interestingly, the high volatility in the period 2006–07 was largely attributed to Zambia's improved external sector performance and reduction in its external debt. These developments have led to large increases in Zambia's net foreign assets, which have been feeding into broad money and hence the high level of volatility.

17.4 CHALLENGES TO MONETARY POLICY

Clearly, monetary policy has performed quite well in Zambia over the period 1992 to 2007. However, the formulation and implementation of monetary policy, even (if not more so) in a liberalized financial system, has not been without challenges. There are several challenges that monetary policy has had and will have to contend with.

First, the underdeveloped nature of the financial system in Zambia is in itself a major challenge. In the first instance, the Zambian financial system, as in most developing countries, is dominated by commercial banks, monetization of the economy is quite low (as measured by M2/GDP which averaged 213.53 over the period 2002 to 2007), cash is the dominant means of making payments, and has a high degree of market segmentation. This entails that the effectiveness of monetary policy instruments is limited.

The secondary market for government debt is also yet to be developed. Until then, the secondary market will continue to place limitations on the efficient functioning of the primary market, as most investors are not prepared to invest in new bond issues unless these can be sold at short notice and at reasonable cost. The lack of an active secondary market in turn means that there is some inflexibility in using government securities to regulate money supply. In addition, the nascent stock exchange means that this too has yet to claim its rightful place in the economy.

Second, developments in the external sector are a constant threat to macroeconomic stability in general and the implementation of effective monetary policy in particular. The fact that the economy is once again becoming quite dependent on the production and export of base metals (in particular, copper) makes the economy susceptible to the phenomenon of 'Dutch Disease'. Meanwhile, managing the potential booms and busts is not an easy challenge to meet. In addition, as a non-oil-producing country, Zambia like other oil-importing countries has to bear the brunt of constant increases in international oil prices. It goes without saying that the full impact of the increases in oil prices is felt throughout the production, transportation and retail systems of the economy.

Third, arising from the substantial debt relief that the country has received and continues to receive, and the generally improved macroeconomic environment, the potential for marked aid and capital inflows has been created. The need for sound management of the resultant exchange rate pressures and the attendant pass-through effects can hardly be overemphasized.

Fourth, strengthening and staying the course with regard to the recently achieved fiscal prudence as well as forging relatively stronger coordination between fiscal and monetary policies is an equally challenging task in the period ahead. At the same time, it is important that the central bank will formally be accorded operational autonomy.

Fifth, according to the FinScope Survey for Zambia of 2006, 67 per cent of the Zambian adult population has no access to financial services. Undoubtedly, this is an extremely important challenge of improving access, both for economic growth and for all. However, with it comes another challenge for monetary policy – the ability to balance the potential conflict that pursuit of this objective will present for monetary policy.

Finally, in this era of globalization and ever continuing improvements in information and communication technologies, gone are the days when countries could be insulated from developments in other parts of the global economy. This therefore calls for constant vigilance and actively seeking better ways of managing national economies.

17.5 CONCLUSION

It is quite clear from the above discussion that the economic reforms that the country has undergone over the period 1992 to 2007 have begun to bear fruit. The economy has steadily grown, averaging about 5 per cent in the period 2002 to 2007. Inflation has been coming down, reaching single digits in 2006 and 2007. The exchange rate of the kwacha against major currencies has strengthened and relatively stabilized. Fiscal policy performance has improved markedly. Commercial banks' nominal lending interest rates have been trending downwards, although the spread and the real lending interest rates are still considered relatively too high. International reserves have also increased substantially. In a nutshell, the country is now enjoying relative macroeconomic stability. The appendix provides a summary of these and other developments during the review period.

The discussion has also brought out some of the major challenges that monetary policy has had and will have to contend with in the period ahead. The importance of effective monetary policy can hardly be overemphasized. It has a lot to offer in terms of economic growth and poverty reduction through stable and reduced inflation. A strong anti-inflationary policy will however require a broadening and deepening of the financial markets and thus expansion of the instruments. In this context, the Bank of Zambia will need to continue to intensify the use of indirect instruments, such as open market operations, and reduce reliance on direct instruments. An enhancement of confidence in the internal and external value of the kwacha will also help the central bank to strengthen the market for medium- and long-term government securities so as to broaden the available options for open market operations and reduce the sensitivity of the government budget to short-term fluctuations in interest rates.

Dealing with external sector developments, particularly volatile international oil and metal prices, is a major source of challenges to the performance of monetary policy in terms of maintaining inflation in single digits. Managing the effects of globalization will equally be quite challenging.

Much has been achieved in financial sector reform as outlined above, but the scope for financial deepening and development exists. Challenges to develop the financial system will be with us for some time to come. The capital market is nascent, but a start has been made upon which further developments can be made, particularly now that the privatization programme is almost completed following the successful sale of the mines.

Developments in the financial system are critical for the effective implementation of monetary policy and the achievement of sustainable growth in the long term. Given the undeveloped nature of Zambia's financial system, it is evident that the diversification and strengthening of financial institutions, instruments and markets must be regarded as a prerequisite to further economic development. In this regard, the government-approved Financial Sector Development Plan, among other things, provides a good framework for focused development of the financial system, such as the improvement of financial services to the unbanked population in the rural areas of the country. Bearing the foregoing in mind, the role of the central bank as a key player will continue to be crucial to the achievement of the economic objectives of the country as envisioned in the Vision 2030 long-term plan, expressing Zambians' aspirations by the year 2030, and as envisaged in the Fifth National Development Plan, 2006–10.

APPENDIX 17.1

Table 17A.1 Zambia: selected economic indicators, 2000–07

	CPI inflation (%)	Weighted average lending base rate (%)	Real GDP growth (%)	Per capita GDP growth (%)	Change in annual average exchange rate (%)	CA/ GDP (%)	International reserves (US$ million)	External debt (US$ billion)
1992	180.7	59.3	–1.8	–5.2	167.2	–9.1	–	7070
1993	128.1	113.3	6.5	0.3	162.9	–8.1	192.3	6835
1994	38.3	70.6	–3.5	–1.9	49.2	–8.7	268.1	6565
1995	46	45.5	–2.5	–5.1	29.3	–8.3	210.5	6483
1996	35.2	53.8	6.9	4.4	38.3	–6.1	211	6710
1997	18.6	46.6	3.3	0.9	8.9	–6.1	237.9	7267
1998	30.6	31.8	–1.9	–4.2	41.6	–13.1	68.6	6666
1999	20.6	40.4	2.2	–0.2	28.2	–17.0	45.3	6378
2000	30.1	39.1	3.6	1.1	30.3	–18.8	268.3	6334
2001	18.7	45.9	4.9	1.8	16.1	–20.1	116.5	7116
2002	26.7	45.3	3.3	0.1	19.3	–17.3	464.8	6936
2003	17.2	40.5	5.1	1.8	9.9	–15.9	247.2	6039
2004	17.5	30.9	5.4	2.1	1.0	–10.7	312.2	7113
2005	15.9	28.2	5.2	2.0	–6.6	–9.6	312.2	5056
2006	8.2	23.2	5.8	2.7	–19.3	–0.6	706.4	1496
2007	8.9	18.3	6.2	0.9	11.4	–7.7	1087.8	2083*

Note: *Excluding private sector debt, external debt reduced to US$676.5 million by end-2006.

Source: Central Statistical Office and Bank of Zambia.

NOTE

* I wish to acknowledge the support and valuable research assistantship of Ivan Zyuulu, Benjamin Musuku and Simacheche Dinde. However, the views expressed in the chapter are mine and do not necessarily reflect the official position of the Bank of Zambia.

BIBLIOGRAPHY

Alexander, W.E.A., T.J.T. Balino and C. Enoch (1995), *The Adoption of Indirect Instruments of Monetary Policy*, Washington, DC: International Monetary Fund.

FinScope Survey for Zambia (2006), 'Measuring Financial Access in Zambia', FinScope Zambia 2005 Report, prepared by FinMark Trust for the Government of the Republic of Zambia Financial Sector Development Programme Secretariat and DFID/Sida, November.

Government of the Republic of Zambia, *Enhanced Structural Adjustment Facility Policy Framework Paper, 1999–2001*, prepared by the Zambian authorities in collaboration with the IMF and the World Bank, available at: http://www.imf.org/externel/NP/PFP/1999/Zambia/index.htm.

Government of the Republic of Zambia (1999), *Letters of Intent*, 1999–2007.

Honohan, P. and T. Beck (2007), *Making Finance Work for Africa*, Washington, DC: World Bank.

Kalyalya, D.H. (2001), 'Monetary Policy Framework and Implementation in Zambia', Paper presented at the South African Reserve Bank Conference on Monetary Policy Frameworks in Africa, 17–19 September, Pretoria, South Africa.

Laurens, B.J. (2005), *Monetary Policy Implementation at Different Stages of Market Development*, Washington, DC: International Monetary Fund.

Mehran, H., P. Ugolini, J.P. Briffaux, G. Iden, T. Lybek, S. Swaray and P. Hayward (1998), 'Financial Sector Development in sub-Saharan African Countries', Occasional Paper 169, Washington, DC: International Monetary Fund.

Ng'ambi, C.N. (2005), 'The Changing Landscape of the Foreign Exchange Market in Zambia over the Last Forty Years and the Challenges for the Future', in *Facing the Challenges of the 21st Century*, Bank of Zambia 40th Anniversary Report, Lusaka, Bank of Zambia:

Senbet, L.W. and Isaac Otchere (2005), 'Financial Sector Reforms in Africa', Paper prepared for the Annual World Bank Conference on Development Economics (ABCDE), Dakar, Senegal, January.

Index